THE
SHAAR
PRESS

THE JUDAICA IMPRINT
FOR THOUGHTFUL PEOPLE

INCLUDES **20** ESSAYS BASED
ON THE TEACHINGS OF
HAGAON HARAV YITZCHOK HUTNER זצ"ל

A
SHAAR
PRESS
PUBLICATION

BEYOND TIME

THE MYSTERY AND MEANING OF THE JEWISH FESTIVALS

RABBI PINCHAS STOLPER

Published by **SHAAR PRESS**
Distributed by MESORAH PUBLICATIONS, LTD.
4401 Second Avenue / Brooklyn, N.Y 11232 / (718) 921-9000

Distributed in Israel by SIFRIATI / A. GITLER
6 Hayarkon Street / Bnei Brak 51127

Distributed in Europe by LEHMANNS
Unit E, Viking Industrial Park, Rolling Mill Road / Jarrow, Tyne and Wear, NE32 3DP/ England

Distributed in Australia and New Zealand by GOLDS WORLD OF JUDAICA
3-13 William Street / Balaclava, Melbourne 3183 / Victoria Australia

Distributed in South Africa by KOLLEL BOOKSHOP
Shop 8A Norwood Hypermarket / Norwood 2196, Johannesburg, South Africa

ISBN: 1-57819-744-9 Hard Cover

Printed in the United States of America by Noble Book Press
Custom bound by Sefercraft, Inc. / 4401 Second Avenue / Brooklyn N.Y. 11232

ביהמ"ד גבול יעבץ
ברוקלין, נוא יארק

דוד קאהן

בס"ד

When an approbation is given to a young man's scholarly work, the phrase חָדָת מָלֵא יָשָׁן (a new vessel containing old wine) is commonly used. To my mind one can also use as an encomium the phrase יָשָׁן מָלֵא חָדָת (an old vessel containing new wine) when describing Rabbi Stolper's masterful presentation of his Rebbe's Torah. Our sages admonish us, concerning Torah, that בְּכָל יוֹם יִהְיוּ בְעֵינֶיךָ כַּחֲדָשִׁים (the words of Torah shall appear to you as new) and Rabbi Stolper fulfills this desideratum admirably by presenting "old" Torah with a fresh perspective.

It goes without saying that Rabbi Stolper's original insights are intellectually stimulating which both scholar and layman can enjoy.

I rejoice that my dear friend has not lost his prolific talent to present Torah truths in beautiful idiom.

דוד קאהן
חונה פ"ט

Approbation of Rabbi David Cohen

Vaad L'Hatzolas Nidchei Yisroel

Rabbi Moshe M. Eisemann

of Stam Gemilas Chesed Fund, Inc.   Tax Exempt #22-2371275
401 Yeshiva Lane • Baltimore, Maryland 21208 • Tel: 410-484-7396
Fax: 410-486-8810 • E-Mail: eisemann@erols.com
*In order to be received, all e-mails must contain
the word "Kosher" within the Subject line*

January 23, 2003

Dear R' Pinchos:

I have always felt that one of the greatest miracles of Chanukah is that year after year people find and explore new, as yet untrodden paths, branching off from the well worn roads that all of us know so well.

I imagine that anyone who feels inspired to write and publish thoughts on the *mo'adim*, faces this struggle. He does not simply want to repeat what has already been said. If he were to do that, he could save himself the trouble of writing. On the other hand he knows that חדש אסור מן התורה and the last thing he wants to do is to pass on insights which, to borrow a phrase from the Chazon Ish in a critical assessment of a new book, אין בו ממה שנאמר למשה מסיני.

The solution of course lies in asking the right questions which, by definition, will always be new questions. It is to be expected that every generations sees things from its own unique perspective and that is as it should be. Again by definition, freshly minted questions will yield freshly minted answers. These will be new only in the sense that a polished diamond is new. Facets of the old are revealed which had always been there but which needed the deft hands of the polisher to make them really sparkle.

You have displayed the sure touch of the gifted craftsman. Your work has a lasting beauty which will give pleasure and inspiration to many generations of entranced readers..

We are all grateful to you. לך בכחך זה!

In friendship:

Moshe M. Eisemann

Approbation of Rabbi Moshe M. Eisemann

CONTENTS

* Based on *Pachad Yitzchok* by Rabbi Yitzchok Hutner, זצ״ל

III. Rosh Hashanah

IV. Yom Kippur

V. Succos and Shmini Atzeres

VI. Chanukah

* Based on *Pachad Yitzchok* by Rabbi Yitzchok Hutner, זצ"ל

VII. Purim

VIII. Passover and Lag B'Omer

* Based on *Pachad Yitzchok* by Rabbi Yitzchok Hutner, זצ״ל

IX. Shavuos

X. Tishah B'Av

XI. Yearning for Redemption

XII. Conclusion

Index

---

* Based on *Pachad Yitzchok* by Rabbi Yitzchok Hutner, זצ״ל

AUTHOR'S PREFACE

▶ Allowing the Holidays to Transform Our Lives

t was in my parent's home that I first delighted in the joy, anticipation and festive celebration of the holidays. But it was only when I began to attend the scholarly lectures of my Rosh Yeshivah, *Hagaon* Rav Yitzchok Hutner, *zt"l*, that I was introduced to the penetrating, profound, original and moving depths of their meaning. Following the tradition of the great Chassidic masters, much of his piercing teaching on Jewish ideology and historiography revolved around the festivals. Each holiday was preceded by a *ma'amar*, an in-depth scholarly lecture. On the eight-day festivals of Passover and Succos, there was a new *ma'amar* each evening. This process continued over many years, well beyond my days as a student in the Mesivta Rabbi Chaim Berlin and Kollel Gur Aryeh. Whatever independent thinking and writing I have done concerning the holidays was inspired by his teachings.

The holidays are G-d's great gift to the Jewish People. They are our map through time, our beacon through history, the master plan with which we build a bridge through the divide of human events to mankind's ultimate destiny. The holidays also direct each individual to experience and relive the critical formative events of Jewish history. This experience enables us to transform our lives by attaching ourselves to G-d's goals for each individual Jew, for *Klal Yisrael* [the Nation of Israel] and for all humanity.

The holidays are much more than family, parties, prayer and ceremony. We are commanded to make them an adventure of heart, mind, spirit and intellect. If during the holidays you have not journeyed with our People through the great events of Israel's ancient days; if you have not been transported and transformed by adventuring through Creation, Exodus, Revelation, rebirth and the Messianic challenge; if you have not advanced spiritually and intellectually — you have missed the sublime opportunity inherent in each festival.

The holidays enable each of us to learn from our People's rocky journey through history. Each holiday teaches us how to internalize the lessons of Jewish history and make them an integral part of our inner selves. In this way, we succeed in harnessing the past to our personal goals and the goals of our Creator. If history does not speak to us, if we do not learn from the events of the past, what value is there to history and to the heroic efforts of the valiant generations that preceded us?

Unlike people who wander through time lonely and lost, each Jew has been given G-d's greatest gift: the opportunity to connect with the momentous events of history, and to unite with our ancestors and with G-d. We are given the chance to transform our own lives and, through responsible activism, transform history.

The purpose of this book is to present a variety of adventures through time — insights into each holiday that will uplift, inspire and motivate you to become active in the effort of the Jewish Nation to perfect the world and transform it into the G-dly Kingdom.

▶ Why This Book Contains Twenty Chapters Based on the Teachings of Rabbi Yitzchok Hutner, *zt"l*

Interspersed in this book are essays adapted by the author from the words of Rabbi Hutner, *zt"l*, one of the greatest and most original Jewish thinkers and teachers of our time. Each essay is freely translated from the original Hebrew, because Rabbi Hutner's writings do not lend themselves to literal translation. His rich and penetrating writing is part philosophy, part poetry, part mysticism and part piercing analysis. It was my privilege to sit transfixed as Rav Hutner introduced me, and his thousands of other students, to the world of Jewish thought and ideology. He uncovered the structure, logic, purpose and goals of our holidays, bringing them to life by revealing their inner dynamic and depth. He demonstrated how the holidays are the textbook as well as the classroom of Jewish ideology. He showed us how they underscore the structure of human life; how they are linked to each other like the workings of a perfectly balanced clock; how they form a ladder for us to climb from a simple awareness of Creation to the pursuit of human fulfillment and ultimately to the realization of the purpose of G-d's Creation.

I have included adaptations of these essays in this book because his lectures form the inspiration for everything I have written. I have attempted to present his ideas as I understand them. Obviously, while these adaptations/translations are a tribute to my teacher and rebbe, they are also an attempt to help the reader understand the source of my inspiration. Without Rabbi Hutner's thoughts, mine would have remained barren.

For many years, it was my privilege to hear the Yom Tov [holiday] presentations of my rabbi and friend, Rabbi Dovid Cohen, at Congregation Ge'vul Ya'avetz. Rabbi Cohen's penetrating insights and interpretations of the holidays have been both enlightening and inspiring.

This book consists of many "stand alone" chapters. The reason is that many people may read a given chapter or only a

few chapters at each sitting. In order to preserve the readability and integrity of each chapter, some repetition from some chapters to others is inevitable. In any case, our Sages taught that review and repetition is the essential handmaiden of Torah knowledge.

ACKNOWLEDGMENTS

An enormous investment of time and resources was required to make this book a reality. I am indebted and grateful for the generous support, friendship and encouragement of the following individuals:

▸ To Those Who Made Dedications:

Rabbi Meir A. Babad, Dr. Benjamin and Ellen Befeler, Jack A. and Marilyn Belz, Dr. Ronald and Raina Berger in memory of Sam Berger *z"l*, Howard Zvi and Chaya Friedman, Dr. Stanley and Marla Frohlinger, Paul and Rachel Glasser, H.B.S., Dr. David L. Hurwitz, Aaron and Malka Lampert in memory of *Avraham ben Aharon Shlomo Halevi* Lampert z"l,

Joseph and Julia Macy, Martin and Elizabeth Nachimson, Jack and Gita Nagel, Harry Zvi and Helen Ostreicher, Stuart and Lise Panish, Thomas W. and Miriam Pearlman, Eric and Gale Rothner in memory of *Aviva Esther bas Yisroel Avraham* Miretsky *z"l*, Larry A. and Shelly Russak, Lee C. and Ann Samson, Jay and Jeanne Schottenstein, Marvin and Jean Staiman, Sol and Ruth Teichman, Gary and Malka Torgow, *Le'iluy Nishmas Ya'akov ben Yonah z"l* by his granddaughter and her family; Heshy and Debbie Wengrow.

▶ I also Extend Heartfelt Appreciation to:

Mark I. and Joanne Bane, Rabbi Herschel and Shirley Berger, Steven and Linda Brizel in memory of *Yitzchak ben Zelig* Brizel *z"l, and Ya'akov Yitzchak ben Shmuel* Brizel *z"l*, Allen and Judith Fagin, Sheldon and Joan Fliegelman, Mark and Linda Karasick in memory of Joseph Ulevitch, *Yoseph Refael ben Issar z"l*, Leonard A. and Aliza Kestenbaum, Gerald and Phyllis Lerhman, Dr. Noah and Ellen Lightman, Moshe and Dena Luchins, Werner and Rachel Rosenbaum, Leonard Rosenthal, Sheldon and Hedda Rudoff, Jack and Rashie Schnell, Frank and Rosalyn Snitow, Marcel and Paula Weber, David S. and Grace Weil.

▶ And with gratitude to the following friends who also encourage and support my other literary efforts:

Moshe Alon, Fred and Susan Ehrman, Ernie and Regina Goldberger, Lothar and Sue Kahn, Paul and Cheryl Rodbell, Larry A. and Shelly Russak, Lee and Ann Samson, Jay and Jeanne Schottenstein, Leon Wildes.

There are four special individuals whose loyalty, friendship and dedication made possible the completion of this volume. They are **Harriet Bachman, Laura Berkowitz, Shelly Fliegelman** and **Ruthy Ungar.**

This book benefited from the diligent and conscientious devotion, sensitivity and patience of wonderful people who took the time to read and review sections of it and whose many wise suggestions are deeply appreciated: **Rabbi Leibel Rutta, Rabbi Sholom Morrow, Rabbi Dr. Aaron Lichtenstein, Rabbi Eliakim Willner,** my son **Rabbi Akiva Stolper,** my daughter-in-law **Channah Lee Stolper,** my son-in-law **Rabbi Zev Cohen** and my daughter **Michal Cohen.**

My admiration and gratitude go to a rare *talmid chacham* **Rabbi Yaakov Homnick,** whose insight, brilliance, depth and scholarship are awesome. It was he who did the final editing on the chapters based on Rav Hutner's works.

No one could have asked for a better editor than **Charlotte Friedland,** whose clarity of vision, depth, talent, sensitivity and idealistic professionalism kept me on my toes and did so much to bring out the best in my writing.

My deep appreciation for the advice, support, friendship and many kindnesses of the creators of the "ArtScroll Revolution," **Rabbi Meir Zlotowitz** and **Rabbi Nosson Scherman.**

I recall with deep gratitude the inspiration and zealous devotion to Jewish tradition of my late father, **Rabbi David Bernard Stolper** זצ״ל and of my mother **Mrs. Nettie Stolper,** תבלחט״א, who resides in Jerusalem.

No other wife would have allowed her husband to turn the dining room table into a writer's habitat for months on end (and I have two studies). I dedicate this volume to **Elaine,** my truest critic, whose patience and support made it possible. She personifies the nobility, *chessed* and insight of the Jewish wife, mother and grandmother. May we be worthy to merit the continued growth and achievements in Torah and *Yiras Shamayim* of our children and grandchildren.

May the Torah learning engendered by this volume add to the *tefillos* of the *tzibbur* for the *refuah sheleimah* of our daughter,

Malka Tova bas Chaya. May she, her husband Rabbi Dr. Chaim Kaweblum, and their children enjoy Hashem's blessings for many years to come.

Songs and praise to the most Mighty and Kind, the *Ribono Shel Olam* Himself, who has given me the *z'chus* to witness His miracles, to dwell in the tents of His Torah and to be His agent in person and through my pen.

Shevat 5763/January 2003
Pinchas Stolper

I INTRODUCTION

OUR
HOLY DAYS:
LOOKING FOR
THE TRUTH

1

Throughout our brief journey on earth, most of us read books and articles on philosophy, psychology, history, sociology, medicine and science. Our goal is to uncover the secret of life, to unravel the mystery of creation. Each time we open a new book or publication, we are attempting to find new ways to grow, to heal, to help, to understand. We attempt to dig deeper into our psyches. Thinking people engage in a never-ending search to uncover the mysteries and intricacies surrounding us so as to understand the building blocks that constitute our world.

Most of us are searching for the "black box" which contains the ultimate formulas and plans of reality. We hope to discover design, order and pattern. We realize that we are face to face with an exquisite and expertly designed structure which dwarfs the inventive ability of all the human engineers, architects, biologists, mathematicians, physicists, psychologists and sociologists combined, from the beginning of time to this day. As we dig deeper, the world is revealed as more complicated and more intricate than we ever imagined. As we continue our search, we discover infinite layers of wisdom and brilliance throughout creation.

For example, think of how the body reacts when you cut your finger: An army of tiny "doctors," "engineers," "builders" and "biologists" are mobilized to draw up a master plan and to import building materials with which to repair the cut. They then go about building a bridge across the torn divide. Most of us take healing for granted. We say, "The cut healed." We forget that in human terms, it's as though the Verrazano Narrows Bridge collapsed, and in just a few days it was rebuilt.

Discerning minds realize that once we acknowledge the existence of a world of design, art and engineering, we must also acknowledge a Designer, an Artist, the creative, active Mind of a super genius beyond human imagination and comprehension. Some people would rather avoid that thought.

I have told you all this because I hope that you are a seeker of truth. And I hope that you will want to read and reread this book, for it is an adventure into the mind of G-d, as He expresses it to us through the Torah. The festivals are much more than days of joy, celebration, prayer, ceremony and family. They are G-d's "black box:" They reveal G-d's ultimate formula for humanity and plan for history.

In this book, we will journey through Israel's early history. We will discover formulas for transforming our lives. By studying the holidays, secrets of life and the mystery of Creation will be revealed. You will learn how to become G-d's partner in the renaissance of the Jewish nation and ultimately of all mankind.

An example of this depth is offered in the following two paragraphs adapted from *Michtav Me'Eliyahu,* a book written by Rabbi Eliyahu Dessler who in turn had been inspired by his mentor, Rabbi Zvi Hirsch Braude. He offers a new way to view the festivals:

A Jew moves through time in a cycle we call the year. [It helps to envision an analog clock with calendar dates marked off instead of numbers.] Time does not pass. It is we who pass through time. Each year, we arrive at the same point in time that we left the previous year. Each festival is a "stop" on life's journey. Each stop has its own particular spiritual potential and influences. For instance, all of our Passover stops represent one Passover. When we arrive at the Passover stop, the [spiritual potential of the] day imbues us with the ability to experience freedom and the birth of the Jewish nation in the same way that our ancestors experienced freedom when they left Egypt.

Each year's Passover stop is designed to allow us to add to the treasure trove of experiences and insights we developed during previous Passovers, so that each year witnesses the maturation and growth of our personal Passover structure. So it is regarding the Sabbath and each of the holidays.

May your reading of this volume inspire you to read and study the many great and classic works as you explore the depths of Jewish thought.

THE WHY OF THE YOM TOV EXPERIENCE

he holidays of the Jewish year afford each individual the opportunity to experience *the totality of Jewish history* each year. This annual holiday cycle forms a hermetic unit, with a beginning and a conclusion. Each festival records seminal events in the history of our people. Imprinting the lessons of the past on the consciousness of the Torah People is the Torah's formula for influencing the choices we make in the present.

Through this process, the Torah molds and creates the future. The present and the future are rooted in the beginning. The tree bears fruits by keeping its roots vibrant. The proper observance of the festivals enables us to relive and re-experience each key event through which the Jewish nation was created and molded. In this way these events remain vibrant and alive, so that they effectively imprint their searing message on our consciousness, individually and as a people. Jewish thought is rooted in history; it is a philosophy that demands action and deeds. The Sabbath and holidays propel us forward, towards the day of Messianic fulfillment.

Jewish history is the recounting of the efforts of a G-d-conscious collective of individuals, who through the drama, trauma and experience of the Exodus were fashioned by G-d into a unique nation. Unlike any other nation in the world, the Jewish Nation was created with a specific goal and purpose. It is a "founded nation," established at the behest of G-d by Abraham to accomplish an ideological, societal and universal goal. At the Exodus, the Israelites who were committed to Abraham's ideology followed Moses and Aaron into the desert. There the newly freed slaves, who had suffered under the yoke of Pharaoh, would rejoice as they learned of the responsibilities of freedom which were intrinsically connected to their obligation to obey their loving and benevolent Master, G-d Himself.

The purpose of the Exodus was to enable the Jew to learn how to serve G-d, not to improve his physical lot or to conquer territory. The newly born nation braved the forbidding desert in order to receive the Torah. The goal of the desert journey was to train the liberated slaves to become a Torah nation dedicated to becoming G-d's instrument for the perfection of all of humanity.

The Jewish festivals are cyclic microcosms (miniature worlds which annually repeat their cycle) that encompass the totality of the human historical experience. It is for this reason that the Jewish year has two beginnings: Rosh Hashanah, which celebrates the creation of the Universe and the emergence of mankind; and Passover, which celebrates the birth of the Jewish Nation. The holidays, when observed to their fullest, are the creative womb that nurture the Messianic era of the future. The holidays nourish, sustain and create the Jewish reality. Only a people that centers its life around the experiences of its history, that cherishes the memories of its past; that learns from both its failures and its triumphs, that understands the need to sanctify time, and that toils to attain the perfection of the individual, family and society can possess the blueprint for building the Messianic society.

The goal of the holidays is to transport us from slavery to liberation; from the sojourn through the desert to the receiving of the Torah; and then up to and through the conquest of the Land of Israel to the building of the *Beis Hamikdash*, the Holy Temple in Jerusalem. It was in this crucible that the Nation of Israel was molded and formed. Each holiday constitutes a way station from the Exodus, each holiday is a marker on mankind's greatest and most significant journey. The Jew wasn't only freed from slavery. Most importantly, the Jew turned his back on the alluring and corrupt pagan civilization of Egypt, to create a new vibrant righteous society.

The process of unloading the negative influences of Egyptian society constitute the bulk of the Torah's narrative, beginning with the Book of Exodus through the end of Deuteronomy. The story of the Exodus, *Yetzias Mitzrayim*, recounts the struggle of a slave nation to become the central player in the Divine drama in which man escapes the magnetic allure of paganism and achieves spiritual wholeness. In the desert, the Jews accepted Divine direction, overcame sin, temptation and backsliding, cleansed itself of sin, regained G-d's favor and finally became worthy of entering the Land of Israel, the locale where the ideal Torah society was to be created.

The holidays and their elaborate observances challenge and motivate each Jew to internalize the lessons of our forefathers, experience their struggles and emerge as mature, responsible, G-d-fearing, Torah observant individuals.

In a nutshell, how do the holidays and special fast days achieve this purpose?

Passover recollects the birth of Israel as a nation, the acceptance of G-d's sovereignty and the rejection of Pharaoh's corrupt civilization.

Shavuos re-enacts the Sinai Revelation of G-d's word, i.e. the giving and receiving of the Torah, which is the guidebook for how to serve G-d and create the ideal society.

On the **Seventeenth** of the Hebrew month of **Tamuz,** Israel sinned by worshipping the Golden Calf and Moses smashed the first Tablets of the Covenant.

On **Tishah B'Av,** the Ninth of Av, Israel sinned again by accepting the distressing report of the spies who discouraged them from entering the Land of Israel.

On the first day of Elul, Moses ascended Mt. Sinai for the second time.

On **Rosh Hashanah,** the day on which mankind was created and is judged, the scales of justice tipped in Israel's favor after the sin of the Golden Calf. (Like the Children of Israel at Mt. Sinai, on Rosh Hashanah man acknowledges G-d as Creator and King.)

On **Yom Kippur,** the Day of Atonement, Moses descended Mt. Sinai holding the second Tablets of the Covenant. This was a Divine indication that G-d had forgiven Israel's sins. On this day, Israel was cleansed and born again as it accepted the Torah for a second time.

Succos celebrates Divine protection in the desert. It is the holiday on which the repentant individual and nation joyfully celebrate their ability to overcome sin and be restored to G-d's favor.

Hoshanah Rabbah is the last day for repentance, the day on which we anticipate the coming of the Messiah.

Shmini Atzeres/Simchas Torah anticipates the final victory of human history and the rebuilding of the Temple, when our hopes and dreams are realized and civilization achieves its goal and purpose. It is the day for anticipating the coming era of the Messiah.

The holidays are times to rejoice, to enjoy the blessings of home, children and family. The goal of this book is to help you become more deeply aware of the ultimate purpose and goal of each holiday. Each holiday affords one the leisure to celebrate and enjoy its observances but also to *think*, to study and to delve more deeply into the unique meaning and lesson of the day. Most importantly, we have the opportunity to emerge from each holiday spiritually energized, motivated to apply its lessons to the tasks of life and to commit ourselves as a partner in the enterprise of rebuilding the Torah People into a more effective instrumentality for *tikkun olam*, for the remolding of our world as the Divine Kingdom.

My hope is that the experience of each Yom Tov will succeed in stimulating you to achieve a deeper and more mature appreciation of its lessons and goals. The Torah tells us "*V'samachta b'chagecha*,[1] and you shall rejoice in your festivals." May you discover the true joy of each holiday through the exhilarating magic and depth of its unique challenges and observances.

---

1. *Deuteronomy* 16:14.

OUR PAST IS OUR FUTURE:
THE INNER MEANING OF JEWISH HISTORY AND THE JEWISH FESTIVALS

The lessons of history dare not be ignored. He who ignores history is destined to repeat its mistakes out of ignorance. But he who is conscious of history is able to overcome the errors of the past and build the new, enlightened future. Jews are given the option: learn from the past — remember the Egyptian bondage and the Exodus — or be forced to relive the bondage and remain "slaves" to the empty idols of our own times. In the western world, these idols are the false values of our materialistic, alien, secular society. Or we can opt to become liberated, independent and free. Our Sages teach, "No one is truly free, except for the person who makes Torah study his major occupation."[1] Each of our festivals recalls a seminal event in the history of our people. The Jew is always remembering, always conscious of history. How does the memory of the events of the Exodus from Egypt enable the Jew to accomplish today's goals of healing an ailing society and bringing about the era of the Messiah?

How do our festivals contribute to the perfection of man and mankind? What is the relationship between history and morality? How do our festivals promote the creation of a society that lives in harmony with Divine imperatives? Why is all of Jewish life considered "a remembrance to the Exodus from Egypt"? Why does history play such a prominent role in our Torah and in the holidays that form the infrastructure of the Jewish year and Jewish existence? These crucial questions will be answered throughout this book. First, we must understand what the Jew's relationship with the past is and what it is not.

There are people who view Judaism as a rigidly congealed tradition focused on the ancient past alone, who disdain it for being concerned with preserving the uses and prerogatives of yesterday. In fact, however, the opposite is true. Judaism has very little interest in the past per se. Judaism relates to the past only to the extent that the past is concerned with the future and provides guideposts for building the future. Judaism views "man" as a continuum whose present and future are extensions of the past. The present is the fleeting fiction between past and future. Since the future is not yet here, "man" is the sum total of his individual and collective memory and experience. In order to propel us into the future, the Torah preserves only those pivotal and formative events of the past that are needed for the molding of the present and the future.

No Jewish practice, *mitzvah* or festival is observed today *only* because of what happened in history. True, the Torah is historical; it is based on scrupulously preserved, Divinely revealed historical truth. In fact, since man is a highly subjective and fallible recorder of history, we can speak of only revealed history as true and objective. Jewish practices and observances are rooted in historical events because these events are the foundation for contemporary, societal value structures on which to build the redeemed world of tomorrow, the "*olam b'malchus Sha-kai.*" Imprinting the spiritual lessons of past history on the consciousness of a people in order to influence the choices of the present is the Torah's formula for creating tomorrow. The end is rooted in the beginning — without the beginning; the end cannot take root and blossom. Our festivals are beyond mere commemoration: They call upon us to feel and relive the events, moods, associations and circumstances of the past, so that they become alive again in the present. It demands that we hear the voices of our Sages as they bore into the depth of events and bring us the nuggets of insight and understanding that are the essence of the festivals.

In the process of recording history the Bible is highly selective. This is why only sixty-six chapters are preserved of Isaiah and only three of Habakkuk, from their lifetimes of Divinely inspired speech. These were preserved not for their literary or historic value but because they are ceaselessly contemporary, because their message is eternally valid and addresses all generations, because they link the past to the future and transform the personalities of the past into living members of the dramatic cast of future events.

Unlike other religions whose roots are in mythological mystery or pagan magic, Judaism is rooted in history because only a world-outlook that sprouts from the very origins and roots of human experience can be relevant to man. This is true because man, as stated above, is the product and sum total of historical antecedents which catapult him into the world of the future. Jewish philosophy is related to, and distilled from, live events, from the experiences of a living historical people. This is why the bulk of the Five Books of Moses is biography and history, and not "law" as is commonly assumed.

Jewish philosophy, rooted as it is in time and history, insists that history has direction, purpose and goals that ceaselessly advance man toward the day of Messianic fulfillment. History is not an aimless meandering of tragic error and brutal human suffering. Nor is man so hopeless that, as in the Christian view, he is totally dependent on otherworldly supernatural redemption.

Redemption and the Messianic kingdom in Jewish thought are primarily the responsibility of man: Torah and *mitzvos* are man's G-d-given instruments for the perfection of the world and the restoration of Eden. With them, he must lift himself up by "his own bootstraps" to bring Redemption. Only when man chooses the right paths will he merit the coming of the Messiah.

Our name, Israel, derives from our forefather, Yisrael, who obtained that distinctive princely title by struggling with both G-d and man and prevailing in both instances. We, too, must maintain the struggle within ourselves and with society so that the Israel in us all will prevail over the Esau who wages unceasing battle for domination. The Messiah will come, our Sages tell us, when "Israel will fully keep two Sabbaths, one following the other."[2]

The Kingdom of G-d, the reign of justice, "the beating of swords into plowshares and spears into pruning hooks" is man's responsibility. The world is redeemable and perfectible — and man has been placed in it to improve, correct and perfect the world as the Kingdom of G-d. My Rosh Yeshivah, Hagaon Rav Yitzchok Hutner, *zt"l*, once told me: "*Mashiach kimt nit; m'darf em brengen* — the Messiah will not come [of his own accord]; we must bring him."

This is not to question that G-d alone is the ultimate redemptive force of the world. The master plan is His alone; the identity of the Messiah is His secret, yet to be revealed. And the Messiah himself will be anointed by G-d alone. But the agent for fulfillment is man, not G-d. The responsibility is man's, not G-d's. The King Messiah will not be a "G-d-Man" with superman qualities. On the contrary, the Messiah is Man, intensely, superbly man. He is so great, so holy, so selfless and so knowledgeable that men and women, attracted to his knowledge and charisma, will freely choose him as their king. But always, mankind will build the kingdom — not by magic, but through the ongoing process of perfection of self, society and environment.

History, insofar as the Jew finds it relevant, is the recounting of the efforts of a collective of individuals, who became a nation after the Exodus, received the Torah and set forth to bring about world Redemption. It is the re-telling of events that constitute a pattern — a formula — for bringing about the fulfillment of that process which was set in motion by the first Jew, Abraham, and by the first Jews, the people liberated from Egypt. The Jew lives with the assurance that "*Ma'aseh avos siman le'banim*," i.e. that the experiences that molded our fathers set the pattern for the future history and fulfillment of their children.

How is all of this accomplished? The first step is through the study of Torah, which dwells so elaborately on history and towering historic personalities. A pattern for correct living is acquired not only through the discipline of laws and rules, but through the example of living personalities and the lessons of historic events.

But a problem arises. How are we to make these personalities and their experiences, trials and triumphs, part of our own lives and personalities? In a word, how can we become our ancestors' successors and disciples, so as to be able to fulfill their goals? This question takes us to the second step: immersion in a total Jewish environment. How can we regain in some measure the experiences of the past? How can we recreate for ourselves the environment of Judaism's formative and crucial events? Only through the observance of Shabbos and *moadim*, our Sabbaths and festivals, through which we recreate, relive and re-experience the formative events of Jewish history.

The festivals reveal the national character of *Klal Yisrael*, the Nation of Israel, in all its majesty. It is these experiences that molded our national character. The festivals reveal the relationship and the ties that bind the Nation of Israel to G-d.[3]

Other utopian efforts consistently fail, while the Jewish Messianic dream remains ever vibrant, fresh and forceful. This vitality stems from three unique characteristics that distinguish Jewish Messianism:

First: While non-Jewish revolutions often succeed in uprooting the corruption of a given society, disillusionment soon sets in and the citizens wake up to discover that the former rot is rapidly replaced with equally obnoxious evils. Communism, "the god that failed," is a classic example. To establish a beautiful garden, it is far from adequate to uproot noxious weeds. Above all else, it is necessary to possess the expertise and the will with which to design, create, plant and sustain the beautiful garden.

Second: Utopian concepts are invariably constructed on political or economic formulas that generally employ a single component and logic. But life's realities are multi-phased, going well beyond cold logic. In contradistinction, the Jewish Messianic concept utilizes the total gestalt of human experience — mind, emotion and environment.

Finally: The secularist pursues and worships an illusion called "progress," a concept which sets forth the dogma that the first human beings were primitive and barbaric, while we moderns are advanced sophisticates, capable of creating the ideal society. Secular society posits history as advancing and progressing in a straight line from primitive ape to civilized modern, while Jewish thought views history as a cycle which begins with Adam and Eve — individuals who were on the highest human and spiritual plane — and will conclude with the Messiah — the most exemplary and accomplished human being. Much of Jewish life (as is true of all life) revolves around cycles, history, the year and its festivals — and the week with its Sabbath. Judaism recognizes that to aspire toward utopia, mankind must reach back to Genesis, to its exalted beginnings, to the most ancient man, Adam, who stood at the pinnacle of human perfection prior to his sin.

How is the ideal, Messianic society created? Only a nation that centers and concentrates its life around Messianic days possesses the blueprint for building a Messianic world. Only a people that dreams of "tikkun olam," the fulfilled and perfected Messianic world, possesses the formula and vitality to rebuild society as the Kingdom of the One G-d. My Rosh Yeshivah told me on another occasion: "Mashiach brengt min nor mit chutzpah — The Messiah does not come [of his own accord]; he must be brought with daring, imagination and audacity."

An ideal society does not sprout out of the ground, nor does a people create the Kingdom of G-d from theories and concepts. The prophesied society in which "swords will be a beaten into plowshares" requires a human laboratory, a committed core of leadership that lives on a high plane and cultivates an existence of spirituality and high purpose. The Jewish Messianic dream and the ideal Jewish reality are nurtured by the festivals and the Sabbath. These come with cyclic regularity into our weed-strewn lives, offering us a foretaste of the World to Come, "may'ain olam habah." These are days in which we set aside the secular to immerse ourselves in the holy. On the Sabbath and festivals we envelop ourselves in the Messianic environment. The Sabbath is a weekly reliving and experiencing of world history: Through it, we remind ourselves of our obligation to serve as the heart and soul of the Divine charge to bring history to fruition.

The festivals follow the same cycle as the Sabbath — from birth of Israel to fulfillment of its purpose.

Passover, the first festival of the Jewish year, marks the birth of the Jewish People and sets the pattern for the succeeding holidays — Shavuos and Succos/Shmini Atzeres. Passover is no mere commemoration of historic events. Its basic premise is echoed in the words of the Haggadah: "In each generation, every person must see himself as though *he too* went out of Egypt." We say the blessing, "Blessed are You, who redeemed *us* and redeemed our fathers from Egypt."

The ritual of the Seder allows each participant to relive and experience liberation. We eat matzah, charoses and *maror* (bitter herbs) because *we* were slaves in Egypt, because we yet lack redemption. Without a sense of identification with the liberated, and without reliving the experiences of their liberation, Passover has limited value. Observed properly, it becomes a vicarious, experiential, collective reliving of the Exodus.

Shavuos, the second festival, does not commemorate the giving of the Torah; it calls on us to *experience and relive* the receiving of the Torah. For this reason, there are no special rituals of Shavuos in our day, because its focus is exclusively on Torah. Each individual can experience in his or her own consciousness the unique and awesome act of receiving of the Torah.

Succos, the third festival, completes the cycle with a variety of graded purposes. First, we experience the life of the homeless stranger; the desert wanderer whose only protection is the frail, thatched *succah*, a temporary dwelling, a symbol of exile and total dependence on G-d's beneficence. Second, we experience the ascent of the Jewish People to the Land of Israel. The *esrog* [citron], *lulav* [palm branch], *hadassim* (myrtle branches) and *aravos* (willow) are held together, symbolizing the unity of the many groupings of G-d's people. We gather Israel's many fruits, symbolized by the *esrog* [citron] and *lulav* [palm branch], universal symbols that represent various levels of human attainment.

Finally, as we reach the crescendo of the festival cycle, we reach the pinnacle of the year with Shemini Atzeres and Simchas Torah, days somewhat similar to Shavuos in that they do not require specific rituals. If we have internalized the lessons of the Succos observances, and made them part of our psyche and life's purpose, we dance and sing with abandon on Simchas Torah (the culmination of the year's events), as though to declare, "I have freed myself of all enslavement. I have fully accepted Your Torah. I have cleansed myself of the filth of exile. I have entered Your Holy land. I have built Your Temple. I have participated in the perfection of society. I have prepared myself to welcome the Messiah a world not yet aware of the challenges and responsibilities of the great Divine adventure."

Journeying through our festivals, we will arrive at the full Redemption of Israel and mankind. This journey can be completed by our generation only if we have fully identified with the spiritual adventure of those who took the very first steps. If we relive their experiences and learn the lessons of their triumphs and their failings, we too will succeed in being liberated from the chains that bind us to the false values of western civilization; we too will receive the Torah; we too will resist the temptations of materialism's Golden Calf; we too will enter the Promised Land and we too will be participants of the rebuilding of the Temple on Mount Zion. These events will be the ultimate sign that G-d once more dwells among man and that we have established the Kingdom of G-d on this earth.

Ultimately, this kingdom will be created by those who presently participate in its building. The Messianic revolution is brought about not by slogans, rallies, petitions or political revolutions, but by dwelling in G-d's Kingdom, by building and planting from within. "*Yismechu be'malchuscha* — those who reside in Your Kingdom, the Kingdom of Shabbos and Yom Tov, are those who will merit the ultimate joy." This is the secret of Jewish Messianism. When G-d's Chosen People throws off its lethargy and dynamically blossoms and grows from within, it will be capable of building that Kingdom for the benefit of all mankind.

1. *Ethics of the Fathers* 6:2.
2. *Shabbos* 118a.
3. *Ohr Chadash.*

THE JEWISH HOLIDAYS AND AGRICULTURE

During the Biblical period, as long as the Jews lived in the Land of Israel, the survival of all people was intimately tied to the local agriculture. If the fields failed to produce, the people starved. The modern global economy, where produce is shipped from one country to the other worldwide, and where few of us derive our livelihood directly from agriculture, did not exist until recently.

When local agriculture was the prime source of sustenance, life revolved around the seasons and the anticipated success of crops. The severe storms, floods, droughts, locusts or other pestilence was the constant fear of the farmer, his family and the entire population. Life depended on nature and the Master of nature, G-d above.

Agriculture requires faith. The very act of planting seeds in the ground represents a supreme act of faith. When seeds are planted, not only do they disappear from sight, they undergo a process in the ground that can only be called decay. It is only after much toil and anticipation that the seeds burst forth in what is essentially a resurrection. This joyous result, however, is never guaranteed and can be thwarted by many factors. The farmer, more than anyone, realizes that his prosperity is dependent on G-d. When the people of an entire nation understand that the very food sustaining them is a blessing directly from heaven, their faith is reinforced with each harvest.

For this reason, the agricultural calendar is a mirror image of the Jewish historical/spiritual calendar of festivals. As the earth orbits, each season of the year inspires and produces the conditions necessary for both physical and spiritual events. It is no accident that our people's great historical events, commemorated by our festivals, took place in tandem with specific seasons of the year. It is part of G-d's great plan that history and nature combine. It was G-d who saw to it that Israel's liberation and birth took place in the springtime, when nature is liberated from the hibernation of winter, when the trees and fields are reborn.

The Hebrew language — in which every word has deep meaning — contains key words that provide evidence that the events of history and the events in nature are intimately related to each other and reflect the same reality. The meaning of the Hebrew word *zeman* [time, season] is derived from *mezuman* [prepared]. *Shanah* [year] takes its meaning from *l'shanos* [to change or repeat]; and *chodesh* [month] is related to *chadash* [new and renewal]. The festivals are called *moadim* [meetings, a time when people gather]; they are also called *chagim*, from the word *chug,* [a circle or cycle] because they return with regularity each year.

The three major festivals reflect the seasons:

Passover, called in the Torah *Chag Hamatzos,* the festival of unleavened bread, took place in the *chodesh he'aviv,* the month of springtime, the appointed Hebrew month of Nissan.

Shavuos is "the festival of weeks" [a week is a *shavuah*]. Shavuos is also called *Chag Habikurim,* when the first offerings [*bechor*] of the new wheat crop were brought to the Holy Temple in Jerusalem.

Succos, the festival whose name means "booths" (in which we dwell for the duration of the holiday), is also called *Chag Ha'asif*, "the festival of ingathering (of crops)."

In addition, though not Biblically ordained, Chanukah and Purim take place during the winter, when the earth is cold and dark. Both are festivals of exile in which the Jewish People fought spiritual destruction and the threat of genocide.

The success of the Holy Land's agricultural seasons added greatly to the joy of each festival. It opened the hearts of the Jewish People to understand that the Divine blessing of rich crops dovetailed with the blessings He bestowed upon the nation with the historical miracles of the Exodus, the Revelation at Mount Sinai, forgiveness on Yom Kippur, the conquest of the Land of Israel and the realization of Israel's dreams and aspirations as the People of G-d.

Though today we no longer feel the agricultural cycle directly, it is still true that the success of harvests globally provide our food; and despite advanced technology, it is possible for entire nations to starve. In the western world, our celebrations tend to emphasize other aspects the holidays. Yet we would do well to be aware that the changing of the seasons and the bounty bestowed upon us in Israel are closely linked to timely spiritual opportunities that are eternal.

II | SHABBOS, THE SABBATH

THE DAY THAT LEADS US TO ETERNITY

5

hen Alexander the Great arrived in the Land of Israel with his Greek armies, he saw Jews for the first time. The Greeks were shocked when they observed that nearly everything came to a halt on Saturday. They thought the Jews were lazy. The notion of a Sabbath — a day dedicated to rest and spirituality — was totally foreign to the Greek mind. Today, Shabbos lives and thrives while the world of the ancient Greeks can be found in museums, ruins and books few people read.

No ancient nation prior to the Jews had a day of rest, and no society since has successfully replicated or properly understood the Jewish Sabbath. As G-d stated in Genesis, "It is a sign between Me and you:" The Sabbath is to be an exclusively Jewish institution. The Moslem Friday and Christian Sunday are at best imitations, counterfeit borrowings from the beautiful, deep and rich table of the Jewish Sabbath's delicacies.

Generally one cannot appreciate or understand Shabbos unless one has lived and experienced it. No written word or flowery description can capture its true essence. For so many who previously stood on the outside, one taste of an authentic and joyous Sabbath was sufficient to convince them that they had tasted something that is not of this world, *may'ain olam habah* [it is a taste of the World to Come] and that Shabbos is worth every sacrifice in order to earn its weekly joy, fulfillment and heightened spiritual existence.

Shabbos promotes and facilitates the idea that man is at his best when he is spiritual. Judaism is the only civilization that assigned and promulgated a full day of genuine spirituality each week by putting aside *all else* so that the mind, heart, soul and intellect might rule.

The power, vigor and tenacity of Shabbos in Jewish life is so strong that a Jew is defined as practicing and observant if he is *Shomer Shabbos* — a keeper of the Sabbath laws. No other *mitzvah* comes close as a sweeping blanket definition of the loyal "halachic Jew," i.e. observant of Torah law. The paramount significance of Sabbath observance is demonstrated by the fact that the Ten Commandments contains but *one* commandment which can be defined as religious ritual, namely, Shabbos observance. The Sages noted that, "the weight of Shabbos is equal to that of all the commandments."[1]

By pursuing a life of spirituality, we attach ourselves to G-d and assure ourselves eternal life in the spiritual realm. What are some of the signs that the Sabbath and the pursuit of eternity are synonymous? The Sages speak of Shabbos as *may'ain olam habah*, a foretaste of the World to Come, the world of spirituality that continues after one's death. The mystical work *Zohar (Bereishis)* says that, "Shabbos is a sample of the world of the future."

The fact that Shabbos is the only time Jews proclaim (in the *Shmoneh Esrei* of *Minchah*), "You are One and Your name is One," in the present implies that the Sabbath exists on a plane above and beyond time — that in observing Shabbos we are elevated beyond time and above history to the level of Messianic existence. It is only on Shabbos at *Minchah* that we experience a heightened elevated reality — a meta-historical existence in which we vicariously experience that future time when *G-d is One*. We might point to *Sh'ma Yisrael,* the Jew's most pronounced proclamation that G-d is One, but the Torah commentator par excellence, Rashi, explains that the meaning of *Sh'ma* is that G-d, who is our G-d, *will become One* only when all of mankind accepts G-d as King over all the earth, i.e. Hashem who is our G-d *will become One* only when mankind accepts G-d in keeping with *Zechariah* 14:9, "Hashem *will be* king over all the earth *on that day*. Hashem will be One and His Name One."

The story is told of the king of a tiny kingdom who invited all of his subjects to a weekly celebration on Wednesday nights between 9:00 P.M. and 12:00 A.M. At first, everyone in the realm came. As the months went by, the number of attendees dwindled. One day, one of the wealthiest of the king's noblemen decided that he too would arrange for a weekly celebration at the very same time as the king's party. He, however, outdid the king in every way and served an even more lavish and regal dinner. The very next week, the king posted a guard at the palace door to record the names of all those who attended his party, instead of the nobleman's. Only those who attended the king's party *that night* were allowed to attend in the future. They became the king's intimate confidants.

So too with the Jewish People and the Shabbos, as G-d stated in the Torah, "It is an eternal sign, exclusively between Me and the Children of Israel, to attest to the fact that in six days, G-d created the heavens and the earth, and on the seventh day He ceased from His creative labors and called it Shabbos." Those who faithfully observe the Sabbath as G-d commanded will merit a place in G-d's kingdom. Those who allow themselves to be lured away from Shabbos forfeit the "eternal sign" between themselves and G-d.

On Shabbos, we discover and develop our true inner selves — our spiritual selves. Instead of being a person consumed by the physical, instead of being totally wrapped up by our desire to capture and conquer the physical earth, we develop our *neshamah,* our spiritual side. We become better able to control and overcome that part of us that wants to hoard things, most of which we surely don't need and certainly can't take with us to the World to Come, *olam haba.*

Shabbos facilitates man's ability to be his very best, as far removed from the animal as possible. This goal demands placing maximum emphasis on the spiritual — which we do by using the many gifts that G-d has given us to pursue spiritual goals. When we pursue spirituality, we are attaching ourselves to G-dly goals; we become eternal, somewhat like G-d Himself. In effect, we insure that our souls will never die. If we want to find our way to the spiritual world that our Sages call *olam haba* — or if we wish to create the *olam haba* in this world, i.e. the Messianic era — we must invest ourselves totally in Shabbos, the day of spiritual perfection and completion which is *me'ein olam haba* — a taste of the World to Come.[2]

Many of us find it difficult to refrain from discussing material things on Shabbos, whether it is our business, our profession or the market. The Torah says, "You shall labor for six days and complete all of your work."[3] Is it possible to complete all of our work in six days? Can we stop on a dime when Shabbos arrives? Obviously not: On the material level, our work is never done. What can we do? When Shabbos comes, we should adopt the mindset of relating to our work *as though* our work is completed.[4] This is accomplished by putting our professional and business activities out of our minds. By adopting the attitude that our work is the *means* and Shabbos is the *end*, the goal of our work-a-day week, we develop the ability to overcome the temptation to trivialize and secularize our Shabbos. "The test is: Do thoughts of our work week invade our Shabbos — or does the spirit of Shabbos permeate our week in such a way that we will be able to take our minds off business on Shabbos?"[5]

The above description does not imply that Shabbos is not a day for pleasure. To the contrary, our Sages require that we honor Shabbos with good food, an attractive table, fine dinnerware and linen, with the best that we own. We also dress in honor of Shabbos and arrange our homes so that it befits a day of *oneg,* pleasure. This understanding is derived from the words of the prophet Isaiah: "You shall call the Shabbos *oneg* — a pleasure in honor of G-d's holy day."[6]

Pleasure has a dual meaning: physical pleasure as well as the spiritual pleasure. The spiritual delight results from being close to G-d.[7] The holiness of Shabbos is so intense that it is able to absorb our physical pleasures, transforming them and merging them with the spiritual dimension of Shabbos. The Sages note, "One Shabbos is a sixtieth of the World to Come."[8]

The more a person appreciates the essence of Shabbos, the better he or she is able to transcend the boundaries of the every day. Genesis 2:3 says that G-d blessed the Shabbos [*veyevarech*]. Blessing implies expansion, unlimited opportunities for spiritual growth and progress. But a day is limited in time. How can Shabbos afford us unlimited opportunities for growth? The answer to this question, says noted *Mussar* thinker Rabbi Eliyahu Dessler, is that in bringing us close to G-d, Shabbos is beyond time.[9] The experience of Shabbos makes it possible for a human being to transcend the limits of time on both the physical and spiritual plane. "The true blessing of Shabbos is the expansion of our consciousness from preoccupation with the trivialities of this world to immersion in the limitless spiritual world. This is the 'inheritance without bounds,' which is promised to the person who takes pleasure in Shabbos."[10] Here, too, we are forging links with *olam haba*, the World to Come — the "*Yom Shekulo Shabbos*, the day which is totally Shabbos," without any end or boundaries.

▸ The Secret of Shabbos

In the world of science, things are of value only when we are able to describe or measure them. In contradistinction, in the world of the spirit, things are most valuable when they are indescribable. The essence of Shabbos is its ability to free us from the narrow straits of materialism and attach ourselves to the endless values of the spiritual. The prohibitions of "work" on Shabbos are designed to facilitate our ability to pursue this goal, to help us detach ourselves from the world of physical creativity so that we can enwrap ourselves in spiritual creativity.

This is why in Hebrew we call the Sabbath "*Shabbos Kodesh, the holy Shabbos.*" Holiness means separation from the everyday, from the profane. Holiness aspires the world of spiritual goals. Shabbos is "G-d's day" — the day that emphasizes the unique relationship between G-d and Israel. G-d promises, "Shabbos is a sign between Me and you that I [G-d] will make you holy."[11]

This relationship between G-d and Israel in the context of Shabbos is unique. It is also private and personal. It is the secret reward for keeping Shabbos, which the Talmud tells us is not revealed: "The reward for observing Shabbos He did not make known to them."[12] To again quote Rabbi Dessler: "It cannot be revealed because we are speaking of the holiness of Shabbos that is experienced in the secret recesses of our heart. If it were ever revealed or articulated, it would cease to be a unique, personal, inward experience of 'being.' Once Shabbos emerged into the outside world, it would never be the same. This is a quality that Shabbos shares with *olam haba.*"

Our attitude to Shabbos and our manner of observing it demonstrate our true attitude to spirituality. Are we spiritual beings — or are we so very material that the spiritual does not speak to us and does not penetrate our being? This is the "sign between G-d and us," the sign which points to our true selves, the sign which reveals the true nature of our inner being.

▸ The Conclusion of Shabbos

The concluding moments of Shabbos are the time of its deepest spirituality. We literally have arrived at the apex of the holy day. If we have spent our Shabbos enjoying its spiritual opportunities, by *Minchah* time we are primed to experience moments paralleling the coming Messianic era. At the third meal, we have the ability to be transported spiritually above and beyond time to the presence of the Messianic King. We are, as is movingly depicted in the hymn of the third and final Shabbos meal, "... members of the Divine Sanctuary who yearn to see a miniature presence of the Heavenly glow, who long to be part of the angelic assemblage."[13]

Soon, we will arrive at the foreboding moments of the departure of the Sabbath. Holiness wanes and the travails of the workweek loom ahead of us. Our moods change. At the conclusion of Shabbos, we hold the cup of wine, the *Havdalah* candle and the spice-box and exclaim, "Behold, G-d is my salvation. I will trust. I will not fear." The Sabbath has passed. Darkness has descended. The promised Messiah, the day that is forever, is gone.

The initials of the instruments of the *Havdalah* ceremony — *yayin*, wine; ***besamim,*** spices; ***ner***, a candle; and ***Havdalah***— spell *Yavneh*, the town which served as the focal point for the revival of Jewish life immediately after the great tragedy of the destruction of the Second Temple in the year 70 CE. *Yavneh* can also be pronounced *Yibaneh*, which means "it will be rebuilt." Our fear results from our disappointment and frustration that *this* Sabbath did not continue. We fear exile and alienation. We fear our endless enemies. We fear the continued absence of the Holy Temple from its site and the absence of the *Shechinah* [the majestic presence of G-d] that dwells in the Temple.

Yet we trust that someday "it will be rebuilt," as symbolized by *Havdalah*. When the great day comes, we will merit greeting the King Messiah. We know that some day soon, Shabbos will not end with *Havdalah*, but will continue forever as the *Yom Shekulo Shabbos*, as the anticipated day that will continue eternally to be Shabbos.

We have a Divine promise: "If you will preserve the Shabbos lights, I will show you the glowing lights of Zion." Another rendering of this concept is stated in the Jerusalem Talmud, "If all of Israel will observe two consecutive Sabbaths, we will be redeemed immediately."[14]

▶ An Additional Thought

Our detractors often challenge us, "What proof do you have for all the laws you observe?" While many books have been written in support of the authenticity of our tradition, one simple sentence should suffice: "Only G-d could have thought of the Shabbos."

It is inconceivable that a human being could have invented something so brilliant, so compelling and so decisive. Even if a human mind could have conceived it, who could have succeeded in convincing an entire nation of stubborn, critical and rebellious people to undertake the observance of a day that, on one hand, is so exacting, so filled with legal minutia; and on the other hand, is so joyous, so fulfilling, so utterly necessary to mental health and spiritual balance? Only One, the unique One, the Holy One, Blessed is He, Himself.

1. *Shemos Rabbah* 25.
2. *Zmiros Mah Yedidus.*
3. *Exodus* 20:9.
4. *Michtav Me'Eliyahu II* 14.
5. *Seforno: Genesis* 20:9.
6. *Isaiah* 58:13.
7. *Zohar III* 946.
8. *Berachos* 57b.
9. *Michtav Me'Eliyahu II* 15.
10. *Shabbos* 118a.
11. *Exodus* 31:13.
12. *Beitzah* 16a.
13. *B'nei Heichala.*
14. *Jerusalem Talmud Ta'anis* 1a.

SHABBOS IN A NEW LIGHT

6

"**A**nd G-d examined His creation and saw that it was very good."[1] Did G-d not know that His own creation was the essence of goodness? The Hebrew word "*vayare*" in the Torah is usually translated to mean "He saw." But it can be read differently — not He *saw*, but He *demonstrated* that it is good. It is good because G-d is goodness; therefore His creation is good. It is now up to man to make this goodness even better.

"And G-d 'rested from His creative efforts [*vayishbos mikol melachto*].'"[2] What was missing in the world? Shabbos, a day of withdrawal from physical creativity, which would allow for spiritual creativity.

"And you shall do *all* your work."[3] How is it possible to finish all creative efforts right before the arrival of Shabbos? Just because Shabbos has arrived, does that mean that my business deal has been completed? That I have finished writing my term paper? That I completed building my home, or my skyscraper? The answer to these questions is that just as G-d called a halt to physical creativity, Shabbos demands that we, too, call a halt to creativity. Once we enter the environment of Shabbos, we must behave *as though* our work has been completed.[4] This is a tall order, a most difficult expectation. But that is the challenge of Shabbos — the ability to unplug our minds from our daily chores and apply ourselves to the effort of building our inner spiritual world.

On Shabbos we call a halt to physical creativity — to mastery, invention and routine; to our enslavement to the world of things; to our careers and ambitions. We learn to desist from creativity and to act *as though* all of our tasks, projects and obligations have been completed. By behaving in this fashion, we imitate the actions of our Creator.

If we appreciate that the goal of Creation was Shabbos — and that the culmination of history will be the *Yom Shekulo Shabbos*, the establishment of the Messianic era that is *totally* Shabbos, we will then have harmonized our personal goals with the goals of our Creator. We will have demonstrated that spirituality is on the highest rung of our life's agenda.

To the average outsider, a description of the Jewish Sabbath — with its many restrictions and observances — sounds difficult and arcane. To the Orthodox Sabbath observer, however, Shabbos is the most pleasant, enjoyable and rewarding of days. How many times have you heard: "I just can't wait for Shabbos;" or "If it weren't for Shabbos, I just couldn't make it;" or "How in the world can those who don't have Shabbos manage to keep up the same demanding pace day after day?"

Shabbos is the most civilized innovation in all of human history. Most ancient societies were based on slavery, and slaves worked every day, all day, till they dropped. Israel's Sabbath is for all — men, women, children, the rich and the poor, the indentured and the free. It is the most democratic, liberating institution of mankind. Most societies denied their poor a day of rest, not only because they saw no reason to give the poor such a magnanimous and unnecessary gift, but because of the fear that a day of leisure would allow for the emergence of dangerous and revolutionary thoughts and plots.

Shabbos innovated the concept that spirituality, literacy, learning, leisure, recreation and family are the right and obligation of all — no matter how low, poor or uneducated. On Shabbos, assembled around the festive Shabbos table, with its challah and wine, meat and fish — every man is a king and every woman is a queen. Even the children feel like little princes and princesses. Somehow, the magic ingredients of Shabbos transform everyone — granting every person a reprieve from drudgery.

Shabbos created a society in which every person is free and endowed with dignity for one day each week. Every person could enter the magic Kingdom of Shabbos. You might say that Shabbos was mankind's first Bill of Human Rights.* It was only because the laws of Shabbos are so all-encompassing, strict and precise — so universally applicable to all — that they grant rights, privileges, obligations and dignity to every single member of society without exception. Leisure is the sine qua non for human creativity. Only a people that feel inwardly free, equal and privileged feel free enough to emulate the creativity of G-d.

Shabbos teaches that the world had a beginning, that there is a Creator. Because the world was created by a moral, loving and purposeful G-d, it follows that Creation has a purpose, and

---

* Even in Greece, the home of democracy, only 10% of the population was entitled to vote. In ancient Israel, where learning and intellect were valued above money, social standing or power, every child had the opportunity to be literate and to become a leader of society. The concept of universal continuous education *as a right* and a duty for all was born and nurtured by the Jewish Nation in a world where these ideas were unknown. Often these ideas were two or three thousand years too early, so far as most nations of the world were concerned. Where else was all this possible?

Moreover, the Jewish People was, and continues to be, the first human society to so value universal education that it insisted on it as a universal and obligatory pursuit for all. Education, the knowledge of Torah and the respect for knowledge was so sacred that it became the obligation of the government and of all society to safeguard, so as to make knowledge available to all — without exception. Remember that universal education was introduced into the United States only some 120 years ago. Throughout history, many kings and their aristocracy were illiterate. Knowledge in all its aspects was restricted to the few, guarded as a possession and an asset belonging to members of private and privileged guilds that were not to be shared with anyone but the elite, who were entitled to it through inheritance or purchase.

that life too has a purpose and a goal. Shabbos is the central day of the Jewish week. It is a day that celebrates all of human history; it directs all people to creatively and purposefully fashion their lives, the lives of family members and all of society. The Sabbath is the laboratory for creating the ideal and perfected society.

Shabbos is a foretaste of the Messianic era. In this laboratory, each individual is expected to *experience Shabbos* in order to live and taste the Messianic way of life within the environment of the family. The very structure of Shabbos rests on the three pivotal events of history. The first aspect is the *first* major event in world history — the culmination of Creation by G-d. The second celebrates the Revelation experience when the entire Jewish People received the Torah at Mount Sinai. The third and final aspect of the Sabbath is an event still in the future: the coming of the Messiah and the arrival of the Messianic era.

It is for the above reason that the Sabbath includes three prayer services, each of which celebrates each of the above three themes. (See the central text of the *Ma'ariv, Shacharis* and *Minchah Shmoneh Esrei* prayers in the *siddur.*) There are also the three meals, where the songs we sing dwell on the theme of each meal and prayer.

The Jewish People not only anticipates salvation, it also *lives* salvation by observing the Sabbath, the Messianic day. When the Sabbath is observed fully in law and in spirit, each person vicariously experiences each of the three key events and concludes the day with the exhilaration of one who has greeted the King Messiah.

---

1. *Genesis* 1:31.
2. *Genesis* 2:2.
3. *Exodus* 20:9.
4. *Rashi Exodus* 20:9.

SHABBOS AND THE JEWISH MESSIANIC QUEST

7

n a world filled with terror, hatred, hunger and strife, the Jew retreats each week to the only genuine island of sanity remaining in this mad world: the Sabbath. How does Shabbos illuminate the task of the Jew? Through the concept of *tikkun olam*; by making this world a G-dly, exalted place. The Jewish Messianic dream remains vibrant, fresh and forceful due to its unique characteristics.

Judaism teaches that Messianism must be more than a concept, a dream and an ideal. It is necessary to live and experience this ideal — to demonstrate that the ideal is viable, that it is applicable to human beings and to human society. Only then will we be capable of inspiring others to help create the ideal, Messianic society.

Only a people that dreams of *tikkun olam* — a fulfilled and perfected world — is able to build a society as the Kingdom of the One G-d. The task of the Jew in this world is to proclaim the unity and Oneness of G-d — Omniscient and Omnipotent. Yet nowhere in the weekday prayers does the Jew proclaim that G-d is One. In our daily prayers, the blessing preceding *Sh'ma Yisrael* clearly describes our task as "*l'yachedchah b'ahavah,* to unify [G-d] with love." Our task is not solely to proclaim His dominion over all mankind, but to actively unify, to carry forward the task of unification with our efforts and deeds.

If we examine the meaning of *Sh'ma* as defined by Rashi, the prayer speaks in the future tense. *Sh'ma* proclaims that, "*Hashem Elokeinu,* G-d who is our G-d" [i.e. the G-d of those who accept His Kingdom today] will become "*Hashem Echad,* One G-d," tomorrow. We are charged with the task of teaching mankind to accept the One G-d as theirs, and we will then be able to "crown" Him as King over all the earth. Only when mankind accepts His authority will G-d become recognized as *Hashem Echad,* the One G-d.

There is but one exception to this rule: The "Messianic day" called Shabbos, an experiential foretaste of the Messianic future. If you truly envelop yourself in the environment of Shabbos — if you live its history — if during the *Ma'ariv Shmoneh Esrei* you experience the creative power of G-d, the Creator; if during the *Shacharis Shmoneh Esrei* you experience G-d, the Giver of the Torah; then by the time *Minchah* arrives you will have reached a special plateau. Suddenly, you will find yourself proclaiming, as is stated in the *Minchah Shmoneh Esrei*, "*Atah Echad v'Shimcha Echad,* You [G-d] are One and Your Name is One," *now*, in the present, at this very moment. It is as though the Messiah were standing before us at that very moment, as though each and every Jew were committed to do his bidding.

"*Umi ke'amcha Yisrael, goy echad ba'aretz,* Who can be compared to Your Nation Israel, a unique and united nation on earth?" Each week, Shabbos enables us to experience the Messianic life in the expectation that we will soon teach all of mankind to recognize the One true G-d.

This insight is confirmed by the Sfas Emes who writes that, "The children of Israel possess a portion of G-d's unity — even in this world — through the power of the *neshamah yeseirah,* the 'additional soul' [inherent in every Jewish individual] that reveals itself on the holy Shabbos, the day on which the Torah was given. The Torah says: '*Shabbos hayom laShem*, Today is the L-rd's Sabbath.' Therefore, we are able to proclaim in the present, 'You are One, and Your Name is One, and who like Your People, Israel, is one unique nation on earth?'"[1]

The *Shabbos Mussaf Shmoneh Esrei* introduces a new and almost shocking element into the Shabbos formula. "*Yismechu be'malchuscha shomrei Shabbos v'korai oneg*, Those who keep and preserve Shabbos, who proclaim it a joy, reside in Your Kingdom." In other words, a Sabbath-observant Jew resides in a unique kingdom on earth, the Kingdom of Shabbos. Every Jew has the opportunity to enter and reside there every week. In this Kingdom, G-d is One.

Those who lived through the era of the Holocaust; the miracle of re-established Jewish sovereignty in the Land of Israel; the glory of Jerusalem reunited; and the even greater miracle of a regenerated, resurrected world of Torah study and observance, recognize that we live in the eye of a storm. Something over-whelmingly great is happening around us. The Jewish world is undergoing a revolutionary transformation and Torah observant Jews are prime movers in this dynamic process.

No longer are we observers of history sitting on the sidelines as we were for so many generations. Today, we, the *Am HaTorah*, the Nation of the Torah, are again the molders of history. We are charged by the Master of nature and of history to be the creative force in a rebuilt world molded on the pattern and blueprint of Torah. Once again, a window of redemption has been opened before us, large enough for us to sense the potential of the ren-aissance and victory of a regenerated Torah people. Yet it is suf-ficiently fragile for us to realize the awful tragedy should we, G-d forbid, falter and fail. This success or failure depends on the nature of our response to the fate of the masses of Jewry who are threatened with spiritual genocide, those whose Jewish future hangs in the balance.

The posture of American Jews, a posture of business as usual, takes little cognizance of the rapid disintegration and demise of scores of communities. Irresponsible decisions not only promote further abandonment of Jewish tradition, they strike at the viability of Jewish families and communities who are rapidly abandoning their Jewishness. The blindness of the bulk of American Jewry to its own tragedy has turned it into a practitioner of self-immolation.

An ideal society, a Kingdom of G-d, can be created by only those who reside in the Kingdom of the Sabbath. Without Shabbos and its living message of a regenerated and united Jewish People, all talk of Jewish renaissance and unity is a sham. Shabbos contains the secret of the Jewish tomorrow.

One day, Elijah the Prophet will return to herald the coming of the Messiah. Each Jew will rush forward to grasp his hand and say, with tears in his eyes, *"Sholom aleichem, Eliyahu HaNavi!"* Some he will embrace, but others might receive a cold stare and the rebuke, "Where were you when you were called upon to make my coming possible?"

THE KING'S PALACE IN THE HAVDALAH SPICE BOX

8

The unusual design of the spice box traditionally employed for *Havdalah* at the conclusion of the Sabbath must be more than a coincidence. Beyond its utilitarian function of holding the spices, it is often adorned with objects not generally found in the synagogue or the Jewish home. Perched on top of a silver tower waves a silver flag, inscribed with the Star of David. Under the tower is the spice container itself. On its four corner posts on the top of the box are unfurled four additional silver flags. Underneath the box four bells are affixed on each of the four corners and on one side of the box there is a single door. This door is not only the entrance to a spice box; it is also the gateway to the palace. I have seen similar spice boxes in homes, synagogues and museums with the repetition of similar themes: flags, bells, turrets, towers and palace doors. These are objects strange to the homes of an exiled people whose monarchy ceased to exist 2,000 years ago. What does the unusual form of the traditional spice box signify?

The conclusion of the Sabbath presents dual and contradictory themes: fulfillment and disappointment. Hidden within the Sabbath experience resides the hope that this Sabbath will never end, that this Sabbath will be the harbinger of an era that is "*Yom Shekulo Shabbos*, a day that is continuously Sabbath." Shabbos is the core and the foretaste of Messianic fulfillment. The Jew yearns for the ongoing Sabbath, the Sabbath that will never end. We anticipate "a day" that is continually spiritual, a Sabbath day that is the first day of the Messianic era, a day which inaugurates "the life of the world of the future."

The concept of the ongoing Sabbath is rooted in Jewish law as much as in Jewish ideology and thought. Notwithstanding the setting of the sun, a dark sky and the technical beginning of a new day at nightfall — the Sabbath regulations and the prohibition of creative work continue in force until the recitation of *Havdalah*; or at least by the individual articulating an abbreviated formula of the *Havdalah* by stating the words, "*Baruch Hamavdil bein kodesh l'chol*, Blessed be He who distinguishes between the holy and the common." Built into the structure of the Shabbos, then, is a unique feature: Shabbos continues in force — until man calls it to a halt.

Had this week's Sabbath continued of its own volition, it would not be necessary to call it to a halt since the Messianic era would now be with us. The arrival of the Messianic era is symbolically represented by a special meal that follows the end of each Sabbath, the *Melaveh Malkah*, the festive meal designated to "escort the Sabbath Queen." It is also known as *Seudah De'David Malkesa*, the banquet of David the King, i.e. a banquet sponsored each week in the name of King David, the forefather and harbinger of the King Messiah. Interestingly, this is the only Jewish meal that has two names, each of which represent its two contradictory themes. At the very same moment that we bid farewell to the Sabbath Queen, we also "celebrate" the coronation of King David, whose descendent will be the Messiah.

The *Havdalah* service reminds us that while this Sabbath has passed, another will soon follow. While the Messiah did not come this week, he will surely be with us next week. The Messianic promise will be fulfilled when one special Shabbos continues — and does not cease. When the Sabbath ends, darkness, disappointment, despair, even fear set in: We anticipate another week to be lived in exile, another week without the fulfillment of the Messianic promise. The *Havdalah* service begins with words of the prophet Isaiah, designed to cast away this despair and fear. "G-d, He is my salvation; I will trust and will not fear, for G-d is my strength and song, He is my salvation."

Even while *Havdalah* bids farewell to the Sabbath through the words of the *Havdalah* service, at the same time the physical symbols used in the *Havdalah* ceremony indicate the coronation of the Messianic King. Symbolic of confidence and hope, *Havdalah* anticipates a promising future. Casting away the fear and gloom that invariably set in with the departure of Shabbos, *Havdalah* holds forth the promise of the coming of the Kingdom of G-d and the Messianic era.

And it is for this reason that the *Havdalah* spice box often assumes the shape of a palace — the palace of the Messianic King. Flags, turrets and bells are symbols of royalty. They herald the arrival of the King. Hidden in each Jewish home is a subtle reminder that while the nations of the world may flaunt their royal families, palaces, armies, flags, power and sovereignty, true royalty and sovereignty are destined for the Jewish People, who will one day establish the "Kingdom of Heaven on earth."

Spice, too, is symbolic of royalty. It helps to refresh the despairing soul, just as wine is a symbol of richness and blessing. The flame of the *Havdalah* candle assures us that just as light was G-d's first creative act, an everlasting Divine light will soon dispel the world's darkness.

The inner structure of the Sabbath reflects this hope. The Sabbath is a microcosm of the Divine historic plan; each Sabbath calls upon each Jew to experience and internalize world history in capsule form. Each of the Sabbath's three meals and three prayers celebrate the elements of a three-stranded universal history.

Shabbos links the creation of the world "in the beginning" with the Revelation of the Torah, the instrument for achieving individual and world perfection, and to the coming of the Messiah, the era in which the Torah of peace, spirituality and harmony will dominate the affairs of mankind. This will be the "era that is all Sabbath, *Yom Shekulo Shabbos*."

The Sabbath is both the vehicle for achieving human perfection as well as an experiential foretaste of that perfection. The Messianic era is in itself Sabbath, as it will mark the expansion and extension of the Sabbath experience from one day each week, from a minority of a tiny people to all of humanity and for all time. This condition is called the Kingdom of G-d.

Each of the three Sabbath prayers and meals is devoted to one of the themes of Shabbos. The first prayer celebrates Creation. As stated in *Ma'ariv* following *Kabbalas Shabbos*, "You have sanctified to Your Name the seventh day, marking the end of the creation of heaven and earth... .By the seventh day, G-d had completed His creation which He had made."

The second prayer, which appears in the Sabbath morning service, celebrates the Revelation of Torah: "Moses rejoiced with the gift bestowed upon him, for You called him Your 'faithful servant.' You placed on his head a glorious crown as he stood before You on Mount Sinai when he brought down in his hand the two tablets of stone."

The third prayer, the theme of the Sabbath *Minchah Shmoneh Esrei*, describes the Messianic era: "You are One, and Your Name is One, and who like Your People Israel — a unique nation on the earth? ... The Messianic era is one of true and genuine rest, a rest that yields peace, tranquility, serenity and confidence, a perfect rest with which You are pleased."

Havdalah and its royal palace of spices celebrate the Messianic day when the Shabbos will not end. On that day, the descendant of David will preside over a transformed humanity. On that day, *Havdalah*, which distinguishes between Shabbos and the other six days of the week, will no longer be required. Shabbos will be forever.

How can we bring about that day? By learning the lesson of the *Havdalah* prayer. "Blessed is G-d, who distinguishes between the sacred and the profane, between light and darkness, between Israel and the nations."

UNDERSTANDING THE DUALITY AND UNITY OF SHABBOS

9 Based on *Pachad Yitzchok:* Shabbos 2

▸ Introduction

This chapter is an eye-opening study of the inner meaning of Shabbos. While it offers spiritual and intellectual rewards, it is not easy reading. (It is, in fact, the most intricate chapter in this volume.) It considers, how does one relate to the dual expressions of Shabbos? Are they contradictions, poles apart, or do they constitute a unity? The most significant expression of this duality is the command *"remember"* [*zachor*] (the Sabbath day) that appears in the text of the Ten Commandments, as related in Exodus, and the command to *"safeguard"* [*shamor*] (the Sabbath day) that appears in Deuteronomy. A second duality is articulated in the Shabbos Psalm —*"Mizmor Shir,* A Psalm and a Song of the Sabbath Day." We will also discover how our fear of G-d and love of G-d are integral parts of our Shabbos experience.

▸ Part One

"Whoever neglects to say 'true and certain,' *emes ve'yatziv,* when praying in the morning and 'true and faithful,' *emes ve'emunah,* in the evening *Ma'ariv* prayer (both prayers immediately follow the *Sh'ma*) has not fulfilled his obligation".[1] This is reflected in the verse, "to declare your love in the morning and your faithfulness in the night."[2] Rashi explains that "true and certain" is entirely devoted to the love G-d showered on our forefathers when He took them out of Egypt and split the Reed Sea, while "true and faithful" includes our anticipation of the future fulfillment of G-d's promises to "redeem us from oppressive kings and tyrants, to grant us life and to lead us to victory over our enemies." While these prayers are said daily, they derive from Psalm 92, "A Psalm and a Song of the Sabbath Day" where the verse "to declare Your love in the morning and Your faithfulness in the night" is found. This teaches us that kindness in the morning and faithfulness at night represent both a principal and corollaries. The principal forms part of the song of the "Sabbath Queen," while the corollaries affect our daily behavior.

In order to understand the relationship between the antecedent and its consequences, we must introduce the words of our Sages who state that Shabbos is filled with dualities.[3] The duality of the Shabbos observance is *shamor ve'zachor,* safeguard this and remember. One of these words appears in each of the two texts of the Ten Commandments.[4] The duality of the Shabbos song is a "psalm and a song." To understand our Sages, let us investigate the implications of the dual nature of "safeguard and remember" and of "a psalm and a song." In this way, we will identify the factors that constitute the duality of Shabbos.

We cannot begin our analysis without first correcting a misconception regarding the subject of "the awe of Heaven." This misconception is so widespread that even the author of a Kabbalistic work attributed his mistaken remarks to an authoritative source. These are his words:

We must understand that the attributes of love, graciousness and compassion that are to be found in man are present only due to his G-dly soul. What is not present in G-d is the quality of awe. Under no circumstances can we ascribe awe to G-d. We therefore say, "that G-d has nothing in this world but The Awe of Heaven."[5] While other attributes possessed by man have their source in G-d, awe does not.

The author of these words takes for granted that awe cannot be equated with the ways of G-d. *This assumption is incorrect* and indicates a mistaken grasp of G-d and His attributes.

This is the correct general principle: Every possible action of man's service of G-d has a corresponding quality among G-d's attributes. This follows from the fact that man's capacity to serve G-d is founded on the reality that man is created in the image of G-d; therefore how can any impulse in service of G-d exist in man without the existence of a corresponding attribute in G-d, as expressed in G-d's behavior toward His world?

▸ Part Two

Let's now see how we can resolve this matter: The Ramban, in his commentary on *Yisro*, writes[6] that "love" is at the root of our service to G-d when we observe the positive *mitzvos*, while our observance of the negative *mitzvos* originates in the quality of awe. The Ramban's intention is not to tell us that the intellectual motivation for the performance of *mitzvos* is love while the intellectual motivation for the avoidance of transgression is fear. Just as love motivates us to fulfill the will of the object of our love, it similarly obligates us to be careful not to do anything contrary to G-d's will. Conversely, just as awe impels us to avoid things that are contrary to G-d's will, it also constrains us not to be lax in fulfilling G-d's will. Therefore, the Ramban is not speaking of intellectual motivation; he is referring to the spiritual forces that stimulate our positive or negative behavior in the service of G-d. Just as there exist physical forces in nature that cause matter to expand, there also exist physical forces that cause matter to contract. Similarly, there are spiritual forces that cause expansion and others that contract or contain.

As regards the person who serves G-d, we see that love has an expansive effect. Love motivates man to act in honor of G-d, while awe causes man's psychic powers to contract as a way of advancing the honor of Heaven. This is what the Ramban means when he says that, "love is the inner motivation for the fulfillment of the positive *mitzvos*" so that when powers of expansion motivate one's soul, a force emanates from the soul that propels man in the direction of positive action. Awe, on the other hand, leads to the avoidance of sin. When inwardness rules a man's soul, his faculties are contained and an inactive state holds sway.

We have elsewhere explained why the term, "Awe of Heaven [*Yiras Shamayim*]" is used in place of "Awe of G-d's Name [*Yiras Hashem*]." There is no equivalent when speaking of love. Nowhere do we find the term, "Love of Heaven [*Ahavas Shamayim*]" used instead of "Love of G-d's Name [*Ahavas Hashem*]." This fact requires an explanation. Our general effort to avoid the mention of G-d's actual "Name," and our constant use of other references to G-d, implies a withdrawal, the narrowing of the outgoing tendencies of the soul in a manner similar to the experience of the Sinai Revelation, where "they [the Jewish People] stood at a distance."[7] This retrenchment is, in essence, the Awe of Heaven. Thus, to create asymmetry between the phrase and its message, *Chazal* invented a way in which even the form of the phrase would constitute a performance of the *mitzvah* of awe. Using the term "Heaven" conveys a trepidation of saying "G-d."

It is for this reason that the quality of awe expresses itself in two ways: either as the "Awe of G-d's Name" or as the "Awe of Heaven," while the quality of love is stated *only* as the "Love of G-d's Name (*Ahavas Hashem*)." The Awe of Heaven is a quality of the soul which allows it to limit the universe for the sake of "the glory of Heaven."

▶ Part Three

et us proceed in our search for the quality of awe among the attributes of G-d. The Sages explained His name *Sha-dai* as a reference to, "*She'amar L'olamo Dai: G-d said to the world, 'it is sufficient.'*" During Creation, the universe was in an expanding state until G-d declared its creative expansion to be sufficient, *dai*.[8] This quality is one of the many characteristics of G-d's conduct of the world that corresponds to man's Awe of Heaven. Just as G-d acted to restrain further creativity in His universe for the purpose of furthering the honor of Heaven, so too does the person who serves G-d restrain his own inner world in order to further the honor of G-d. This limitation is descriptive of the Awe of Heaven.

We are now able to shed light on the concept of the duality of the commandments of Shabbos. G-d's limiting of Creation is alluded to by both "The heavens and the earth were completed"[9] and "the L-rd completed His creative efforts." Without this characteristic, the universe would have continued to expand and would never have attained completion. The verse *"and the L-rd completed"* therefore refers to G-d's command "enough/sufficient." As an immediate result of the command "it is sufficient," the seventh day was sanctified with a holiness acquired through *limiting* creative effort. Just as the universe was created through the declaration "sufficient," so too was the sanctity of Shabbos created through an act of sanctification based on "cease and desist, *dai*," i.e.: Creation is complete; it has attained its maximum allowable expansion. We now see that creative expansion and its negative — desist from further expansion — are intertwined in bringing about the sanctity of Shabbos.

This is the source of the concept that safeguard [*shamor*] and remember [*zachor*] were said concurrently, as one word.[10] "Remember" includes the positive *mitzvos* of Shabbos, while "safeguard" includes the negative *mitzvos*. Both were said concurrently. This is the uniqueness of Shabbos: the realization of the duality of Shabbos, that two become one when they unite the expansiveness of love and the inwardness of awe. In effect, the commandments rooted in love and the commandments rooted in awe were expressed simultaneously. *Safeguard* and *remember* were linked to each other so that whatever is contained in one is contained in the other.[11]

So far as the sanctity of Shabbos is concerned, the *distinction* between the attributes of love and awe were suspended. The sanctity of Shabbos rests on the *combination* of expansion and compression, of love and awe. All who are totally dedicated to the service of G-d can appreciate this to its fullest. How? They also taste love in the restrictions of Shabbos and awe in the positive *mitzvos* of Shabbos. Now we can understand what the Sages mean when they say that all the aspects of Shabbos and her *mitzvos* are dual. Now, we can move from the duality of the *mitzvos* of Shabbos to the duality of the Song of Shabbos: "*Mizmor Shir,* A Psalm and a Song of the Sabbath Day."

▶ Part Four

Just as expansion and contraction are significant modes in the emotional realm of serving G-d, these trends have a place in the intellectual service of G-d. For example, the Maharal[12] states that one is forbidden to do a favor for someone who does not recognize the obligation of gratitude.[13] This, despite the fact that we practice altruism to emulate Him, and we note that He bestows much good even upon the ungrateful. This indicates to us that we can only imitate behavior of G-d that we can understand.

The mode of G-d's compassion that we can appreciate, and consequently emulate, is the intuitive path of "good for the righteous and suffering for the sinner."[14] His other way, less common but still fairly frequent, of "good even for the sinner" is perceived by the human mind as arbitrary, and is not subject to imitation.[15] That mode sometimes even extends to "suffering of the righteous," which is certainly incomprehensible to our limited grasp.

The rationale for the above Divine behavior is hidden from us. Indeed, as we grow in our appreciation of the ways of G-d, our relationship to the One Above reveals itself as increasingly dual, consisting of two contrasting aspects. One is our perception of identity with G-d in our striving to emulate G-d. The other is our realization of His exaltedness and the impossibility of any genuine human association with Him. The first describes the forward advance of the intellect; the second describes an intellect in retreat.

To return to our former terminology, the first direction is the intellect's expansion, the second is its contraction. There are two antithetical movements as regards the laws governing the intellect, much as we found regarding the imperatives directed at the emotional obligations of the person who serves G-d. We earlier referred to the two emotions of love and awe. Now we encounter the intellectual counterpart: "The secrets of the universe belong to G-d, while that which is revealed belongs to us and our children." (Yehudah Halevi said, "How can I find You, Your place is concealed and hidden; yet how can I not find You – Your glory fills the universe?"[16])

▶ Part Five

The above provides the key to understanding the verse titled "A Psalm and a Song of the Sabbath Day." This is one of the few psalms whose contents contain no reference to the topic noted in the psalm's opening sentence. The first verse says, *"A psalm, and a song of the Sabbath day"* while the balance of the chapter never once mentions Shabbos. It deals exclusively with G-d's conduct regarding "when the wicked bloom like grass and the doers of iniquity blossom."[17] What does this verse teach?

Even though the *mitzvah* of joy on Shabbos is only found in the Prophets,[18] it originates in the Torah, in Genesis, where the Torah speaks of the concluding moments of Creation. Here is what the Torah says: "And G-d saw all that He made and it was very good — and He ceased and He sanctified."[19] We see that the rest and the sanctification [*Kiddush*] of Shabbos came by way of the observation "it was very good," which relates to the entirety of Creation. Just as our resting on Shabbos and our sanctification of Shabbos are models of the "resting" and the sanctification of G-d Himself on the seventh day of Creation, so too is our *Oneg Shabbos* [Sabbath pleasure] a model of the observation "very good" with which G-d viewed His universe at the conclusion of Creation.

The Sages interpret *vayechulu*, ["and He ceased"] metaphorically as the completion of a residence.[20] They compare it to a king who, upon seeing the palace he built, acknowledges that it finds favor in his eyes. Just as he is pleased with it today, he adds, "would that it be G-d's will that this palace will continue to bring joy all the days of my life!"[21] This aspect of the appreciation of the universe lies at the heart of the word *vayechulu*, "and G-d completed," which introduces the sanctity of Shabbos. The degree to which a person is resentful concerning the way events unfold in the world, to that extent he lacks appreciation for the sanctity of the Shabbos. (The more frustration and anger a person harbors concerning his own life, to that degree he has less Shabbos.)

▸ Part Six

The discerning reader will realize that the verse, "it is good to praise G-d"[22] which follows immediately after the words, "A psalm and a song of the Shabbos day," is intimately related to the "very good" found where Scripture discusses the sanctity of Shabbos. This reader would understand that the mode of God's conduct that allows the sinner to receive goodness is intimately connected with the "very good" at the conclusion of Creation and the institution of the holiness of Shabbos. (See Genesis 1:31.) So long as an individual does not understand that the flourishing of sinners is for the ultimate purpose that "their destruction will be forever," his feeling of contentment toward the Author of Creation is corrupted. His resentment darkens the "very good" that introduces the sanctity of Shabbos and celebrates the completion of the Divine palace. Thus, the psalm that deals with the ultimate destruction of sinners in the face of their present flourishing is transformed into a Song of the Shabbos day: "… A boor cannot know, nor can a fool understand this: When the wicked bloom like grass and the doers of iniquity blossom — it is to destroy them eternally." The recognition of this fact *is* the song of the Shabbos Queen.

We are now ready to study the duality of the Song of Shabbos. We have already seen how the duality of the *mitzvos* of Shabbos derive from the integration of the expansive "rise and do" expression of love with the contractive "do nothing" expression of fear. "'Remember' and 'safeguard' were said simultaneously." We have also seen how the two movements that constitute love and awe are among the emotional qualities of the individual who serves G-d and constitute the perception of identity with G-d and the recognition of His exaltedness.

▶ Part Seven

The foregoing discussion serves as a foundation for a deeper understanding of the joy of Shabbos. Just as the *mitzvos* of Shabbos are dual in that they include the two motions in which the service of G-d is grounded, so too is the *mitzvah* of Shabbos joy dual through its inclusion of these two motions as one. But while the actual *mitzvos* of Shabbos unite the motions of expansion and contraction as they affect psychic emotions and their resultant physical actions (love and awe, positive commandments and negative commandments), they also unite them as they affect our intellect and our beliefs (hidden and revealed, identity and exaltedness). As we have said, so long as our acceptance of the mode of behavior characterized by "the suffering of the righteous and the good awarded the sinner" is not on the same self-evident basis as our natural acceptance of the more palatable behavior characterized by "good for the righteous and suffering for the sinner," our soul is not yet prepared to delight in the Shabbos. We then find that the two normally opposing motions of expansion and contraction that govern the intellect of the servant of G-d emerge as twins in the *mitzvah* of Shabbos joy.

▶ Part Eight

In light of the above profound appreciation of Shabbos joy, we now understand the two-fold terminology that is used in the Song of Shabbos. "*Tov le'hodos laShem,* it is good to give thanks to G-d, *u'Le'zamer le'Shimcha Elyon,* and to sing praise to your name O Most High." The phrase, *le'zamer,* songs of *zimrah,* means a song of praise to G-d. *Zimrah* connotes praise. The word *zimrah* has another meaning. It also means to prune, to separate from the life source, as in the *zomer* [pruning] type of forbidden Shabbos work, which is included in one of the 39 forbidden Shabbos labors. This usage is found elsewhere in the Bible as well. The dual meaning of the root *zamor* can best be understood when we realize that praise becomes glorification of the Divine when the one who praises stands in such wonderment before the exaltedness of the object of his praise that he no longer perceives his own being as possessing consequence. He figuratively diminishes his own essence. Praise and extirpation share a common root, because the obliteration of the lower ranking person's sense of self as he perceives it in the face of his commander, is in itself an act of praise for the commander. *Zimrah* does not refer to praise in a general sense. It specifically describes praise that is expressed in the form of a song. While praise generally expresses a lower ranking person's self-negation before his commander, *zimrah* as praise is an expression of pleasure during self-negation before the commander. Here we see the difference between ordinary song and *zimrah*. In worship, song is an expression of pleasure at the perception and feeling of G-d's exaltedness, awesome power and wonderment. We therefore see that the expression of pleasure and expansiveness in worship is the very content of song, while the song that expresses pleasure at the contractive movement is called *mizmor*.

Since we have now learned that the central point of Shabbos joy is the intermingling of these two classes of joy, both *shir* and *mizmor* join together to constitute the Song of Shabbos as they form the single unit called the *psalm/song* of the Shabbos day.

The word *vayechulu* ["and G-d concluded"] also has a dual implication. On one hand, it implies conclusion. On the other hand, it implies a wedding, a joining together [*kallah/kellulos*]. Shabbos rest derives from *vayechulu*, conclusion, while Shabbos joy derives from the celebration and coming together of a wedding.

▶ Part Nine

The word *vayechulu* has an additional, third meaning. *Vayechulu* also implies consolidation and inclusiveness [*lichlol, hiskallelus*]. Each of the two original meanings implies the reconciliation of opposites so that they form one inclusive unit. Just as Shabbos rest is seen as the concluding aspect of *vayechulu* — which denotes one unit of expansion and contraction as they affect our emotional qualities and our behavioral patterns (remember and safeguard said as one) — so does the *Oneg Shabbos,* as a festival of marriage (completion), form one unit of expansion and contraction. But this time, they affect our beliefs and our thinking, *mizmor* and *shir/song* as a single word, as *psalm/song,* a *mizmor/shir* to Shabbos. The holy composer continues; he arranges his song/psalm into two stanzas. "The first is a song of expansiveness. The second is a psalm of inwardness. ...It is good to praise G-d and sing a *miz-*

mor to Your holy Name." The same enjoyment that I feel as a perception of intimate identity with G-d, I also feel when I stand in wonderment at His distance. "To recount Your love [*chessed*] in the morning and Your faithfulness at night." The Sages explain that *"chessed* in the morning" refers to prior redemptions,[23] which are manifestations of the *tzaddik*, the righteous person, who enjoys the good. The "faithfulness at night" refers to past and present states of exile, instances of the righteous who experience evil. The intent of this verse is to teach that although the articulation of the morning's love and the faithfulness at night are two separate categories of service to G-d, the first is an expansive movement brought about by the perception of identity, while the second is an inward movement caused by a feeling of wonderment at G-d's distance. Nevertheless, they find themselves united in the song of the Shabbos Queen. For so long as "Your faithfulness at night" is not voiced in the same clear and self-evident manner as "Your love in the morning," there is no place for the *Song of the Holy Shabbos Day* in which the enjoyment of identity and the enjoyment of wonderment are fused together to form the *mizmor/shir,* the *psalm/song.*

▸ Part Ten

We now return to the beginning of our study. "Whoever neglects to say the prayer 'true and certain' in the morning and 'true and faithful' in the evening has not fulfilled his obligation." Generally, the love of the morning and the faithfulness of night are divided between appropriately designated times — true and certain in the mornings, and true and faithful in the evening. However, in the structure of the sanctity of Shabbos, this distinction is dissolved, since all the affairs of Shabbos, both its *mitzvos* and its song, are dual in nature. The sanctity of the Shabbos structure interweaves the two aspects of the duality into the single word, *psalm/song.*

A close and careful perusal of the Psalm, "A Psalm/Song of the Shabbos Day" in the context of our present discussion will be most enlightening to the reader, for what we have been taught shines with the light of the sanctity of the Shabbos Queen.

1. *Berachos* 12a. Rashi, ibid., explains that this requirement includes the entire text of the blessing that begins *"Emes ve'yatziv," "Emes ve'emunah"* and ends *"Ga'al Yisrael."*
2. *Psalms* 92:3.
3. *Yalkut Shimoni* on *Tehillim* 92:2.
4. *Exodus* 20:8 and *Deuteronomy* 5:12.
5. *Shabbos* 31b, see also *Berachos* 33b, "All is in the Hands of Heaven except the Awe of Heaven."
6. *Exodus* 20:8.
7. *Exodus* 20:15.
8. *Chagigah* 12a.
9. *Genesis* 2:1-3.
10. *Rosh Hashanah* 27a.
11. *Berachos* 20b.
12. *Gur Aryeh/Bereishis* 2:5.
13. *Sotah* 14a, *Rambam Hilchos De'os* 1/5 and 6, *Pachad Yitzchok, Pesach* 18.
14. *Berachos* 7a.
15. *Deuteronomy* 29:28.
16. *Kol Shirei Rabbi Yehudah Halevi,* Tel Aviv, 5706, Vol. 2, p.121.
17. *Psalms* 92:8.
18. *Isaiah* 58:13, *Shabbos* 118b.
19. *Genesis* 1:31.
20. *Midrash Tanchuma Bereishis* 2/*Sheiltos of Rabbi Achai Ga'on.*
21. *Bereishis Rabbah* 9:4.
22. *Psalms* 92:2.
23. *Berachos* 12a.

III ROSH HASHANAH

ISHMAEL AND *U'VECHAIN*: TWO KEYS TO ROSH HASHANAH

10

▶ Who is Ishmael?

We all know what happened to Ishmael, Abraham's first son through his second wife Hagar, the Egyptian princess. Based on her astute observations, Sarah was convinced that Ishmael and his Egyptian mother were dangerous and harmful influences on her son, Isaac. Ishmael the cynic is described by the Torah as "mocking," which denotes that he transgressed the three cardinal sins: idolatry, adultery and murder. G-d commanded Abraham to banish Ishmael from his home. Ishmael and Hagar had to go — despite Abraham's reluctance. But Sarah knew, and G-d confirmed her conclusion, that if not removed, Ishmael would have the audacity to claim that he was Abraham's spiritual heir, thus aborting Abraham's mission on earth. Once Abraham learned that the expulsion of Hagar and Ishmael was G-d's Will, he complied at once.

On their return journey to Egypt, Hagar and Ishmael lost their way. Eventually, their ample supply of water was consumed. Ishmael became dangerously ill. Hagar abandoned Ishmael, but G-d heard his cries and sent an angel to rescue him from death. The angel promised Hagar that Ishmael would survive and become the father of a great nation.

According to the *Midrash*, the angels pleaded with G-d not to perform a miracle to save Ishmael, because his offspring would someday persecute and murder Jews. G-d responded by saying that He would judge Ishmael solely in accord with "his present deeds." The *Midrash* explains that Ishmael had repented, which is demonstrated by the term the Torah uses to describe his condition, "*ba'asher hu sham*" — G-d judged him "in his present state."[1]

The question we must answer is why did the Sages choose this story for the Torah reading of Rosh Hashanah? Weren't there more important and more relevant readings available? Wouldn't the Torah passage about the creation of Adam and Eve, their sin and banishment from the Garden of Eden, be much more appropriate?

The answer to this puzzle is that the story of Ishmael personifies the purpose and challenge of Rosh Hashanah, possibly more so than any other incident in the Torah. No one was more evil and wicked than he. In addition, Ishmael grew up in Abraham's home and knew the meaning of righteousness, justice, kindness, ethics and morality. He witnessed the exemplary and idealistic behavior of his father. No one else on earth was raised or trained in a finer, more spiritual, caring and inspirational home, yet Ishmael rebelled against Abraham. He rejected both his teachings and his mission.

At that moment of extreme danger to his life, however, Ishmael did *teshuvah,* he truly repented his evil deeds. G-d judged him "as he was" at that moment, a righteous person. More precisely, by definition *teshuvah* includes a resolve to remain righteous in the future, to utilize one's potential for the good. This is precisely the challenge and opportunity of Rosh Hashanah. No matter how sinful and evil we may be, G-d is prepared to grant us continued life *if* we acknowledge G-d as our Father and King, *if* we are prepared to renounce our past and undertake the obligation to become a new and different person. Even though Ishmael failed and returned to his life of crime and evil, his story perfectly describes the challenge and purpose of Rosh Hashanah.

▶ What is *U'vechain?*

The central prayer of each day is *Shmoneh Esrei*, the silent standing prayer. The first three paragraphs and the last paragraph of *Shmoneh Esrei* never change. Only the middle paragraphs change on the Sabbath and the holidays. The key message of all special holy days in the Jewish year can be discerned by examining the middle prayer of the *Shmoneh Esrei* of that day.

Rosh Hashanah and Yom Kippur have their own unique text. This text reveals the goal and message of Rosh Hashanah. This message consists of three paragraphs, each of which begins with the word *U'vechain*, usually translated as, "And so too." In common Hebrew usage however, the word *u'vechain* has a stronger meaning. It is used in the sense of "and what do you plan to do about it?" I believe that this translation of *u'vechain* holds the key to the challenge of Rosh Hashanah. Without, "and what do you plan to do about it," the three paragraphs appear to be in reverse order. In addition, their meaning is somewhat muted.

The first paragraph sets forth the universal Messianic goal of Jewish existence. *"G-d, instill Your fear on all Your creations and Your dread on all existence. Let everyone revere You and prostrate themselves before You. Let all mankind become a single united society which will do Your Will wholeheartedly..."*

Now, how will all of this happen? The second paragraph explains that this is the mission and responsibility of the Jews. *U'vechain* – What will the Jews do to make it happen? The answer is in the second paragraph:

"G-d grant stature to Your nation, renown to those who revere You, good hope to those who seek You, gladness to Your land [of

Israel], *joy to Your city* [Jerusalem] *and fulfillment to David Your servant* [the Messiah]…"

Finally, who will inspire, teach, motivate and train the Jews to carry out their responsibility? Again, *U'vechain* — Who will do it?

The righteous will see and be glad, the upright will exult and the devout will rejoice. Evil will be silenced, and wickedness will evaporate.

When? When the righteous, the upright and the devout of the Jewish People fully understand that salvation is their task. Finally, when all of the above takes place:

G-d will reign as King over all creations on Mt. Zion, the resting place of Your glory, and in Jerusalem, Your holy city.

Essentially, the above key paragraphs tell us that G-d is prepared to grant each of us a new lease on life *if* we are prepared to acknowledge G-d as our King and agree to live in such a way that we will help bring about the fulfillment of His plans for the Redemption of mankind.

A final note: In the above prayer to G-d, He sees us as His partners — in keeping with Psalm 68:35 which instructs us to "give strength to G-d." Since G-d is all-powerful, why does He need our puny strength in order to accomplish His goals?

That is the entire point of Creation. Man was created with free choice and the challenge is to exercise it wisely. It is *our* ability to choose G-d as King that *makes* Him King. It is our partnership in His enterprise to transform the world that *makes* His agenda meaningful and significant. It is only *here* on earth that G-d is King, because nowhere else do people exist who can make a free choice as to whether they will submit to G-d's Will or rebel against it.

When Rosh Hashanah is long gone, we must remember the lesson of Ishmael: that G-d stands ready to forgive us if we truly repent our wrongdoings. And the word *u'vechain* must continue to reverberate in our minds. So, knowing that G-d waits for your repentance, what do you plan to do about it?

---

1. *Genesis* 21:17.

THE ROLE OF FEAR ON ROSH HASHANAH

The Days of Awe begin with the recitation of the penitential *Slichos* prayers that are initiated on the evening following the Sabbath preceding Rosh Hashanah. The key prayer of the first *Slichos* service is the hymn *B'motzei Yom Menuchah* (which means "at the conclusion of the Day of Rest"). This prayer describes the mindset of the Jew at the beginning of the season of repentance: It speaks of "shuddering, trembling and shaking before G-d's wrath, like a woman who is fearful in the moments prior to the birth of her first child."

The image of a woman about to give birth is extremely powerful. The young woman is anticipating a major transformation in her life, the birth of her first child. This is the most exciting and eventful day in her life. While she anticipates much joy, she is also filled with trepidation, fearful of what her fate might be should something go wrong. The fear of disaster weighs on her mind.

This analogy describes our own situation on Rosh Hashanah, a day filled with trepidation and hope, a day which offers us the opportunity for positive transformation, a day on which we also fear failure as we stand before our King in judgment. Rosh Hashanah is the day of new opportunities and beginnings.

In his *Sefer HaMitzvos* (the book which examines each of the 613 commandments) the Rambam, one of the greatest halachic authorities of all time, prepares us for the awesome responsibility of Rosh Hashanah:

> *We are expected to be fearful of G-d's judgment, not like those who deny* [G-d's sovereignty] *who merrily go about their way; who think of every life challenge as an event that "will just happen, as though by accident." For this reason the Torah states, "You shall fear the Lord your G-d," to which the* Tanna, *Yossi ben Yossi, comments, " 'To fear the L-rd your G-d' is not a warning, but a command." It is one of the positive commandments. There are those who turn their backs on the Torah: The sinner says, "I will manage just fine, I will follow my heart's desires." This person is an* apikores — *one who denies G-d.*[1]

The great commentator, Rashi, is struck by the strength of G-d's justice in the following passage.

> *You are all standing today before Hashem your G-d, your leaders, your tribes, your elders and your officers, all of Israel — so that you will enter into a covenant with Hashem, your G-d, and accept the oath that Hashem, your G-d, made with you today in order to establish that you are His People, so that He will be your G-d...*[2]

Rashi asks why this sentence is juxtaposed with 98 curses and punishments that will befall Israel if they violate the Sinai Covenant. The faces of the people turned white upon hearing the curses. They said, "Who can bear these?" Moses began to console them by saying, "You are still standing today even though you have deeply angered G-d. He has not destroyed you.

Behold you exist in His presence." Rashi is teaching us that the point of the Torah's curses is for Israel to fear sin, but not to despair. The fear of these punishments arms Israel with the strength to resist sin. An effective warrior requires training, weapons and courage, just as the woman who is about to give birth has prepared for any eventuality by engaging the finest doctor and hospital possible. The warrior also requires fear, because without it, he will not be able to steel himself psychologically or physically for the trauma of battle.

What we are describing is one of life's stark realities: Fear is a mechanism that helps us cope with danger. We have all heard of average people who performed heroic deeds that far exceeded their strength when faced with the challenge of saving a life. Fear of disaster pumps the adrenalin that makes the impossible possible.

Fear is so essential that on Rosh Hashanah we actually pray that G-d instill fear into mankind. The major theme of the Rosh Hashanah and Yom Kippur *Shmoneh Esrei* prayer is, "Hashem, our G-d, instill Your awesome fear upon all Your creations and Your dread on all that You have created." Without fear of punishment, human beings cannot function on a high moral level. Awareness of our deep-rooted fear enables us to create our own inner awe of G-d's power. The Torah teaches, "You should fear the Lord your G-d." Our task on Rosh Hashanah and Yom Kippur is to assemble our own experiences of fear and use them to create a higher and deeper level of the awe of Heaven.

Rabbi Mattisyahu Salomon, the *Mashgiach Ruchani* of Beth Medrash Govoha in Lakewood, New Jersey, asked the following question: Why is it that so many people display no evidence of fear on Rosh Hashanah? His reply is that our inclination for evil "speaks to us" and says, "You are not any less a righteous person now than the person you were a year ago, and yet you are still alive — you have survived." This rationalization creates within us the false confidence that we can get away with our sins, that we have no cause for worry.

In light of the above, how are we to understand the teaching of the Rambam that "if a person's sins are judged to be greater than his positive deeds on Rosh Hashanah, he will die immediately"? The Ravad in *Yevomos* explains this concept. No person knows when his last day will be. The judgment on Rosh Hashanah does not necessarily imply that the evil person will die *immediately*. It does teach us that a person, who, for example, originally had been allotted 80 years of life, may have five years deducted from his allotment. In other words, the sentence may not be carried out immediately — but it will be carried out.

We can understand this situation with the following illustration: Human beings should see themselves as though they are part of a school of fish swimming in the middle of the ocean. The fishermen have cast a very large net around them. Many hours pass before the fish are aware of the fact that the net has been cast and has locked them in on all sides. The fish swim about merrily, unaware of impending disaster. Suddenly, the fishermen pull the net tight, and the fish discover that they have been caught, with no escape possible. In the same way, a person will not be aware as to whether or not he had a "good" or a "bad" Rosh Hashanah: He does not know if the Heavenly court subtracted or added a year (or ten years!) to his life. What we do on Rosh Hashanah gives us the opportunity to escape the net.

The bottom line is that we must be sensitive to the demands of Heaven and take them seriously. We must constantly ask, "What does G-d ask of us?" We must be aware of the reality of Heavenly judgment. We must be infused with a sense of trepidation and dread. If we think maturely, fear is a great gift. It allows us to prepare for the year to come. It allows us to own up to our failures and our acts of omission, to our laziness and lack of responsibility. It impresses us with the fact that there is a King and a Judge who loves us but who also expects us to toe the line. It enables us not to be treated by the Heavenly court like those who scoff and deny G-d, who go their merry way without an awareness of the fact that there is a Divine ear that hears and a Divine scribe who writes. It is for this reason that it behooves us all to "shudder, tremble and shake" in anticipation of G-d's wrath on Rosh Hashanah.

This chapter was inspired by Rabbi Mattisyahu Salomon.

1. Commandment #4.
2. *Deuteronomy* 29:9-12.

WHY DOES G-D REVIEW US AS THOUGH WE WERE SHEEP?

12

O ne of the most awesome and moving of the Rosh Hashanah prayers is *U'nesaneh Tokef*, said during the *Mussaf* prayers:

Let us relate the power of this day's holiness — for it is awesome and frightening. All mankind will pass before You like b'nei maron, *like members of the flock. Like a shepherd pasturing his flock, making the sheep pass under his staff, so, too, will You review, count, calculate and consider the soul of all living beings. At this time You will decide the needs of all of Your creatures and inscribe their verdict.*

This expression *b'nei maron* is taken from the Mishnah.[1] The Mishnah tells us that, "On Rosh Hashanah all mankind will pass before G-d like *b'nei maron.*" The Talmud[2] elaborates on this unusual phrase and offers three meanings:

What does "b'nei maron" mean? First, we translate it to mean "k'vnei amarna, like a flock of sheep." Second, as Raish Lakish says, "It means 'like the ascent to Beis Maron.'" Third, Rabbi Yehudah says in the name of Shmuel, "It means k'chayalos Beis David, like the troops of the House of David.'"

How can we understand the message behind this cryptic term, *b'nei maron,* in the light of the three definitions offered by our Talmudic Sages? What mysteries lie behind this phrase that holds the key to the process of judgment on Rosh Hashanah?

▸ How Are We Like Sheep?

The first definition offered by the Talmud is "like a flock of sheep." This phrase indicates that each person will be examined in accordance with a uniform standard applicable to all. When a shepherd evaluates his sheep, he employs but one standard. Are they healthy enough to go to market? Is the wool of sufficient quality? Sheep have a second quality — they follow their leader. The purpose of these analogies is to instruct us that each human being has similar needs and is judged using a similar standard. To what degree do you follow the 613 commandments? To what degree did you contribute to the needs of the community? To what degree did you follow the Torah's standards of truthfulness, ethics, morality and charity?

▸ Standing Alone

The second definition offered by the Talmud is "like the ascent to Beis Maron," i.e. The House of Maron. In the Talmud,[3] the ascent to Beis Maron is described as entailing traveling through a narrow mountain pass, traversable by only one person at a time. The emphasis here, therefore, is on the individual. Just as each human face is uniquely different, so too is each human being different. As the Mishnah states, "For this reason man was created alone, as a single being, to instruct us concerning the greatness of the Holy One, Blessed be He. A person mints coins using the same mold. The result is that all coins are exact replicas of each other. But the Supreme King, the Holy One Blessed be He, formed every human being using the mold of the first human being, yet not one of them resembles his fellow. This is to instruct us that every individual is obligated to say, 'For me alone was the world created.'" Therefore, we must recognize that each person is endowed with special talents and tasks that he alone can fulfill.

Each human being is obligated to bring those talents to fruition. Rabbi Israel Salanter, the founder of the modern *Mussar* [ethical] movement, taught that the greatest sin a person can commit is to allow his talents to remain unused and not find ways to develop them to their fullest possible potential in the service of his Creator. This explains the analogy of the "ascent to Beis Maron." Beis Maron was a famous mountain landmark in the Land of Israel. To climb it, one had to negotiate a narrow road that could be passed by only one person at a time. *B'nei maron,* therefore, teaches that each human being will be judged based upon the Divine assessment of that person's unique talents, potential, circumstances, trials and means.

▸ A Soldier in David's Army

The third definition offered is "as a soldier in the army of the House of David." It was David who was chosen to establish the royal house from which the Messiah will eventually be born. It was the House of David that built the First Temple. During the lifetime of Solomon, David's son, all of the conditions that will prevail in the Messianic age were established for the first time in history. These conditions have not yet been re-established: All of the Jewish people lived in the Land of Israel; the Jewish state controlled all of the Biblical territory of the Land of Israel; the Temple of Jerusalem was fully built; the priestly service was observed; all Jews were Torah observant; the Jews had defeated all of their enemies and peace prevailed in the Land of Israel. The task of each Jew is to be a soldier in the "Army" of King David, to do what only he or she is able to do to establish G-d's Kingdom on earth.

The Mishnah is obviously not describing three different types of Jews. It is challenging us with three standards by which each Jew will be judged on Rosh Hashanah. We may summarize them in this way:

Did you observe all of the Commandments and obligations expected of each and every Jew?

Were you creative and responsible in your own right, based on your unique talents, capabilities, challenges, opportunities and means?

Did you understand that the obligation of a Jew is to serve as "a soldier in the army of King David?" In other words, did you try to bring closer the day when the ideal conditions that prevailed in King Solomon's day will again prevail, bringing about the Redemption of all mankind and the coming of the Messiah?

When each Jew stands before G-d in judgment on Rosh Hashanah, he is should think in terms of these question, for on this basis he will be judged.

---

1. *Mishnah Sanhedrin* 4:5.
2. *Rosh Hashanah* 1:2.
3. *Rosh Hashanah* 18a.

THE PURPOSE
OF THE DAYS
13 OF AWE

To understand the method and purpose of the Days of Awe, the *Yamim Nora'im*, we must first find an answer to each of the questions below.

Question 1: Why do the Ten Days of Repentance begin with Rosh Hashanah, the Day of Judgment and of the coronation of G-d as our only King? Wouldn't it be more logical that they begin with Yom Kippur, the Day of Atonement? Shouldn't we first identify our sins, atone for them and cleanse ourselves before we stand before G-d in judgment, celebrate the creation of mankind and crown Him as our universal King?

Question 2: The same question relates to the Ten Commandments, which are more than a group of basic laws. They involve a pact undertaken by the eternal G-d and the Jewish Nation. Don't the Ten Commandments appear to be out of order? One would think that first we should accept the second five commandments, which renounce murder, robbery, immorality, swearing falsely and coveting the property and wives of our neighbors. By accepting these commandments, we vow to behave as civilized human beings. Once we become *menschen*, we would then be in a position to consider the philosophical and theological concepts of belief in G-d set forth in the first five commandments.

Question 3: Why must the central declaration of Jewish faith, the *Sh'ma Yisrael*, begin with, "*Hear, O Israel*?" Wouldn't it be adequate to simply declare, "*Hashem Elokeinu, Hashem Echad*, The G-d who is the G-d of the Jewish People, is the one G-d." Or alternately, "Hashem is our one and only G-d. He will *become* One when all mankind accepts His authority as ruler" (as interpreted by Rashi).

Question 4: Why do we say *Yizkor*, the prayer for the departed, which invokes the presence and memory of our departed parents and close relatives, on Passover, Shavuos, Succos and Shmini Atzeres, but omit *Yizkor* on Rosh Hashanah, when we feel the absence of our departed parents more intensely than at any other time of the year?

Question 5: The above questions also relate to the structure of Torah itself. Rashi asks this question on the very first page of the Torah, "Why does the Torah begin with the story of Creation, then relate the events of the lives of the founders of our People and only much later instruct us concerning the laws and commandments G-d expects us to observe? Shouldn't the commandments and laws come first?"

Before answering these questions, let us consider the following fictional story: An ancient, benevolent and beloved king had a favorite daughter. One day, his daughter was murdered by an uneducated, uncouth peasant. The peasant was arrested, tried, convicted and sentenced to death. The laws of the kingdom, however, demanded that only the king could sign and authorize the execution order. When the document was presented to the king, he refused to sign it at that time, but directed that it be put aside in a safe place. The king then directed that the murderer should be rehabilitated and educated in the kingdom's finest schools. The peasant took to his studies with vigor and soon became a respected doctor who was now able to live "the good life." It was only when the murderer became an educated professional who appreciated the finer things of life, a person who had cultivated his new identity, that the king signed the execution document.

The point of the story, and the key to the above questions which relate to the Ten Days of Repentance, the Ten Commandments, *Sh'ma Yisrael*, *Yizkor* and the Torah itself, is that in each case priority must be given to identifying the individuals involved and the nature and quality of their commitments and relationships.

Our primary concern as Jews must be the identity and commitment of each individual and the depth and nature of our relationship with G-d. It is only when this relationship is identified and described that it is possible to proceed with an agenda or program. Now let us look at the elements of the five questions posed above.

▸ Rosh Hashanah

Rosh Hashanah marks the creation of the first human beings. It is therefore the time for establishing and renewing the relationship between man and his Creator. Rosh Hashanah is the time we acknowledge G-d as King. Do I follow His rules? Do I look to Him as a Father who is merciful, compassionate and caring? What conclusions will G-d reach when He judges my behavior? Our task is to reinforce our relationship with G-d by promising that He can expect us to change and improve in various areas. It is also a time when we can appeal to G-d to extend our life and grant us mercy based on the tenor and quality of the relationship. Are we ready to change, or have we just paid lip service? Do we understand that during these special days G-d is especially close, receptive, caring and demanding? All depends on what we say and do on Rosh Hashanah.

▶ The Ten Commandments

The purpose of the first five commandments is to establish our relationship with G-d and determine His expectations as they relate to this relationship. This flows from the fact that the Ten Commandments weren't simply "given." Prior to proclaiming the commandments, the Jewish People undertook a contract or covenant with G-d. It is the first five commandments that establish the terms of this contract.

▶ *Sh'ma Yisrael*

Sh'ma Yisrael is much more than a declaration of the acceptance of the one, unique, all-knowing G-d. It represents an affirmation on the part of each Jew and a commitment to our fellow Jews. When we say "Hear, O Israel..." we are also addressing Israel, the ancient father of the Jewish People. In saying *Sh'ma Yisrael*, we are telling him that despite 2,000 years of persecution, we are committed to the agenda of *Sh'ma Yisrael*. It is more than a declaration of faith. It represents the acceptance of G-d as King. We undertake to observe His commandments. We are committed to spreading His doctrine, faith, ideology and message to all Jews. When this is accomplished, it will trigger the acceptance of G-d as King by mankind. *Sh'ma Yisrael* is not lip service. It demands serious commitment.

▶ *Yizkor*

The existence of every Jew derives from the efforts of our parents and the generations that preceded us. This is an essential message of Rosh Hashanah. The presence of parents and grandparents is *so strong* that there is no need for a special prayer to invoke it. Therefore, saying *Yizkor* would be redundant.

The recitation of *Yizkor* is more than a spiritual reunion with parents and grandparents. It represents an acknowledgement of generational continuity. It reinforces the awareness that we are not detached individuals: The striving of all the generations who preceded us must continue through us.

▶ The Torah

The reason for the sequence of the Torah chapters is by now obvious. The story of Creation, the history of the formative years of the Patriarchs, the descent to Egypt and Egyptian slavery are crucial to our understanding of the instruction that is derived from the lives of the great personalities who set the Jewish Nation on its path through history. Before we can accept the laws of the Torah, which are enumerated in the later books, we must first understand our identity and our unique relationship with G-d.

Each of the above examples points to the fact that for the Jews, the greatest joy of life is in the relationship we create with G-d and the knowledge that G-d is close to us, cares for us, loves us and is concerned with each of us. G-d has entrusted each Jew with a unique personal mission that is a part of the overall mission of the Jewish People, but is nonetheless uniquely suited to the talents and personality of each individual Jew.

Many people feel the guiding Hand of G-d in their lives. Our life's history represents the effort of G-d to speak to us and to guide us along life's path. Judgment on Rosh Hashanah is the greatest evidence of G-d's caring, closeness, love and concern. What we do — or don't do — matters to G-d, and this knowledge makes our lives so different from the lives of those who are unable or unwilling to study and observe His Torah.

The Jew does not live for himself. Our task is to do "the will of G-d." Otherwise, we become a rudderless, directionless, aimless group of chaotic individuals, not the Nation of Torah, the Nation of G-d. Judgment on Rosh Hashanah provides the unique privilege of living in the shadow of G-d, in His palace and as part of His Kingdom. Judgment implies purpose, structure and direction. G-d unifies us, ties us together and forms us into one body, one Nation, one People.

This awareness of man's need to maintain an intimate relationship with G-d and to be constantly accountable to G-d is described in an amazing story concerning the Chofetz Chaim, one of the greatest Jews of all time. When Chofetz Chaim's daughter married, he gave the young couple his attic as their residence. He stipulated one small condition. He needed the use of the attic for one night each month. The couple readily agreed to the condition and arranged alternate sleeping arrangements for that night. One night, the husband needed to return to the house in order to retrieve a forgotten object. Upon approaching the steps of the attic, he heard the Chofetz Chaim pacing the floor and speaking out loud. The Chofetz Chaim continued his pacing through the night, and the young man was appalled to hear his father-in-law recounting to G-d each incident in his life, each crisis, each time G-d's love helped him, from early childhood until his old age. He recalled each date, each situation and the way in which Divine intervention made the crucial difference. To the Chofetz Chaim, Rosh Hashanah happened every month.

It is not our past deeds that are the crux of Rosh Hashanah. It is who we are as we stand before G-d on that day. G-d is concerned with our potential and our determination to use the talents, personality, energy and willpower we possess in order to become the kind of person He wants us to be and we want to be. That is all that matters. On Rosh Hashanah, mankind was born. On this day, we have the ability to return to our source, to be born again. G-d is examining the nature of our commitment to use our potential to build the kind of world our Torah describes.

CHESSED: THE ESSENCE OF JUDAISM

14

Based on *Pachad Yitzchok:* Rosh Hashanah 1

hessed is benevolent, altruistic love — the type of love that seeks to give what is in the recipient's best interest, without expecting or needing thanks, payment or reward.

Chessed love, like all love, needs to be expressed. Love can exist only if there exists a beloved — someone to love. G-d created the universe and mankind in order to be able to express His great quality of *chessed*. The purpose of Creation was to give G-d an avenue through which to shower His love. Creation was itself an act of *chessed*.

Chessed is the basis of creation, the building block of the universe. *Chessed* is therefore the foundation upon which all other ethical and moral qualities rest. It was only after *chessed* provided the mortar for *building* the universe that other Divine qualities, which were needed to *maintain* the universe, were revealed. Many Divine qualities are apparent to us when we observe the way in which G-d governs His universe, but G-d's quality of *chessed* can be understood most readily when we study Creation. G-d has many qualities that He employs in governing the universe; however, His quality of *chessed* was and is the basic ingredient in its creation.

Man was created for one purpose: to delight in, to learn from, and to emulate G-d. As with all moral and ethical qualities, we learn them by studying Torah as well as by imitating G-d's qualities and traits. If we hope to elevate and refine our personalities, the major component must involve our effort to imitate our Creator. As our Sages taught, a person must say, "Just as You, G-d, are merciful, so too must I be merciful; just as you feed the hungry, so too must I feed the hungry," etc. When we educate ourselves in the laws of *chessed* and emulate G-d's quality of *chessed*, we not only mold our personalities, we also deepen our awareness that we are created in His image. As we attain higher levels of *chessed*, we actually create our inner world and discover our true selves. In the process, we recreate ourselves in G-d's image and become more G-d-like.

The Talmud teaches, "A person who does not engage in acts of *chessed* is regarded as someone who does not have a G-d."[1] Without *chessed,* there could have been no Creation. Without man performing acts of *chessed*, there is no place in the world for the Creator. By not doing *chessed*, we in effect banish G-d from the world. In refining and perfecting our personalities, it is important not only to understand *chessed* from a conceptual viewpoint, but also to recognize that *chessed* imposes obligations on us. Our responsibility is to identify with G-d — the fountain of *chessed* — by imitating Him through the performance of acts of *chessed*. *Chessed* is a major obligation of each human being.

Our father Abraham was the first person to understand that G-d created the world through *chessed*, and that it is our obligation to emulate this quality. How? Abraham intensely studied the world and came to discern the Master Architect and Builder of the universe. In seeing the genius of Creation, Abraham also realized that it was a product of G-d's *chessed*, and that G-d's intention was to bestow love and kindness on His creation.

Abraham understood that in order to identify with G-d the Creator, he and his descendants would need to emulate His quality of *chessed*.

We, the descendants of Abraham, therefore observe the covenant of *chessed*, G-d's covenant with Abraham. As the Talmud teaches, "Raish Lakish said, 'Our brethren who bestow love and kindness are children of a People who bestow love and kindness.'"[2] We are loyal to G-d's covenant with Abraham when we follow His path of *chessed*, as is written, "For I have known Abraham in order that he will be able to command his descendents to follow My path by acting with righteousness and justice."[3]

We celebrate Creation, and thank G-d for creating the universe, each and every day. We also observe a special holiday that specifically celebrates creation — Rosh Hashanah. Actually, Rosh Hashanah celebrates the creation of man, who is the crown and culmination of Creation. With the creation of Adam and Eve on Rosh Hashanah, Creation was completed. As suggested above, love can exist only if there is a beloved. G-d created man so as to have a unique being — one who himself possesses G-dly qualities — on whom to shower His love.

We honor our Creator and His Creation each day by performing acts of *chessed*. How much more so are we obligated to reaffirm our loyalty to G-d, our Father, King and Creator on the very holiday that celebrates the creation of mankind? The prophet Nehemiah instructed the Jews prior to Rosh Hashanah, "Eat gourmet foods and enjoy sweets, but also send gifts to the poor."[4] Nehemiah teaches us that acts of *chessed*, such as helping the needy, are integral to the observance of Rosh Hashanah. Indeed, no enjoyment or celebration can be truly complete without acts of giving and sharing.

Deeds of *chessed* honor the sanctity of Rosh Hashanah for another reason too. When *chessed* penetrates the human psyche, it becomes the moving force of an individual's personality. From the moment *chessed* gushes from the heart, it activates, motivates and enriches one's personality. In this way, with each act of *chessed*, the human soul recreates the universe. This is why acts of *chessed* are especially important on Rosh Hashanah, the holiday of Creation.

Chessed, while central to Rosh Hashanah, is integral to all of our holidays, and indeed to every aspect of our lives. We are commanded to invite the needy to our Passover *sedarim*; we are instructed to send gifts to the poor on Purim; we are told to be charitable to the orphan and the widow, and in general to treat others with the same care as we ourselves would want to be treated.

Rosh Hashanah also has an additional special and unique quality. All the other holidays celebrate events that took place after Creation was completed. Rosh Hashanah is the one exception.

Rosh Hashanah not only celebrates Creation itself, it also highlights the dual aspects of man's relationship to G-d. G-d is our King, but G-d was not king until He created man, for to be a king, one must have subjects who accept him as king. We can understand our relationship to G-d our King, because the events of the world since the moment of Creation are known to some extent. But Creation itself, which is described only cryptically in the Torah, is a mystery unknowable by mankind. This is the basis of Rabbi Levi's teaching that "Until the seventh day of Creation, the glory of G-d the Creator is to be found in the concealed, while from the seventh day on, the glory of G-d our King is to be found in the revealed." Thus, Rosh Hashanah serves to remind us of our responsibilities to G-d, Who is both our Creator and our King. Our obligations are to heighten and raise the honor of G-d the Creator regarding the mysteries of the universe (which are beyond our understanding), and also to increase the authority of G-d the King regarding the revealed aspects of events that took place following Creation.

The mystical and concealed aspects of Creation are central to Rosh Hashanah. The rays of spiritual light that come to us on Rosh Hashanah are lights of Creation. But we already have seen that it is both mysterious and unfathomable to man. The spiritual lights of Creation reveal that, "The glory of G-d is found in the hidden." Everything that deals with coming-into-being contains elements of Creation, and everything that relates to Creation is by its nature concealed and hidden. Whether we are speaking of Torah or of human events, the glory of G-d the Creator is to be found in those mystical events that are hidden.

The unknowable, hidden aspect of Rosh Hashanah is emphasized by the distinctive phrase, *"Tik'oo bachodesh shofar bakeseh l'yom chagenu,* Sound the shofar on the new moon at the concealed time of our holiday."[5] Each month, the moon is hidden from view. Each month, the moon renews and reveals itself. From this we learn that *bakeseh,* meaning covered and hidden, is a major theme of Rosh Hashanah. The holy lights of Rosh Hashanah radiate to us through a concealing cover. Rosh Hashanah is the only holiday that celebrates G-d's concealed creativity. Even though we are incapable of understanding the mysteries of Creation, we can and should celebrate and absorb the spiritual lights that shine forth from Creation.

Rabbi Hutner once stated that the concealed nature of Creation is the source of the laws of *tznius,* modesty. We must treat everything that relates to Creation, especially the relationship of man and woman that leads to the creation of children, in a hidden and private fashion. If we are to be partners with G-d in recreating the world by starting families, then we must do so in keeping with the concealed nature of Creation. Only then can the glory of Creation truly shine through.

To summarize: The quality of *chessed* is the cement with which G-d created the world and mankind. Abraham realized this and understood that mankind must worship, emulate and serve G-d. We emulate G-d and serve Him by performing acts of *chessed.* One way to perform *chessed* is to share what we are and what we have so that we can help those who have special needs. Rosh Hashanah, which celebrates the creation of mankind, is the holiday of G-d's concealed light. Through G-d's covenant of *chessed* with Abraham, we, the descendants of Abraham, join with G-d in continually renewing and recreating the world. We emulate G-d not only by performing acts of *chessed,* but also by being His partner through our acts of elevating, refining and sanctifying our lives and the lives of others.

▶ Concluding Comment

I t is only in recent times that science has revealed the unbelievable intricacy of design of a single cell, the unbelievable expanse of the universe, and the magnificence of any one of thousands of biological mechanisms such as the eye, the brain or the reproductive system. Anyone who thinks that all that we see could have come about without the genius of a Master Builder, Artist, Architect and Inventor — the Creator Himself — is practicing self-deception.

It is generally our practice to pronounce one blessing on a *mitzvah*. Circumcision, however, is unique in that in addition to the first blessing on the circumcision itself, we also recite a second blessing — "Who commanded us to initiate the infant into the covenant of our father Abraham." This second blessing teaches us that circumcision is not only a *mitzvah* which we are commanded to perform, it also demands that every Jew identify with the covenant of Abraham and be included in it. In other words, the *Bris Milah,* the covenant of *chessed* of our father Abraham, obligates each and every Jew to become an active practitioner of Abraham's quality of *chessed.*

---

1. *Avodah Zarah* 17.
2. *Kesubos* 8b.
3. *Genesis* 18:19
4. *Nehemiah* 8.
5. *Psalm* 8.

WHAT "GOOD" IS SIN?

15

Some people think sin is good, but those are not the kind of people who are reading this.

Most of us agree that serious sin is not identified with good citizens or fine people, but with gangsters, racketeers and "shady" characters. We agree too that it is found not in our homes, synagogues or schools but in hideouts and hangouts. And yet, sin is the central theme of the holiest days of the year, when the best and finest people gather in the synagogue to ask G-d to forgive our transgressions.

Why should good people be concerned with sin and repentance? The answer is that, in the eyes of G-d, each and every human being has in some way sinned; therefore, every person — even the greatest, most pious and learned — must come before G-d to repent. To sin is to be human; it is hard to avoid. Only G-d above and animals on earth are free of sin: G-d, because He is perfection and goodness, animals because they lack values (such as good and evil) as well as the freedom to choose and assume responsibility for their deeds.

▶ A Tug of War

The question is: Why did G-d create man's life as a constant tug of war between good and evil, between judgment and instinct? King Solomon states that no man can totally escape sin.[1] If that is so, sin must serve an important role in the life of man, even in the lives of men and women who are essentially good — even in the lives of religious and righteous people.

To understand how sin operates in our lives, and how it is understood in Jewish tradition, we must take a deeper look into the meaning of Rosh Hashanah and Yom Kippur. These holidays deal primarily with the Kingship of G-d, the nature of man and the G-d-man relationship. These days are not devoted simply to achieving deeper spirituality and awe of Heaven. Their focus is on the action program each person must undertake, by examining his deeds and returning to G-d in a spirit of atonement.

The central theme of Rosh Hashanah and Yom Kippur, the "Days of Awe," is the recognition that the Almighty is supreme and that we must accept Him as our King. Each Jew must acknowledge that the wisdom and Will of the Creator is to be found behind the seeming accidental occurrences of life; and that our fate is determined by G-d's Will alone. The prayers and practices of Rosh Hashanah in particular are designed to impress upon us an awareness that this world, which often gives the appearance of being chaotic, disorganized and in complete disarray, operates in accordance with rules, order and system.

What appears to us to be bewildering disorder, in truth, is the unfolding of G-d's plan for history. Through Torah study, we come to understand that the creative force in our lives is an infinitely wise King and Creator, who brought this world into being with purpose, goals, meaning and direction. The duty of man and the very purpose of man's creation and continued existence are to achieve the fulfillment of this goal. The blueprint and road map is the Torah, revealed at Sinai to our fathers and transmitted to their children and children's children after them. If we acknowledge this, and become deeply aware that this world is ruled by an eternal King and that we are all His subjects, then we will come to realize that whatever takes place in our lives is either the Divine response to our actions, by way of the rewards and punishments through which G-d tests and refines our integrity and loyalty, or the cause-and-effect consequences which follow our accomplishments or failures.

▸ Why is there Reward and Punishment?

Why does G-d use a system of reward or punishment? Is it to "settle a score," to restore "the balance of justice," or to frighten us into obedience? There is something that is deeper and more subtle involved here. In the promise of reward and the threat of punishment, G-d wants us to hear a call to personal growth and development, to examine our deeds and motives, to weigh our values and priorities. Often this reward or punishment cannot be immediately detected and is kept in abeyance for some future time. But the promise must bring fulfillment, if not now, then later: if not in this world, in the next.

To the observant Jew each *mitzvah* is not only a duty that brings reward, but is also a reward in itself. This works through a simple process. The performance of a *mitzvah* elevates the performer spiritually and makes possible the observance of other, possibly more difficult *mitzvos*. The doing of *mitzvos* trains our minds and bodies to a life of discipline and action that must be tempered by planning and thought. By reaching for the highest plane, we can also cope with the daily and the ordinary. We come to live more sublime lives, where each deed and each day is part of a greater plan, where even the smallest act achieves meaning. Why? Because the deed becomes an integral unit in a great and meaningful pattern, just as each piece in a jigsaw puzzle is part of a larger picture. Instead of floating aimlessly in a great sea, we realize that life leads to a specific port; that in the great journey of life G-d, has reserved a special place for each and every one of those who are sensitive to His Will and purpose.

To give this idea added emphasis, our Sages taught that, "The reward of one *mitzvah* is another *mitzvah*." This teaches us that the fulfillment of human existence is not greater material comforts and pleasures, but rather the growth of our ability and the enhancement of our capacity to live a life of Torah and *mitzvos* on higher and higher levels. Living "the good life," as set forth by the Torah, becomes our goal and aspiration. Although it comes slowly, reaching these goals becomes our greatest reward. When G-d rewards us each year with renewed life and health, this is not necessarily a pat on the back, but a grant of another opportunity, a new chance to continue to grow and develop further. And if we have not yet earned this reward of health and life, then even through our declaration of good intentions we might receive another chance for achievement. The greatest challenge is to grow, to find inner strength, to discipline mind and body to overcome the obstacles of laziness and habit, and to discover new inner resources, so that greater challenges may be met with greater competence and renewed enthusiasm.

▸ Climbing a Ladder

To clarify this concept, let us picture life as a ladder. (Recall the famous ladder in Jacob's dream, with its "legs on the ground and its head reaching up to the heavens.") We are told to climb to Heaven on this ladder, away from our base animal and physical nature. The higher you climb, the harder you fall, if you slip. But you cannot rise unless you first fall, and once you fall, you thank G-d that you have not broken your neck and that it is possible to begin the climb all over again.

"Had I not fallen I could not have risen; had I not sat in darkness, I would never have learned to appreciate the light of G-d."[2] In reference to the above statement, the Bible speaks of two different types of light: A psalm states, "G-d is my light." This means that generally speaking, when I don't sin, G-d is my light. Yet, even when I sin, there is hope, for the prophet Micah says, "Even when I sit in darkness, G-d is my light." This is the second type of light.

Another point we should appreciate is that all Jews, no matter how great or small, are on the same ladder, all facing challenges and offered opportunities. The difference is only in the nature of our response.

The analogy of the ladder indicates that in a certain sense, what is sinful for one person is not necessarily sinful for another. This in no way means that one person has an obligation to perform a *mitzvah* while the other does not. Rather, it refers to the quality and intent of two people performing the same *mitzvah*. While everyone is expected to observe Shabbos, eat only kosher food and be truthful, one person may be at the bottom of the ladder, having just now begun to observe these *mitzvos*, while another may be many steps ahead. Each time one performs any *mitzvah,* the performance of that *mitzvah* raises the performer one spiritual step. When, for example, one observes Shabbos with greater fervor and has trained himself to purer thoughts during Shabbos, and has delved deeper into the meaning of the Shabbos commandment, then his *mitzvah* of Shabbos has taken on deeper significance and meaning.

A person who reaches higher and then falls down is, in a sense, committing a sin. If, for example, a person on a high level goes down one step and another person on a lower level climbs up one step and both meet on the same level, the one who has climbed up has earned reward while the one who has fallen has begun to move in the direction of sin, even though the two stand on the same step. While at the outset each *mitzvah* makes substantially the same demands on each person, each person is on his own, based on the factors mentioned above.

This is the meaning of the rabbinic teaching that "the consequence of sin is more sin." Each deed brings with it other deeds, with yet additional deeds that flow from them. Once you have set out in the direction of sin, you are in danger of sinning again. If you fear the punishment of sin, the greatest fear should not be the suffering of pain or death, but the personal downfall and diminishment that involves the weakening of our freedom and free choice. Instead of rising on the ladder of spiritual growth, the sinner is brought down toward the animal level, where instinct, desire and lust rule. Instead of ruling instinct, instead of taming and disciplining desire through Torah wisdom, the person comes under the control of those very instincts. Freedom is lost when we are caught in a chain reaction. Once one starts to fall, it is hard to stop.

▸ Fear of Falling

t is not the fear of pain, death or sorrow that frightens us as much as the fear of falling; of shrinking our human selves; of losing the strength of our personalities, our consciousness, freedom and awareness; of becoming less today than we were yesterday. The severest Divine punishment is our downfall, for by falling we fall away from the Divine, and demonstrate our inability to meet the challenges of life and G-d's call to live the Torah life. Two elements constantly battle for dominance within us: our drives and instincts on the one hand, and our mind and willpower on the other.

Our progress is measured by the degree to which we are able to overcome one obstacle after the other, and finally reach our goal. If the obstacles persist in standing in our way, we have lost life's battle or, at best, we stagnate. In the end, the person who achieves is not the individual who walks on the flat terrain, but the individual who has trained himself to climb higher and higher mountains.

In the book of Ecclesiastes, King Solomon (the wisest of all humans) relates our lifelong struggle to find meaning and purpose in life. His final sentence summarizes his search: "The sum of the matter, when all is considered, is this: Fear G-d and observe His commandments, for that is the essence of man."[3]

Our constant confrontation with sin determines and guides our path through life. Sin had its purpose: Without it, we would be robots. Real people must use the challenge of sin to overcome challenge and grow.

---

1. *Ecclesiastes* 7:20.
2. *Micah* 7:8.
3. *Ecclesiastes* 12:14.

LINKING ROSH HASHANAH TO THE EXODUS

O ne of the favorite "insights" of non-believers is their oft-repeated claim that our holidays originated as agricultural festivals. Only "later," they claim, did "the rabbis" superimpose historical or spiritual meaning upon the festivals. That nature and history are indeed one; that they have one source; that there is harmony and unity in the physical and the spiritual universe, requires belief that G-d is real, that G-d designed both nature and history in one context. Nature and history as a unified whole is seen by our detractors as being much "too advanced" for a "5,000-year-old G-d."

As the Creator of Nature and the Master of History, G-d designated specific times of the year for the budding of vegetation or the freezing of the ground. Jewish tradition, history and experience long ago recognized that these seasons are likewise suited for the budding of human events or the freezing or unfreezing of human destinies.

This pattern of changing seasons in nature and in history, of specific days with built-in potential for good or evil, reward or punishment, obedience or rebellion, follows consistently each year, from Creation through the end of time, through all generations and in all eras. It is a pattern that governs each and every year as the seasons change and the world turns. We will, therefore, discover that while the festivals of the Jewish year mark certain outstanding events, such as the Creation of the world, the Exodus from Egypt and the Giving of the Torah, they also invariably mark other significant historical events as well, events which preceded the major outstanding historical event for which each festival is best known, as well as events which took place at a later time or will yet take place.

▶ Our Keys to History

An archaeologist uncovers the various generational layers of ancient cities, studying the city's history as revealed by each strata of rubble, attempting to uncover the ideological, national or sociological thread which unites the city from the day of its founding up to its final destruction. To understand Jewish history and Jewish historical thought, we must search for the key events of each holiday in each layer and stratum of history.

When we study the Written and Oral Torah and its many commentaries, when we research carefully, we discover that significant events took place in each major era of history on each and every Jewish festival. This information is stated explicitly or implicitly in the Torah, in the Talmud and the *Midrashim*. Sometimes, it was passed through the generations as an oral tradition to be revealed by a commentator who felt that the information needed to be imparted to a given generation. Thus, each festival — Rosh Hashanah, Yom Kippur, Passover, Shavuos, Succos/Shmini Atzeres, and all the fast days — recall occurrences that took place at the time of Creation, during the period of the Patriarchs, events from the Exodus through the building of the Holy Temple and in succeeding periods as well. One major event always stands out, however, and the festival is known primarily for that one significant event.

That Passover, Shavuos and Succos are tied to the generation of the Exodus is well known. Even Yom Kippur fits into the pattern of the Exodus, as it is the day on which Moses descended from Mt. Sinai for the second time to deliver the Second Tablets of the Covenant. The giving of the Second Tablets indicated that G-d had accepted the penitence of the Children of Israel and had forgiven them.

There would appear to be a significant exception to the above statement, as Rosh Hashanah has no seeming connection with the events of the Exodus at all. Its central theme relates to the Creation of Man, the Coronation of G-d as King over mankind and the anticipation of an era in which all of mankind will accept and recognize G-d's Kingship. But here, too, consistent with the axiom spelled out above, there is an Exodus connection and if we search our sources we will find it. This connection is implicit, in that the *Kiddush* of Rosh Hashanah follows the uniform festival text by stating that the day is "a holy convocation, a memorial of the Exodus from Egypt."

Let us look deeper. Rosh Hashanah is the day on which man was created. It is also the day on which the first man sinned and repented. It is therefore the day man first rebelled against his King — and again accepted G-d fully as his King.

The link between Rosh Hashanah to the Exodus is to be found again in the commentary of Rabbeinu Nissim (Nissim ben Reuben Gorondi, 1310-1375, of Cordoba and Barcelona), known as the "Ran." In his Talmud commentary, tractate *Rosh Hashanah* (page 3, side 1), he teaches that the Divine scale, which had until that day been weighted in favor of the destruction of the Jewish People, began to tip in the opposite direction on Rosh Hashanah.

A review the circumstances is in order: The Jews left Egypt on Passover. Seven weeks later, they completed the *Sefirah* count and on Shavuos they received the Torah. Moses then went up on Mt. Sinai to receive the Tablets of the Ten Commandments.

During this forty-day period Moses remained atop Mt. Sinai, where G-d instructed him in the Torah. He descended Mt. Sinai on the 17th of Tamuz, saw the sin of the Golden Calf and broke the original Tablets. He went up again to the top of Mt. Sinai and remained for an additional forty days. There he pleaded with G-d to forgive the Jews. He came down a second time on Rosh Chodesh Elul. That same day, G-d told Moses to again go up the mountain. The Talmud tells us that he came down with the second pair of Tablets and arrived in the camp of Israel on Yom Kippur. This was a Divine sign that G-d had forgiven the Jews for their earlier sin of the Golden Calf.

But it was on Rosh Hashanah, as indicated by the Ran, that the fate of the Jewish nation was determined, when the scales tipped in favor of life. "And it would seem that from Rosh Hashanah up till Yom Kippur, G-d began to accept the repentance of Moses" on behalf of the Jewish People, states the Ran, and "on Yom Kippur He accepted their repentance completely." The Ran provides the missing link proving that the Exodus and Rosh Hashanah are closely related.

REMEMBER US TO LIFE: ZOCHREINU L'CHAIM

17

"Remember us to life, O King who desires life, and inscribe us in the Book of Life, for Your sake, O living G-d."

Unfortunately, most translations barely skim the surface of this High Holiday prayer. It should be obvious that if the intention of this prayer were to ask G-d to grant us life in the coming year, there is no need for so many words and so complicated a sentence. What is the true meaning of this prayer?

The key to the prayer lies in the last two words, *Elokim chaim*, which mean much more than "a living G-d." I believe that the meaning of these words is "G-d whose essence is life." What is the definition of "G-d whose essence is life?" I believe that it cannot refer to physical or biological life. What we are being told is that not only is G-d life itself, the Creator of life, but that the life we are asking for must, in some way, emulate G-d's "life." For this reason, the prayer begins by saying, "*Zochreinu l'chaim, Melech chafetz ba'chaim*, Recall us for life, King whose greatest desire is that we should want to emulate [Your] form of life." G-d wants us to be much more than creatures that eat, sleep and reproduce. He wants us to be close to Him, to maintain an intimate relationship with Him, to develop ourselves to a point where we succeed in overcoming our earthbound limitations and aspire to spirituality and eternity.

And when that day comes, G-d wants our relationship with Him to continue beyond our earthly existence. G-d is hoping that the experience of Rosh Hashanah will help us refine ourselves to the point where our greatest wish will be to create intense and intimate channels and relationships with Him, so that while we are still on this earth we will have prepared ourselves for the day when our souls will return to their source and be reunited with G-d. He wants us to live that kind of existence that is the *real life*, the life that is not tied to this earth; the life that is eternal; the life that is far more spiritual than the life we live on earth. G-d wants us to yearn for a life that we cannot even imagine, but which must become our greatest wish and aspiration.

When we pray, we must believe seriously that G-d both listens and reacts. We must understand that when we die, our soul is liberated from its earthy bonds and begins to live its true life. There is but one proviso: This can happen *only* if during our sojourn on earth we develop the spirituality and refinement that will enable us to live beyond this life. For example, if our prayers are mere words, if we are not actually speaking with G-d, then they are of little true value. If, however, our prayers express our deep-felt and most important aspirations, then we will, after death, have acquired the ability to maintain our link to G-d and our ability to communicate with him. We are given the gift of being able to transform ourselves in this world so that we will be able to live in the next world. This is our major task. Once we reach the next world, we are unable to transform ourselves. We are, in essence, whatever we have already made of ourselves in this world.

We must also remember that while we are on this planet we have the choice to live two kinds of life — a physical/animal life, or a spiritual life. Obviously, this is not a one or the other proposition, but a question of where we place the emphasis. As the Sages taught: "Prepare yourself in the foyer so that you can merit to enter the great palace."

EXPLORING
18 THE SHOFAR

The sounding of the shofar on Rosh Hashanah can be understood as a response to the creation of the first human being that took place on that day. When G-d created the first person, the Torah says, "G-d *blew* into his nostrils the soul of life." The first human is the only creation among all of G-d's creations into which He *blew* a Divine soul.

At the moment that G-d infused a soul into the first person, G-d became King. Only the human being possesses a Divine soul as well as the ability to freely choose his or her course of action. This is an ability that G-d shared only with the human race. This power of free choice gives human beings the ability to accept or to reject G-d's Kingship. The essence of true sovereignty takes place when the subject says to his king, "I have chosen to serve you of my own free will."

What is the underlying power of reciting a blessing prior to eating something we are about to enjoy? The blessing removes the fruit from obscurity, it bestows on it new meaning: Now it plays a role in G-d's Kingdom. The food is brought into focus — it is now identified as having been created by the King to serve man's needs. When we recite a blessing over a food, upon seeing lightning or putting on new clothing, we do more than express our gratitude and reliance on G-d. What we are doing is removing the object from insignificance and pointing to it as a creation of the Divine King. We are pointing to G-d's Kingship and acknowledging Him as King and Creator. Most people simply see food as food, and no more. The Jew sees evidence of G-d's sovereignty and love of mankind.

The shofar arouses in us the remembrance of the day of our creation and the awareness of our relationship with our King. We intensify our awareness of our past, present and future dependence on G-d. In this sense, the shofar is similar to the Sabbath. The Sabbath celebrates our past, present and future; it awakens us to experience and explore the three key, pivotal themes in human history: First, that G-d is King — that the creation of the world and of mankind required a Creator, an Architect, a Builder. Second, that the Torah is mankind's roadmap and constitution. Third, with the anticipated arrival of the Messiah, G-d will become King over all the earth. It is only when man acknowledges G-d's Kingship that he realizes his own responsibility to make known the oneness of G-d.

The prayers of Rosh Hashanah are also centered on these three key components:

Malchuyos — Kingship: G-d is King and Creator. We freely acknowledge G-d as King.

Zichronos — Remembrances: The obligation to be continuously aware of the giving of the Torah at Mt. Sinai.

Shofros — The Great Shofar will be blown on the day of the Messiah's arrival. This is the day of our final Redemption. The sound of the shofar and the raising of a banner will herald the gathering of all of Israel's exiles in Jerusalem.

What is the true role of the shofar? It awakens us as to the nature of our potential. It reminds us that we are capable of returning to the exalted station of the first human being, who was created without sin. The reason Rosh Hashanah is centered on the individual is to motivate us to understand that each individual has the ability to accomplish the goals of Rosh Hashanah in his or her own life.

On Rosh Hashanah we anticipate the coming of the Messiah and pray for his coming. It is not sufficient to *hope* for the coming of Israel's Messiah. Each Jew must also feel a personal responsibility to bring about the coming of his own personal "messiah" within his own being. What does this mean? Each person is called "a miniature world." In the framework of our life, each of us is capable of achieving the goals G-d has set for the entire universe. Each person is born. (This recalls Creation.) Each person must receive a Torah education (corresponding to Revelation). And each person must perfect his own personality and character so as to use his talents and potential to become a force for the maximum good (corresponding to the coming of the Messiah).

The coming of the King Messiah is a national concept, an event that will happen in the future life of the Jewish Nation. As pointed out above, every Jew can regard his own spiritual growth in this context as well — as though his "personal Messiah" has appeared. When we have all achieved this breakthrough, the Messiah will come for all Jews. When? "*Today*, if you hearken to My voice!" (Psalms 95:6)

SANCTIFYING TIME

19

▶ Time and Change

We generally like to think of time as something constant and undeviating, as an unending stream we use when and how we see fit. It seems, however, that G-d arranged reality differently. It is He who structured time and filled it with meaning. We go to sleep at night and wake up to a new day with new strength and vigor, ready to take on new challenges that the exhaustion of the previous day made impossible. If we are normal, we cannot ignore or conquer the night — eventually we must sleep. We must renew ourselves. As we shall explain, G-d built the divisions of time into nature. While we may try to overcome time, it is impossible to ignore its demands.

As we move from the day to the week, we see that the concept of the week was instilled into the first man and has become the universal inheritance of all of civilizations. This "Jewish" invention is honored universally: Indeed, the Biblical week is now the week of all mankind.

The month is also built into nature through the moon, which to human eyes appears to disappear and reappear each twenty-nine or thirty days. The monthly renewal of the moon is indicated in the Hebrew word *chodesh*, month, which is rooted in the same word as *chadash*, meaning new. The year is also enshrined into the annual cycle of the sun, which determines the four seasons that govern nature and complete the annual cycle of holidays and events. No one even *tries* to have more than one birthday per year!

The intrusion of nights, days, weeks, months, seasons and years shatters our illusion that time is insignificant in our lives. The changes and shifts of time are a constant reminder that G-d wants us to be aware of the march of time. Most of all, G-d wants us to value time, to respect time, to sanctify time. The injunction to "Remember the Sabbath to keep it holy,"[1] indicates that it is we who must make time holy by sanctifying it. And it is we who trivialize, defile and waste time by ignoring its potential for sanctity.

Our lives and aging bodies also remind us that, like the day and the year, our lives are dynamic and finite. Our lives consist of an ever moving cycle which transports us — like it or not — from infancy, to childhood, to adulthood, to old age and finally to unavoidable death. The time we are allotted on this earth is finite. We may want to live forever, but only fools ignore reality. The years pass with shocking speed.

The way we *use* time is left to our own volition to a large degree. The holidays are reminders that we are obligated to conserve time and make time holy just as G-d sanctifies time by giving us the week with its Shabbos and the year with its festivals. We too must follow G-d's example and zealously sanctify each precious minute. We Americans are masters at squandering our time, as though we are capable of renewing or reclaiming it. We choose to forget that time passes once.

"It is G-d, who, through His constant supervision and wisdom, brings about the evenings, opens the gates of sunrise and sunset, changes the seasons, orders the changing of the heavenly guard, the stars and the constellations, and creates day and night. He is the Master of nature; Master of Legions is His Name."[2]

Let us not forget that the term Rosh Hashanah — the "head of the year" — does not appear in the Torah or in Tanach. The Torah calls this day *Yom Teruah* — the day of the shofar blasts, a day on which we crown the Divine King by sounding the shofar, a day on which we recall and mark the creation of mankind. The shofar awakens us from our lethargy and urges us to acknowledge the constant urging of the King to sanctify our daily lives. It is He who calls upon us to review the crises and challenges we faced last year and the year before and to hear His call that we examine and change the way we use the precious gift of time.

The day of mankind's birth, Rosh Hashanah, is the day on which G-d judges us. It is the time that is ripe for the Divine plan for the world to be reevaluated, for the progress and conduct of the players to be judged, for the players to be reminded that our King, Father and Creator has expectations and demands. G-d expects us to respect and maintain His timetable, and be sensitive to the potential of this special day to evoke change.

The Torah also calls Rosh Hashanah *Yom Hazikaron* — the day of memory and recollection. Judaism calls on Jews to be aware of the fact that each of us is a link in a chain that stretches from the day of Creation to the End of Days. *Zikaron* is more than the memory of things past — it demands that we be aware, that we recollect the challenges, achievements and failures of those who preceded us. It reminds us of our obligation to strengthen the chain of Jewish history and to extend it until it reaches its goals.

For some, time is an illusion. For Jews, time is holy; it is the key to reality. How we use our time and our lives defines and describes us as we stand in judgment on Judgment Day.

Each of us is given a limited number of years. Some of us receive a gift of forty years, some sixty years and some, ninety or more. Each year presents us with a new opportunity to scale a higher and more difficult mountain. If each year we find ourselves standing on the same level as we stood last year, we have failed. In our effort to scale our spiritual and intellectual mountains we are judged by the degree to which we have applied new thoughts, knowledge, judgments and efforts, more so than the degree to which we have actually changed.

It is effort and intentions that count. If we fail to make the grade despite our best efforts, it may well be that G-d has other plans for us. The Hebrew root of the word *shanah* — *shin nun* — appears to be a universal vehicle for bringing about change and transformation. *L'shanos* means to change. *Shaynah*, sleep, transforms a person's exhaustion so that he awakens refreshed. *Shane*, tooth, transforms food to a state where the body can digest and utilize it. *L'shanein* is to study or review information which is then changed from something external to something absorbed and internalized in our memory as information and knowledge. Finally, *shanah*, year, calls on man to undergo internal transformation. That is why the word for year in Hebrew is *shanah*. Liberally translated, *Rosh Hashanah* means "the time to use our heads so that we will take advantage of this special opportunity to make a sincere effort to change." In effect, we decide to sanctify our time by using it as G-d intended.

▶ An Additional Thought

The accepted practice of a person who faces judgment is to wear black, to wrap himself in mourning, to neglect his hair and fingernails, for he dreads the unknown results of the judge's decision.

Not so the Nation of Israel! "'What other nation is like this one — Israel — that understands its G-d?' We wear white, groom our hair and fingernails, eat, drink and rejoice on Rosh Hashanah, confident that the Holy One will perform a miracle [of forgiveness] for us."[3] If this is so, why don't we wear elaborate, colorful clothing? To do so might appear overconfident, implying that we do not fear G-d's judgment sufficiently, that we are insensitive to the danger surrounding us.

According to Rabbi Shlomo Luria (Maharshal), wearing white also demonstrates awareness of the day of death, for we are buried in white shrouds. If we keep in mind that someday our soul will return to G-d, we will be more careful in our actions and strive harder to live our lives as He has instructed us in His Torah.

1. *Exodus* 20:8.
2. From the *Ma'ariv* prayer.
3. *Tur Orach Chaim* 581, from the *Midrash.*

IV YOM KIPPUR

YOM KIPPUR: THE SECOND CREATION OF MAN

20

There is an interesting parallel between Rosh Hashanah/Yom Kippur and Passover/Shavuos. Rosh Hashanah celebrates the creation of mankind. When man sins, he loses his majesty and his glory. He is then banished from the Garden of Eden. Yom Kippur restores man to his former state. He is forgiven. Rosh Hashanah and Yom Kippur teach that man can restore his former majesty and that he can be forgiven. When man again wins G-d's confidence and love, G-d gives man His most treasured gift for the second time: the Torah.

How is Yom Kippur connected to the giving of the Torah? On Yom Kippur, Moses came down from Mt. Sinai the second time with the second set of Tablets. Both Yom Kippur and Shavuos are days on which the Torah was given.

With the birth of the Nation of Israel at the time of the Exodus, G-d's plan for mankind was again launched. Passover, therefore, celebrates a second creation, the creation of the Jewish People, a nation that would carry out G-d's purpose for mankind. Forty days after the Exodus, on Shavuos, the Jewish People received G-d's greatest gift — the Torah. Here, too, sin intervened. On his way down from Mt. Sinai forty days later, Moses saw the Jews dancing and reveling around the Golden Calf. Realizing that they were no longer on the same high spiritual plane they had been just forty days previously, he smashed and broke the Tablets. G-d, in His anger, wanted to destroy the Jewish People.

Both Rosh Hashanah and Yom Kippur are days of creation. On Rosh Hashanah man was created pure, but he sinned. On Yom Kippur, G-d forgave and recreated the Jewish People. This time, Moses taught them that it was possible to regain G-d's favor. G-d had created a new reality — *teshuvah,* repentance. *Teshuvah,* which literally means to return, enables man to reinvent himself by regretting his sins and by asking G-d for forgiveness. *Teshuvah* represents a new creation of man. Yom Kippur, which reenacts Israel's acceptance of G-d's punishment and admonition, provides man with a formula for obtaining forgiveness. "Repentance, prayer and charity avert the evil decree" (as stated in the *Mussaf* service of Rosh Hashanah and Yom Kippur). It describes a new gift, a new reality and a new creation: the ability of man to slip and fall, then rise up and again win the favor and acceptance of G-d.

Rosh Hashanah celebrates Creation. Yom Kippur celebrates atonement, forgiveness and the gift of Torah. On Rosh Hashanah, G-d alone is King, but on Yom Kippur, man becomes G-d's partner in the effort to perfect Creation.

Passover is linked to Yom Kippur through the giving of the Torah on Shavuos, which was nearly cancelled due to the crisis caused by the Golden Calf. When Moses ascended Mt. Sinai a second time, he descended with the second Tablets on Yom Kippur. In this way, Yom Kippur compliments both Rosh Hashanah and Passover. It is the advent of the creation of *teshuvah* on Yom Kippur that allowed the continued existence of the Jewish People and the continued celebration of both holidays of Creation, Rosh Hashanah and Passover.

TESHUVAH: A NEW CREATION

21

Based on Pachad Yitzchok, Yom Hakippurim 1

▶ Introduction

y linking *teshuvah* to the power of creation, G-d calls upon us to recreate ourselves. Once we "do" *teshuvah,* the person who sinned yesterday no longer exists: He is reborn through his reacceptance of the Torah and *mitzvos.* By cutting his connections with his sinful past, the *ba'al teshuvah* is seen by G-d as a new individual. To achieve this status on Yom Kippur, repentance for individual sins is not sufficient. A comprehensive examination and reconstruction of our personalities is required, so that a new self can emerge. *Teshuvah* on Yom Kippur is not a process of becoming a better person; we must become a new person.

▸ Yom Kippur, The Day of *Teshuvah*

"On that day, He will forgive you, to purify you of all your sins. In the presence of G-d purify yourselves."[1]

Rabbeinu Yonah[2] observed that the statement, "in the presence of G-d purify yourselves," is not a promise, but a special command to perform *teshuvah*. When is this *mitzvah* performed? On Yom Kippur.

The term employed for the *mitzvah* of *teshuvah* year round is, *ve'shavta*, "you shall return."[3] On Yom Kippur the Torah commands: "purify yourselves."

We do *teshuvah* all year — but Yom Kippur is the *day of teshuvah*. The emphasis is on total purification on this day.

This difference between the *teshuvah* we do year round and the special *teshuvah* of Yom Kippur is emphasized by the language of Rabbeinu Yonah.[4]

> *Many steps lead to* teshuvah, *but depending on how high an individual climbs, to that extent he will draw closer to G-d. Each* teshuvah-*step brings partial forgiveness, but the soul is "purified" only when a person purifies his heart.*

Think of a garment that needs laundering. A little washing removes some dirt, but fully laundering will clean the entire garment. Every *teshuvah* effort removes some "dirt," bringing about some forgiveness. However, the restoration of the soul to its original pure state by wiping the slate clean requires that total *teshuvah* takes place. This "full cleaning" is the task and goal of Yom Kippur.

▸ The Special Quality of *Teshuvah* Prayer

How is the above reflected in the unique prayers of the *teshuvah* season? The elevated quality of our prayers at this time is especially pronounced. Just as G-d's closeness to us during the atonement period helps us in our *teshuvah* effort, that proximity also assists us in achieving greater elevation in prayer.

The Rambam says this explicitly:

> *Even though* teshuvah *and beseeching are always effective, during the ten days between Rosh Hashanah and Yom Kippur* teshuvah *is of the greatest significance and is accepted instantly, as is stated by Isaiah (55:6), "Seek the Lord while He can be found, call on Him while He is near."*[5]

The special character of prayer during the *teshuvah* season points to the fact that praying for success in achieving *teshuvah* is an intrinsic element in the quest for *teshuvah*. Rabbeinu Yonah enumerates prayer as the fifteenth element in the steps required for *teshuvah*. He teaches that prayer for *teshuvah* is a unique and integral part of the process.

▸ The Unique Character of *Slichos* Prayer

A primary example of the unique character of prayer during the Ten Days of Penitence is the *Slichos* service, the special early morning penitential prayers universally observed for centuries. *Slichos* are formulated and structured so as to parallel the order of the daily prayers. How? We open the *Slichos* with *Ashrei*. *Slichos* concludes with *Nefilas Apayim (Tachanun)* and *Kaddish Tiskabel*. This sequence is unique to the *Slichos* prayers of Elul and Tishrei and is not found in other prayers that relate to family, health or sustenance.

▸ The Repetition of G-d's Name in the Thirteen Attributes

The unique core of the *Slichos* prayers are the Thirteen Attributes of Mercy which G-d taught Moses: "*G-d, G-d, L-rd, compassionate and gracious, slow to anger, abundant in kindness and truth; preserver of kindness for thousands of generations, forgiver of iniquity, willful sin and error, and Who cleanses."*[6] Why do the Thirteen Attributes begin with a double repetition of G-d's name? The Sages[7] explain: The first Name of G-d speaks of G-d before man sins, while the second Name of G-d speaks of G-d after man sins and does *teshuvah.*

But a question arises. Doesn't *teshuvah* derive from the last of the Thirteen Divine qualities: *venakay*, He Who cleanses? Don't the rabbis teach, *menakay Hu lashavim*, "He [G-d] cleanses those who return?"[8] An explanation is provided by the Maharal:

> *He who does* teshuvah *for all his sins derives his* teshuvah *from the second Name of G-d; while the individual who does* teshuvah *for [only] some of his sins derives his* teshuvah *from the Divine quality "venakay, He who cleanses."*[9]

▸ *Teshuvah:* A New Creation

The power of *teshuvah* which derives from the second Name of G-d is not expressed in words or terms which can be defined or translated, or which relate to G-d's attributes of "patience" or "slowness to anger." On the contrary, the power of *teshuvah* derives from the ineffable Name of G-d that defies translation. (*The four letters: Yud, Kay, Vav, Kay.*) [Note that the second and fourth letter of G-d's Name is *Hay*, the fifth letter of the Hebrew alphabet. Since it is prohibited to spell out G-d's Name, we substitute *Kay* for *Hay*.] This indicates that *teshuvah* was not created among the original forces that govern the world. It is a new creation.

What is the import of the ineffable Name of G-d used in this prayer? That G-d is the giver of life and existence; that He creates reality and renews existence every minute by actualizing it from the potential to the actual. (In Hebrew, creation that results from G-d's command, creating something out of nothing, is called *yaish may'ayin*; i.e. *ex nihilo*.) Since there is no terminology to describe total *teshuvah* other than by invoking the ineffable Name of G-d, we conclude that *teshuvah* is an *ex nihilo* creation.

Teshuvah therefore represents a second "edition" of Creation, the new creation of a new world: a world in which it is possible for sin to be totally eradicated. What is the sequence of events? The first "edition" of Creation existed until Adam sinned. Man's first sin marked the end of the first "edition." G-d then created a new world, a world in which *teshuvah* is possible, a second edition as defined by the second Name of G-d. Since our present world is the "world of *teshuvah*," it is governed by the Divine quality characterizing G-d as "slow to anger." It is a world in which G-d patiently anticipates *teshuvah*, in which the sinner is able to return. Without *teshuvah*, G-d's qualities of patience and slowness to anger are of no consequence. If a person could not change his status from thief to *ba'al teshuvah*, what point is there to G-d's "patience" or "slowness to anger?" From the moment one sins, the world which existed before the sin is destroyed and a new world of potential *teshuvah* is created.

▸ Yom Kippur's Goal: To Return to the Status of Man Prior to the First Sin

The Maharal teaches us that G-d's attribute, "Who cleanses" indicates that G-d also cleanses those who do *teshuvah* on only a portion of their sins. But did we not say that the second Divine Name following man's sin refers to man's opportunity to do *teshuvah* for *all* of his sins? Does not the creation of the new world of *teshuvah* derive from the second Divine Name? Isn't its purpose to enable the sinner to return to the station of man "prior to Adam's sin" in such a way that the second Divine Name restores man to the state he occupied at the time of his original creation?

Created anew, man and all of Creation can now aspire to return to their station prior to the sin. The "Second Name of G-d" following the sin, says the Maharal, relates exclusively to the person who does *teshuvah* for all of his sins. But without *venakay*, "He who cleanses," there would be no provision for partial *teshuvah* for specific sins. Only the option of total *teshuvah* and the total cleansing of the soul would remain. The attribute of "He who cleanses" became a reality only after the creation of the new world of *teshuvah* which makes possible the correction of specific sins.

▸ The Unique Difference of *Teshuvah*-Related Prayer

How does prayer operate in the world of *teshuvah*? The Sages teach that G-d criticized Moses for praying when the Egyptians pursued Israel at the moment of the splitting of the Reed Sea. G-d challenged Moses, "Why do you cry to Me?[10] Saving Israel depends on Me, not on you."[11] Why does saving Israel depend exclusively on G-d? Because the splitting of the Reed Sea was a condition built into Creation. The Torah says, "and the sea returned to its original power," *l'eisano.*[12] *Eisano* has a double meaning: first, a stipulation "contracted" with the sea at the time of its creation;[13] second, that events built into Creation are beyond the reach of prayer.

From this we deduce the deep difference that exists between *teshuvah*-related prayer and prayer in general. *Teshuvah's* relationship to Creation is far more significant and intimate than the relationship of the splitting of the Reed Sea to Creation, because *teshuvah* implies the possibility of the creation of a new world. When the first world ended with Adam's sin, a new "*teshuvah* world" had to be created. Since *teshuvah* was not created by the first Divine Name, *teshuvah* does not derive from the original Creation prior to Adam's sin. It therefore follows that *teshuvah*-related prayer does not derive from general prayer, which involves material concerns stemming from the first Creation.

▶ G-d Taught Moses A New Kind of Prayer

Regarding general prayer, the Torah commands, "You shall serve the Lord your G-d"[14] — which signifies prayer, according to the Rambam.[15] Yet, when Moses prayed that G-d accept the *teshuvah* of the Jewish Nation following the sin of the Golden Calf, "G-d passed before Moses and proclaimed..."[16] The Talmud[17] teaches that, "G-d passed before Moses enwrapped in a *tallis* as a prayer leader and taught Moses a new form of prayer." Why was Moses not taught this new form of prayer at the very same time G-d commanded him concerning general prayer? Because prayer for *teshuvah* emerged from the trauma of the Golden Calf tragedy. *Teshuvah* prayer relates exclusively to *teshuvah*, with no connection to general prayer. Just as we have prayer suited to the "first world of the Divine Name," there is also prayer suited to the "second world of the Divine Name."

Furthermore, the innovation of a special *teshuvah* form of prayer was so unique that it was not sufficient for G-d to simply teach it to Moses. A demonstration was required. The Torah describes this demonstration:

"... and G-d descended in a cloud and stood with him there and He called out with the Name of G-d."[18] As noted above, the Talmud presents the image of G-d enwrapped in a *tallis* as a congregational prayer leader. The rabbis teach that this new form of prayer had to be explicitly demonstrated, for otherwise it could not exist.

We must pray for Divine assistance for forgiveness, just as we pray for all our needs, because we are not naturally aware of the power of *teshuvah*. Our souls required this special revelation to awaken us to the unique innovation of *teshuvah*-related prayer.

The innovation of *teshuvah* is G-d's second greatest creative act, second only to the miracle of Creation. Just as it is impossible to pray regarding Creation itself, it follows that prayer for repentance would also be impossible. We are able to pray for repentance only because "G-d enwrapped Himself as a prayer leader" and taught us a special order of *teshuvah*-related prayer. Prayer for *teshuvah* is a special innovation. We now understand why *Slichos* possesses all the trappings of established prayer *(i.e. Ashrei, Tachanun,* and *Kaddish Tiskabel)*. This is because it exists as a parallel prayer, a complete unit of prayer unto itself.

▸ The Unique Nature of Fasting on Yom Kippur

With the above in mind, let's examine the Yom Kippur fast. *Halachah* requires that we "enact a fast day in the face of crisis, since fasting is one of the methods of *teshuvah*."[19] As Yom Kippur is our day of *teshuvah*, it might appear that it is similar to other public fasts that also are used as a means to accomplish repentance. The Rambam, however, indicates that this is not the case:

"Yom Kippur requires a unique positive commandment: *lishbos* — to desist [from eating and drinking]." Just as on the Sabbath we desist from certain activities, on Yom Kippur we desist from consuming food and drink.[20] This is supported by *Halachah 5*: "It is a *mitzvah lishbos* (to desist in Sabbath-like fashion) from the other Yom Kippur prohibitions in the same fashion as we desist from eating and drinking." Clearly, the other fasts (Tishah B'Av, the Fast of Esther, etc.) have no relationship to the term *lishbos*, to rest, to desist from.

▸ The Second Giving of the Torah Took Place on Yom Kippur

Finally, as much as Yom Kippur is Israel's day of *teshuvah*, it is also the day the Second Tablets were given. The Jewish People heard, "I am the Lord your G-d" (the first of the Ten Commandments) on two occasions: first, on the 6th of Sivan (on Shavuos)[21] and the second time, on the 10th of Tishrei (Yom Kippur).[22] Following the first revelation, the Children of Israel sinned by worshipping the Golden Calf and then repented. When they completed the process of *teshuvah,* they received the Second Tablets.

For this reason Yom Kippur is called "the day of the marriage of the Jewish People to G-d, since it is also the day of the giving of the Torah." This is explained by the Mishnah[23] "The day of 'His' wedding: this is the day of the Giving of Torah."[24]

From the *teshuvah* process that took place following the sin of the Golden Calf we learn that *teshuvah*-related prayer requires its own source. Because the world of *teshuvah* represents a new "edition" of Creation, it required its own form of prayer as well as its own Receiving of the Torah. It follows that the purpose of the fast of Yom Kippur is not to deny the body sustenance and lessen its strength, as on other fasts. Its purpose is to enact a Sabbath-like "rest" from eating and drinking. Just as the sixth of Sivan (Shavuos) was the day of receiving the Torah prior to Israel's sin, Yom Kippur is the day of the receiving of the Torah in the new world containing the new Creation, i.e. *teshuvah.* Yom Kippur is not the day for *teshuvah* as much as the day on which the Children of Israel accepted the Torah in the new world of *teshuvah.* This was the day of the "marriage" of Israel with G-d. As the world of *teshuvah* was not a continuation but a new creation, it required its own unique form of prayer as well as its own unique form of the acceptance of the Torah.

The world that preceded sin is celebrated with both physical and spiritual enjoyment, for the body had not yet been corrupted. Shavuos is therefore "*lachem,* for you," celebrated for "your benefit" and with joy. Yom Kippur is unique in that it is "*laShem,* for G-d's sake" alone. It is totally devoted to the spiritual. On Yom Kippur we separate ourselves from *lachem*, from all self-benefit, from eating, drinking, etc. Contrary to the public fasts on which we negate our bodily needs, Yom Kippur emphasizes the positive needs of the soul. On Yom Kippur, the Yom Tov of *teshuvah*, the creation of the new world that anteceded sin is celebrated by relating exclusively to the needs of the soul.

▶ The Unique Nature of Yom Kippur's Prohibitions

Let us study the words of the *Ohr Same'ach*.[25] He instructs a sick person who suffers from a dangerous illness and must eat on a Yom Kippur that falls on Shabbos, not to recite the Shabbos *Kiddush* because the very character of Yom Kippur encompasses the Sabbath as well. How is such a Shabbos sanctified? A Yom Kippur-Shabbos is sanctified by refraining from eating food — in order to concentrate on the spiritual purpose of man. This halachic decision attains greater clarity when seen in the following light.

Yom Kippur does not demand denying the needs of the body as a method of atonement. The reason we desist from eating is *because food is not a requirement of the soul*. Fasting on Yom Kippur relates more to the receiving of the Ten Commandments on that day than to any specific act of repentance. This is the meaning of the Rambam's statement that, "the command of Yom Kippur is to 'rest' from eating and drinking" (and not the self-denial of fasting). The Rambam therefore titled his compendium of Yom Kippur laws *Hilchos Shevisas Asor,* Laws Concerning the 'Rest' of the Tenth Day. Included in the same category are "resting" from labor and "resting" from eating.

This conclusion confirms our earlier point: Just as the purpose of resting from labor on Yom Kippur is not self-denial, the purpose of not eating and drinking on Yom Kippur is also not self-denial. Yom Kippur casts a new light on the concept of "rest," which reflects on Shabbos as well.

▶ Teshuvah on Yom Kippur Demands Total Purification

Rabbeinu Yonah emphasizes the special *mitzvah* of attaining purification on Yom Kippur through *teshuvah* because Yom Kippur is the day of the Giving of the Torah. Indeed, the Torah was given as the result of the completion of the process of *teshuvah*. The essence of Yom Kippur is that *teshuvah* is intrinsically linked to the giving of the Torah, at which time the Jewish People was both "married" to G-d and recreated.

Teshuvah on Yom Kippur demands total, not partial, purification. Rabbeinu Yonah explains the verse in Psalm 51:4, "Abundantly cleanse me from my iniquity and purify me from my sin." He teaches that even though every act of *teshuvah* brings forgiveness, it does not result in purification. If our goal is purification, we must meet the condition of "abundantly cleanse me." The essence of Yom Kippur is the forgiveness and atonement brought about through total cleansing that makes us deserving of a renewed acceptance of the Torah.

1. *Leviticus* 16:30.
2. *Sha'arei Teshuvah*, Chapter 2:5.
3. *Deuteronomy* 3:2, 4:31. *Sha'arei Teshuvah, Sha'ar* 1,1.
4. *Sha'arei Teshuvah, Sha'ar* 1, 9.
5. *Hilchos Teshuvah*, Chapter 2, Halachah 6.
6. *Exodus* 34:6.
7. *Rosh Hashanah* 17:2.
8. *Yoma* 86:1.
9. *Nesivos Olam, Nesiv Hateshuvah*, Chapter 6.
10. *Exodus* 14:15.
11. *Rashi, Exodus* 14:15; *Mechilta.*
12. *Exodus* 14:27.
13. *Shemos Rabbah,* 21:6.
14. *Exodus* 23:25.
15. *Rambam* Chapter 1 *Hilchos Tefillah, Halachah* 1; *Talmud Ta'anis* 2:11.
16. *Exodus* 34:6.
17. *Rosh Hashanah* 17:2.
18. *Exodus* 34:5.
19. *Rambam,* Chapter 1, *Hilchos Ta'anis, Halachah* 2.
20. *Rambam,* Chapter 1, *Hilchos Shevisas Asor, Halachah* 4.
21. *Exodus* 20:2.
22. *Deuteronomy* 5:6.
23. See *Talmud Ta'anis* 26:b.
24. *Ta'anis* 30:2.
25. *Avodas Yom Hakippurim,* Chapter 4, *Halachah* 1, by Rabbi Meir Simchah of Dvinsk.

V
SUCCOS AND
SHMINI ATZERES

AN IN-DEPTH LOOK AT SUCCOS AND SHMINI ATZERES

▶ Is the Yearning for the Messiah both National and Personal?

Why is time divided into years? The reason is that each year opens a new chapter in our lives by providing new opportunities for change, improvement and growth. Each season of the year presents us with new opportunities, new moods and new insights. As the seasons change, we change We are affected by the snow, cold and darkness of winter. We feel nature burst forth after its winter sleep. The year in nature and the year in our historical, spiritual life both have a beginning and a conclusion. Nature and history travel on parallel tracks toward the goal set forth by their Creator. This is why each of our holidays is tied to a season. If we are sufficiently sensitive, we can use the seasons and the holidays to change and grow as human beings and as Jews.

▸ Why Are The Festivals Tied to Nature?

t is by design that Passover takes place in the springtime. It marks the birth of *Am Yisrael,* the nation of Israel, just as spring marks the rebirth of trees, gardens and fields after their winter sleep. Nissan, related to the word *nes*, miracle, is the first month of the Jewish year, the month of beginnings. Israel was born when nature reawakens and planting begins. Shavuos is the festival of [spring] harvest, a time of maturation, growth and development. For this reason, the Torah was given on Shavuos, because it was at Sinai that the mission and nature of the Jew was set and defined. Succos is the festival, "when the [fall] harvest is gathered from the fields."[1] The Torah is speaking both of the harvest of the fields as well as the "harvest" of our lives. The harvest is completed on Succos, as the summer draws to its end, when the produce is gathered into the storehouses. Only then is the planting process finalized and confirmed. Succos, therefore, represents the end of time, the fulfillment and culmination of history.

Both Chanukah and Purim take place during the winter, when the days are cold and short, when night comes early, when the ground sleeps and freezes. Chanukah and Purim are holidays of exile, of the night, when the Greeks attempted to destroy Israel spiritually and the Persians plotted to destroy Israel physically. They provide flickers of light and hope in an otherwise bleak terrain.

▸ Defining Succos

ow do we define Succos? No simple definition will suffice. The difficulty is that Succos (and Shmini Atzeres/Simchas Torah, which cap Succos at the end of its week-long observance) is the grand finale of the entire year. It brings to fruition the message and the challenge of each of the festivals. Succos brings two festival cycles to a simultaneous conclusion.

What are the festival cycles? The first is the *Shalosh Regalim*, the "pilgrimage festivals:" Passover, Shavuos and Succos. Succos also concludes the second holiday cycle of the *Yamim Nora'im*, the Days of Awe. On Rosh Hashanah, man was created and we recognize our Creator as King; on Yom Kippur, cleansed of our sins, we are born again; and on Succos, cleansed of our sins, we reach the pinnacle of joy and fulfillment. Succos concludes on its seventh day, also called Hoshanah Rabbah. Shmini Atzeres and Simchas Torah constitute a holiday separate and apart, marking the initiation of a new era — the celebration of the completion of the annual Torah cycle and the coming of the Messiah, the goal of all human endeavors. Indeed, it celebrates the victory of good over evil in the End of Days.

▸ How Does Succos Relate to both Holiday Cycles?

Victorious over our sins, we come before G-d on Succos to offer thanksgiving. Having survived the travails of forty years in the desert, on Succos our ancestors celebrated their survival through G-d's protection. We also celebrate Israel's conquest of the Land of Israel and the building of the Temple, the symbol of human fulfillment, spirituality and perfection. The final day of celebration is Shmini Atzeres/Simchas Torah, a day the Torah added to the Succos season that celebrates the coming of the Messiah. Indeed, Shmini Atzeres/Simchas Torah sees the Jew dancing with G-d and His Torah, not in celebration of historic events such as the Exodus or Revelation, but in anticipation of the perfection of man and the coming of the Messiah that will take place in the future.

▸ Shmini Atzeres: A New Age for Mankind

The name Shmini Atzeres contains the key to its significance. Note that the Hebrew number, *sheva*, seven, represents completeness [*savayah*: satisfied], while *shmoneh* [*shemen*:

fat/oil] represents something extra, a step beyond completeness. Seven (the seven days of the week) marks the completion of Creation and the Sabbath rest. Succos (a seven day festival) denotes completion and the arrival of Redemption. Shmini Atzeres — literally the Eighth Day of Assembly — is a day that on one hand is the eighth day in relation to Succos, but on the other hand is defined by the Torah as "a holiday in its own right." It represents a new age, the era of actually living in a redeemed world — the Messianic age. Even though it is tied to Succos, Shmini Atzeres is separate and apart from all the other holidays. It is a world of its own, and unlike all the other holidays, Shmini Atzeres/Simchas Torah celebrates and anticipates the future.

In view of the fact that the holidays exist on both the national and the personal level, we vicariously live the future Redemption when we celebrate Shmini Atzeres/Simchas Torah. At the same time, each individual celebrates his or her personal "redemption." Shmini Atzeres becomes a day on which each individual celebrates his own personal growth and transformation as a result of the experiences beginning with Elul and the *Slichos*.

The above explanation indicates why *esrog, lulav* and *succah* cease to be observed on Shmini Atzeres. In our minds, the *succah* has been replaced with the Messianic Third Temple and the *esrog* and *lulav* have been realized and actualized through the unity of all Israel with the arrival of the Messiah. While these events have not yet taken place, we celebrate as though they have. We live in a day that is raised beyond reality and above history. We live beyond time! It is indeed a taste of the World to Come.

We can now understand why our Sages gave the second day of Shmini Atzeres the additional name Simchas Torah, a day of supreme joy with our Torah. Since the Torah is the very essence of the Jew, by beginning its reading cycle once again, we emphasize the meaning of Shmini Atzeres as a day of "the new heavens and the new earth."[2] Interestingly, while the high emotional moments of the year take place during the *Neilah* prayer on Yom Kippur and on the first Seder night, Simchas Torah has the same mystical and magical pull as *Neilah* and the Seder. Many Jews feel in their very bones the heightened joy and spirituality of the Messianic day.

Our holidays not only recall the events of the past, they primarily call upon us to reenact each major historic event in Jewish history, to experience each event anew and to absorb the lessons of each event into our consciousness. In Jewish thought, the coming of the Messiah represents both the perfection of each man and woman as well as the perfection of the Jewish People and of the entire human race. While we anticipate and work for the perfection of world society, and while each Jew endeavors to make his/her contribution to that event, each person is endowed with free will, and possesses the ability to transform the quality of his or her own life. On Simchas Torah, each Jew should be able to celebrate his own "Messianic transformation," or at least celebrate the specific steps he or she has taken in that direction.

▸ Ultimate Joy/Ultimate Victory

Why is Succos singled out by the Torah to be called *Z'man Simchasenu*, the Festival of our (ultimate) Joy? Are all the festivals not joyous? Succos is singled out because the highest human joy is the intensification of man's relationship with G-d. On Succos, that relationship reaches its pinnacle.

There are only two Torah-prescribed *mitzvos* for which a person uses his entire body. The first is *mikvah* and the second is *succah*. Just as a person enters the *mikvah* and emerges reborn, so, too, when the Jew leaves the *succah* on *Shmini Atzeres*, he emerges reborn and enters a new world, the world of Messianic perfection. There, in the world of Messianic perfection, all of Israel will enter, with their entire bodies, the rebuilt Temple and the united *Eretz Yisrael.*

The prayer of Succos, "May the Almighty rebuild the fallen *Succah* of David," teaches that the fallen *succah* is analogous to the Jerusalem Temple, the "Succah of David." Our Succos prayer to G-d therefore, is, "Please rebuild the Temple, restore the House of David and reestablish his Kingdom."

The final war in the End of Days is called the War of Gog. The word *gog*, says Rabbi Samson Raphael Hirsch, comes from the Hebrew word *gag*, roof. The nations of the world insist that they represent the "roof" of civilization, the pinnacle of human achievement, that their conception of civilization will ultimately dominate the world. The Jew, however, insists that when the fallen *Succah* of David is rebuilt, the roof of the rebuilt third Temple in Jerusalem will become the "roof" of the entire world.

The weekly cycle of the Sabbath and the two annual cycles of our holidays convey two ideas. First, that the cycle of life's events will recur next week as well as next year. If we failed to grasp the message of the last cycle, there will be a new opportunity as each new cycle repeats itself. G-d constantly provides us with new chances and new opportunities.

▶ An Opportunity for Rebirth

The cycles of the year also teach us that even if we fail to achieve the final victory, even if we fail to bring the Messiah and to perfect society in our own lifetime, we can succeed in doing so with our *own lives,* because each individual represents a miniature world. Each individual can experience rebirth through repentance. Each individual faces the challenge to become a *ben* or *bas Torah*, to strive for redemption and to have the Torah mold his or her life and personality. Each individual has the ability to strive for and achieve a higher degree of perfection. Each individual has the opportunity to aspire to a level of Messianic existence in his own lifetime through a constant struggle for self-improvement. If we have accomplished even some small measure of growth at the conclusion of the holiday cycle, we have cause to celebrate.

1. *Exodus* 25:15.
2. *Isaiah* 66:22.

THE END OF DAYS AND THE COMPLETION OF MAN'S MISSION

23

A s we've noted in previous essays, Succos/Shmini Atzeres/Simchas Torah completes one of the holiday cycles as the last festivals of the year, if we consider Passover the first festival.

Israel was created on Passover. At the moment of Israel's birth we ceased being slaves to Pharaoh and became the servants of G-d. On Shavuos, Israel received the Torah and was taught the method, content and goal of our mission. On Succos we return to our King and report: "We have accomplished our mission."

Israel's holidays are rooted in the annual agricultural cycle to teach us that G-d is the Master of both nature and history and that both nature and history are elements of the same human reality. Both nature and history anticipate the fulfillment of the goals of Creation. As Succos reaches its finale on Simchas Torah, we anticipate the ultimate celebration of the achievement of the goals of history. In effect, Simchas Torah is the celebration of the coming of the Messiah. At that time, the vision of the Torah and the prophets will have been fulfilled: The Torah, its People, its ideology, its method and its law will be triumphant. Indeed, G-d will have become King over all the earth.

As the last festival of the year, Succos anticipates and celebrates the ultimate victory of Israel and its Torah. The *esrog, lulav, hadassim* and *aravos* are the symbols of Israel's victory. They are multifaceted universal symbols that celebrate the roots the Jewish Nation has struck in the Land of Israel and they express our gratitude to G-d for the bounty of the harvest and of life. By binding the four species together, we also celebrate the unity of all Jews. We celebrate, if only symbolically, the gathering of the fruits of the Land of Israel and the unity of the Jewish People, even if this unity is not yet a reality but a hope. For this reason, all Jews come before G-d on Succos in celebration, even if they have not fully accomplished its goals in their own time.

By celebrating the "completion" of the goals of history we learn to understand the nature of our task. Succos speaks to us both as individuals and as a nation. Succos is unique in that it is the only festival that belongs to both holiday cycles. Indeed, it completes *both* holiday cycles of the *Shalosh Regalim* and the *Yamim Nora'im*.

Coming right after Yom Kippur, Succos is the holiday of the *ba'al teshuvah*, the repentant and reconstructed Jew. Cleansed and repentant as the result of our efforts on Rosh Hashanah and Yom Kippur, we observe Succos and behave as though we, and *all* Jews, have returned to G-d, at least to some degree. It is our hope that if the message and purpose of Yom Kippur weren't completely absorbed, maybe it will begin to take effect when we celebrate Succos together with repentant and not-yet-repentant Jews.

Succos is therefore the holiday that celebrates human transformation. On Succos we acknowledge that it is *possible* for a person to change, to bend his character, to accomplish that which all of Israel will accomplish in the End of Days, when the Torah's message penetrates and transforms all of mankind; when all war, idolatry and hatred is abolished and all Jews are once again gathered in the Land of Israel and the Temple is rebuilt. At that time, Israel will become the exemplar of human achievement, a fully spiritual people. At that time, the Messiah will be crowned as king — which means that G-d will have been crowned as King of all mankind.

Why is Succos described as the holiday of "triumph" over the nations of the world? Does the Jew hope to conquer the other nations? No. Succos anticipates the day on which the Jewish Nation will stand triumphant, separate and distinguished from the other nations. Why? Because Israel's ideology, morality and spiritual message of peace will have "conquered" the minds of all men and women.

▶ Succos: The Holiday of Joy

Why is joy so deeply associated with Succos? Why is it the only holiday called "the season of our joyous celebration"? True joy is the product of each person's newly reestablished relationship with G-d. It results from our successful *teshuvah,* from repenting our deeds and reformulating and elevating our personalities.

Joy and repentance [*simchah* and *teshuvah*] are major themes of the *Simchas Beis Hasho'evah*, the Water Drawing Celebration that took place in the Holy Temple on Succos. This celebration was the greatest human expression of happiness, the high point of Succos. On this occasion, everyone who had repented sang, "Happy is our old age which has atoned for the sins of our youth!"[1]

▶ G-d's Thirteen Attributes of Mercy

The central prayer of Rosh Hashanah and Yom Kippur is the recitation of the "Thirteen Attributes of G-d's Mercy." On his descent from Mount Sinai, Moses observed the people engaged in the sin of the Golden Calf. He immediately smashed the Tablets of the Covenant and after ridding Israel of the troublemakers, again climbed to the pinnacle of Mt. Sinai to plead for G-d's mercy and forgiveness. G-d instructed him that whenever Jews seek forgiveness, they should recite the "Thirteen Attributes of G-d's Mercy." Our Sages teach that G-d made a Covenant with Israel: anyone who recites the "Thirteen Attributes of G-d's Mercy" will not be turned away empty-handed.[2]

This awesome prayer of repentance opens with the repetition of G-d's ineffable Divine Name, "Hashem, Hashem." The Sages teach that the first Divine Name applies to a person before he sins, and the second Divine Name applies to a person after he has sinned and repented.[3] The second Name of G-d has special significance. All the other attributes of G-d can be translated into any language, except for the four-letter name of G-d. Each of the attributes relates to various aspects of G-d's qualities, "Merciful, gracious, long suffering," etc., and can easily be applied to our lives. But the ineffable four-letter name of G-d can neither be translated nor understood in human terms. It defies translation. This "Name" is the source of repentance and teaches that every Jew is capable of repentance — and indeed that every Jew will return to G-d on the day of the Messiah's arrival. On that day all of mankind will have accepted His authority: "G-d will be One and His Name One."

---

1. *Succah* 53a.
2. *Rosh Hashanah* 17b.
3. Ibid.

THE MYSTERY OF THE *ESROG* AND *LULAV*

▸ Deep Torah Structures Unravel the Mystery of the *Esrog* and *Lulav*

One of the most dramatic and mystical demonstrations of the truth, accuracy and unity of the Torah is found in a series of multi-layered phenomena hidden deep in the Torah's text. They reveal some of the mysteries associated with the observance of *esrog* and *lulav*, the four species of plants that, together with the *succah*, are the heart of the observance of the joyous festival of Succos.

These plants are called "the four species." They are: *lulav* [a date palm], *hadassim* [twigs of the myrtle tree], *aravos* [brook willow branches] and *esrog* [citron]. They are taken in hand each day of the eight days of Succos (except for the Sabbath), until and including the eighth day — also called Hoshanah Rabbah. Interestingly, the Torah clearly commands us to hold the four plants, but does not always clearly identify each of them. In Leviticus (23:40), the Torah says, "On the first day you shall take the fruit of the *hadar* tree, branches of palm trees, boughs of thick trees and willows of the brook, and you shall rejoice before the L-rd your G-d for seven days." The unwritten Torah, namely the Talmud, instructs us that the *hadar* — literally the beautiful tree — is the citron or *esrog*; and the "boughs of thick trees" are *hadassim,* or myrtle.

From the above we see that the actual words, *esrog, lulav* and *hadas* are not explicitly mentioned in the Torah. We are about to explore whether there is clear literary evidence hidden somewhere in the Torah text that this is exactly what G-d commanded.

Obviously, we have always relied on the Unwritten Torah for direction. We know that when Moses brought us the Written Torah, he defined for us those areas where the Torah employs language that would benefit from precise definition. A positive answer to our question would provide clear evidence that the Written Torah and the Unwritten Torah (often called the Oral Torah, i.e., the Mishnah, the Talmud and its commentaries) are one and the same and not "inventions of the rabbis," as is claimed by some of our detractors. In other words, is it possible that the words *esrog, lulav, hadas* and *aravah* are actually to be found in the Torah text by way of "hidden" word or letter patterns that tell the full story of the four species?

There is also a second challenge. In many *siddurim*, there is a special voluntary prayer — a *"Yehi Ratzon,* May it be G-d's will" — that many people recite before reciting the blessing on the four species. This prayer, which is heavy with Kabbalistic implications, was introduced by the seventeenth-century master of Kabbalah, Rabbi Nassan Hanover, and first appeared in his book, *Sha'arei Zion* (Prague, 5422/1662). The Kabbalah teaches that each of the four species is identified with a letter of the four-letter Name of G-d, which we never pronounce. The prayer is:

> *May it be Your Will,* Hashem *my G-d, and G-d of my*
> *forefathers, that through the fruit of the* esrog *tree,*
> *the date palm branches, the twigs of the myrtle tree*
> *and the brook willows, the letters of Your unified*

*Name may become close to the other, so that they,
(i.e., the letters of G-d's Name represented by the
four species) will become united in my hands in
order to make known that Your Name is called upon
me, so that evil forces will be afraid to approach
me. My intention is to unify the Name of the Holy
One, Blessed be He, and His Presence with awe and
love in order to unify G-d's Name,* Yud-Kay *with* Vav-
Kay *(kay represents the letter hay) in perfect unity.*

What evidence do we have from the Torah that the four let-
ters of G-d's Name are associated with the four species? What
Torah source is there for this association, other than the
Kabbalistic *Zohar?*

Now, to a third challenge: The Vilna Gaon states that the four
letters of G-d's Name are associated with four of the Five Books of
the Torah: The letter *Yud* with *Bereishis* [Genesis]; the letter *Hay*
with *Shemos* [Exodus]; the letter *Vav* with *Bamidbar* [Numbers]
and the final *Hay* with *Devarim* [Deuteronomy], and that these letters are also associated with the *mitzvah* of the four species.

In order to unravel this mystery, we need two additional ingredients; firstly the number 13, which is associated with G-d's
"Thirteen Attributes of Mercy," which are recited during the
morning prayers on Rosh Hashanah, Yom Kippur and Succos.
Also, we must include the numerical value of the Hebrew word for
one — *echad* (G-d is One and His Name is One). *Aleph* is numerically one; *ches* is numerically eight; and *daled* is numerically four.
Therefore — 1+8+4=13 (i.e. the Thirteen Attributes of Mercy).

The answer to all of the above questions is revealed through a
literary and numerical phenomenon that is deeply embedded in
the first two and the last two Books of the Torah.

▸ The Literary Formula

et us begin by counting from the beginning of the first Book,
Genesis. Count the word *Elokim* [G-d] thirteen times (i.e.

the first thirteen times this word appears), and then, count the letter *ayin*, the first letter of *aravah* (willow) ten times. Ten is expressed numerically as the letter *yud,* the first letter of the four-letter Name of G-d. From the next *ayin* (i.e., the eleventh letter *ayin*), count 49 letters. The 50th letter will be *reish*, the next 50th letter will be *veis,* and the next 50th letter *hay*, thus spelling *ayin*, *reish*, *veis*, *hay* = *aravah* (willow).

Then we go to the second Book, Exodus, which principally deals with the birth of the Jewish People. We count the first thirteen words that mention the Jewish People in any form (*B'nai Yisrael, Yaakov* [in Exodus, this is an illusion to the Jewish People] *ha'Ivrim, ha'Ivrios*), then we count the letter *lamed* — the first letter of *lulav* [palm] — five times because the second letter of G-d's unpronounceable four-letter Name is *hay*. The numerical value of *hay* is five. From the sixth *hay,* count 49 letters and the 50th letter will be *vav*, the next 50th letter will be *lamed*, the next 50th letter will be *veis,* thus spelling *lamed, vav, lamed, veis* = *lulav* [palm].

We move on to the fourth Book, Numbers, where the key subject matter is the *Ohel Moed* — the Tent of Meeting (i.e., the *Mishkan*, the portable Tabernacle.) Here we count this word thirteen times. The third letter of G-d's name is *vav,* so we count the letter *hay* five times. Counting each 50th letter, the word that emerges is *hay, daled, samach* = *hadas* (myrtle).

In the fifth Book, Deuteronomy, the key word is *Hashem Elokeinu*, the Lord our G-d, or *Elokim*, G-d. Count these words thirteen times. The fourth letter of G-d's name is *hay*, with the numerical value of five. We count *aleph* — the first letter of *Elokim* — five times, again counting each 50th letter. The word that emerges is *aleph, sav, reish, gimel*, or *esrog* (citron).

To sum up: we have found the four words, *aravah, lulav, hadas* and *esrog* within the text of the Torah as part of a deep structure that bridges four Books of the Torah and reveals the various associations we discussed at the beginning of this essay, all of which concern the unity of the four letters of G-d's Name and G-d's "Thirteen Attributes of Mercy."

Amazingly, this complex and compelling equation was discovered by Rabbi Dov Ber Weismandl prior to World War II, in an age before computers existed. Now that we live in the computer age, how many additional structures will we find which confirm the unity of the Torah text, the unity of the Written and Unwritten Torah and even the accuracy of rabbinic concepts — mystical and otherwise — in the Talmud, *Midrashim* and *Zohar* that have not yet come to light? These revelations are becoming part of our Torah experience thousands of years after the Divine giving of the Written and Unwritten Torah.

DISCOVERING
HOSHANAH
RABBAH

The big crowds of Rosh Hashanah and Yom Kippur have long dispersed. To most American Jews, Hoshanah Rabbah is a day like any other, its great drama and significance a secret known to very few. Even among religious worshippers, the drama and pageantry of Hoshanah Rabbah prayers are usually rushed through as an intrusion of still more, difficult to understand mystical Hebrew poetry into an already extended Chol Hamoed Succos morning service.

It is the morning of Hoshanah Rabbah, the final day of Chol Hamoed Succos, the day prior to Shmini Atzeres and Simchas Torah. The average synagogue has a few more than its regular complement of morning worshippers, but few people are aware of the fact that this day has special meaning — that it is a miniature Yom Kippur, and is even more significant than the preceding days of Chol Hamoed Succos.

The moving *hakofos*, a march consisting of nearly every worshipper holding the *esrog* and *lulav* while circling the *bimah* seven times instead of the usual once around of Chol Hamoed, culminates in the mysterious beating a bundle of five willow branches on the floor. These tend to be performed almost perfunctorily. The worshipers are almost afraid to pause, to grasp what they are doing. Just another fifteen minutes of difficult Hebrew poetry and strange pageantry and the long service will be over.

▶ King David, The Mystical Guest

"Hoshanah Rabbah" means The Great Redemption. It is the wrap up day of the Succos holiday, the near culmination of the Jewish year, an emotional apex, a day of high anticipation, expectation and hope, a Yom Tov of majestic grandeur. Some Jews stay up all night the night before to recite the entire Book of Psalms. On this night, the last night of Succos, King David is the mystical "guest" in the *succah*, the last of the series of seven great *ushpizin*, or spiritual *succah* guests. On each night of Succos we mystically invite another father of our nation as our guest: Abraham on day one, then Isaac, Jacob, Joseph, Moses, Aaron and finally David. It is as though we are saying to them, "We have guarded your trust through the ages, we have persevered and we are striving for the ultimate Redemption, just as you did."

▶ Is There an Eighth Guest?

On the next day, Shmini Atzeres/Simchas Torah, we will bid farewell to the *succah*. Nonetheless, on Shmini Atzeres, "the eighth day" appended to Succos, there is an unspoken eighth guest, a mystery guest. We discover this guest in the *haftarah* (reading of a section of Prophets) of Shmini Atzeres, which

recalls King Solomon, the son of David, and describes the dedication of Solomon's Temple. Is not Solomon, the son of David, the
next in line to be our guest in the *succah*?

The *succah* is a temporary dwelling; fragile, frail and open to
the elements. The Holy Temple, however, was a strong, stone
building. Our prayer throughout Succos, in fact the very theme of
Succos, is, "May the All-Merciful rebuild for us the fallen *Succah*
of David." This expression, first used in Amos 9:11, alludes to the
weakness of the royal House of David during the Exile as the
"fallen *succah*."

On Hoshanah Rabbah, we anticipate the coming of the
Messianic Redeemer, the son of David. We "hear" his footsteps. A
"messenger" arrives to inform us to prepare for his arrival — that
he will arrive soon, within hours, even minutes. (This allusion is
found in the theme of the Hoshanah Rabbah *hakafos* in which we
identify the voice of the messenger as that of the prophet Elijah.)
This is the day of his arrival. Tomorrow, he will be among us. We
will soon be invited to attend his coronation. Tomorrow, we will
sing and dance in his presence, holding the Torah aloft, ready to
live a new life in the presence of G-d's anointed Messiah. We pray
that tomorrow the Messiah will replicate the deeds of his ancestor, Solomon, by rebuilding the Temple and heralding a new era.

This is why Hoshanah Rabbah is called by the Sages, "the day
of the delivery of the message of each individual's final fate to the
Heavenly Angel." Is this not why Hoshanah Rabbah is the last day
to "do *teshuvah*," to repent, prior to the great celebration of
Shmini Atzeres/Simchas Torah? Furthermore, the *teshuvah* of
each individual is linked to our national aspiration to see the
coming of the Messiah. We have been waiting for this day for
2,000 years. Are we ready for it? Are we ready to greet him?

Each year, we hope that *this* Hoshanah Rabbah is the last day
of an era, for it is almost the last day of the holiday cycle, simultaneously closing the series of the three pilgrimage festivals, the
Shalosh Regalim, and the *Yamim Nora'im*, the Days of Awe. The
next and final day, we pray, Shmini Atzeres/Simchas Torah will
initiate the Redemption, the Messianic era when a new historic
era will begin.

Why is this fact not explicitly stated? Why is it clouded in thick veils of secrecy? The answer is that nearly everything relating to the coming of the Messiah was concealed by our Sages from public view. They feared, and for good reason, that the masses would over-anticipate the arrival of the Messiah, especially during times of great crisis, and would believe in false messiahs. This concern proved to be quite true throughout our history, bringing nothing but grief, suffering and persecution.

All Jewish history (and all of the cycles of Jewish life) is rooted in the anticipation of the perfection of man, the obliteration of false ideologies, the coming of the Messiah. If we are sensitive, we see in the daily *siddur* and in the Jewish calendar all of Jewish history, which begins with Creation, discovers its purpose in the Exodus from Egypt and the Revelation of the Torah and is fulfilled in the building of the Temple and the Messianic Redemption.

The events of the Hebrew month of Tishrei constitute a series of interrelated events that build to the great climax. In many ways, Hoshanah Rabbah is a miniature Yom Kippur — it is the last day to repent prior to the final celebration. Note that the *shliach tzibbur,* the prayer leader, wears a white *kittle*, the Yom Kippur garment, and that the prayers are a mixture of Yom Tov, *teshuvah* and Messianic anticipation — all integrated into the service of one magical day.

Once the King Messiah arrives, he will find us either worthy or unworthy — either we will enter Shmini Atzeres repentant or we will be found unworthy to greet the Messiah, unworthy to participate in rebuilding the Temple, to celebrate in the Rejoicing of the Torah or to enter the Land of Israel. On Hoshanah Rabbah, the last day for repentance, the heavenly messenger will deliver the "note" upon which our fate has been inscribed.

As we put down the *esrog* and *lulav* for the last time after marching around the altar seven times, we pick up the *Hoshanah* bundle of five *aravah* [willow] branches. They are called *Hoshanos*, redeemers, and become our vehicle for imploring God that He find us worthy of receiving the Messiah.

Following *Mussaf*, the voice of the prayer leader rises. We hear the following electrifying words, describing the declaration of the coming of the Messiah: "*Kol* [a voice] *mevasser* [brings tidings], *mevasser* [again, brings tidings]; *ve'omer* [and proclaims]." Proclaims what? "*Kol dodi hinay zeh ba*, Hark! The voice of my beloved is coming, skipping over the mountains, jumping over the hills."

Filled with emotion, we continue to pray:

> *Open for us the gates of heaven —*
> *Saving God save us —*
> *I hear my Beloved; His voice is near.*
> *Let the trumpet sound — He knocks —*
> *Exult and be joyful —*
> *A man has sprung forth —*
> *He is King David Himself. Rejoice!*
> *Up, rise, no longer be buried in the dust:*
> *Awake and sing, you who dwell in ashes.*
> *The desolate Jerusalem shall rise as he becomes king,*
> *He who is a tower of strength brings deliverance to his King.*
> *Bringing tidings, he declares:*
> *God shall extinguish the wicked as He shows kindness to David his King.*
> *Bring Redemption to the Eternal Nation,*
> *To David and his seed forever —*
> *Hark — the voice is bringing good news!*

You actually feel the drama, it is as though the Messiah is but steps away. You challenge yourself; "Am I really prepared to meet him?" How will you respond if he looks into your eyes and asks, "What have you *done* to make my coming possible?"

And then, you take the *aravah* bundle tightly in your hands and beat it on the ground, demonstrating your desire to destroy evil and to accept the Divine Will. This is an act of welcoming the Messiah, of telling him that you are prepared to do his bidding.

Tomorrow, on Shmini Atzeres/Simchas Torah, you will begin a new life. You will, as Solomon did, worship in the Temple and dance with the Torah. All of the symbols of Succos — *esrog, lulav, succah, ushpizin, aravos* — are now discarded. All that remains is the redeemed, cleansed Jew, reunited with G-d and His Torah. All the external symbols have become unnecessary. We have internalized the message and symbols of Succos. We are reunited with our fellow Jews and with all of Israel. As the *Zohar* proclaims, "*Kudsha Brich Hu, Yisrael v'Oraisa chad hu!* G-d, Israel and the Torah are one absolute unity."[1]

All the holidays, beginning with Passover, lead to Hoshanah Rabbah. On this day, the humble hear His voice, on this day the messenger of the Great King arrives. Tomorrow I will cling to G-d and His Torah. Tomorrow we will build the Third Temple — the symbol of the new world. The Days of the Messiah will surely arrive if we learn to rebuild our lives by internalizing the lessons of our holidays.

Our holidays are not riveted to the past. Nor are they celebrations or commemorations of historical events alone. The past interests the Jew only to the extent that it influences the present and provides guidelines and motivations with which to mold the Messianic future.

The Torah commands us concerning Succos: "And you shall rejoice in your festival — and you shall be exceedingly joyous." The joy of Succos thus reaches its climax with the exceeding and ultimate joy of Shmini Atzeres/Simchas Torah.

Interestingly, the festivities of Simchas Torah on Shmini Atzeres are of neither Biblical nor rabbinic origin: They were instituted by the Jewish People. Simchas Torah grew out of their sense of the special bond between Israel and the Torah on this day. Bursting with internal joy, they had no choice but to add a new dimension to the final festival of the year. They had just now completed the year-round reading of the Torah. They were ready to begin reading it again. They were dancing, singing and rejoicing as they held the Torah aloft. Indeed, it is the day of the rejoicing of the Torah, literally Simchas Torah.

It is one thing to live in the spiritual world created by our festivals, and another to realize that so much remains to be done before we merit the ultimate celebration of the coming of the Messiah.

▶ An Additional Thought: Why Do We Beat the *Aravah*?

I have always asked myself, what is the meaning of the strange and paradoxical practice of beating the willow/*aravah* bundle on the ground on Hoshanah Rabbah morning? Where else do we "desecrate" a *mitzvah* object by beating it? Rabbi Yehoshua Ben Levi describes this practice as a "custom of the prophets." Yet, no explanation is offered. We know that the major theme of the message of the prophets is overcoming sin and punishment in order to achieve salvation and final Redemption. The key to the beating of the *aravah* must therefore be found in this prophetic message.

I offered the following two explanations to my Rosh Yeshivah, Hagaon Rabbi Yitzchak Hutner, *zt"l*. He responded with enthusiastic approval, "*Yafeh darashta,* [Your insight rings true]!"

We are standing at the precipice of Messianic anticipation. We hold in our hands the symbol of Divine Redemption — the *aravah* bundle with which we have implored, "*Hoshanah* — Redeemer, redeem us!" We are about to welcome the Messiah with shouts of joy. All of this is taking place, of course, on the level of meta-history — on the anticipatory level of holidays that are vehicles for living above and beyond history, for reliving the past and anticipating future redemptive historical events. Our hope and anticipation are high.

But, what of reality? What of tomorrow? Where indeed is the Messiah? Look around. Where is this redeemer who will salve Israel's pains? Where is the instant solution to assimilation, disintegration, disaffection and intermarriage? It is one thing to anticipate the Messiah's coming, to jump and dance and hope; on the other hand it is amply clear that he has not yet arrived. The worshipper who is in tune with the message of the day and the reality of the present is overcome by a sense of deep frustration and fear. He needs a release for his anger, despair and frustration. He beats the *aravah* bundle, by way of release. The Redemption is still a dream — the reality is far off.

A second reason: We are all familiar with the famous rabbinic analogy that compares the four components of the *esrog* and *lulav* to the four types of Jews. The *esrog* has taste and fragrance — it represents the Jew who is both learned in Torah and is observant of the commandments. The *lulav* only has taste — it represents the Jew who is learned, but short on deeds. The myrtle/*hadassim* have fragrance but no taste — it represents the Jew who is long on deeds, but deficient in Torah knowledge. The willow/*aravah* has neither taste nor fragrance. It is lacking on all counts — it represents the Jew who possesses neither intellectual Torah attainments nor *mitzvos* — deeds and accomplishments. Bound together, the four species represent the entire Jewish People united before God on Succos, the festival of spiritual victory over evil. But separated, the *aravah* stands alone as the symbol of the Jew who has acquired neither Torah nor *mitzvos.*

Tomorrow is Shmini Atzeres/Simchas Torah. Tomorrow we will "celebrate" the coming of the Messiah. I have undergone months of preparation, from Elul through Rosh Hashanah, from the Ten Days of Repentance to Yom Kippur. I have atoned. I have achieved forgiveness. I experienced and celebrated Yom Kippur and Succos in order to experience my rebirth as a new person, refined, perfected, cleansed before God.

After all my effort, after months of prayer, fasting and breast-beating, of saying, "I have sinned" — I am about to join the entire Jewish People in welcoming the King Messiah. But am I ready? Have I truly changed? Or have I remained an "*aravah* Jew" — an empty vessel, possessing neither Torah knowledge nor *mitzvah* accomplishment? Realizing my failure to reach my potential, realizing that much of my *teshuvah* and atonement were merely talk, realizing that I am still a critical, arrogant, intimidating, unrepentant, self-serving, controlling, petty person, I acknowledge that I deserve a beating. How could I not have changed? How is it possible that I remained an *aravah* Jew despite my many efforts and good intentions? Therefore, I take the *aravah* in hand and beat it until its leaves fall off. Symbolically, it is myself I am beating. Hopefully, next year I will reach higher.

---

1. *Zohar Achrei Mos* 73.

THE DEEPER MEANING OF SUCCOS

26 Based on *Pachad Yitzchok*, Rosh Hashanah 10

▸ Succos: A Rabbinic Tale

wo accused officers appeared before their king to be judged. When one officer emerged from the palace smiling, with his sword held high, it was no longer a question as to who was vindicated.

On Yom Kippur, Israel and the nations of the world are judged by the King of Kings. Who is vindicated? G-d commanded, "And you shall take on the first day" an *esrog* and a *lulav*.[1] When the Jew emerges from judgment following Yom Kippur with *esrog* and *lulav* held high in his hand, is there any doubt as to who was vindicated? (*Midrash*)

What is the point of this tale? It is to convey the intimate connection between Yom Kippur and Succos. What other possible connection could there exist between a solemn day of repentance and fasting and a joyous festival of thanksgiving and celebration?

To understand this connection, we must first examine the two interlocking holiday cycles of the Jewish year. The first cycle consists of the three Pilgrimage Festivals, the *Shalosh Regalim*: Pesach, Shavuos and Succos. The second cycle consists of the Days of Awe, the *Yamim Nora'im*: Rosh Hashanah, Yom Kippur and Succos. What makes Succos unique? It is the only holiday that is found in both cycles; only Succos relates to both cycles. Succos also brings both cycles to a simultaneous conclusion as the Jewish holiday year reaches its climax.

What is the principal relationship between the *Yamim Nora'im* and Succos? Succos emphasizes the distinction between Israel and the nations of the world. We don't yet know who was vindicated, Israel or the nations of the world. The trial begins on Yom Kippur; Israel does *teshuvah* and emerges vindicated on Succos. (We must remember that the annual holidays are a microcosm of world history, beginning with Creation and ending with Redemption. The struggle takes place every year; the challenge is ongoing. Neither the nation nor the individual "know" who was vindicated.)

▶ *Teshuvah* is a New World

> (For a fuller explanation of the *teshuvah* concepts below, see chapter 21, "*Teshuvah*: A New Creation.")

Teshuvah is not only the major force that makes the continued existence of the world possible; it also represents a new world and a new creation. The meaning of the Divine Name *Havayah* (*Yud, Kay, Vav, Kay* i.e. Hashem) is Creation, the constant recreation of the universe from nothingness to existence. Because this Divine Name signifies Creation, it specifically relates to *teshuvah*, a totally new creation in itself.

Why is this creative name of G-d, *Havayah*, mentioned twice in the prayer, "Hashem, Hashem," the Thirteen Attributes of Mercy? (Since the name of G-d is not to be pronounced, we substitute the word Hashem — the Name.) The cosmos created prior to Adam's sin derives its power and strength from the first rendition of the Name, *Havayah*. After Adam sinned and repented, an entirely new world, the world of *teshuvah*, had to be recreated and sustained by the creative force of G-d's Name, *Havayah*. *Teshuvah* renewed and transformed all of Creation. The ability of a human being to cleanse himself of his past transgressions and to be reborn without bearing the stigma of his old crimes carries with it revolutionary consequences, including the way in which we relate to G-d in prayer.

▸ *Teshuvah* and Prayer

The obligation to pray is derived from the Torah passage, "And you shall serve the L-rd your G-d." Our Sages teach that "serving G-d" refers to prayer. Prayer impacts on all of mankind's needs, both physical and spiritual. However, when it came to repentance, Moses had to be taught a new method of prayer.

The Torah teaches, "And the L-rd passed before Moses and proclaimed the Thirteen Attributes of Mercy."[2] Rabbi Yochanan taught, "Were this not explicitly stated in the Torah, it would be impossible [for us] to say it. G-d wrapped Himself in a *tallis* [symbolically, of course] much like a prayer leader and demonstrated to Moses a new method of prayer." He said to him, "Whenever Israel sins, let them perform before Me this order [of prayer] and I shall forgive them."[3]

Why was this new method of prayer introduced at this moment? Why didn't G-d teach the Thirteen Attributes to Moses earlier, when He taught him about prayer generally? Regular prayer, which belongs to the original world of Creation, is both inadequate and ineffective against sin, which cannot be resolved in the context of that world. G-d had to teach Moses a completely new form of prayer that would be effective in a world of sin, and to teach man that through this special prayer he would be capable of repentance. The new world of *teshuvah*-prayer has the power to rejuvenate all things that are soiled by sin. When we pray for repentance, our eyes discover an incredible new world and we begin to realize that the true creative force of the universe is G-d's willingness to grant man forgiveness for his sins.

The revelation of Torah to the Jewish Nation represented the recreation of mankind prior to Adam's sin. But the Jews *did* sin, forcing Moses to smash the Tablets, and for G-d to want to destroy the Jewish Nation. It was here that G-d decided to innovate a new creation of *teshuvah,* a method by which the entire nation could repent, wipe the slate clean and begin anew. This national, communal *teshuvah* is the major function of Yom Kippur and the Thirteen Attributes of Mercy prayer.

There are times when even prayer is not effective. When the Jewish People had its back to the Reed Sea they prayed for salvation, but G-d criticized Moses, "Why are you crying to me?"[4] The Sages explain that prayer could not bring about the splitting of the sea because this event had already been set into the original plan of Creation. Prayer only relates to events which are yet to be determined in the give and take of this world. Similarly, for man to achieve *teshuvah,* G-d needed to create a new entity. This was precisely what G-d did when He taught Moses a new form of prayer, the Thirteen Attributes of Mercy. But it was not sufficient to teach Moses a prayer for *teshuvah*; G-d had to create a totally new form of prayer and demonstrate its unique method to Moses.

▸ Yom Kippur and the Giving of the Torah

We may ask the following question: We understand why the First Tablets of the Covenant were given on Shavuos, fifty days after the Exodus from Egypt, but why were the Second Tablets given on Yom Kippur? Why is it necessary that Yom Kippur commemorate the giving of the Torah? The answer is that Yom Kippur is designated as a day of atonement because on that day in history Israel achieved forgiveness for the sin of the Golden Calf and once again merited the gift of Torah. Just as *teshuvah* requires a new Creation and a new method of prayer, the day designated for *teshuvah* also requires a new day for the giving of the "second" Torah.

Solomon's Song of Songs, the *Shir Hashirim*, says, "Go forth daughters of Zion, gaze upon King Solomon, upon the crown with which his mother coronated him on the day of his marriage, on the day of the gladness of his heart." Our Sages teach, "On the day of his marriage," refers to the Giving of the Torah.[5] Rashi explains that this giving of the Torah refers to Yom Kippur, when the Second Tablets were given.

From the above, we learn of the necessity for rebirth and transformation. The person who does complete *teshuvah* is a reborn person. His new world is unrelated to his previous existence. He is similar to the proselyte who severs his relationship with his previous existence after his conversion. While the physical world may look the same following *teshuvah*, the inner spiritual world is new and fresh. The soul is recreated and pure. At that point, the soul is ready to reaccept the Torah, and at that point the Torah can be given again.

▸ Clouds of Forgiveness

Now that we have been introduced to the world of *teshuvah*, we can understand the inner meaning of Succos. The *s'chach* covering our *succah* surrounds us with the Clouds of Glory that protected the Jewish People when they left Egypt.[6] The obvious question is, why doesn't this commemoration take place in the month of Nissan, when the clouds first appeared, instead of in Tishrei? How do the clouds of Tishrei relate to the desert event they commemorate?

The Vilna Gaon explains that the celebration of Succos does not only commemorate the Clouds of Glory that surrounded the nation in Nissan. Specifically, it marks their return after their disappearance as a consequence of the sin of the Golden Calf. When the Jewish People sinned, they were no longer worthy of Divine revelation or protection. The Clouds of Glory disappeared. Now began the long *teshuvah* process which culminated in Moses descending Mt. Sinai on Yom Kippur with the Second Tablets — proof positive that a new world of *teshuvah* had been inaugurated.

On the 11th of Tishrei, the day after Yom Kippur, we read "*Vayakheil Moshe*, and Moses gathered" the Jewish People for the building of the *Mishkan*, the Tabernacle. During the three days that followed, the entire nation was deeply occupied with gathering the materials needed to erect the *Mishkan*, a dwelling place for the *Shechinah* [G-d's holy presence]. These preparations were completed on the 15th of Tishrei (Succos). At that point construction began — and the Clouds of Glory returned.[7]

We now understand how Succos relates to *teshuvah* and to Yom Kippur.

The Clouds of Glory not only protected the Jewish People, they also signified forgiveness. Once again, Israel became G-d's Chosen People. As soon as the Jewish People repented and received the Torah anew, they were given the *Mishkan,* a spiritual center where repentance could be attained whenever they sinned. The rebirth of the Jewish People and the renewal of their status as G-d's Chosen People is the essence of Succos. "*Atah bechartanu*, You have chosen us," recited on all holidays, refers to the first selection of Israel and belongs to the first name of G-d, the first Divine Name, *Havayah*. Succos represents the second *Havayah*, the name of G-d in the recreated world of forgiveness and repentance. What joy could be greater than the rapprochement between Israel and G-d?

▸ The Song of the *Ba'al Teshuvah*

Joy and repentance (*simchah* and *teshuvah*) go together. The Rambam teaches that every *mitzvah* must be performed joyously. Rabbeinu Yonah teaches in *Sha'arei Teshuvah* (4:8) that the joy of the *ba'al teshuvah* cannot be separated from *teshuvah* itself. Joy is not simply an added dimension; it is an integral part of *teshuvah*. The suffering of sin can be erased only through the joy of knowing that G-d has forgiven.

Now we can understand the Rambam's teaching that we must be especially joyful on Succos, *Ve'hayisa ach samei'ach*. The Rambam teaches, "Although it is a *mitzvah* to be joyous on each of our festivals, on Succos there was extraordinary joy in the *Beis Hamikdash*."[8] On Succos the *ba'al teshuvah* sings a special song. His joy is unparalleled and unmatched.

Succos, therefore, is the time when we stand in the presence of G-d as a nation of *ba'alei teshuvah*. On Succos, the world of sin is replaced by a new world of forgiveness and purity. Just as repentance creates the special joy that comes from knowing that one has been forgiven, Succos also generates special joy — the joy of an entire nation that has been forgiven, reborn and chosen by G-d once again. During the celebration of the Water Libation Ceremony, the central source of holiday rejoicing in the *Beis Hamikdash*, the joy of Succos overflows.

▸ A New Danger Lurks

While there is no greater joy than the joy of *teshuvah* and no greater cleanliness than the purity of the cleansed sinner, this joy carries a danger as well. Every awakening and purifying force meets an opposing counteracting force. We know that the creation of man involved his being singled out from the rest of Creation: "You singled out man from the beginning and chose him to stand in Your presence" (*Neilah* service). At that moment, the angels stood before G-d demanding, "Who is man that you are so mindful of him, who is the son of man that he is so important?"[9]

At the splitting of the Reed Sea the moment Israel was liberated from Egypt, an opposing voice was heard: "Why do you favor these over those (Israel over the Egyptians)? Have not both sinned?"[10]

The rebirth of a newly repentant Nation of Israel awakens similar opposition. Even on Yom Kippur, when the Jewish People stand trial before G-d, Israel must respond to the prosecutor who represents the nations of the world. In this struggle, it is unclear who is vindicated. Suddenly Israel emerges with its "weapons," the *esrog* and *lulav,* held aloft. At that moment, it is clear who is the victor; it is clear who is G-d's Chosen.

▶ The Victory Of *Teshuvah*

What arguments do the nations of the world bring to this trial? What is their claim? What accusation do they believe will defeat Israel in the new world of *teshuvah*?

The answer to this question will be found in the final and ultimate confrontation between Israel and the nations of the world in the End of Days. The nations will complain that G-d has played favorites; G-d has treated Israel differently. If justice is to be meted out on the basis of free will, Israel seems to be an exception to this rule. After all, we are taught that in the End of Days *teshuvah* is inevitable: "When all of these things will come upon you in the End of Days, you will return to the L-rd your G-d and obey His voice."[11] "And it shall come to pass on that day that a remnant of Israel will return."[12] The fact that *teshuvah* must take place in the End of Days would appear to favor the argument of the nations. How will Israel triumph in the great courtroom of the End of Days? How will ultimate justice be carried out when Israel's return to G-d appears to be inevitable and inescapable?

▶ The Final Test

In response to the protest of the world's nations, the evidence of Succos will be offered. After the final battle, the *esrog* and *lulav*, the weapons of Succos, will be held aloft. While these weapons will be no longer needed in battle, they will eloquently testify who has been vindicated.

How does this satisfy the just arguments of the nations of the world? The answer calls for a glimpse into the world at the End of Days, as described by our Sages. "At that time, G-d will bring a *Sefer Torah*, hold it in His bosom and declare, 'Everyone who studied the Torah should come and claim his reward.' Immediately, the nations of the world will come to claim their reward. The nations will plead, 'Offer us the Torah and we will obey it.' G-d will say to the nations, 'You are foolish. Whoever prepared food on the eve of the Sabbath will eat on the Sabbath, but those who did not prepare on the eve of the Sabbath have nothing to eat on the Sabbath. The End of Days is the Sabbath of the world. It is now too late to begin to study Torah or observe *mitzvos*. Nevertheless, I will offer you an easy *mitzvah* called *succah*. Go, observe it.' Quickly, the nations will build *succos* on top of their roofs. But G-d will make the sun shine hot — and the nations will kick the *succah*, and leave it."[13]

The distinction between Israel and the nations is the strength of the statement, "He who prepares on the eve of the Sabbath will eat on the Sabbath." Even though Sabbath — the End of Days — has arrived and there is no further need for weapons because the struggle is over, whoever "fought" with these weapons on "the eve of Sabbath" when we were dependent on effort, struggle, labor and battle, and was victorious, will "eat on the Sabbath." The victor will wear his crown and the weapons of yesterday will, in the End of Days, become ornaments of victory. He who emerges from the king's palace with his weapons held aloft will be vindicated.

1. *Leviticus* 23:40.
2. *Exodus* 34:6.
3. *Rosh Hashanah* 17b.
4. *Exodus* 14:15.
5. *Ta'anis* 26b.
6. *Succos 11b.*
7. See the commentaries of the Vilna Gaon on *Shir Hashirim* 2:17 and Rashi on *Exodus* 35:1.
8. *Hilchos Lulav* 8:12.
9. *Psalms* 8:5.
10. *Midrash Rabbah, Shemos* 21:7.
11. *Deuteronomy* 4:30.
12. *Isaiah* 10:20-22.
13. *Avodah Zarah* 3a.

WHY DID THE "LOWER WATERS" CRY?

Based on *Pachad Yitzchok*, Rosh Hashanah 13

▶ The Source of Succos Joy

Joy is located in the heart. Our Sages teach that joy also requires outward expression, such as eating meat, drinking wine, singing songs, and playing instrumental music.[1] The Water Libation Celebration that took place in the *Beis Hamikdash* on Chol Hamoed Succos added a new dimension to joy. What is the meaning of this unique celebration? The rejoicing at the Water Libation Celebration involved drawing water from the wells beneath the Temple Altar and then pouring them on the Great Altar.[2] This ceremony has its roots in the "separation of the waters" into "upper and lower waters" which took place on the second day of Creation.[3]

> *G-d said, "Let there be a firmament in the midst of the waters, and let it separate between waters and*

waters." So G-d made the firmament and separated between the waters that were beneath the firmament, and the waters that were above the firmament and so it was.[4]

Rashi explains that the upper firmament includes the rain, oceans, seas and rivers. The lower waters run underground. Relegated to a position below ground, they "cried out": "We, too, want to serve our King in His presence." In order to console them, "the lower waters" were promised that they would be poured on the Temple Altar during the rejoicing at the Water Libation Celebration on Chol Hamoed Succos.

The above Rashi expresses a spiritual concept. To understand it, we must examine why the daily song of the Levites each *Yom Sheini*, the Second Day of the week,[5] (the day G-d "divided Creation and ruled over it") began with, "Great is the L-rd and worthy of much praise."[6] There is clearly a connection between the daily events of Creation and the prescribed daily song of the Levites in the *Beis Hamikdash.*

▸ The Song of the Kingdom of Heaven

From this we see that even though the song of the Kingdom of Heaven, "The Lord reigns supreme"[7] is not sung until the Sixth Day, the root of this song is found in the song of the Second Day. Human qualities have their parallel in the physical world; and choice is the defining quality of man. Since choice is rooted in the fact that man is both spiritual and material, our Sages teach that human choice is rooted in the division of the world into "upper and lower waters." The Song of the Sixth Day is revealed in the mystery of the division that took place on the second day of Creation. This is why the Song of the Sixth Day, which celebrates the Creation of man, who is endowed with free choice and is capable of voluntarily accepting upon himself the obligations of the Kingdom of Heaven, is "The Lord reigns supreme."

▸ Why Did the Lower Waters "Cry"?

Why did the lower waters "cry"? As noted above, they lamented the fact that they could not "serve our King in His presence." Since man's ability to choose relates to the division of the upper and lower waters, we may infer that the concept that "it would have been better had man not been created"[8] is tied to the cry of the lower waters who mourn this division. Would it have been better had man not been created? Doesn't man's free choice open opportunities for sin?

Sin is not only a possibility; it is a certainty. As the Sages taught, "No man ever existed who was so righteous that he never sinned."[9] It is not in our immediate power to correct that reality. We can only regret this taint upon Creation, which we express by shedding tears. Thus tears represent our desire to extend the horizons of choice, to occupy a world in which sin is no longer inevitable. Just as the ability to choose is rooted in the division of the waters, the tears that accompany this quality are rooted in the "tears" of the lower waters, deprived of the ability to "serve our King."

▸ The Significance of the Water Libation Celebration

Now we can understand the Succos Water Libation Celebration, when the lower waters were raised to the Altar so that they too can "serve the King in His presence" with dignity and honor. The mystique of this honor is that the Water Libation is brought by sinners, people previously alienated from G-d. The Water Libation Celebration creates an honor for the *ba'al teshuvah* higher than that accorded to those who are already close to G-d.

This unique honor helps us understand the correlation between the concept of the "consolation" of the lower waters with the timing of this ceremony on Succos. The consolation of the lower waters is that the privilege to ascend the Altar is *exclu-*

sively theirs. On their trip to the Altar, the lower waters undertake a difficult journey. They ascend great distances from the depths of the earth. Their arrival on the Altar represents the reward granted those who are distant over those who are near, of those who triumphed through much inner struggle and effort. Why does this event take place on Succos? On Succos, all Israel has achieved *teshuvah* (due to the recent Yom Kippur) and merits the honor of sitting in the shade of the Divine Clouds of Glory — the *succah*.

▸ Tearful Joy

"**M**y eyes pour forth torrents of water because they did not observe your Torah."[10] Why does Tehillim say, "*they* [i.e. my eyes] did not observe" instead of "I did not observe?" Rabbeinu Yonah writes in his Fourth Principle of Repentance:

> *In the battle of repair vs. ruin, each organ has its own…rules. And while this applies to each organ, we witness the true expression of this principle when we examine the eyes. As a rule, crying denotes sorrow while laughter denotes joy. However, tears of joy are unique. They display a deeper joy than even the joy of laughter. The special characteristic of tearful joy is that it takes place right after the sweetening of the sorrow that preceded it. When sorrow turns into joy, the joy is deeper. …Turning mourning, sorrow or pain into joy deepens the joy. The special depth of this joy then appears on the cheeks in the form of joyful tears…[11]*

The power of *teshuvah* is its ability to transform rebellion into submission and alienation into intimacy. Tears are unique in their ability to express both joy and sorrow. Tears, then, express the dual interrelated concepts: "It would have been better had man never been created — but now that he was created let him be meticulous in his deeds."

Tears best express the sorrow of the person who realizes he has sinned as well as the joy he feels when he accomplishes *teshuvah.* Explaining "Rivers of tears run down from my eyes because I did not observe your Torah," Rabbeinu Yonah speaks of "displaying joy at the moment of atonement": The agony of sin and the joy of atonement are two sides of the same coin. The same eyes that bring forth tears over the agony of sin, bring forth tearful joy when atonement takes place. Regret produces atonement because regret not only brings about submission; it also transforms rebellion into submission.

Atonement gives rise to "rivers of water" because it reverses sadness and turns it into joy. Forgiveness not only brings about return, it turns alienation into intimacy. Overcoming an opposing force represents a deeper and greater achievement than never facing a challenge. The submission of an individual who previously rebelled against G-d, who cursed and rejected the Torah, is deeper than the individual who accepted the Torah's demands at the outset.

▶ The Consolation of the Lower Waters

This is the "consolation" of the lower waters that takes place during the Succos Water Libation Celebration. The "tears" of the lower waters, their piercing plea, "We too want to serve our King in His presence," cannot be consoled until the arrival of Succos, when G-d's Clouds of Glory surround the People of Israel. In the quality of G-d's Glory the power of the alienated over those who are intimate is revealed — the power of the lower over the higher. In the very shadow of G-d's Clouds of Glory the lower waters ascend the Altar — an unprecedented action. As a result, the bitter entreaty of the distant and alienated is transformed into torrents of water — joyful tears. These tears of joy are the joy of the Water Libation Celebration.

▸ Throwing Flaming Torches

As part of this unique ceremony, "Men of piety and achievement would dance with flaming torches in their hands."[12] The use of flaming torches relates exclusively to the Water Libation Celebration. Light creates glory — as the prophet Isaiah said, "With lights give glory to G-d."[13] The Water Libation is a unique celebration, different from all others because it lies at the foundation of G-d's honor and glory in this world. Only when G-d's glory is expressed with the bright light of flaming torches do we perceive the special significance of those who had been distant from Him yet through their *teshuvah* achieved greater stature than those who had always been close to Him.

In the future, G-d will initiate a dance for the righteous and He will "sit" in the center.[14] The circle dance at the Water Libation Celebration is an expression of the joy that reveals the glory of He who "sits" in the center.

"With torches give glory to G-d." May we merit both light and enlightenment.

---

1. *Pesachim* 109a, *Succah* 51a.
2. *Succah* 51b, also see Rashi.
3. *Midrash Vayikrah* 2:13, *Rabbeinu Bachayei*, also Rashi.
4. *Genesis* 1:6, 1:7.
5. *Rosh Hashanah* 31a.
6. *Psalms* 48:2.
7. *Psalms* 93:1.
8. *Eruvin* 13b.
9. *Ecclesiastes* 7:20.
10. *Psalms*119:136.
11. *Sha'arei Teshuvah*: Gate 1:15.
12. *Succah* 51a.
13. *Isaiah* 24:15.
14. *Ta'anis* 31a.

SUCCOS:
FORGING ISRAEL'S FUTURE

28 Based on *Pachad Yitzchok*, Rosh Hashanah 9

▸ Knowledge and Succos

hen the Torah speaks of the Passover Exodus it employs the term *remembrance;* when its subject is Succos, the term used is *knowledge*: "So that your descendants will *know* that I caused the Children of Israel to dwell in *succos* when I brought them out of Egypt."[1] Why is knowledge, rather than remembrance, essential to Succos?

The principal expression of joy on Succos took place at the *Simchas Beis Hasho'evah*, the rejoicing at the Water Libation Celebration in the Holy Temple during the intermediate days of Succos. The Mishnah relates that, "He who has not seen the rejoicing at the Water Libation Celebration has never witnessed true joy."[2] The Mishnah then provides us with the following description of the Water Libation Celebration.

*They sounded trumpets until they reached the gate
facing east. When they arrived at this gate, they
turned their faces from east to west, facing the
Temple, and said, "In the days of the First Temple
our fathers stood on this spot with their backs to
the Temple and their faces to the east. They then
worshipped the sun."*

The Talmud[3] describes the degenerate depths of this
obscene and insolent idol worship. "They uncovered themselves and defecated downwards." i.e.; as they worshipped the
sun, they degraded themselves. "But as for us, our eyes are
turned toward the L-rd."[4] This indicates that at one point the
hideously degrading Ba'al Pe'or idol worship had found its way
into G-d's Temple. This reference to a shocking incident of blatant idol worship which took place in a previous generation
strikes us as highly inappropriate, especially since it took
place during the festive Succos holiday, at the very moment
reserved for the rejoicing at the Water Libation Celebration.
This celebration highlighted Succos as the joyous festival of
the penitent, who had been cleansed of their sins just a few
days before, on Yom Kippur.

▸ The Festivals and Nature

The answer to this puzzle will emerge from our study of the
three pilgrimage festivals that required every adult male to
travel to Jerusalem to celebrate Passover, Shavuos and Succos.
The Torah describes each festival by placing emphasis on the
agricultural character of each: Passover is the holiday of spring,
Shavuos is the holiday of early harvest, while Succos, in late summer, is the holiday of the ingathering of grain and fruit. The
Maharal explains these festivals in his *Sefer Ha'gvuros* with the
following description:

A messenger makes contact with the person who sent him on
his mission at three crucial moments: a) When the agent is

appointed to carry out his mission; b) When he is in the midst of carrying out his mission; and finally c) When the agent returns to his master and reports, "I have successfully completed your mission."[5]

This principle is then applied to the pilgrimage holidays. These three festivals revolve around three pivotal events.

Passover — the Jewish Nation was created and was appointed as G-d's messenger to the nations of the world. Passover is therefore the festival of birth and beginnings.

Shavuos — the holiday of early harvest. After the Exodus, the spiritual efforts of the Jewish People galvanized them to take on G-d's mission. The Torah was then revealed to them at Mt. Sinai and Israel was instructed how to accomplish its mission.

Succos — the final harvest. Israel will ultimately report to G-d the successful fulfillment of its mission at the End of Days, when the Messiah arrives. This is the theme of Succos, the time when the fruits and grains of the field have been fully gathered into storehouses and are safely in the possession of their owners.

▸ Succos and the End of Days

What will take place at the End of Days and what unique role does *succos* play in the fulfillment of Israel's mission? The Book of Nehemiah[6] describes the return of Jews to the Land of Israel from the Babylonian captivity. Under the leadership of Ezra, "All of the returnees built *succos* and dwelt in them. The Children of Israel had not done so from the days of Joshua the son of Nun until that day, and there was great rejoicing." This passage is extremely puzzling. Is it possible that the *mitzvah* of building and dwelling in a *succah* went unobserved during the nine centuries that elapsed from the time of Joshua to the time of Ezra? Obviously, this verse has a different and much deeper meaning: The emphasis of the verse is not on the dwelling in *succos* per se but on the "extremely great rejoicing."

▸ The Return to the Land

The return of the Jews to the Land of Israel in the time of Ezra involved enormous sacrifice and engendered much gratitude to G-d. Foreign peoples had been imported to repopulate the Land of Israel and it had become desolate. The returnees were those who excelled in their love of G-d. Although the Jewish nation indeed had observed the *mitzvah* of Succos throughout its history, it had not achieved an intimacy with G-d since the time of Joshua — until the era of the returnees. Our Sages teach that this verse in Nehemiah describes an unprecedented act performed by Ezra and the sages of the *Anshei Knesses Hagedolah*. (This body of Torah scholars was the supreme civil and spiritual authority of the Jewish People when they returned from the Babylonian exile.)

▸ Breaking the Magnetic Power of Idol Worship

Through the power of intense prayer, the pious *Anshei Knesses Hagedolah* appealed to G-d to abolish the one major flaw that was the Jewish Nation's undoing during the period of the First Temple, namely, the passion of so many Jews for idol worship. The abolition of the passion for idolatry represented a unique fulfillment of the *mitzvah* of Succos, whose purpose is to recall G-d's protection of the Jewish People in the desert. The abolition of the magnetic power of idolatry is described in the Talmud and elucidated by the Maharal. No similar event is described by the Torah or in Jewish tradition from the beginning of time until our time.

Why is this event so unique and unprecedented? There is no instance in the history of man of the total excision of a major negative human trait or passion. The abolition of this trait should have occurred at the End of Days, the era of the Messiah. As Israel's prophets teach, the abolition of the "evil inclination" and the "turning of our stone hearts to human hearts" constitute the fulfillment of the End of Days. These prophecies are a major component of the fulfillment of Israel's mission. The abolition of the passion for idolatry is a significant element in this process. It is part of the success of the mission that Israel will report to G-d. This unique event took place on Succos precisely because the sanctification of humanity at the "End of Time" is part of the fulfillment of Israel's mission celebrated on the Festival of Succos. It is for this reason that the Torah describes Succos as the festival of ingathering (both spiritually and physically), *Chag Ha'asif*.

▸ Succos: The Holiday of the End of Time

Succos, as the holiday of the "End of Time," annually and in human history, includes elements of nature and history: Physically, it is celebrated at the end of the summer, the time of ingathering the summer crops; spiritually, Succos concludes the annual Jewish holiday cycle and celebrates the ultimate coming of the Messiah. The results of the year's agricultural efforts are collected and brought into the house to sustain each family through winter. In a spiritual sense, this is also a time for ingathering and reaping the rewards of spiritual growth and transformation. This fulfillment brings great joy.

The Rambam, in his *Laws of Lulav*, gives this characteristic of Succos special emphasis. "While there is a commandment to rejoice on each of the festivals, on the festival of Succos there was exceptional joy, especially in the Temple." The Rambam then proceeds to describe the rejoicing at the Water Libation Celebration.

The Maharal explains that the extreme joy of Succos derives from the fact that it is the finale, the apex and fulfillment of all the holidays.[7] As Rashi explains, "The joy of the Festival of Ingathering is greater than the joy of either the spring or the harvest festivals."[8] Indeed, the inner soul of the joy of Succos is reserved for the rejoicing at the Water Libation Celebration, the ceremony that specifically relates to the fulfillment of the Jewish mission and the announcement to the Master of the World that the goal of Creation has been achieved.

We now understand the significance of the Talmud's description of the ugly incident of idol worship in the First Temple and the mention of this event as part of the rejoicing at the Water Libation Celebration. It is striking that the passion for idolatry was forever banished by way of the unique prayers of the *Anshei Knesses Hagedolah* and not through national self-discipline or repentance. After this point in history, Israel's prophets and sages never again condemn the Jews for succumbing to idolatry. *This was the only instance in human history when human nature was changed*, and when a portion of the mission of Israel was fully accomplished. This great event represents the inner core of the rejoicing at the Water Libation Celebration. The celebrants would turn from east to face west and recite, "When our forefathers were at this spot, they turned eastward and prostrated themselves to the sun. But as for us, our eyes are turned toward the L-rd."

▶ Fulfilling Israel's National Mission

L et us return to the beginning of our study — to the change of emphasis from *remembrance* on Passover to *knowledge* on Succos. The Torah uses the following language when commanding us to observe the Succos festival. "When I liberated Israel from the Land of Egypt, I caused them to dwell in *succos*." We see here that the Torah goes beyond commanding the Jew to dwell in a *succah*, it emphasizes that the *succah* is linked to the Exodus.

According to the Maharal, the above distinction has the following meaning. "The fall ingathering of Israel follows Israel's springtime. Dwelling in a *succah* is related to the Exodus because the fulfillment of Israel's mission is tied to the initiation of Israel's mission. The ingathering of Israel is intrinsically tied to Israel's springtime."[9] Knowledge is therefore more appropriate to Succos than remembrance. Why? When we speak of the past, we must remember. Succos, however, brings the past into the future. Succos describes and motivates the Jew's effort to mold the future, to fulfill Israel's national mission. The completion of our mission, while tied to the past, requires an awareness, a knowledge of the steps needed to achieve that mission. In effect, G-d is telling us, "I caused Israel to dwell in *succos* [that it would be cognizant of its responsibility to actively bring about the fulfillment of its mission]."

Remembrance therefore befits Passover, while knowledge befits Succos. Passover describes events that took place in the past, while Succos projects Israel into the future. For Israel to someday be able to say to G-d, "I have fulfilled Your mission," requires much more than a memory of the past: It requires insight, knowledge and understanding.

---

1. *Leviticus* 23:43.
2. *Succah* 5:1.
3. *Succah* 51b.
4. *Succah* 53b.
5. *Sefer Ha'gvuros,* Chapter 46.
6. *Nehemiah* 8:17.
7. *Gevuros Hashem,* 46.
8. *Genesis* 1:7.
9. *Gevuros Hashem,* 46.

SHMINI ATZERES: THE PINNACLE OF THE HOLIDAY CYCLE

After the last day of Succos, the Torah instructs us to observe a festival that is not given a name or a reason. The Torah does not even call it a *chag*, a festival, even though all the usual festival laws are to be observed. The Torah says, "On the eighth day, there shall be an Assembly for you; you may not do any Yom Tov-like work."[1]

It is possible that the Torah found no cause for calling it a *chag* because its very essence and function is that it concludes all the festivals of the year. It is the capstone of the festival year. It brings to conclusion both the pilgrimage festival cycle and the Days of Awe cycle. In essence it is the *chag* par excellence because all of the cycles of the Torah pour into it. Note that Shmini Atzeres, unlike all of the other festivals, does not have special observances of its own. There is no matzah, no *succah*, no historic reference.

The Hebrew word *chag* is related to *chug*, a circle. Therefore, it is not necessary to call Shmini Atzeres a *chag* because its very essence is to be a circle — to conclude a full year of circles — and to enable a new holiday circle to begin anew. In order to better understand Shmini Atzeres/Simchas Torah, we need a brief recapitulation of the events that lead up to Shmini Atzeres.

▶ The Jewish Festivals: A Unified, Interlocking System

The festivals of the Jewish year constitute a unified, coordinated and harmonious interlocking system. Each holiday relates to a historical event, each event flows from the event preceding it and each of the holidays relates to the next. The holidays progress from the birth of the Jewish Nation to the ultimate fulfillment of its mission with the coming of the Messiah. Because the holiday cycle has a beginning and a conclusion, and because the holidays relate to each other much like the components of a finely tuned timepiece, we may not tamper with the holiday cycle by either adding or subtracting holidays.

Each holiday is paired with the one that follows it; for example, Passover celebrates the physical birth of the Jewish People, and Shavuos, which follows it seven weeks afterward, celebrates Israel's spiritual birth, the conclusion of the process that was initiated on Passover.

Succos, which follows Shavuos, not only celebrates the Divine protection of Israel in the desert where they dwelt in physical *succos* and were protected by the *succah* of the Divine cloud, it also celebrates the conquest and settlement of the Land of Israel, the Divinely defined locale where the liberated nation is charged with creating the ideal Torah society. Finally, Shmini Atzeres/Simchas Torah caps Succos, which marks and celebrates the coming of the Messiah and the initiation of the

Messianic age. Even though the Messiah has not yet come, we anticipate his coming by experiencing a meta-historical day, enabling us to experience in a spiritual, vicarious sense the ideal for which we strive. Much like Shabbos, Shmini Atzeres/Simchas Torah offers a "taste" of the world of fulfillment and perfection.

▶ Interconnected Cycles

The holidays consist of two coordinated, interconnected cycles. While each cycle operates independently, it also merges with the second cycle on Succos. (*Chag Ha'asif*, the holiday of gathering or combining, belongs to both cycles.) Each cycle begins independently, but merges as both cycles simultaneously achieve their goals. They join when they reach Succos.

The second cycle begins with the month of Elul and Rosh Hashanah. On Rosh Hashanah, mankind was created and acknowledges G-d as King. Rosh Hashanah is the first day of the Ten Days of Repentance, which concludes on Yom Kippur. Man is able to achieve forgiveness on Yom Kippur, having acknowledged G-d as King and Creator on Rosh Hashanah.

How did Yom Kippur become the day for atonement and forgiveness? On that day G-d accepted Israel's repentance for the sin of the Golden Calf. On Yom Kippur Moses descended Mt. Sinai for a second time, and for a second time he held in his hands the Tablets of the Covenant, the "Ten Commandments."

Just as the Jewish Nation was cleansed of its sins on Yom Kippur when G-d granted them the gift of repentance and the formula for achieving it, each individual Jew can be cleansed of sin on Yom Kippur. The repentant Jew is then able to enter the holiday of Succos — the joyous holiday of the repentant Jew — and celebrate in the presence of G-d, in His Temple, with the *esrog* and *lulav*, the fruits of the Holy Land, and in his *succah* (which teaches us that our homes and physical possessions are temporary, while our relationship with G-d is forever).

What was to have been achieved on Shavuos, and was subsequently soured by the sin of the Golden Calf, was set right on Yom Kippur. It was on Rosh Hashanah that Adam and Eve sinned by eating the fruit of the forbidden tree, and were banished from the spiritual Garden of Eden. In both instances, repentance was achieved on Yom Kippur.

The day prior to Shmini Atzeres is the last day of Succos. This day has a special name, Hoshanah Rabbah, the day of the Great Redemption. Hoshanah Rabbah is the day on which the "heavenly messengers" finally deliver the "note" containing the verdict of each Jew to the heavenly throne. On the historical plane, it is the final day for repentance, and the day before the coming of the Messianic era on Shmini Atzeres/Simchas Torah.

▸ Shmini Atzeres: The Crown of Both Holiday Cycles

The key to understanding both cycles is the least understood holiday of all, Shmini Atzeres. (The second name of Shmini Atzeres is Simchas Torah.) While usually thought of as the eighth and last day of Succos, in reality, Shmini Atzeres is a separate holiday unto itself. Shmini Atzeres is the crown of the entire holiday system, representing the accomplishment and fulfillment of all the holidays of the year.

While each of the holidays is rooted in history, in that each relates to a historical event which Israel already experienced, Shmini Atzeres is meta-historical — beyond and above history. Shmini Atzeres celebrates an event that has not yet taken place — the coming of the Messiah. Keep in mind that, in the national Jewish sense, the Jewish year begins with Passover, not Rosh Hashanah. Passover is the spring festival, the first historical event in the life of the Jewish People. The month of Nissan, in which Passover falls, is called by the Torah the first month, the beginning of the year. "This month is to you the first of months, the first of the months of the year."[2] Shmini Atzeres is the very last festival of the year. Life begins with spring and ends with the winter, and winter begins right after Shmini Atzeres.

▶ Shmini Atzeres: The Crown of Rosh Hashanah

G-d's original intent was that Rosh Hashanah would be celebrated as the celebration of the creation and grandeur of man. However, when Adam and Eve sinned, the *chag* [festival] aspect of Rosh Hashanah became "*bakeseh*," covered and hidden. The Psalms teach, "On the first day of the month, blow the shofar *bakeseh*,"[3] i.e. conceal the festival aspect of the day. Shmini Atzeres became the festival that Rosh Hashanah was originally intended to be. Do we not need a *chag* to celebrate the majesty and creation of man? How do we know that Shmini Atzeres is that festival? Because the Temple sacrifices of Shemini Atzeres are precisely the same as the sacrifices of Rosh Hashanah. The Temple services were meticulously planned to evoke the essence of each holiday. That Rosh Hashanah and Shmini Atzeres are observed with the same service is no coincidence.

Yom Kippur and Succos witnessed man's return to G-d. On Shmini Atzeres we finally feel fully cleansed; we find our true inner self and we are able to properly celebrate the creation and majesty of man. Shmini Atzeres is the day on which all of the holidays reach their apex. It is on this day that we celebrate the fulfillment of man's historic role.

The *Midrash* teaches that after the Succos festival, G-d did not wish the Jews to return to their homes following their pilgrimage to Jerusalem. G-d "said" to them, "Remain one more day: Let this day be a day of intimacy between Israel and G-d." This is how the concept of Simchas Torah, the rejoicing of the Torah, became a permanent feature of the last festival day. The absence of symbolism and of specific observances on Shmini Atzeres/Simchas Torah is intentional. The addition of the concept and name Simchas Torah are also intentional.

▶ Shmini Atzeres: The Day of Total Fulfillment

What should a Jew do on this day of ultimate joy, on the day on which we celebrate, at least in a spiritual sense, the arrival of the Messiah? We no longer require the external symbols of Succos — the *succah* and the "four species" — because we have internalized the meaning of each of these symbols. They are no longer outside of us; now they and their message have been absorbed into our minds and hearts. We are now ready to rejoice and dance, because we have lived to see that the Nation of Israel, the Torah and G-d are finally truly united in an eternal and unbreakable unity. The goals of the Torah and of the Jewish People have been achieved. What greater joy can there be?

---

1. *Numbers* 29:35.
2. *Exodus* 12:2.
3. *Psalms* 81:4.

VI CHANUKAH

THE MODERN
CHALLENGE
30 # OF CHANUKAH

▶ The Modern Challenge of Chanukah

What *is* the essence of the human being? What makes us unique? What is the core of our *Tzelem Elokim*, our having been created in the image of G-d? Is it not in discovering our true hopes, dreams, ideals and goals? But even if we are clear as to what these are, what is the quality of our hopes and dreams? To what degree do they motivate our actions and determine our thoughts?

What dominates our lives — our pursuit of money, power and possessions, or the spiritual quest of the Torah Jew to forge an intimate relationship with G-d?

If I would ask you — given the world, as we know it, given the dangers that face our People — what are the dreams that fill your heart on Chanukah? Wouldn't you agree that it is the yearning that the miracles G-d performed for our fathers, the heroic Maccabees, would happen in our day, at this time?

As a child in 1939, I watched my father cry as he sat at his radio and heard news of the early stages of the Holocaust. It was then that I developed the habit of standing in front of the Chanukah menorah, of staring at its tiny lights, of trying to comprehend their message. I remember repeating over and over again, "Hashem, please do it again. We need Your miracles today, as much as the Maccabees did 2,000 years ago."

▶ The Uniqueness of the Chanukah Celebration

The text of the *Al Hanissim* prayer indicates that the primary miracle of Chanukah was the military one. The prayer makes it clear that the victory of a small band of righteous people over overwhelming forces of evildoers was possible only because of G-d's miraculous intervention. This gives rise to three questions:

1) Why do we celebrate a great military victory with fragile, tiny flames? Surely there should be a symbolism more in consonance with the nature of the miracle.

2) Since the primary miracle was the military one, why did the Sages choose to institute an observance — that of the Chanukah menorah — which commemorates a secondary miracle, one that took place *after* the victory?

3) What was G-d's message to the Jewish People in this form of miracle: that oil sufficient for one night glowed for eight? No miraculous manifestation of G-d's Will is without a message. Indeed, this is the miracle that we commemorate in tangible form for eight nights. It is obvious that it represents the essence of Chanukah.

▶ The Flame and the Spirit

The answer to all three questions is the following: Flame is a physical manifestation of the spiritual, "*Ki ner Elokim nishmas adam* — the candle of G-d is the soul of man." Like the human spirit, a flame can die or soar; it can be extinguished easily or it can light up the entire world, if provided with sufficient fuel. The essence of the Jew is his spirit. The basic and essential miracle of Chanukah commemorates the steadfastness, resilience and unprecedented self-sacrifice of the Jewish spirit, the stubbornness of a "stiff-necked people" in the face of fierce opposition, persecution and overwhelming military might.

In its deeper meaning, the miracle of the oil sufficient for one day was a reflection of the underlying miracle of Chanukah: the resurrection of the will of the Jewish People to resist the efforts of the Greeks and their Hellenist allies in their attempt to destroy the Torah way of life. Just as the Holy Temple oil had been defiled by the Greeks, the spirit of the Jewish People also had been defiled by them. Almost no one remained who possessed the will to wage the battle for G-d and His Torah. No one believed that resistance was possible. For all intents and purposes, the Greeks and the Hellenists were victorious. For a moment in time it appeared as though the entire Jewish People had succumbed to superior internal and external forces. Scores of thousands of Judean families had been Hellenized or intimidated into accepting the decrees of the Greeks which forbade the study of Torah and the observance of *mitzvos.* The light of the Jewish People was all but extinguished, its spirit depressed, its hope lost.

▶ Jewish History Stood Still

I n the midst of this hopeless, desperate situation, there arose a family of priests, Matisyahu and his five sons, who advocated armed rebellion. Not only did they battle the Greeks, they also fought their fellow Jews who had caved in to the pressures and had adopted the Greek way of life. The Greeks had conquered the entire civilized world. They were not satisfied merely to have conquered the Jews: They now wanted to turn the Jews into Greeks. They could not tolerate the fact that the Jews saw themselves as unique, as G-d's Chosen People. The family of

Matisyahu, the Hasmoneans, was the only pure, undefiled flask of holy oil remaining among the Jewish People.

The First Book of Maccabees describes the Greek anti-Torah edicts which lasted 52 years, and the Jewish response: "And Matisyahu, their father, cried out with a loud voice saying, 'Everyone who is zealous for the Torah, who is determined to maintain G-d's Covenant, follow me.' At this point he, his sons and a small band of followers fled to the mountains, left all they possessed in the city and unfurled the banner of resistance and revolt."

Before they could successfully unfurl the banner of revolt, the Maccabees (the sons of Matisyahu and their army) had to revive the will and spirit of the Jewish People. They had to reawaken the Jews' faith in G-d so He would become their ally. In the *Al Hanissim* prayer we read: "*Ravta es rivam*, You [G-d] fought *their* battles." Once we were prepared to go to war on G-d's behalf, G-d battled on our behalf.

Matisyahu's family of *Kohanim* was the one bit of sacred, undefiled Jewishness later symbolized by the one tiny vial of undefiled sacred oil that had survived the defilement of the Jerusalem Temple. It was that one undefiled family that succeeded in rekindling the pure flame of Torah, which in turn revived the spirit of the Jewish Nation and its determination to resist its enemies for all time.

It is this victory, the victory of the Jewish spirit and intellect, of indomitable faith and determination, which we celebrate with the kindling of the Chanukah menorah. It is the victory of the Maccabees over Jewish depression and despair. It is this spiritual obstinacy and the call for religious and military resistance that G-d acknowledged with the miracle of the flask of oil.

▶ Chanukah Today

The miracle of Chanukah repeats itself in each generation, "in those days and at this time." The revival of Torah in our day is no less a miracle; the odds are no less formidable and the faith and determination that is required is no less.

The forces of Western civilization — which place materialism, secularism and technology above spiritual Torah values — are Greek philosophy in modern dress. The adoption by masses of Jews of secular values and immoral lifestyles mimics the Hellenization of Jewish society in ancient times. Secular philosophy, which denies the uniqueness and supremacy of Torah and the reality of G-d's Will, remains our greatest enemy. We sing in the Chanukah hymn *Ma'oz Tzur*, "*Yevanim nikb'tsu alai*, Greeks have overwhelmed me." This challenge describes the plight of the majority of Jews today; they are overwhelmed by the secular, technological life around them. But if we can succeed in rekindling the light of authentic Judasim as did the Maccabees, we too, can succeed in replicating the miracle of Chanukah.

Let us not mince words. Something ominously frightful is enveloping all of *Klal Yisrael*, the Jewish People. A massive spiritual decline is overtaking significant segments of the world Jewish community. Recent sociological studies indicate that in ten years a majority of American Jews will cease to be Jewish. A million and a half American Jewish children are not receiving a meaningful Jewish education. The intermarriage rate is well over 52%. A million Jewish children in Israel can't tell you the meaning of *Sh'ma Yisrael*. They are totally alienated from their Jewish heritage despite the fact that they live in what is supposed to be a Jewish state.

What is different today is that, for the first time, many secular Jews also realize it. For the first time they, too, are beginning to acknowledge that they are unable to insure Jewish survival without calling upon the resources and strength of the ancient ideals and practices of Torah Jewry.

Now let's flip the coin to the other side. The accomplishments of the American and Israeli *teshuvah* [return to Judaism] movements — in terms of their impact on people's lives and on Jewish communities — is unique and unprecedented. Suddenly, during the 1960s and '70s, a new and unexpected voice was heard. It was the voice of youth speaking out on behalf of *kedushah* and *mitzvah* observance. Yeshivos and women's seminaries catering to the needs of Jews searching for their spiritual roots became fixtures in the Jewish world. *Teshuvah* programs for youth and adults were established. It was found that when Jews experience the warmth and truth of Torah, they are attracted to Judaism despite the competition of an earthy, materialistic popular culture.

Our Maccabean ancestors call to us from their graves: "Repeat the miracle of Chanukah, 'in those days, in our time.'" The question is, who will respond to their call?

The sixth chapter of Exodus states that G-d replied to the cries of the Jews enslaved in Egypt, saying, "And I also have heard the cry of the Jewish People." The Chasam Sofer asks, "What is the meaning of, 'and I *also* have heard?'" He then answers the question, explaining that a transformation had taken place among the Jews. They began caring about each other and performing acts of kindness for one another. Jews began hearing each other's cries and began praying for each other and for the entire Jewish People. Most importantly, they stopped speaking *lashon hara*, harmful and hateful speech one against the other. New camaraderie took hold and unity emerged. Only then did G-d respond to their prayers. Only when they heard each other's pleas and responded through exemplary behavior did G-d come to their assistance — saying, "I, too, have heard their cries."

In speaking of Chanukah, the *Shulchan Aruch* asks, "What is the essence of Chanukah?" Its reply is, *"D'lo mispdei bay*, It is forbidden to mourn or be depressed during Chanukah." The Maccabean victory grew out of the fact that the Jewish People discovered its inner strength to overcome despair and depression, to fight against unbelievable odds. Undeterred by the vast number of assimilated Jews, the Maccabees overcame intimidation and lethargy. Can we, in our day, unfurl the banner of the Maccabees? Can we call out to our fellow Jews, *"Mi Lashem alei* — Whoever believes in our cause, join us"? The Maccabees reversed the Hellenist tide of their generation and brought about miracles. It is our duty to do no less.

WHY DID THE GREEKS FORBID TORAH OBSERVANCE?

31

I n order to understand the miracle of Chanukah, it is essential that we comprehend the root cause of the attempt of the Greeks and their Jewish collaborators to forbid and destroy traditional Jewish life. What were the weak points in the Jews' spiritual armor that made them vulnerable to the Greek efforts to undermine and destroy their spiritual life? What failings and sins made them defenseless, susceptible and exposed to the harm that was directed against them? Once we gain this understanding, we will be able to fathom the Chanukah miracle. To complete the picture, we must understand that the Maccabean uprising not only brought about the defeat of Israel's enemies, it also stimulated a spectacular turnabout, strengthening the renaissance of Jewish life and Torah study. To begin our inquiry, we must first seek the roots of Chanukah in the Torah.

▶ Chanukah Has Roots in the Torah

The Torah often speaks of events that will take place in the future. Some of the Torah's predictions of future events are clear, while some consist of hidden references that were uncovered and clarified by our Sages. Among these is a reference to the wars of the Maccabees in Deuteronomy 33:11, which Rashi translates as follows: "Hashem [G-d] will Bless His army, and favor the work of His hands. He will strike down His opponents to the loins and strike His enemies so that they will not be able to rise again." This is part of the blessing Moses gave to the tribe of Levi before his death. Rashi states that the *Chashmonai,* i.e. Yochanan the High Priest, the father of Matisyahu and his Maccabean sons, are destined, hundreds of years later, to wage war against the Greeks. He therefore prayed for them because the core of the Maccabean Jewish fighting force would constitute barely a handful of individuals. This force consisted of the twelve descendants of *Chashmonai* and Elazar, one of the Jewish resistance heroes against the Greeks, who fought against tens of thousands of Greek soldiers. This is why the Torah says, "G-d will bless his army and favor the work of his hands." Moses prophesied that the core of the Jewish resistance against Greece would rest on the shoulders of these valiant and determined individuals who had no previous training in weapons or war.

▶ What Was the Essential Miracle of Chanukah?

Judea had long been a vassal state to Persia and had not had an independent government or a standing army since the destruction of the First Temple and the exile to Babylonia. Nor did the Jews possess arms of any kind, or the skills with which to manufacture armaments. The Jewish fighters would be compelled to oppose massive, well-equipped Greek armies composed of seasoned, professional soldiers who were led by highly trained and experienced generals. Rashi is teaching us that the *willing-*

ness of the Jews to take up arms and engage in what was, to any rational mind, a hopeless and futile effort, especially in keeping with the nonexistence of a Jewish army, was of a miraculous and heroic nature. The ability of the Maccabees to create a guerilla force and to wage a successful war against unbelievable odds was the essential miracle of Chanukah. It was the Maccabean belief that G-d would stand by their side so that the people could be restored to their status as the Torah Nation that gave them the spiritual strength with which to do the impossible. The flame of Judaism was nearly extinguished. This tiny group was determined to reignite it, come what may.

▸ What Was the Root Cause of the War Against the Greeks?

The next question is, what was the spiritual root cause of the Jewish war against the Greeks? How did the Jews sin? Why did G-d punish the Jews? The Jews were fighting in order to reverse the edicts of the Greeks that forbade the practice of the Jewish religion. The Greeks wanted the Jews to make themselves subservient to the Greek way of life. Why did G-d allow the Greeks to proceed with their anti-Jewish plans? What was the root cause of these edicts? In what way did the Jews fail so as to deserve G-d's wrath and this terrible punishment? Rabbi Yoel Sirkis (the Bach), a famous commentator on the *Shulchan Aruch* and the Talmud, teaches that the Greek edicts resulted from the general neglect and sloppiness of the *Kohanim* as regards the Temple service (*hishrashlus ha'Avodah*). This would point to the existence of a similar lack of enthusiasm in the observance of *mitzvos* among most Jews.

The powerful effect of Greek civilization, which aggressively attempted to foist itself on Jewish civilization and corrupt it, weakened the loyalty and resolve of significant numbers of Jews, even of those Jews who remained fiercely loyal to the Torah. The Jews had failed to take the Temple and its service sufficiently seriously. It was for these reasons that the Greeks were able to order an immediate cessation of the Temple service. In fact, a *Breisa* [a rabbinic tradition from the time of the Mishnah] teaches that the initial decree of the Greeks compelled the Jews to stop the daily *Tamid* sacrifice in the Holy Temple. In addition, Antiochus and his assimilated, Hellenized Jewish advisors understood that the Jews possessed a special *mitzvah* that protected them, namely the daily lighting of the Temple Menorah. The Torah commands, "You are to light the eternal flame." So long as the Jews kindled this flame, the Jews remained invincible and eternal. It was at this point that the Greeks proceeded to defile all of the flasks of pure Temple oil.

▸ Why Were the Maccabees Victorious?

The Jews mended their ways and repented by displaying a readiness to sacrifice their lives to protect the Temple and uphold its service. Only then could G-d bless them with a series of amazing victories through the instrumentality of the Priestly Maccabees and many of their fellow Priests and Levites who maintained the Temple worship service. This is the reason that the Chanukah miracle took place in the Temple. The Temple miracle was in response to the heroic, self-sacrificing idealism of the Maccabees. This miracle, which took place with the restoration of the lights of the Temple Menorah, happened *after* the Temple was recaptured and cleansed by the Maccabees. It acknowledged the miraculous revival of Jewish life and the readiness of the Jews to sacrifice their lives for the restoration of the Temple service and the integrity of Torah life.

This theme of Jewish neglect of the commandments and the inevitable Heavenly retribution is constantly to be found in the books of the prophets. Taking the Torah for granted and exhibiting a lack of zealousness in worship and observance has always been the inner cause of Israel's crises, which, in this case, resulted in a major confrontation between the Maccabean Jews and the Greeks. While the confrontation was military, the root cause was spiritual and ideological.

The influence of the Greeks on all the peoples of the ancient civilized world was deep and profound. Greek had long become the spoken language of the entire Near East and Mediterranean Basin, so much so that 150 years prior to the Chanukah confrontation (in approximately 285 BCE), the Greek king of Egypt, Ptolemy II, compelled the 70 members of the Sanhedrin to translate the Torah into Greek, called the Septuagint. Much of the Jewish intelligentsia of the time was highly proficient in the Greek language and had read the works of the major Greek philosophers. From the time of the conquest of the ancient world by Alexander the Great, Jews began to develop a measure of comfort with the Greek lifestyle that was much more damaging than the American Jews' involvement in American civilization today because it involved a strong pagan element.

▸ The Imprint of the Sages

One of the unique features of Chanukah is that there is very little discussion of Chanukah in the Bible or the Talmud as distinguished from the other holidays, which are discussed at length in the Torah, the Tanach, the Mishnah and the Talmud. It would appear that the Sages were not anxious for later generations to become absorbed in the intricate study of the interplay of Greek and Jewish ideologies that led to the repression of Jewish observance. On the other hand, there are a number of non-biblical, historical books written during the period of the Second Temple, such as the books of Maccabees I and II and the historical books of Josephus Flavius, which go into considerable detail concerning the historic events that led up to the Chanukah victory. These sources are, in large measure, at the root of the secularization and trivialization of one of our most spiritual festivals. They dwell on the religious, political and military aspects of Chanukah but lack serious depth in fathoming the spiritual and intellectual bedrock of the revolt, and do not contain the imprint of our Sages as to the deeper spiritual meaning of

Chanukah. Many Jews celebrate Chanukah without having any clear idea as to its true meaning. Each "branch" of the Jewish People has interjected its own ideology into Chanukah, turning it into the holiday of "lights," nationalism or religious freedom. But none of these rewrites fit. Only our Sages, employing few words, have revealed the inner message and meaning of the festival.

While the causes of the saga of Chanukah were religious, political and ideological, historical books are incapable of expounding on the inner-spiritual roots of the events and the deep ideological, intellectual and spiritual nature of the Jewish response. It is only in the writings of *Chazal*, the Sages of Israel, that these events come into focus. They elucidate the meaning of the conflict of Jewish and Greek ideologies as a prototype of the many future struggles that will challenge the Torah People during their 2,000-year exile. Conscious of this perspective, the Jews were able — with some notable exceptions — to successfully resist the efforts of their opponents throughout history.

▸ A Final Thought

It has been pointed out by Rabbi Mattisyahu Salomon, the *Mashgiach Ruchani* of Beth Medrash Govoha of Lakewood, that even today, most observant Jews are guilty of *hisrashlus ha'Avodah*, neglect of the Temple Service. How? A significant section of our daily prayers are devoted to the *Avodah*, the "prayers" that speak of the ancient Temple Service. Because *Shacharis* is often rushed, it has become the practice of many to skip this portion of the service. In a spiritual sense, however, this recitation takes the place of the Temple Service and is a strong force in bringing about the restoration of the *Beis Hamikdash* and its Service speedily, in our day.

This is an admonition we should all take seriously. It requires an additional few minutes to say these words of the Temple Service, but it sends a powerful message. May it be Hashem's will that He favor us and restore our ancient glories.

WHY DID THE GREEKS STOP THINKING?

32

Among the ancients, only the Athenian Greeks and the Jews attempted to answer life's ultimate questions. The Greeks created a theology, a philosophy and a grand civilization whose economic base was the enslavement of the majority of the residents of Athens. Looking at it from a twentieth century perspective, Athenian democracy guaranteed the rights of only the male aristocracy, who constituted 10% of the population. The balance — foreigners, women, slaves, the landless — had no rights. Yet its democracy was a cut above the autocratic monarchies of its contemporaries.

My first trip to the Acropolis of Athens, a flattened mountain-top on which the remnants of enormous pagan temples remain, took place during the summer of 1999. This world famous group of buildings provided a deeper appreciation of the grandeur and power of the only other civilization which attempted to do that which the ancient Jews succeeded in doing: to think — to seek and provide answers for man's quest for truth and purpose.

▸ The Jewish Confrontation with Greece

The Jewish confrontation with Greece and its successor empire, Rome, led to a long series of bloody wars and revolutions, most of which tragically ended in the Jews' defeat. Both Greece and Rome repeatedly sought to subdue the Jews, primarily by attempting to force them to abandon their faith, philosophy and way of life. The Greeks and Romans vehemently rejected the Jewish concepts of G-d, faith, morality, Creation, ethics, equality and philosophy.

The Chanukah victory marks Judaism's successful confrontation with Greek ideology and power. The Greeks attempted to obliterate Jewish civilization through force, by imposing the death penalty on any Jew who would teach or observe key aspects of his religion. Subsequently, the Romans fought two bloody wars to subdue Jewish resistance and repeated uprisings. They, too, forbade Jewish worship and the study of Torah. In the wake of the first war in 70 CE, the Romans destroyed the Jerusalem Temple and forbade Jewish observance. Again, in 135 CE, they brought their best generals and armies from as far as England to totally subdue the Jewish revolt led by the great Jewish general, Bar Kochba, and his rabbinic sponsor, the great sage, Rabbi Akiva. Bar Kochba's defeat left hundreds of thousands of Jews dead. The Land of Israel lay in shambles and was desolate for the next 1,900 years.

▸ Greece and Rome Today

Ancient Greece and Rome no longer exist. Despite nostalgic pretenses, today's inhabitants of Rome and Greece have very little genuine connection with the ancient Greeks or Romans.

Nor do they in any way retain or relate to the culture and heritage of the ancient Greeks, despite their wishful thinking. Their connection with ancient times was severed by the conquest of their lands by barbaric hordes and by other cultures and empires, as well as their later adoption of Christianity. We find the ancient Greeks and Romans today in the dust of archaeology, in their literature, their art, and in history books. Their civilization is long dead. The great minds of Sophocles, Socrates, Plato and Aristotle have long lost their attraction for modern philosophical thinkers.

▶ How Did the Jews Defeat the Greeks and the Romans?

In a deeper and much more ultimate sense, both Greece and Rome were defeated by the Jews when the former nations totally abandoned their pagan beliefs, thought system, mythology, philosophy and social structure, and in a limited form, accepted the world view of the Jews. Today's Greeks and Romans are descendants of people who converted to Christianity in the fourth century of the Common Era and, in so doing, accepted major principles of the Jewish Bible as the new basis for their lives. Notions of universal human equality, universal Sabbath rest, the significance of family, of one all-powerful G-d, morality, a spiritual afterlife, the concepts of salvation, messiah, creation and so much more, were Jewish "innovations" the Greeks and Romans had rejected for many years and later accepted when they adopted Christianity.

While the differences and disagreements between Judaism and Christianity are fundamental, broad, and deep, nonetheless at least in certain terms, Christianity represents the attempt of a deviant Jewish sect to disseminate and impose their altered form of Judaism on the world. The fact remains that by accepting the Bible, the Greeks accepted a revolutionary change in their way of life and in the way they worshipped. Basically, this represented an acceptance of a somewhat "Jewish" viewpoint of life and the abandonment of their own.

▶ Five Unanswered Questions

During my brief visit to their country, I asked a number of Greeks who seemed intelligent and educated:

Why did the Greeks adopt the Jewish worldview after so fiercely opposing it?

What happened to the intellectual impulses that had fired and motivated the Greek search for truth?

Why didn't the era of the great Greek philosophers continue through the ages as it did for the Jews, to whom thought has always been at the core of their lives?

Why didn't their adoption of the Jewish Bible (through Christianity) lead to a further study of Judaism and a refinement of their religious faith? It must be noted that the Egyptian, Babylonian, Phoenician, Mesopotamian and Persian religious systems were basically copycat pagan systems which revered and searched for the Divine, but did not have a clue as to where to find it. These nations left no meaningful religious literature, indicating the absence of a serious attempt to create a worldview that dealt with life's basic issues. In contrast, the ancient Greeks, basically the Athenians, created a literature and thought system that demonstrated a serious search for truth. Why did this search stop at Christian dogma and not seek deeper truths?

Furthermore, if the Greeks and the Romans were convinced that their paganism and all the ancillary societal, philosophical and religious approaches with which they had experimented failed to offer satisfactory answers, why did they accept Christianity which, at best, was extremely superficial? The Greek population did not study the Jewish Bible, the Jewish thought system and the *mitzvos* with the same depth, seriousness and scholarship with which they created their own thought system and writings at the height of their culture. In addition, they infused their own version of Christianity with generous doses of their discarded pagan thought and practices, which included familiar vestiges of their abandoned and rejected culture.

In other words, why didn't the Greeks utilize their piercing, intellectual powers to follow the path of their initial confrontation with Judaism to its logical conclusions by adopting the pure monotheism of Judaism together with its all-encompassing and rich system of literature, thought and *mitzvah* practice? One would expect that a nation which had developed a unique form of intellectualism that at one time pervaded the entire known world would try to continue that tradition.

We know that many individual Greeks and Romans did, in fact, do so. According to some sources, including Josephus, thousands of Romans, including prominent members of the aristocracy, converted to Judaism. But they did not create a lasting indigenous movement.

▸ Western Civilization and Judaism

Finally, why is it that there is no contemporary attempt to confront this mystery? Why does a major portion of the civilized world practice religions that drew their power and strength from Judaism; that attempted in some limited form to emulate the exemplary life of the Jews they met throughout Palestine and the Diaspora — and stopped at the point of a serious, in-depth study of the Jewish viewpoint? It is estimated that following the *Churban*, the destruction of Jerusalem, the Holy Temple and the Jewish state, Jews constituted 10% of the population of the Mediterranean basin. Why did relatively few Greeks and Romans in ancient times have the courage and intellectual honesty to fully examine the root source and foundation of their newly adopted lifestyle?

▸ Why Did the Greeks Stop Thinking?

Interestingly, the people to whom I posed these questions acknowledged that the questions were valid. They pressed me to propose answers. I replied, "Follow the example of your ancestors, Sophocles, Plato and Aristotle, and search for answers. Ask yourselves the following questions: Why are the Jews an eternal people who, despite the attempt of the Greeks, Romans, Persians, Egyptians, Babylonians, Assyrians, indeed almost every empire, to destroy them, remain a dynamic and critical force in the world today? Why is Greece today a backward country with so little to show of its former greatness and grandeur? Finally, why aren't these questions posed and why is there so little search for truth?"

A final comment: Today's Greece is a pathetic shadow of ancient Greece. It is a drab, colorless, country that lacks serious power, industry, technology, creative thinkers, religious or secular leaders. Its ancient writings have left no living heritage. All that remains is the memory of their past. Who today has taken the place of the ancient Greeks and attempts to complete the task they initiated?

What Christianity provided for them was a half-baked, semi-pagan, semi-monotheistic system that led Europe into the Dark Ages. For generations, thought, inquiry, literacy, education, philosophy, technology and science were suppressed. Their ancestors' thirst for truth was squelched and almost all voices of creative scholarship or intellectualism were stilled.

▸ The West's Dead End

The West has by now come to a philosophical and theological dead end. It has, however, accomplished two things — it has abandoned the iron vise of paganism and has hitched its wagon to a weak derivative of Judaic monotheism. It has also co-opted the Bible as its wellspring of inspiration and values. Yet, it has consistently ignored Judaism's Oral Tradition and the many Bible commentaries that succeed in converting the Bible from a sealed and enigmatic text to one which, in its original Hebrew, provides refreshing, meaningful answers and truths. Unable to face the contradictions and inconsistencies of the Christian scriptures and the horrific record of Church corruption, prejudice, inhumanity, hatred, narrowness and anti-Semitism which have plagued so much of its history, Western civilization — for all its glowing technological achievements — refuses to think through its adoption of monotheism to a logical conclusion.

We know that the day will come when the truths of Judaism in their pure form will be understood and accepted by the world-at-large. And while it's true that Jewish scholars debate whether the introduction of Christianity was a step toward or a step away from that goal, some of the concepts that originated in Judaism have replaced the totally pagan ideas in the Western world. Perhaps the world will start thinking again. Perhaps it will take outright miracles to begin that process anew. In either case, the Jewish People must continue to set a moral, ethical, intellectual and spiritual example that cannot be ignored or denied by anyone. In that way, the pure truth of Torah will be recognized when the right time comes.

FOR TORAH TO SURVIVE, IT IS NECESSARY TO SACRIFICE

33

The Jewish conflict with Greece represented the first instance of a foreign power demanding that Israel betray its Torah. The Jewish response was to fight to the death; but this happened only once the Jews realized that the very survival of the Jewish People was at stake and that there was no alternative.

The Greeks were determined to destroy traditional Jewish religion. They demanded that the Jews abandon their ancestral faith in its entirety. The response of the Maccabees and their followers called for total loyalty to G-d and to the uniqueness of the Jewish Nation as the Torah Nation. The Maccabees realized that victory demanded a readiness to sacrifice one's life rather than betray the Torah. At first, too few Jews understood what the goals of the Greeks and their "left wing" secular Jewish allies truly were, but once the stakes became clear, more and more people joined the Maccabean brothers in their uprising.

▸ How Purim and Chanukah Differ

The Purim crisis differed from the Chanukah crisis. While Haman wanted to destroy the Jewish body, the Greeks wanted to destroy the Jewish soul. The battle lines formed slowly because most Jews did not at first understand what was at stake. The Jewish rebellion did not materialize until the Greeks actually insisted that the Jews betray their claim to a unique relationship with G-d and demanded that they turn their backs on their heritage entirely by accepting the Greek way of life. The Greeks essentially demanded that the Jews write a "giant sign" on the horns of their oxen stating: "I am no longer loyal to the G-d of Israel." (This would be equivalent to our putting a huge sign to that effect on the windshields of our cars.)

▸ The Readiness to Sacrifice

Because the Jews refused to obey, because of the Jews' readiness to sacrifice their lives to defend and uphold their spiritual identity, as was done by thousands of loyal Jews throughout the Chanukah saga, they created an indelible, lasting and historic impression. Through the events of Chanukah, we see the actualization of the teaching of our Sages that "the events that were experienced by our forefathers are an eternal signpost for their children." Just as our patriarch Jacob earned the name *Israel* as the result of a life and death struggle with the Angel of Esau, so too did the Maccabean struggle cause the title "Israel" to be confirmed forever as the name of the Jewish nation.

The confirmation of this title was the result of the Jews' life and death struggle with Greece; it was the reward for their readiness for total self-sacrifice in the battle for Jewish spiritual survival. When the Jews chose loyalty to G-d over every other value in life, it was then that G-d forever chose the Jews.

Let us distinguish between the Jews becoming the Chosen People at Sinai and the concept expressed above. The Ramban and Rav Tzadok of Lublin teach that the Divine promise became eternally permanent in the great battles with the Greeks and Romans over Jewish survival. The Covenant between G-d and the Jewish People is eternal; for when He made the Covenant with the Jews, G-d clearly knew that Israel would be tested and would stand up to the challenge. When the Jews indeed fought for their spiritual survival, G-d's promise was vindicated. The bond between the Jewish People and G-d that began at Mount Sinai is compared to a wedding. A marriage becomes binding under the *chuppah*; it becomes eternal when it survives crisis. This was a love that was solidified through sacrifice. When they experienced their own resilience under impossible oppression and witnessed their miraculous survival, this love then became the eternal possession of the Jewish People.

CHANUKAH AND THE SYRIANS

34

▸ How Did the Syrians Find Their Way into Chanukah?

All Jewish sources describe Chanukah as a conflict between Israel and Greece. Yet, I recall that as a child that whenever Chanukah was discussed in speeches, in the press or in publications we were told that Chanukah was the celebration of the victory of the Jews over the Syrians. The obvious answer is that in the 1930s and '40s Reform spokesmen dominated English language Jewish literature and the Jewish media. Reform spokespeople and educators could not conceive or tolerate the idea of Judaism in confrontation with Greek culture. Greece was idealized as the fountainhead of Western civilization, the cradle of democracy, equality, philosophy, art, architecture, music, sports — all the good things of civilization. To their minds, Jews (despite their "authorship" of the Bible and their "invention" of monotheism) were, at best, semi-primitives who could not and would not confront the great and mighty Greek culture. Chanukah was, therefore, described as a conflict with the Syrians: in this way, a major conflict of intellect and civilization between the world's two major ancient civilizations could be downgraded to a minor military skirmish. As a result, Chanukah was trivialized; a major event in world history was relegated to a sideshow of little real importance.

▸ What Was the Real Conflict About?

At the time of the Chanukah rebellion, Greek philosophy, literature, music and architecture had become the pervasive culture of the Middle East, including what is today Syria. The Jewish conflict with Greek culture inflicted significant wounds on Jewish society that almost led to its destruction and disintegration. The lure of Greek sports, Greek mythology and idolatry, the Greek worship of the human body and Greek promotion of many forms of promiscuity sent shock waves through Jewish society.

A sufficient number of powerful and wealthy Jews had accepted Greek ways, some partially and others fully. The Greek military government, headquartered in Syria, was led to believe by Hellenized Jews (including the corrupt High Priest of the Holy Temple) that Greek influence had so weakened traditional Jewish society that if the Greeks forbade the practice of the Jewish religion and instituted Greek idols and worship in the Jerusalem Temple, they would meet little or no resistance. The Greeks acted on this advice and ruthlessly proceeded with their plans.

The masses of Jews, especially those who lived outside the large cities, wanted to remain Torah-observant Jews but lacked the will, the determination, the idealism, the means and the leadership to resist the power of the Hellenized Jewish aristocracy and the Greek military government. The Greek army controlled all public institutions and had the ability to suppress, persecute and subjugate the people. Never before had the Torah People met such determined and massive opposition. The Jews had no army to speak of; the people were traumatized and demoralized. Their spirit deadened, they all but folded in the face of Greek power.

▶ Chanukah: The First Rebellion

Then, out of the blue, the beginnings of a rebellion erupted. Led by Matisyahu and his five sons, a small secret underground army began to coalesce. Believing that G-d would help them face impossible odds, they encouraged young Jews to join their ranks and urged the people to resist the Greek anti-Torah edicts. Thousands of heroes arose, ready to give their lives to sanctify the Divine Name. (The most poignant story, perhaps, is that of Hannah, who was forced to witness the brutal executions of each of her seven sons as they resisted the Greek demands.) Indeed, as we affirm in *Al Hanissim,* "the few defeated the many, and the pure defeated the impure."

Chanukah was the first rebellion of men of faith against a world power that thought it could impose its will and get away with it. As such, through the ages it has inspired many people in countries throughout the world. Chanukah taught that even if they were few, G-d would side with those who were loyal to His Torah and commandments. In the end, Greece and its corrupt pagan society collapsed into the dustbin of history while Torah remains the most dynamic thought system in the world.

THE ETERNAL
MENORAH

35

The golden Menorah in the *Beis Hamikdash* represents the wisdom of Torah. The miracle of Chanukah is the miracle of the Jewish victory over the Greek attempt to force the Jewish People to abandon and forget Torah. Despite the fierce effort of the Greeks and their Jewish Hellenist allies to destroy every shred of Jewish loyalty to Torah, Torah and its wisdom survived and emerged strengthened and vigorous.

When the Romans destroyed the *Beis Hamikdash* in the year 70 CE, its entire elaborate system of worship, sacrifice, music, ceremony and prayer ceased to exist. Only two functions of the *Beis Hamikdash* survived its destruction — the Blessing of the *Kohanim* and the golden Menorah. How did the Menorah survive? It survived through its transformation from an instrument of the totality of the Jewish People, a symbol of *Klal Yisrael*, into an instrument of each individual Jew. Now the Menorah would cast the light of Torah in the home of each individual.

▸ The Temple Menorah in Your Home?

"How would you feel," asked Rabbi Yitzchok Hutner (during a Chanukah lecture in 5739), "if the golden Menorah of the *Beis Hamikdash* were placed in *your* home? You would be overwhelmed, you would not know what to do with it!" This is exactly what happened, and this is the real miracle of Chanukah. The placing of the Chanukah menorah in each Jewish home represents the continuation of the golden Menorah of the *Beis Hamikdash*. The holiness of the menorah in each Jewish home derives from the holiness of the Menorah in the *Beis Hamikdash*. Through the Chanukah menorah, we bring the holiness of the *Beis Hamikdash* and the eternity and indestructibility of Torah wisdom into our homes. Because the Chanukah menorah is today's Temple menorah, we have been granted the right to say in our Chanukah prayer, *Haneiros Halalu,* that which we were able to say only of the Temple Menorah, "These lights are holy, we have no authority to make use of their light, only to look at them."

▸ Why Can't We Use the Chanukah Lights?

Why are we not allowed to make use of the Chanukah lights? Because they represent the "hidden light that was concealed for the righteous in the World to Come."[1] If the Chanukah lights represent the *ohr ganuz*, the hidden light, why are we allowed to see them? Because the light of the golden Menorah represents the eternity and indestructibility of Torah. The light of the Temple Menorah and the menorah in our homes is the light of Torah, which carries the Divine promise that Torah will always succeed in overcoming the attempts of the world's civilizations and their Jewish allies to impose their culture on us, no matter how sophisticated or intellectual they may seem to be. The menorah declares that the Jewish People are an eternal people; that we have survived the attempt of each major world civilization to destroy us and we will continue to do so. It also attests to the ability of the Jewish People who are dedicated to the Torah to defeat our internal enemies, the Hellenists, who in each age undermine and deny the Torah's truth.

The Temple lies desolate and destroyed, but its Menorah lives on — because the Menorah and its light are eternal. The ultimate Temple is the Torah purity of our homes and hearts. It is for this reason that we bring the menorah into our homes and are permitted to see its light.

▸ The Chanukah Miracle

The real miracle of Chanukah is that the Torah survived as a viable force despite the fact that its champions represented a tiny minority of Jewish People. The miracle of Chanukah is the transformation of the *mitzvah* of the communal Holy Temple Menorah into the personal Chanukah menorah lit in each Jewish home. It is the ability of the Jew to bring the light of Torah into his or her home, despite the Greeks' defilement of the Temple and the Romans' destruction of the Temple. The "Eternal People" lives on because Torah is eternal. We live on because we have maintained the light of Torah in our homes and in our hearts in the face of exile and persecution.

The rebuilding of the Temple and the lighting of the Temple Menorah will take place when we succeed in relighting the menorah in the hearts of a majority of Jews. Then we will do precisely what the Maccabees did when the light of the Torah was almost extinguished: we will relight it through our idealism and dedication.

1. *Chagigah* 12a.

THE CHANUKAH VICTORY AND THE CHANUKAH MIRACLE

36

While the Talmud places special emphasis on the miracle of the oil and the lights of the Menorah — thus giving specific weight to the spiritual side of the Chanukah miracle — the Sages of the Mishnah who composed the prayers and blessings associated with Chanukah omitted the miracle of the Menorah and emphasized the military victories.

▸ The Military Victory vs. the Tiny Lights

Examine carefully *Haneiros Halalu* ("These lights..."), which we recite when we kindle the Chanukah lights, and *Al Hanissim* ("Concerning the miracles..."), which is included in the *Shacharis, Minchah* and *Ma'ariv* prayers as well as in *Birkas*

Hamazon (Grace After Meals) during the eight days of Chanukah. It is obvious that our Sages considered the military victories the primary spiritual achievement of Chanukah. Rabbi Tzadok HaKohen Rabinowitz of Lublin, the great Chassidic thinker, writing in his classic *Pri Tzaddik,* says that "the essential miracle of Chanukah is that the *Chashmonaim,* who were so few in number, were able to be victorious over the Greeks who ruled over the entire world and who were overwhelmingly numerous."

While many modern Jews may think of the Chanukah military victory in the context of the victories of great modern armies such as the Israeli Defense Forces or the American army, which would give them a secular or nationalistic coloration, nothing could be further from the truth. When the confrontation between the Jews and the Greeks took place, the Jews did not have a standing army and Judea was a vassal state, lacking political independence. In fact, even after the Chanukah victory over the Greeks, Judea didn't achieve full political independence for an additional 20 years. The Maccabean rebellion was a powerful spiritual, religious and intellectual response to the Greek campaign to destroy Judaism and its adherents. Were it not for the spiritual reasons, there would have been no reason at all for a military confrontation with the Greek authorities.

This analysis is clearly supported by the Book of Maccabees I, which is the major source for the history of those times. The first downhill steps were taken by those Jews who decided to follow Greek ways and were anxious to convince their fellow Jews to emulate them.

▸ The Book of Maccabees I

> *A scion of this stock was that wicked man, Antiochus Epiphanes, son of King Antiochus. He had been a hostage in Rome before he succeeded to the throne in the year 137 of the Greek era.*

At that time, there appeared in Israel a group of rene-
gade Jews who incited the people. "Let us enter into a
covenant with the gentiles round about," they said,
"because disaster upon disaster has overtaken us since
we segregated ourselves from them." The people
thought this a good argument, and some of them in
their enthusiasm went to the Greek king and received
authority to introduce non-Jewish laws and customs.
They built a sports stadium in the gentile style in
Jerusalem. They removed their marks of circumcision
and repudiated the holy covenant. They intermarried
with gentiles, and abandoned themselves to evil ways.[1]

This description of the era might explain why the *Al Hanissim*
prayer, which our Sages inserted into the *Shmoneh Esrei* and
Birkas Hamazon, does not mention the miracle of the oil at all. It
speaks clearly of "the miracles, salvations, mighty deeds, victories and battles that G-d performed for our ancestors in those
days, in this season."

You delivered the strong into the hands of the
weak and many into the hands of the few and the
impure into the hands of the pure. For Yourself,
You created great renown and sanctity in Your
world. And for Your people, Israel, You worked a
great victory and salvation.

Immediately following the lighting of the Chanukah candles on
each evening of Chanukah, we recite *Haneiros Halalu*, which says,
"These lights we kindle to mark the miracles, the wonders, the
salvations and the battles which You performed for our forefathers in those days, at this season."

▸ *There Was No Alternative*

This emphasis stems from the reaction of our Sages to the
Jewish resistance movement that was organized specifical-

ly as a response to the Greek prohibition of the observance of the commandments and the study of Torah. The Greeks converted the Holy Temple into a center for Zeus worship, where they sacrificed pigs and instituted "religious prostitution."

The reaction of the pious population of Judea to these outrageous edicts was one of horror, fear and consternation. When they realized that there was no reasoning with the Greeks or the Hellenists (their Jewish fellow travelers), they knew there was no alternative to a military confrontation. They fought with fury and dedication. They also knew that without Divine support, there was no possible way that they could overcome the mighty forces and sophisticated military equipment of the Greeks. Matisyahu and his sons fashioned the formula with which to unite the people and then confronted the Greek armies. Theirs was a war for spiritual goals.

▸ The Role of the Hellenists

The citation above from Maccabees I refers to renegade Jews, a reference to a significant sector of the Jewish population who promoted the spread of Greek ideas, philosophy, sports and religion among the Jews. *Misyavnim,* or Hellenists, is the traditional name for this group of Jews who wanted to abandon their ancestral religion and absorb the Greek way of life into the body of Israel. It is noteworthy that Rabbi Joseph Ber Soloveitchik stated that when the Sages spoke of the edicts and persecutions of the Greeks, they were alluding to the Jewish Hellenists. It was they who were the force behind the Greek repression.[2]

What caused this confrontation? The Greek king, Antiochus Epiphanes, made a political decision that all nations in his empire were to abandon their local culture and religious practices so as to become homogenized into the Greek empire. He would not have taken these steps unless he had the full backing of the powerful Hellenists who constituted a significant element of Jewish society.

The king then issued a decree throughout his empire: His subjects were all to become one people and abandon their own laws and religion. The nations everywhere complied with the royal command, and many in Israel accepted the foreign worship, sacrificing to idols and profaning the Sabbath. Moreover, the king sent agents with written orders to Jerusalem and the towns of Judea. Ways and customs foreign to Judea were to be introduced. Burnt offerings, sacrifices and libations in the Temple were forbidden; Sabbaths and feast-days were to be profaned; the Temple and its Priests are to be defiled. Altars, idols and sacred precincts were to be established throughout the country; swine and other non-kosher beasts are to be offered in sacrifice. They must leave their sons uncircumcised; they must make themselves in every way abominable, unclean and profane, and so forget the Torah and change all their statutes. The penalty for disobedience was death.

Such was the decree that the king issued to all his subjects. He appointed superintendents over all the people, and instructed the towns of Judea to offer sacrifices, town by town. People thronged to their side in large numbers, every one of them a traitor to the Torah. Their wicked conduct throughout the land drove the loyal Jews into hiding in every possible place of refuge.

On the fifteenth day of the month Kislev, the "abomination of desolation" was set up on the Temple Altar. Pagan altars were built throughout the towns of Judea; incense was offered at the doors of houses and in the streets. All scrolls of the Torah that were found were torn up and burnt. Anyone discovered in possession of a Torah scroll or conforming to a Torah law was put to death by the king's sentence. Thus month after month, these wicked men used their power against the Israelites whom they found in their towns.

On the twenty-fifth day of the month, they offered a sacrifice on the pagan altar, which was on top of the Altar of the L-rd. In accordance with the royal decree, they put to death women who had had their children circumcised. Their babies, their families and those who had circumcised them, they hanged by the neck. Yet many in Israel found strength to resist, taking a determined stand against eating non-kosher food. They welcomed death rather than defile themselves and profane the holy Covenant, and so they died. The Divine wrath raged against Israel.[3]

▸ Only One Nation Refused to Comply

O f all the nations in the grip of the Greek domain, one nation alone offered resistance. Only the Jews insisted on maintaining their own unique spiritual way of life. The prospects of the success of the feeble, untrained and outnumbered forces of the Hasmonean Maccabees were dim. Yet their profound faith, prayers, determination and willingness to die for the cause of Torah-true Judaism evoked the miraculous response of Heaven.

The revolt of Matisyahu and his sons was provoked by the following event:

The king's officers who were enforcing apostasy came to the town of Modin to see that sacrifice was offered, and many Israelites went over to them. Matisyahu [Mattathias] and his sons stood in a group. The king's officers spoke to Matisyahu: "You are a leader here," they said, "a man of mark and influence in this town, with your sons and brothers at your back. You be the first now to come forward and carry out the king's order. All the nations have

*done so, as well as the leading men in Judea and
the people left in Jerusalem. Then, you and your
sons will be enrolled among the King's Friends; you
will all receive high honors, rich rewards of silver
and gold, and many further benefits."*

*To this, Matisyahu replied in a ringing voice,
"Though all the nations within the king's dominions
obey him and forsake their ancestral worship,
though they have chosen to submit to his commands, yet I and my sons and brothers will follow
the Covenant of our fathers. Heaven forbid that we
should ever abandon the Torah and its statutes. We
will not obey the command of the king, nor will we
deviate one step from our forms of worship."*

*As soon as he had finished, a Jew stepped forward
in full view of all to sacrifice a pig on the pagan altar
at Modin, in obedience to the royal command. The
sight stirred Matisyahu to indignation; he shook with
passion, and in a fury of righteous anger rushed forward and slaughtered the traitor on the very altar. At
the same time, he killed the officer sent by the king
to enforce pagan sacrifice, and pulled the pagan altar
down. Thus Matisyahu showed his fervent zeal for
the Torah, just as Pinchas had done by killing Zimri,
son of Salu. "Follow me," he shouted through the
town, "every one of you who is zealous for the Torah
and strives to maintain the Covenant." He and his
sons took to the hills, leaving all their belongings
behind in the town.*[4]

Following the initial Maccabean military foray against the
forces of Antiochus, the Greek generals assembled an army of
40,000 foot soldiers and 7,000 cavalry, augmented by reinforcements from the standing armies of southern Syria and the coastal
regions of Philistia. Against this force, Judah Maccabee assembled a force of 4,000 men, divided into four battalions of 1,000
men each. He then announced, in keeping with the laws of raising
a Jewish army set forth in Deuteronomy 20:19, that "those who

have recently married, built houses or have planted vineyards should leave the army and return home." He exhorted the remaining men to trust in G-d, saying, "It is better for us to die in battle than to witness the ruin of our nation and our Temple."

When Judah ordered his soldiers to attack, he broke the Syrian/Greek orderly phalanxes, which resulted in a panicked retreat. The Jews decimated the entire Greek rear, set fire to the Greek camp and pursued the fleeing enemy, killing 3,000 soldiers during the chase. When the rest of the Greek army saw the fire rising from their retreating forces, they panicked and fled the battlefield.

In the following year, the Greeks sent a stronger force consisting of 60,000 infantry and 5,000 cavalry. By then, Judah had assembled a force of 10,000 loyal Jews.

▶ Judah's Victory

Judah's army attacked the strong Greek force and killed 5,000 soldiers. The Greeks, seeing the determination of the Jews to die rather than surrender, despaired of victory over the rebels and returned to their capital. The above miracles were blatant and visible to all who lived in the Land of Israel at that time. Indeed, the Temple miracle was a significant miracle, but it should be understood that miracles were so common in the Temple that were this one not so symbolically significant and morally important, following immediately after the Maccabean victories and the retaking and cleansing of the Temple, it might have even gone unnoticed. Its symbolism was a message from G-d, whose Presence resided in the Temple, that the willingness of the loyal Jews to oppose the Greeks and the Jewish Hellenists with their lives had the blessing of Heaven. The miracle of the Temple assured the people that this was indeed an authentic and truly miraculous victory that flowed from the devotion of the masses to their spiritual heritage and their love of the Temple and its service.

This is how the Book of Maccabees I describes the victory and the victory celebration:

But Judas [Judah] and his brothers said, "Now that our enemies have been crushed, let us go up to Jerusalem to cleanse the Temple and rededicate it." So the whole army was assembled and went up to Mount Zion. There, they found the Temple laid waste, the Altar profaned, the gates burned down, the courts overgrown like a thicket or wooded hillside and the Priests' rooms in ruin. They tore their garments, wailed loudly, put ashes on their heads and fell on their faces to the ground. They sounded the shofar and the trumpets, and cried aloud to Heaven.

Then Judas detailed troops to engage the Greek garrison of the Citadel while he cleansed the Temple. He selected Priests without blemish, devoted to the Torah, and they purified the Temple, removing to an unclean place the stones that defiled it. They discussed what to do with the Altar of burnt offering, which was profaned, and rightly decided to demolish it for fear it might become a standing reproach to them, because it had been defiled by the gentiles. They, therefore, pulled down the Altar, and stored the stones in a fitting place on the Temple Mount until a prophet should arise who could be consulted about what to do with them. They took unhewn stones, as Torah law commands, and built a new Altar on the model of the previous one. They rebuilt the Temple, restored its interior and consecrated the Temple courts. They renewed the sacred vessels and the Menorah and brought the Altar of Incense and the Table of the Showbread into the Temple. They burnt incense on the Altar and lit the lights on the Menorah to shine within the Temple. When they had put the Bread of the Presence on the table of the Showbread and hung the curtains, all their work was completed.

Then, early on the twenty-fifth day of the ninth month, the month Kislev, sacrifice was offered as Torah law commands on the newly made Altar of

burnt offering. On the anniversary of the day when
the gentiles had profaned it, on that very day, it was
rededicated, with hymns of thanksgiving, to the
music of harps, flutes and cymbals. All the people
prostrated themselves, worshipping and praising
Heaven that their cause had prospered.

They celebrated the rededication of the Altar for
eight days; there was great rejoicing as they brought
burnt-offerings and sacrificed peace offerings and
thanks-offerings. They decorated the front of the
Temple with golden wreaths and ornamental
shields. They renewed the gates and the Priests'
rooms, and fitted them with doors. There was great
merry-making among the people, and the disgrace
brought on them by the Greek gentiles was removed.

Then Judas, his brothers and the whole congre-
gation of Israel decreed that the rededication of the
Altar should be observed with joy and gladness at
the same season each year for eight days, begin-
ning on the twenty-fifth of Kislev.[5]

As Rabbi Tzadok HaKohen Rabinowitz of Lublin points out, following the victory, the people were not required to place themselves in danger for the Temple Menorah. They could have waited
until they had sufficient hallowed olive oil, but their love of G-d and
His sanctuary was so intense that they were determined to restore
immediately the Divine light to the Temple Menorah. When G-d
saw their zealousness and repentance, He responded with the miracle of the oil — an acknowledgement of their atonement and penitence for their previous lack of zealousness and devotion to the
Temple service.

---

1. *Maccabees I,* 1:10:15.
2. Quoted in Rabbi Herschel Schachter's volume on Rabbi Soloveitchik, *Nishmas Harav: Chanukah.*
3. *Maccabees I,* 1: 41-64.
4. *Maccabees I,* 2:15-28.
5. *Maccabees I,* 4:41-59.

INSIGHTS INTO THE CHANUKAH BLESSING

A ccording to the view of the Vilna Gaon, the formulation of the blessing on the Chanukah candles should be "*lehadlik ner Chanukah*, to kindle the Chanukah light," not "*ner **shel** Chanukah*, the light of Chanukah" which is the generally followed text. The difference in wording is subtle, but crucial.

The light we kindle on Shabbos (with the blessing *"lehadlik ner **shel** Shabbos"*) or Yom Tov is a light whose goal is to provide illumination. It is impossible to celebrate in darkness. We light up the house so that Shabbos or Yom Tov can be celebrated. The Shabbos and Yom Tov light is utilitarian.

The light of Chanukah is fundamentally different. It is a unique creation in its own right. It is *Chanukah light*. It is similar to the light of the Temple Menorah, which was not kindled in order to provide illumination. As we know, the Menorah was located in the *Heichal* in front of Holy of Holies. The purpose of the light of the Temple Menorah was to represent the light of Divinity, the light of Divine power, holiness and knowledge. This was the light of the wisdom of Torah, *chochmas haTorah*. The light of Chanukah was a continuation of the light of the *Beis Hamikdash*, a light that represents the inner light, the light of wisdom, the light of Torah.

"These lights are holy. We are not permitted to use them for any purpose, only to gaze upon them" (from *Haneiros Halalu*). These lights symbolize the light of spirituality, the light "concealed for the future use of the righteous." This is the first light that G-d created, even before He created the sun. It is the light of ultimate insight and wisdom, hidden by G-d so that it would only be used by the righteous.

▸ What is Chanukah?

The Gemara asks, "What is Chanukah?" Its response is that we are not allowed to mourn during Chanukah. On a deeper level, this means that we are not permitted to despair or be depressed during Chanukah. This is the essence of Chanukah. The Chanukah victory took place because the Maccabees refused to surrender to despair and depression. Despite the overwhelming numbers, power, arms and military training of their enemies, despite the fact that most of the loyal Jews were in despair, they put their trust in G-d. This was G-d's war, and He alone had the power to bring about victory. "Trust in G-d" is the essential message of Chanukah. As the Chazon Ish* said, "There is no such thing as sadness in this world if you are able to see the inner light of truth."

---

* A towering leader of Torah Jewry of the early twentieth century

HOW A TORAH RENAISSANCE WAS CREATED

Based on *Pachad Yitzchok*, Chanukah 3

▸ Chanukah and The Oral Torah

The Sages searched for a logical reason as to why the Talmudic tractate *Shabbos* begins with a discussion of the laws prohibiting carrying outdoors from indoors on Shabbos. The Maharal offers the following explanation: Since the laws of carrying do not apply on the festivals, the tractate *Shabbos* opens with laws that are unique to Shabbos. Extending this reasoning, the essence of *each* festival is revealed by understanding those laws or qualities that are unique to that festival.[1]

In the Chanukah hymn we sing, "*Az egmor b'shir mizmor Chanukas hamizbayach* — Then I shall conclude with a hymn to celebrate the dedication of the Temple Altar." The dedication of the Temple Altar, which will take place "*az*, then," in the Messianic era, will complete the Temple dedication of the Hasmoneans. Until the Sages had established Chanukah as a festival, the final section of the bridge that spans from the Exodus until the Messianic era had not yet been built. The establishment of Chanukah paved the final section on which the Jews will march in celebration of the dedication of the third *Beis Hamikdash*. Our singing of the Chanukah hymn today denotes the beginning of the process that will culminate in this ultimate dedication.

This idea calls for an explanation. The subjugation of the Jewish People to "four [foreign] kingdoms" is described in the vision of Daniel. Our Sages teach that this subjugation is so fundamental that it is prophetically rooted in the Torah's description of Creation. In the second sentence of Genesis, the four terms that precede "G-d's spirit" — "without form," "emptiness," "darkness" and "the face of the deep" — describe four kingdoms whose reign will precede the coming of the Messiah. "Without form" refers to Babylon; "emptiness" connotes Persia and Medea; "darkness" indicates Greece, which "darkened the eyes of Israel with its anti-Torah edicts"; and "the face of the deep" is Edom (i.e.: Rome/Western/Christian civilization).

The Jews' subjugation to the first three kingdoms took place in the past. We are presently subjugated to Edom/Rome, the fourth and last of the kingdoms. When we contrast our present subjugation to that of the first two kingdoms, Babylonia and Persia, no compelling parallels exist, but we do find significant parallels in our subjugation to Greece.

Our Sages taught[2] that Yose ben Yoezer and Yose ben Yochanan lived during the Greek persecution. They were the very first Sages who were in disagreement concerning a point in Torah law. (The first Torah disagreement relates to a question concerning the "laying of hands" on an animal about to be sacrificed during a festival.) This first Torah disagreement took place precisely when Greece began to "darken the eyes of Israel" through its anti-Torah decrees.[3]

While nothing lasting remained from the conflict with the first two kingdoms, the "Greek exile" is an exception. The goal of Greece was to compel the Jews to abandon the study and observance of Torah. The "darkness" imposed by Greece created forgetfulness. (Note the relationship of the Hebrew words *chashechah* and *shikchah*, i.e. darkness and forgetting.) And forgetfulness caused the first halachic disagreement among the Sages. Even though we were militarily victorious over Greece, a remnant of conflict remained: Henceforth Torah matters became subject to differing viewpoints.

(It is interesting to note that the Jewish victory was not complete until the oppressor had been completely vanquished. The confrontation between history's two great cultures, the Grecks and the Jews, was not concluded until it brought about disagreement among Torah scholars. The Jewish-Greek confrontation was not exclusively military and religious: It was deeply spiritual, ideological, philosophical and intellectual. Paradoxically, the Greek attempt to subdue the Torah by compelling Torah forgetfulness gave rise to a reinvigorated Torah strength that was instigated through the confrontation with Greek thought, values and morality.)

Of even greater significance is that all the disagreements of the Sages concerning Jewish law that were debated from then until today originate in that disagreement, whose source is the Greek effort to force the Jews to forget the Torah. A superficial examination of this occurrence could lead us to the conclusion that the disagreements relating to Torah law are battle scars of the struggle with the Greeks. Today we continue to be embroiled in this tragedy. Our Sages, however, bequeathed to us a much deeper understanding of this phenomenon.

This insight derives from the teaching of our Sages that, "There are occasions when the effort to destroy the Torah actually leads to its preservation."[4] How do we know this? When Moses descended Mt. Sinai and saw the Jews worshipping the Golden Calf, he smashed the Tablets of the Covenant. The Talmud explains that the term that G-d used when speaking about this incident with Moses, "*asher shibarta,*[5] that you smashed," can be rendered as "*yeyasher.*" Therefore, the term used in the Torah indicates that G-d was in effect saying to Moses, "I *commend* you for breaking the Tablets." Our Sages teach that were it not for the smashing of the Tablets, the Jewish

People would have been forever protected from forgetting any aspect of Torah.[6] The breaking of the first Tablets is the original cause of Torah forgetfulness.

A fascinating and novel concept emerges — that Torah forgetfulness can cause the enhancement of Torah. This truth is so significant that it is conceivable that under certain circumstances, as in the case of Moses, one actually deserves to be congratulated for causing Torah to be forgotten.

Our Sages taught, "Three hundred Torah laws were forgotten during the period of mourning for Moses. These laws were restored by Osniel ben K'naz through the use of logical inference."[7] The intellectual effort that brought about the restoration of these 300 laws created a significant body of Torah scholarship. This scholarship came about due to the earlier forgetting of Torah laws. In fact, all disagreements concerning Torah law were caused by Torah forgetfulness. Our Sages teach that despite the fact that there are Sages who say "sacred" and Sages who say "profane;" Sages who say "unkosher" and Sages who say "kosher;" Sages who say "guilty" and Sages who say "innocent," the sum total of their disagreement is that both opinions are "the words of the living G-d."[8] The end of this process is that all legitimate Torah disagreements enlarge and expand the Torah. And all of this Torah scholarship was created as a result of forgetfulness. (Note: While in each case the Sages arrive at a decision as to which viewpoint would be followed in practice, the viewpoint which was not accepted is still to be considered Torah, which means that it must be studied and understood.)

This phenomenon created an even greater innovation: namely, that the power of the unwritten Torah is much more pronounced when there is disagreement rather than agreement. Implicit in the concept that "both 'these and those' are the words of the living G-d" is the principle that even a minority opinion, which does *not* become operative Torah law, becomes an integral part of the corpus of Torah truth, providing it was expressed in accordance with the established rules of Torah argumentation set forth by our Sages. "Indeed, the Torah was given with the express purpose that it be studied and inter-preted by the Sages."[9] The Ramban teaches that "if for any rea-son the Sages of the Torah should gather at a later date and decide that from now on the law will follow the minority opin-ion, in that case the *halachah* [law] changes and the minority opinion becomes Torah-truth." (See the note in *Ohr Yisrael*, Chapter 30.)

The forgetting of Torah caused the flowering of Torah by pro-viding opportunities to uncover new Torah truths which other-wise would have remained concealed. It was an opportunity to reveal the hidden powers inherent in the Torah.

Disagreement reveals the power of the Unwritten Torah more so than agreement. The ongoing debate among the Sages, which establishes Torah law and determines Torah truth, is not just one method among many. Rather, Torah debate and struggle is a unique creation, a constructive method essential to creating Torah values which are not necessarily found in any other Torah source.

The book of Numbers (21:14) says, "And it is therefore told in the Book of G-d's Wars, as an utmost boundary, I have given you the streams of Arnon." The Hebrew words used in that passage *Es vahev = ahavah*, love; and *be'sufah* = disagreement indicate "Love emerging from disagreement."

According to our Sages[10] this means that when a father and son or a rabbi and his disciple vehemently argue over a point in the Torah they appear to behave like enemies; they do not budge from their places until they restore their harmony and love. At first blush it would appear that the purpose of these sentiments is to teach the strength of relationships among Torah scholars. So strong are these relationships that the constancy of their love is guaranteed despite their deep disagreement.

Since we earlier came to the conclusion that Torah debate engenders superior relationships and a higher degree of creativ-ity than can be attained through other types of Torah study, we now see that the love relationship that grows out of bitter Torah disputes intensifies as a result of disagreement. While each one forcefully puts forth his point of view, each becomes a partner in the creation of a new Torah value called the "Battles of Torah" — or "the struggle over Torah Truths."

Let us review our earlier discussion. Torah debates are an intrinsic element of Talmudic disputation that was born in the darkness of the Jewish encounter with Greece. What remains from the redemption from Greece? The victory of the Hasmoneans was a victory over the darkness imposed by the Greeks.

In the struggle with Greece, light was rescued from within darkness itself. Regarding Torah, the Sages taught, "Its abolition was its establishment."[11] "The evil kingdom of Greece arose against your People, Israel, to compel them to forget the Torah" (*Al Hanissim* Chanukah prayer). Thus, in this era of "forgetting," Torah debate brought about a renaissance, a redemptive renewal that restored the clarity of Torah.

Chanukah was the last Jewish holiday to be established. It seals the cycle of Jewish holidays for all times. Chanukah made possible the restoration of the intellectual power of Israel; it created an ingenious Jewish talent. It taught that forgetfulness stimulates renaissance, as demonstrated by the Greek exile. This continued during the Rome/Edom exile, building the bridge that will bring us to the End of Days.

"I will conclude with a hymn of thanksgiving when the Temple Altar is restored" (from the *Ma'oz Tzur* Chanukah hymn). The final triumph of the Messianic era will include our singing of the victory hymn when we dedicate the Temple Altar. This hymn will be the "conclusion" of our Chanukah hymn of today. The forgetfulness of exile will have brought about the full restoration of the glory of Torah.

▶ Concluding Comment

Greece was the first society in history that was not a worshipping society. While Israel based reality on spirituality, Greece was only interested in the material. Greece was self-centered; Israel was G-d-centered. The Greek claim to creativity in philosophy, literature, art, archaeology and architecture is a sham when one understands that Greece was a society based upon the worship of the human body, immorality, prostitution and the mass subjugation of women. The only Greeks who enjoyed rights and privileges were the 10% who were free male aristocrats. The balance consisted of slaves and the oppressed. In the struggle with Greece, light was rescued from within darkness itself. Torah was increased and enhanced as the result of the forgetting of Torah. The Sages taught, "Its abolition was its establishment." Just as the defeat of the Babylonians and the Medes brought about a healing of the subjugation of Israel, in the same fashion the defeat of Greece produced a healing salve that emerged from the plague itself.

1. *Gur Aryeh* on *Maseches Shabbos* 2a.
2. *Seder Hadoros* 4, also *Bereishis Rabbah* 65.
3. *Chagigah* 16a, see *Rashi* and *Tosafos,* also *Temurah* 16a.
4. *Menachos* 99b.
5. *Exodus* 34:1.
6. *Eruvin* 54a.
7. *Temurah* 16a.
8. *Chagigah* 3b, *Eruvin* 13b.
9. *Ramban* on *Deuteronomy* 17:11.
10. *Kiddushin* 30b.
11. *Menachos* 99b.

THE MENORAH AND THE JEWISH MESSIANIC MISSION

39

Based on an unpublished Chanukah lecture by
Rabbi Yitzchok Hutner (5739)

very morning the Jew prays for two qualities, each of which seems to contradict the other. The first request is, "Habituate us in the study of Torah." The second is, "Make the study of Torah sweet and enjoyable."

We pray that Torah become so totally integrated into our personalities that it becomes *habit*. The flip side of the sweetness and pleasure of Torah study is the sweat and effort it demands. Habit is the opposite of effort. The Talmud teaches that when Torah study is not permissible, "we should study Torah through habit" (by reviewing something we know well) to the point where it can hardly be considered Torah "study."[1]

Both habit and effort are required if we are to achieve Torah growth. Habit and effort are not truly at odds. If we study by rote, there is little growth or satisfaction; if there is satisfaction, it requires effort, not rote. Yet Torah growth comes about as the result of our acquiring habitual skills. These skills are the facilitators of intellectual maturation and growth. It is impossible to master any area of knowledge until you have mastered the fundamentals. If the *aleph-beis* is not ingrained in your mind, you can never become an expert reader. This basic principle describes all educational endeavors. You cannot reach for the heights until you have climbed the lower rungs. With each climb upward, the sweetness of the next rung of intellectual discovery unfolds. Indeed, the triumph of Torah in the Messianic age will take place when habit and creativity harmoniously merge and function in a mystical tandem that is beyond our comprehension.

Chanukah initiates our plea to G-d that Torah will become both habitual and creative. The root of the word Chanukah is *chinuch* [education], which we define as habitual education which promotes creative growth.

As we internalize knowledge and transform it into habit, the sweetness of the next step unfolds, thus catapulting the student from elementary to higher education. When we say that a person is of good character, we infer that his fine traits have become second nature. An educated person is one who has mastered his subject to the point where it has become second nature.

Habit liberates our creative powers, thus enabling our Torah study to become pleasurable. How do habit and creativity mesh in the context of Torah? The answer is found in the Chanukah *Al Hanissim* prayer:

> *You enabled the weak to overcome the strong, the holy to overcome the profane. And for Yourself, You created a great and holy Name in Your world.*

For hundreds of years prior to the Hasmonean struggle, Jews proclaimed in their prayers, "You are Holy, and Your Name is Holy." Why did the Chanukah prayer add the phrase, "And for Yourself, You created a great and holy Name in Your world"? Why is this phrase unique to the Chanukah prayer?

Let us look at similar statements. The statement concerning the splitting of the Reed Sea is clear in Nehemiah 9:10: "You made a Name for Yourself on that day"[when You split the sea for Israel]. The splitting of the Reed Sea resulted in the creation of the Jewish

Nation: *Klal Yisrael* was born at that moment, and G-d's Name achieved renown. The prophet Isaiah writes that G-d created the Jewish Nation to sing His praises, i.e. to serve as a vehicle to make G-d's Name known and exalted throughout the world. "I created this Nation so that it would recount My praises."[2]

Referring back to the Chanukah *Al Hanissim*, ("You created a great and holy Name in Your world") we may ask: How was G-d's great and holy Name made even greater on Chanukah? And why do we add the words, "*b'olamecha*, in Your world"?

During the era of the Second Temple, the Jews were saved from many afflictions. Each affliction and redemption was recorded in a Talmudic-period volume called *Megillas Ta'anis* (The Scroll of Prohibited Fast Days). The events described in *Megillas Ta'anis* established days on which Jews are not permitted to fast or eulogize the dead.

As long as the Second *Beis Hamikdash* stood, the Ninth of Av, the Seventeenth of Tamuz and the Tenth of Teves were observed as joyous days, as Yom Tov days. The redemptions and celebrations of those days had their source in the *Beis Hamikdash*. With its destruction, the basis for this joy ceased to exist. The strength and merit of the *Beis Hamikdash* vanished. The days described in *Megillas Ta'anis* were either abolished or were transformed into fast days.

According to the Talmud,[3] Chanukah, too, is mentioned in *Megillas Ta'anis*. Chanukah was established thanks to a redemption that took place during the Second Temple era. Why wasn't Chanukah also abolished as a day of joy? Why do its prohibitions against fasting and mourning remain in force to this day? The Talmud replies that Chanukah differs from the other days mentioned in *Megillas Ta'anis* because it contains *mitzvah* observances, as opposed to the other days described in *Megillas Ta'anis*.

Rashi teaches that the Talmud's reference to *mitzvos* includes all the *mitzvos* of Chanukah: lighting the menorah, reciting *Hallel*, *Al Hanissim*, etc. Chanukah is unique in that it contains these *mitzvos*. Rabbeinu Chananel adopted a radically different approach by teaching that "Chanukah differs in that it contains one *mitzvah* —

the lighting of the menorah." Why does Rabbeinu Chananel place exclusive emphasis on the *mitzvah* of the menorah?

At the beginning of *Beha'aloscha,* Ramban discusses the fact that Aaron, the High Priest, was dejected when the princes of each of the twelve tribes offered sacrifices during the dedication of the *Mishkan* (Tabernacle) and its Altar, while he was assigned no role. Rashi conments that G-d told Aaron, "Your portion is greater than theirs, because you will light the Menorah." The Ramban asks: "Why didn't G-d console Aaron by mentioning the many sacrifices and Temple rituals reserved exclusively for him and the *Kohanim*?" He then explains that the princes brought sacrifices, but that sacrifices will cease when the *Beis Hamikdash* will be destroyed. However, the Menorah will "continue" to be kindled in the form of the Chanukah menorah, long after the destruction of the Second *Beis Hamikdash*. Upon hearing this promise of eternal observance, Aaron was consoled.

The Ramban then quotes a *Breisa* that discusses *Birkas Kohanim*, the Priestly Blessing: "While the *Beis Hamikdash* was the essential locale of the Priestly Blessing, it was also pronounced outside of the *Beis Hamikdash*. It, too, survived the Temple's destruction. The rule which applies to the Priestly Blessing also applies to the kindling of the Menorah." The redemption from Greek oppression highlights these aspects of the *Beis Hamikdash* service that were not to be abolished even after the Temple was destroyed. Rabbeinu Chananel therefore states that "Chanukah is unique in that it contains one *mitzvah*," namely, the kindling of the menorah lights. Chanukah is distinguished from the other redemptions enumerated in *Megillas Ta'anis* in that the kindling of a menorah as a form of service originating in the *Beis Hamikdash* survived the destruction of the *Beis Hamikdash*. To that extent, then, the Temple was not completely destroyed.

In chapter 23 of II Samuel we learn that during one of King David's wars with the Philistines, David's camp was located on one side of the Philistine camp, while the Sanhedrin was located on the opposite side. David proclaimed, "Who will bring me water to drink from the well of Beis Lechem which is at the gate?"

The Sages explain that this is a reference to the Sanhedrin, which was located "at the gate." The Talmud[4] explains this incident as follows: King David had a halachic problem. He asked, "Who will bring me a p'sak (halachic decision) from the Sanhedrin to resolve my question?" Three heroes volunteered to steal through the Philistine camp to bring the "water" King David required. The Tanach says that King David "did not drink of these 'waters,' but poured them as a sacrifice to G-d."

What does this mean? The Sages teach that the three heroes endangered their lives and this is halachically forbidden. The Talmud asks, "What is the meaning of, 'David would not permit himself to drink of these waters'?" It then replies that when David repeated the Sanhedrin's halachic decision, he didn't teach it in the name of those who broke through the enemy lines; instead he repeated it "in the name of the tradition (Mishmei de'Gemara)."

The Mishnah says, "When one repeats a Torah teaching by citing the name of the person who first taught it, he brings Redemption to the world." King David remembered that the court of Samuel the Prophet taught that if someone endangers his life, even for the sake of Torah, we do not repeat halachic decisions in their name. King David realized that this prevented him from teaching this decision in the names of those who had passed through enemy lines to get the p'sak for him. They had violated the Torah mandate, "You shall guard your life very much." That King David was not permitted to transmit the halachah in their name, and was thereby barred from contributing to the Redemption of the world, was a form of punishment resulting from the fact that they had violated a halachah by endangering their lives. Thus, a Torah teaching produced by individuals was transformed into a collective teaching of Klal Yisrael.

Shimon HaTzaddik was the last of the Anshei Knesses Hagedolah, the "Men of the Great Assembly." During this era, the names of individual sages were also not cited. Their teachings are also quoted in the Talmud as collective teachings. The Anshei Knesses Hagedolah is a link in the chain of Torah transmission. While we do not have the key to the spiritual significance of each era of Torah transmission it was necessary that there exist a major era during which Torah transmission be formulated as the collective teaching of the Jewish People. This was a unique and heightened era during which all Torah creativity was collective.

Shimon HaTzaddik was the bridge between the era of the *Anshei Knesses Hagedolah* and the era of the *Tana'im*. The Maharal teaches that Shimon HaTzaddik bridged the era of *collective Torah* with the Torah of the Mishnaic period, in which Torah is always quoted in the name of individuals.

We are keenly aware of the Sages' insistence that each new Torah insight be transmitted with acknowledgment to its originator. *Nachal Yitzchak* by Rabbi Yitzchak Elchanan Spector says that "repeating Torah in the name of its author" not only requires citing the name of the author; it also includes mentioning the names of those who transmitted the teaching from one generation to the next. The Torah of the individual who originated a teaching becomes *his* portion in Torah. Even though our tradition teaches that the souls of all the Jewish people stood at Sinai "as one man with one heart," each Jew was assigned a specific portion of Torah and must claim his portion during his lifetime.

How far does the above teaching go? King David requested of G-d in Psalms,[5] "I want to reside in Your tent forever." The Hebrew word meaning forever is *olamim* (literally, in both worlds). Is it possible for a person to dwell in both worlds? This is what David said to the Holy One, Blessed be He: "May it be Your Will that my Torah teaching will be repeated in my name in this world." The Talmud explains, "Every Torah sage whose Torah is repeated in his name, of him it is said that 'his lips speak from the grave.'" This also refers to individuals who transmitted Torah through the generations; here too it is as though their lips "speak from the grave." Each transmitter "builds" G-d's tent as an eternal tent when he ascribes a Torah teaching to the individual who originated it. Teaching Torah and ascribing it to the individual who originated it is therefore a foretaste of the resurrection of the dead. By citing the author of a Torah insight, the transmitter dwells in G-d's tent for eternity.

Torah demands breadth of understanding. On one hand, one of the greatest periods of Torah transmission was the era of the *Anshei Knesses Hagedolah*, where Torah was transmitted collectively. On the other hand, Torah transmission in succeeding eras was associated with individual Sages, each of whom acquired proprietary rights to his unique Torah portion. The method of Torah transmission of each era created its unique grandeur.

Tosefos[6] teaches that the first disagreement concerning Torah law took place as a result of the confrontation between the Jews and Greece. The Talmud relates that when Shimon HaTzaddik met Alexander the Great, the period of Israel's encounter with Greece began. These were the same Greeks who later, during the time of the Hasmoneans, compelled Israel to abandon Torah and *mitzvah* observance.

The Talmud quotes Mishlei 6:33, *"The candle represents the* mitzvah, *while its light represents Torah."*[7] Just as light protects forever, so Torah protects forever. The strength of Torah lasts forever. Although use of the Temple Menorah ended with the destruction of the Temple, the light of the Menorah lasts forever. One who occupies himself with Torah is protected. Torah study protects us even during moments when we are not engaged in Torah study.

The miracle of Temple oil sufficient for one day that burned for eight days goes well beyond the ability of the spiritual to overcome the physical. Obviously, the G-d who commanded oil to burn can just as easily command vinegar to burn. The miracle of Chanukah was that the Temple Menorah burned not only with the flame of *mitzvah*, but with a flame of the light of Torah, which is eternal.

What is the significance of the Maccabean victory over Greece? Greek wisdom tore chunks from the Torah as it has been doing throughout the ages. The essential Chanukah miracle, greater even than the miracle of the Temple Menorah or the miracle of "the weak and the few who overcame the strong and the many" was the initiation of a new era of Torah learning and transmission. The rekindling of the Temple Menorah on Chanukah represents this new era of Torah transmission. The Temple Menorah was located in the southern side of the Temple. For this reason, The Sages teach: "He who wishes to pursue wisdom should face south"; i.e. the acquisition of wisdom is symbolized by the Menorah itself.

The Talmud asks, "Why is the Torah called 'the Torah of Moses?'" It replies, "because Moses dedicated his life to Torah."[8] The highest level Moses reached is that he "received the Torah on Sinai," not, "This is the Torah Moshe placed before the Children of Israel." Moses' grandeur is, "Remember the Torah of Moses, My servant."[9] The Torah is Moses' Torah.

Another example [of the above] is the psalm that opens with "The psalmist's song at the dedication of David's Temple." The Talmud asks, "Did David build the Temple? Solomon built it!" It replies, "Because David, through much self-sacrifice, devoted himself to the building of the Temple, it bore his name."[10]

The determined dedication of the Jews who confronted the Greeks in order to preserve the Torah initiated a fundamental change in the method of Torah transmission. Wars are hinge periods, and the Talmud mentions more than once that societies are transformed in the wake of war. Indeed, it was the Greek conflict that caused the Torah to become the possession of each individual Jew.

We have already mentioned that the Chanukah menorah is an extension of the Temple Menorah. As we light the menorah, we say, "These lights are holy, it is forbidden to make use of them; we are only permitted to gaze on them." "The rule that 'it is forbidden to use the Chanukah light,'" says the Ran, "derives from the laws governing the Temple Menorah." The Temple Menorah was the flame of *Klal Yisrael* — the Jewish collective. On Chanukah, we place the Temple Menorah in the home of each and every Jew to mark the transition from collective Torah to the Torah of the individual.

The *Beis Hamikdash* is a sacred precinct, *Reshus G'vohah*, sanctified and elevated territory, while the outside world is secular territory. While it is true that "[all of] the earth is the L-rd's," Jewish law defines the world as secular territory. Even if on some level everything in the world is sanctified and belongs to G-d, halachically only the Temple is sacred territory.

On Chanukah, when we install the flame of the Temple Menorah in each Jew's home, each Jewish home becomes sacred territory. G-d said to a dejected Aaron, "Your portion is greater than theirs," because your Menorah will glow forever.

"You created a great and holy Name in Your world," means that G-d's Name is holy not only in the Temple, but also in the home of each Jew. This is accomplished through the annual reenactment of the Chanukah miracle. The Temple Menorah has now become the menorah of each individual Jew. As each Jew installs the sacred menorah in his home, its light spreads from there to the world.

Jews pray each day in *Shacharis,* "Sanctify Your Name through those who sanctify Your Name, and sanctify Your Name in Your world." This means, "Sanctify Your Name through the Jewish People who first sanctify Your Name through its fealty to Torah; and as a result are then able to sanctify Your Name in Your world." We have always said in our prayers, "You are Holy, Your Name is Holy, and those who are holy daily sanctify Your Name." Therefore, "Sanctify Your Name through those who sanctify Your Name" refers to *Klal Yisrael* collectively, while "Sanctify Your Name in Your World" refers to the ability of each Jewish home and each individual Jew to become an instrument for the dissemination of Torah in the world.

The phrase, "You have made for Yourself a great and Holy Name in Your World" refers to the task of each Jew and every Jewish home to serve as an instrument for generating and disseminating sanctity. The collective Torah of *Klal Yisrael* is now the Torah of the individual through the instrumentality of the Chanukah menorah.

"You chose us from among the nations, and gave us Your Torah." The Vilna Gaon taught that each of the above events took place on a different occasion. "G-d chose us from among the nations" took place on the second day of Sivan, when G-d said to Israel, "You shall be to Me a holy nation and a kingdom of priests." "You gave us Your Torah" took place on Shavuos, the sixth day of Sivan, the day of the Sinai Revelation — when the people of Israel heard, "I am the L-rd your G-d."

The Ramban teaches that G-d's election of Israel as his "Chosen People" derives from a Torah teaching: "Not because you are many, indeed you are among the smallest of nations, but because the L-rd your G-d loves you."[11] G-d loves Israel, says Ramban, "because Israel is the fiercest of the nations." How does this fierceness express itself? "Israel possesses exemplary fierceness through its dedication to sanctity." Fierceness is expressed in the ancient Jewish expression, "*Oh Yehudo'ei oh tzelov*, either I remain a Jew or hang me from a tree, crucify me."

"Hang me from a tree" is associated with the word *tzlav,* a cross, the common method by which the Romans executed their opponents during the Second Temple era when they demanded that Jews renounce their faith. "And because G-d loves you," says the Ramban, "you merit to love G-d…The sign of true love is that someone maintains his love under duress, until the very end. This is the source of the closeness [to G-d] of the Jewish People." The Ramban associates the term "*Oh Yehudo'ei oh tzelov*" with "*Atah bechartanu,*" the fact that the Jews are the Chosen People.

The first Jewish encounter with *Gezeras Hashmad* [an edict to betray Torah] took place when the Greeks conspired to force Israel to abandon Torah and *mitzvos.* The Ramban links Israel's election with Israel's persecution, *Atah bechartanu* with *Gezeras Hashmad,* despite the passage of many generations from the time G-d singled out the Nation of Israel until the first experience of *Gezeras Hashmad.* The Ramban states that the willingness of Jews to undergo Roman crucifixion and not abandon Torah is evidence that Israel was "Chosen." "Israel deserves to be G-d's beloved"[12] because of Israel's willingness to die for the Torah.

The Ramban refers to the Talmudic teaching cited previously — *Mizmor Shir Chanukas Habayis L'David* — the song of David's dedication of the Temple. "Why is the Temple associated with David; didn't Solomon build it? Because David totally dedicated his life to its construction." The Torah is called *Toras Moshe*, the Torah of Moses, because Moses was totally dedicated to the Torah. Israel was chosen because the Jews are fully dedicated to sanctifying G-d's Name. Until the era of the Greek oppression it was G-d who loved the Jewish People. During this era the Jewish People demonstrated total love for G-d. The three key phrases, *Oh Yehudo'ei oh tzelov, Gezeras Ha'shmad*, and *Atah bechartenu* now formed one entity.

Through the test of the confrontation with Greece, what is known as "*pulmus shel Yevanim*," Israel was confirmed as G-d's beloved. While Israel was initially chosen as a result of its acceptance of the Torah, it was only through suffering, sacrifice and total devotion that the relationship became firmly established. Israel became Israel by standing firm in the face of intense fire and pressure.

The Ramban teaches that the "Greek Exile" (though the Jews remained in their own land, they were "exiled" in a spiritual sense) was an exile marked by ideological compulsion and oppression. This was a unique and necessary preparation for the Roman Exile (*Parshas Bilaam*). Prior to the Roman Exile, the Jewish People had to be educated and habituated to bear the brunt of persecution. *Oh Yehudo'ei oh tzelov* had to be internalized by every Jew. Through persecution and trial Israel acquired the ability to endure the oppressors who conspired to force them to abandon Torah. This is the meaning of "*Om, ani chomah*, Israel is more than a nation, it is a fortress, a wall." Thanks to its obstinate loyalty, the Jews earned the right to carry the name Israel. It was necessary to brand this quality into the character of the Jewish People. Martyrdom became the response of the Jew to oppression.

The Roman Exile is saturated with Jewish suffering and martyrdom. We see that Torah, which until then was the collective possession of the Jewish People, now became associated with individuals; for example, "Hillel says," "Shammai says." With this, a new manifestation of Torah emerged. The Greek conflict ended the era of the *Anshei Knesses Hagedolah* and initiated a new era of individual transmitters of Torah. Israel ascended to a new stage in the study of Torah: This is the sweetness and pleasantness of being able to say, "The Ketzos says," "The Nesivos says," "Rabbi Akiva Eiger says." The Torah of individuals was an outgrowth of the trial of "either I remain a Jew or crucify me." This is how the Jew steeled himself for the later Roman (i.e., Christian) Exile, the exile in which we live to this day. Unbounded loyalty was now ingrained into the Jewish psyche.

We now see why the definition of Chanukah is *chinuch*, Torah education, which extends from "habituate us to Torah" to "make the study of Torah sweet and enjoyable." Israel became habituated to a thorough identification with and dedication to Torah, even if the price is martyrdom. Torah study made possible the sweetness of Torah growth and creativity. G-d sits on His throne and says, "Eliezer [the son of Aaron the High Priest], My son, is expounding My Torah — Eliezer, My son, is teaching Torah. My Torah is now [called] His Torah."[13]

The Jews became the Chosen People through their readiness to accept the Torah at Sinai. But the sweetness of learning Torah in the name of individual great Sages ("so says Rabbi Akiva Eiger," "so says the Ketzos") came about only when the Jewish People became habituated to bear "either I remain a Jew or crucify me." In the extreme tests of exile, the Jewish Nation became a fortress that could be attacked but not subdued.

From the time of the confrontation with Greece until the destruction of the Second Temple, the Jewish People underwent a major transformation. Until this period, inspiration came from the prophets, from the multi-faceted Temple and from the presence of G-d as a readily apparent force. The Jews were inspired by external experiences. Beginning with Chanukah and the confrontation with Greece, motivation and inspiration had to come from within each individual.

So long as the prophets proclaimed the Divine message, so long as the Temple stood, these institutions carried the Jewish People. They were the source of instruction, inspiration and motivation. The *Anshei Knesses Hagedolah* and the Sanhedrin defined the Jewish People. Then a new era dawned. The Temple Menorah was installed in each Jewish home in the form of Chanukah menorahs; Torah tradition had to be borne aloft by inspired individuals.

This is how Jewry prepared for 2,000 years of exile. Each home was transformed into a Temple; individual Jews demonstrated martyrdom and heroism. Holiness could no longer be obtained from prophets and the Temple, now it had to glow from within. On the other hand, we had also become equipped with the wherewithal to provide that glow.

For 2,000 years, the Torah People confronted the challenge of the fourth exile — Roman and Christian civilization. The exile of Greece was the testing and training ground for this — Israel's longest, most challenging and severe exile of persecution, wandering and oppression.

This is the unique aspect of the Torah of the Messiah. With the coming of the Messiah, habitual Torah and creative Torah will become one in a way which is presently incomprehensible. Our experience will be similar to that of the Jews on Purim who came to understand the Torah more fully, centuries after it was given. The Talmud explains that at Mount Sinai the giving of the Torah was initiated through the proclamation of *"Na'aseh v'nishma* — We will obey and later hear [the explanations]." On Purim, Israel understood the explanations and accepted the Torah [fully] a second time.

Chanukah, the holiday of dedication and education, represents the beginning of *"v'hargileinu,* teach us to habituate ourselves in Torah." This beginning has but one conclusion, one finale: *"Az egmor b'shir mizmor, Chanukas hamizbayach* — We will sing the great song celebrating the dedication of the Altar in the rebuilt Temple."

1. *Berachos* 22.
2. *Isaiah* 43:21.
3. *Rosh Hashanah* 18b.
4. *Bava Kamma* 60b.
5. *Yevamos* 86b.
6. *Chagigah* 16a.
7. *Nefesh HaChaim, Sha'ar* 4:30.
8. *Medrash Tanchuma Beshalach* 10.
9. *Malachi* 3:33.
10. *Mechilta, Shemos* 15:1.
11. *Deuteronomy* 7:7.
12. See *Rambam Balak* 24:2 and *Yisro* 19.
13. *Numbers* 19:3-7.

CHANUKAH AND THE ORAL TORAH

40 Based on *Pachad Yitzchok*, Chanukah 1

t is widely known that the Torah was given to the Jewish People in two forms; the Written Torah, whose letters and words were preserved through the ages precisely as they were dictated by G-d to Moses; and the Oral Torah, through which the expansive application of Torah was revealed to Moses orally. It was then transmitted from generation to generation with the intention that it remain an oral possession of a living people, never to be committed to writing.[1]

The preservation of Torah in its original written form, the opposition to translating the Written Torah into foreign languages, and the resistance to rendering the Oral Torah into written form are all based on a statement of the prophet Hosea (8:12): "If the majority of the Torah were to be put into writing, Israel would be regarded by G-d as strangers."

Our Sages understood this prophecy to mean that were the Written Torah to be translated into a foreign language, or were the Oral Torah put into written form, a gap would be created between G-d and Israel. The translation of the Written Torah into Greek, called the Septuagint, was carried out unwillingly as the result of Greek pressure. It created a measure of estrangement between G-d and Israel.

The *Midrash* teaches that "In the future the nations of the world will write down the Written Torah for themselves."[2] Were the Oral Torah also to be put into writing by the nations of the world (the majority of the Torah is the Oral Torah), the alienation of the Jewish People from G-d would become much more pronounced: The exclusiveness and intimacy of Israel's relationship with G-d would be seriously compromised. When we examine this *Midrash* further, we realize that this is the meaning of the teaching of our Sages that "the Covenant which unites G-d and the Jewish People was established exclusively with the Oral Torah."[3] This is derived from the statement in the Torah: "It was through these words that I concluded My Covenant with you."[4] (Note: The above Torah statement employs the Hebrew words *pi* and *devarim,* mouth and words — a clear allusion to the Oral Torah.)

A covenant not only identifies the parties to an agreement, it also stipulates and identifies those who are excluded. The Torah Covenant therefore stipulates that putting the Oral Torah into written form is clearly forbidden.

To explain this prohibition, we must examine the two blessings we recite in the synagogue over the Torah scroll:

"…G-d, Who chose us from among the nations."

"…G-d, Who gave us His Torah."

The Vilna Gaon taught that each of the above blessings refers to an event that took place at a different time. Israel[5] was *chosen* by G-d on the second day of the month of Sivan,[6] when G-d concluded His Covenant with the Jewish People by saying: "And you shall be unto Me a Kingdom of *Kohanim* and a Holy Nation."[7] The Torah was actually given four days later when G-d proclaimed at Sinai, "I am the L-rd your G-d Who took you out of the land of Egypt."[8]

This Covenant is the source of the prohibition against writing the Oral Torah. Carefully note that this Covenant and its attendant prohibition *preceded* the Revelation of the positive and negative commandments of the Torah. Indeed, they preceded the very giving of the Torah.

From this we see that the prohibition against writing down the Oral Torah is not one among the many prohibitions found in the Torah; it is significantly more. It is integral to the establishment of the very form and content of the Covenant between G-d and Israel.

This point becomes clearer and sharper when we examine the "rules of order" and the conditions laid down by our Sages when they made their first exception to this rule and allowed the writing of the Mishnah. It was the first time any portion of the Oral Torah was put into writing. Upon examination, these rules of order do not appear to be that at all. One rule states that, "The Mishnah is not always written in such a way that it follows a consistent order,"[9] another, "There are deliberate omissions in the phrasing of the Mishnah,"[10] or, "the words of the Mishnah are compact in some places and expansive and wordy in other places."[11]

These "rules" were instituted when the Sages decided that in order to insure the survival of Torah, it was necessary to partially suspend the rules prohibiting the writing of the Oral Torah. In writing it, they integrated the *unwritten* style of the Oral Torah into the Mishnah text to the greatest extent possible. This precaution was to insure that the written Mishnah text would serve simply as an outline that would require the constant presence of mentors and teachers in order to be properly understood.[12] The teacher/disciple arrangement that was so intrinsic and essential to the transmission of the Oral Torah through the generations was thereby built into the new written text of the Mishnah. It guarantees that the *written* Oral Torah remains largely unintelligible without commentaries, teachers and mentors, without the living Sages who continued to be its bearers. These procedures are followed to this day in the written text of the Oral Torah. The Mishnah and Talmud are both designed so as to maintain the spirit and form of a tradition that has remained oral in nature.[13]

Were the prohibition against the writing of the Oral Torah to have been but one among the many prohibitions found in the

Torah, there would have been no need to maintain this prohibition "to the degree possible," since the Sages would be able to rely on the Torah concept, "this is a time to act for the L-rd [which demands a special change in strategy or practice]."[14] The provisions that maintain this prohibition, albeit in a limited form, stem from the fact that the prohibition preceded the giving of the Torah and that it is integral to the Covenant of Torah. Therefore a constant effort must be sustained to preserve the *oral character* of the Oral Torah, even though the Sages were forced to commit a limited part of it to writing to ensure the very survival of Torah.

This is why the Mishnah and the Talmud are nearly impossible to understand without the presence of a teacher/mentor. Many who think they understand the Gemara when studied in translation fail to realize that they have but skimmed the surface: They are far from a full understanding unless they have heard the Talmudic give-and-take from an expert teacher.

This dichotomy between the Covenant of the Torah and the laws of the Torah is also present in the laws of *mesiras nefesh,* which call for the sacrificing of one's life in the sanctification of G-d's name. We observe this distinction when we study the requirement to sacrifice one's life when Torah law so demands (i.e., to avoid worshipping idols or foreign gods, to avoid committing adultery or to avoid the murder of a human being) as opposed to when the requirement to sacrifice one's life comes into play during a period of *shmad,* an era of forced apostasy or conversion. (This would occur when, pressed by a government or foreign power, Jews would by compelled to sacrifice their lives rather than commit an offense that would be considered a minor Torah violation during normal times. During a time of forced apostasy or conversion, this minor transgression — if committed as an act of acquiescence to apostasy — is redefined by our Sages as a major violation.)[15]

Here is an example of such a situation: Suppose that in a certain country where Jews customarily wore black shoelaces, a pagan government suddenly demanded that Jews from now on are to wear green shoelaces as a public indication that they accept idolatry. Under those conditions, wearing green shoelaces becomes a serious offense because it indicates submission to the government's campaign of forcing Jews to accept a different religion or to worship an idol.

While there are certain Torah laws that Jews are permitted to violate during times of religious persecution, these laws may not be violated when their violation would demonstrate a public betrayal of the Covenant of Torah. The law then demands, "Sacrifice your life, but do not submit, *Ya'hareg ve'al ya'avor.*"[16] This readiness to sacrifice one's life under such circumstances has *everything* to do with the preservation of the uniqueness of Israel among the nations and with the preservation of the Covenant of Torah, and little to do with the violation of specific laws.

The Hasmonean willingness to sacrifice their lives went far beyond their concerns for the violation of specific commandments. They sacrificed their lives for one principal reason: to maintain the uniqueness of the Jewish People and the exclusivity of the Jews' Covenant with G-d. The events of Chanukah were not to be written because the very nature of these events are of a "not to be written" character. It is therefore appropriate that the events of Chanukah are not recorded in the text of the Torah or the Bible, but remain orally transmitted. Indeed, the preservation of Torah in its Oral form is the essence of the Jew and the basis of our Covenant with G-d.

Even when the Mishnah briefly discusses the laws of the Chanukah lights, it does so in passing, while discussing other subjects.[17] The Chanukah lights reveal our readiness to sacrifice our lives for Torah. These are lights that symbolize the effort to preserve the oral transmission of the Oral Torah. In the End of Days, Greek culture will cease to "darken the eyes of Israel" through its edicts and influence, or through the impact of the forced translation of the Torah into Greek.

The following is from Section One of Rabbi Hutner's Second Chanukah Lecture:

Israel's ideological struggle with Greece represented the first attempt of an alien nation to tear the Jews from their beliefs, i.e., *shmad*. The threat to Jewish life that demanded *mesiras nefesh,* self-sacrifice, during the events of Purim differs radically from the threat to Jewish life enacted in the events of Chanukah. In the era in which Purim took place, Persians challenged the Jewish possession of the Torah, and plotted to destroy the physical existence of the Jewish People. The Purim victory celebrates the physical survival of the Jewish People as well as a new reacceptance of the Torah (*kiymu v'kiblu*). Chanukah, on the other hand, celebrates the victory of the Jews over the Greek attempt to obliterate Israel's status as G-d's Chosen People, Israel's spirituality and Israel's unique relationship with G-d.

In Jewish tradition, an ideological threat that compels Jews to put their lives on the line to defend their faith creates an everlasting, indelible impression. The willingness of so many Jews to sacrifice and struggle against the enemy of Israel's unique spiritual existence raised Israel to a high level, which is forever inscribed on the collective Jewish consciousness. Just as Haman's threat to the Jews' physical existence caused a renewal of the Torah pact which is everlasting and permanent, so too the readiness of so many Jews to sacrifice their lives during the Maccabean uprising caused the exalted title of "Israel" (which was until that time somewhat tentative) to become everlasting.

Why was it "tentative" until this era? To understand this concept, we must look at the rabbinic teaching that "the experiences of the Patriarchs become a pre-destined marker that will describe the lives of their children."[18] Our forefather Jacob was awarded the title "Israel" as a result of his victorious struggle with the angelic representative of his brother Esau. (The name Israel means, "you struggled with angelic and human ideological forces and prevailed.") Thus this title "Israel" became everlasting and permanent only after the Jews' victorious struggle over the ideological and military forces of Greece. The struggle with Greece is the actualization within the national experience of Israel of the prophetic conflict that had been enacted within the individual experience of Jacob.

Note: In the Talmud, *Yoma* 29, Esther is compared to the dawn: "Just as the dawn concludes the night, so too does

Esther." This means that the events of Purim bring Israel's Biblical miracles to a conclusion. The Sages ask, why exclude the miracles of Chanukah, which took place after those of Purim? They reply that the Purim miracles were meant be written in the Biblical Book of Esther, while the Chanukah miracles are to remain eternally oral.

We might think that the division of Torah into the Written Torah and the Oral Torah relates exclusively to the text of the Torah, but this is not so. We see that the Sages discuss this division in the context of the historic experiences of the Jewish People, indicating that this division goes beyond the division of the Torah text into written and unwritten forms. As noted above, the events of Chanukah were not written because the very nature of these events are of a "not to be written" character.

1. *Gittin* 60b.
2. *Tosefos, Gittin* 60b.
3. *Gittin* 60b.
4. *Exodus* 34:27.
5. *Perush Avnei Eliyahu* on *Siddur Ishei Yisrael* p.21.
6. *Shabbos* 86b.
7. *Exodus* 19:6.
8. *Exodus* 20:2.
9. *Bava Kamma* 102a.
10. *Berachos* 13b.
11. *Jerusalem Talmud, Rosh Hashanah* 3:5.
12. *Rosh Hashanah, Nesivos Olam.*
13. *Temurah* 14b.
14. *Psalms* 119:126.
15. *Sanhedrin* 74b, also *Rambam Hilchos Yesodei HaTorah* 5.
16. *Sanhedrin* 74b, *Rambam Hilchos Yesodei HaTorah* 3.
17. *Bava Kamma* 62b.
18. *Sotah* 34a.

VII PURIM

AN INTRODUCTION 41 TO PURIM

Central to the celebration of Purim is the battle to eradicate evil. Amalek is the world's leading force for evil and Israel's mission is to defeat and eliminate this evil. This battle is 4,000 years old. We are commanded in the Torah to "erase the memory of Amalek from under the heavens, never forget."[1] The battle continues throughout history, for "G-d wages war against Amalek from one generation to the next."[2] While it is sometimes difficult to identify the Amalek in each particular generation, a certain sign that identifies Amalek is that nation's lack of values and uncontrolled evil behavior, usually manifesting itself in an irrational hatred for Jews.

The historic effort of the Jew is to strive to be the leading force for justice and morality in the world. As part of this ongoing battle, Israel is destined to suffer four exiles. Presently, we are experiencing the fourth and last exile, the Exile of Edom (sometimes called the Exile of Rome, which is another name for Esau's progeny). The victory of Israel and the coming of the Messiah in the End of Days is described by the prophet Ovadiah: "Saviors will ascend Mt. Zion [the mountain on which the Holy Temple stood and will again stand] to judge the Mountain of Esau; at that time kingship will exclusively belong to G-d."[3] The obliteration of the memory of Amalek and the judging of Edom will take place on the eve of the End of Days. These are events that will usher the coming of the Messiah and the restoration of G-d's Temple on Mt. Zion.

---

1. *Deuteronomy* 25:17.
2. *Exodus* 17:16.
3. *Ovadiah* 1:22.

THE
42 PURIM MASK

▶ *Megillas Esther:*
A Book that Reveals the Hidden

The word *Megillah* doesn't only mean a scroll, it is derived from the same root as *l'gallos*, to reveal. The Sages ask: Where is Esther to be found in the Torah? They quote the sentence in the Torah, "*Ve'Anochi* **haster astir** *panai,* **I [G-d] will certainly conceal** My Face."[1] (*Astir* contains the same Hebrew letters as Esther.) Purim teaches that even when G-d's presence seems to be concealed, His presence and glory are revealed to anyone who seeks Him.

On Purim, we wear masks to remind ourselves that G-d sometimes seems to be hidden. Paradoxically, G-d's name is not mentioned in the *Megillah*, to indicate that His presence in the events of Purim was hidden. However, when we carefully study the events of the *Megillah*, we succeed in unmasking G-d's presence.

We find G-d through His deeds. G-d is present if we are prepared to look behind the mask — when we search for His presence.

Jews know that G-d may often seem to hide. But even in the worst of times, if we look carefully, we discover that He can be found. Another reason we wear masks on Purim is to indicate that we, too, often hide our real selves. Even when we are cringing, ashamed of our misdeeds, ashamed of our cowardice, hiding behind our masks, we yearn to find G-d and be close to Him. We want to reveal our true selves to Him. The mask creates the illusion that it is possible to hide. Even the first man, Adam, told G-d, "I heard Your Voice while I was in the garden, but I convinced myself that it is possible to hide."[2]

Even when G-d appears to wear a mask, does that mean that He is distant? No. If you see someone wearing a mask, he is obviously near. If you hear his voice, if you discover his presence, you know he is near. G-d wants us to seek Him, to know His name, to know Him through His love, His deeds, His Torah, His Creation. The Purim mask is an illusion. In truth, G-d is very near.

On Yom Kippur, the *Keruvim* [the two angelic figures on top of the Holy Ark in which the stone tablets of the Ten Commandments were kept] embraced in intimacy. On Yom Kippur, G-d allows us to pierce the mask of the *Paroches*, the drapery that conceals the Holy of Holies, to feel, see and experience His nearness. On Yom Kippur, G-d is intimately near.

Our Sages teach that Purim and "Yom Ki'Purim" (Yom Kippur) are mirror images of each other. On Purim, G-d wears a mask, but He wants us to know that the mask is an illusion. Through the *Megillah*, which hides His name, He reveals His presence. Just as He redeemed us in the past, He will do so again when He reveals Himself in the presence of all mankind.

On Yom Kippur, when we stand before G-d as angels, denying our bodies food and drink, we seek spiritual redemption. On Purim we celebrate the physical redemption of Israel. It is celebrated with wine, food and partying. But the true meaning of Purim is spiritual as well. It is a time for us to seek G-d in every event in history and in every occurrence in our own lives. It is a time that we call out to Him, "Please, do not hide Your face any longer! Reveal Yourself in Your power and glory. Make known the force of Your love and justice; end mankind's violence and hatred; and bring us all under the protective wings of Your *Shechinah*."

---

1. *Deuteronomy* 31:18.
2. *Genesis* 3:10.

TO LOVE
A JEW

43

H ow far must we go to love our fellow Jew — any Jew? What is the extent of G-d's love for every Jew?

The Shabbos prior to Purim is called *Shabbos Zachor,* the Sabbath of Remembrance. What do we remember? The attack of Amalek on Israel; the attempt of the nation of Amalek to prevent the giving of the Torah and to demonstrate that Israel is vulnerable; its eagerness to prove that Israel's Divine defenses can be penetrated because there are sinners among them.

How do we remember Amalek's attack? On the Shabbos before Purim we read from the Torah of Amalek's attack on the Children of Israel. This Torah reading is so important that it is incumbent upon every Jew to hear it. So critical is this *mitzvah* that the passage must be read from a kosher *Sefer Torah,* on the Sabbath, in the synagogue, in the presence of the entire community. This is the only Torah reading that is a Divine command, similar to the recitation of *Sh'ma*. Clearly, this reading is more precious in the eyes of G-d than any other Torah reading.

How did Amalek attack Israel? The Torah says that Amalek "attacked Israel's tail" — the stragglers, people who had fallen behind, those who had detached themselves from the main camp of Israel. The commentator Sifri teaches that this means that Amalek attempted to kill those people who had rebelled against G-d, who had removed themselves from the protective "wings" of the *Shechinah*. Another commentary, the Targum Yonason (on *Beshalach*), says that these were Jews who had turned to idol worship and for this reason they had been expelled from the Israelite camp. And it was there, far removed from the protection of the main camp, that Amalek was capable of reaching them.

As the Torah describes, Israel triumphed over Amalek in that battle due to the help of G-d, who took up its defense with ire. But the nation of Amalek was not destroyed, and it has lived on to plague the Jewish People. Four thousand years have passed, and the anger of G-d has not abandoned the battle against Amalek. "G-d wages war against Amalek in each and every generation." To quote the Book of Esther, "The anger of the King did not subside."

Targum Yonason teaches that "the war of G-d against Amalek will not be completed until the generation of the Messiah." Whose honor is G-d protecting with such fury and unrestrained anger? He is protecting the "*nechshalim*," the rebellious, recalcitrant and unrepentant Jews who had fallen behind due to their sins. And why? Because all Jews, without exception, are G-d's children.

The Talmud asks, "How do we know that they are still called sons?"[1] In response, it quotes the prophet Isaiah who called them "Evil sons, rebellious, destructive sons,"[2] but sons nonetheless. The prophet Hosea prophesied, "The day will come that they will not be called 'not of My People' but will again be called 'the children of the living G-d.'" In each generation, G-d battles against the enemies and persecutors of Israel, even when they attack those who are unworthy of His protection.

---

1. *Kiddushin* 36:1.
2. *Isaiah* 1:4.

GIFTS
ON PURIM

Why are we required to send *shalach manos* [gifts of ready-to-eat foods] to our friends on Purim? Why is this Rabbinic law a unique expression of Purim and of no other holiday? The Sfas Emes, the previous Gerer Rebbe, teaches that sending food packages to friends and giving charity to the needy is an expression of our love for our fellow Jew. It is the strength of our love and concern for fellow Jews that empowers us with the ability to defeat Amalek, the unrelenting enemy of the Jewish People. Expressing concern for fellow Jews unites all Jews, making it impossible for the evil forces of our enemies to overpower us. Jewish unity is an absolute requirement if we are to defeat our enemies.

How did Haman succeed in convincing King Achashverosh that it was feasible to enact his edict for total annihilation of the entire Jewish People? He said, "There is a nation *dispersed and spread out* throughout your kingdom whose laws are different from those of all the peoples" (i.e., the Jews are disorganized and disunited). What was the response of Queen Esther? "Go," she told Mordechai, "unite all the Jews. Fast and pray for me." She knew that she must create Jewish unity, because the strength of this unity will bring about a Divine response that will enable the Jews to destroy their enemies.

The practice of gift giving and charity is unique to Purim, observed Rabbi Yitzchok Hutner, because it was on Purim that the Jewish People reaccepted the Torah. (We will soon learn what that means.) Unity is a prerequisite to the giving of the Torah. The Torah records that when the Jews prepared to receive the Torah, "Israel camped against Mt. Sinai." The Hebrew word camped, *vayichan,* is deliberately written in the singular instead of the plural so as to inform us, as Rashi observes, that the Jews assembled at Mt. Sinai "as one man with one heart," fully united.[1]

Just as all of Torah was concentrated in one place at Mt. Sinai, the hearts of Israel were totally united at Mt. Sinai. The giving and receiving of the Torah requires that both the Torah and Israel be united. Each year, when we celebrate the Receiving of the Torah on Shavuos, we attempt to reenact that scene of all Israel standing united at Sinai, by studying Torah all night until the break of day.

The same circumstances that prevailed at the Receiving of the Torah at Sinai also prevail each year as we celebrate Purim. Purim is also a reenactment of the *final* Giving of the Torah. In fact, the Giving of the Torah on Purim completes the historic process of Revelation.

Megillas Esther alludes to this event with the phrase, *"ve'kibale haYehudim la'asos,* And the Jews undertook to continue that which they had initially undertaken."[2] This clearly suggests a more voluntary acceptance of the Torah than at Mt. Sinai, where an element of compulsion was involved. Here too, the key word *ve'kibale,* "and they undertook," is written in the singular to suggest the complete and total unity of the Jews when they again accepted the Torah (on Purim), but this time in a totally voluntary fashion. It is in celebration of this last phase of Revelation, the reacceptance of the Torah, that we send gifts and charity on Purim. Our purpose is to reenact the unity that prevailed among the Jews both when the death threat of Haman was revealed and when the Torah was again accepted during the days of Mordechai and Esther.

Since Purim represents the last Biblical redemption from a threatened and impending holocaust, it also takes place during Adar, the very last month of the year. Because it precedes Nissan, the first month of the Jewish year, it brings us to the birth of the Jewish People on Passover. It is logical that on the day of the last redemption — the day that is involved with the complete destruction of Amalek and anticipates the coming of the Messiah — the Jews would wholeheartedly and voluntarily reaccept the Torah with a special emphasis on the Oral Torah. This is certainly a powerful reason for much joy and for a prayer that the Jewish People will again reaccept the Torah in our day.

1. *Exodus* 19:2.
2. *Esther* 9:23.

THE JOYOUS MONTHS OF ADAR AND NISSAN

O ur Sages teach that, "*Mi'shenichnas Adar marbin b'simchah*, From the moment the month of Adar arrives, we increase our joy." Why is this statement so complicated? Why not simply say, "In Adar, we are joyous"? It would seem that this statement describes a dynamic progression. It has an air of movement. It also seems to link Adar with its companion month, Nissan. In many ways these two consecutive months are one.

Purim, the last festival of Jewish exile, takes place in Adar. Purim is the ultimate holiday of the exile. It depicts the last recorded Biblical occasion during which the hated Amalekites attempted to destroy the Jewish People. In completing the Biblical cycle of holidays, Purim also introduces the new holiday cycle. Right after Adar, we welcome Nissan and then Passover, the birth of the Jewish People and the beginning of the redemption.

The intent of the above rabbinic statement is that once we enter into the presence and environment of Adar, we should anticipate that the joy of Adar will escalate until it links itself with the spirit of Nissan, which brings with it the anticipation of the arrival of Passover. The coming of Nissan prepares us for our anticipated rejoicing at the final Redemption, which our Sages teach will come during Nissan. When we celebrate Purim to mark the (eventual) destruction of Amalek, the classical enemy of the Jewish People, we also anticipate the birth and (eventual) Redemption of the Jewish People. Our joy expands and escalates from Purim to Pesach, to Shavuos to Succos — until the celebration of the coming of the Messiah that takes place on Simchas Torah. In the statement quoted above, the dynamic words *nichnas* [enters] and *marbin* [increases] herald the beginning and increase of our joyous anticipation of the final Redemption.

Our Sages taught, "Begin the study of the laws of Passover 30 days prior to Passover." What day is 30 days prior to Pesach? Purim. This is but another indication of the close connection between these festivals.

THE ESSENCE OF AMALEK'S ENMITY

46 Based on *Pachad Yitzchok:* Purim 1

▸ Confronting Israel's Eternal Enemy

Which is the most despicable of nations? Clearly, it is Amalek — whose very essence is scoffing and derision. "Amalek is the first among the nations; but in the end it is slated for destruction."[1]

The second part of this verse describes the End of Days, when the nations of the world will acknowledge truth, values and goals of significance and will be repaired and sanctified. At that time, anything that is not rectified will cease to exist. Rashi explains this concept in his definition of *Sh'ma Yisrael*:

> *G-d will become One when all mankind accepts His Kingship. Hashem, Who is our G-d now, but is not accepted as G-d by the nations, is destined in the End of Days to become the G-d of all the nations."*[2]

Amalek is the one exception. It is incapable of spiritual repair, even in the End of Days. Since everything that is capable of spiritual repair will be repaired then, Amalek — whose essence is scoffing and cynicism, to whom nothing matters and for whom everything important is trivial — will be destroyed. In the presence of a world that has achieved spiritual completion, there will be no possibility for the continued existence of a nation whose essence is to abhor ultimate significance and spiritual repair.

Why is Amalek called "the first among the nations"? Amalek was the first nation to attack Israel following its exodus from Egypt.[3] While all of the nations are opposed to Israel, Amalek was Israel's first and most determined opponent.

The Torah's instruction that it is a *mitzvah* to obliterate Amalek is found in proximity to the words, "and Jethro...heard all that G-d did to Moses and to Israel."[4] The Sages saw special meaning in this. See *Shemos Rabba* 27:5, which quotes Proverbs (19:25): "Strike the scoffer and the simpleton will become clever; chastise an understanding person and he will attain greater knowledge." The scoffer is Amalek; the simpleton is Jethro. Nothing, not even his own destruction, can correct Amalek because he is impervious to change. Amalek cannot escape his fate. The reason for this is that to the cynic nothing has significance: There are no values or goals of importance. Admonition has no effect on the cynical scoffer who has a false concept of the world.

The halachic rules concerning cynicism are discussed in the Talmud: "Rabbi Nachman said, 'as a general rule, all mockery and cynicism are forbidden except for the mockery of idolatry, which is permitted.'"[5]

It seems fair to assume that mocking evil in general is permitted. So why did the Sages single out idolatry to demonstrate the permissibility of a certain category of mocking? The key is found in the words of Rabbeinu Yonah, who quotes Proverbs (26:21): "A refining pot refines silver, a crucible refines gold; and we know [the degree to which] a person [is refined] by observing his praises." Rabbeinu Yonah understands this verse to mean that a person is judged based on what and whom he praises. To quote Rabbeinu Yonah, "If he praises good deeds, the Sages, the wise and the righteous, we know that he is a good person who is rooted in goodness and righteousness. If, however, he praises despicable deeds or evil persons, clearly he is evil."[6] In other words, a person's character is determined by what a person respects and the values he holds dear.

We can measure our own values by employing the following hypothetical example. We meet two people: One is an accomplished Torah scholar, while the other is an average Jew. We notice that the Torah scholar is in awe when a wealthy individual visits him, while he does not rise when a great Torah scholar visits him. On the other hand, we observe that the average Jew is in awe of the scholar, whom he honors and before whom he rises. Yet he is not in awe when he is visited by a wealthy person. According to Rabbeinu Yonah, in this instance the average Jew is on a higher Torah plane than the scholar. A person's deep sense of humility, as well as self-knowledge and self-worth, relates to the degree to which he defers and submits to people he respects and values.

Such standards are meaningful to a person with a healthy sense of spiritual values. There are, however, some people who constantly struggle with their propensity towards cynicism and scoffing. These individuals do not have an inner sense of values because they are ensnared by an inner voice that propels them to deny the very existence of "importance." This inner voice wishes to tear down the entire edifice of importance. To this person nothing really matters, not even his own life. The purpose of one who gives praise is to enhance the appreciation of importance and meaning, while the scoffer and cynic strive to consistently denigrate values that are truly important.

Let us analyze this further. What is civilization's greatest folly and lie? Without doubt the answer is the worship of idols and false gods. There is nothing of greater importance than what we worship, and there is no greater lie than the false god. The result is that the person who worships false gods has ascribed the highest importance to that which deserves the greatest denigration. The worship of false gods is nothing other than a perversion of importance and spiritual values. The idol worshiper raises the most nonsensical lie to the level of the greatest importance. He has lost the ability to distinguish between reality and illusion. The worship of idols derives from the human ability to raise an illusion that merits derision to the level of significance and importance.

This will explain why the Sages chose the ridicule of false gods as the best example of permissible scoffing. We are encouraged to scoff at evil. The evil we call the worship of false gods — *avodah zarah* — is actually the worship of forces or things that are removed from the world of truth. In other words, they have no basis in reality; they are built on illusion. It is therefore natural for the true servant of G-d to direct his power of scoffing at the greatest lie, the worship of false gods.

Up to this point we talked about employing scoffing for a good purpose, such as deriding the worship of false gods. There is, however, a fundamental difference between our ability to scoff for the purpose of achieving the good and our general ability to scoff. We have learned that ridicule tears down the particular ranking of spiritual values and importance. This applies to all scoffing, even when it serves a good purpose, since scoffing in all instances employs derision.

At its root, there is a major difference between general scoffing and derision for the sake of the true good. General derision tears down spiritual importance; however, the derision of false gods enhances the importance of the good. The essence of deriding the worship of false gods, the appreciation of the power of derision, stems from the power of praise. Even though scoffing at idol worship seems similar to scoffing in general, its root and purpose are fundamentally different.

Generally, mockery and derision aim at increasing cynicism. However, the derision of the worship of false gods upholds and increases the importance of truth. The Ramchal, Rabbi Moshe Chaim Luzzatto, wrote in his classic book *Mesilas Yesharim*, *The Path of the Righteous*, "One cynical remark can push aside a hundred serious remonstrations." The source of this statement is the Talmud: "Just as it is a *mitzvah* to promulgate a directive that will be heeded, so too is it a *mitzvah* to avoid promulgating a directive that will not be heeded."[7] This derives from the Scriptural instruction: "Do not attempt to admonish a cynic."[8] While admonition of a cynic has no effect, the one weapon that can be used against him is the one he himself uses so effectively: ridicule.

Generally, it is important that people have the ability to accept admonition. Cynicism as a personal quality will, however, prevent an individual from accepting admonition. That is because the goal of admonition is to elevate the importance of correcting things that require correction; to get a person to listen, to become serious, to acknowledge that which is true, real and important in a G-d-centered world. By raising our consciousness of what is ultimately important, we negate the ability of our conscience to scoff at or deny the importance of spiritual values. We become ready to accept admonition.

The scoffer and cynic are indifferent to objective spirituality. The inclination to cynicism wastes no time in cutting off our inner sense of spiritual values, importance and significance. One cynical comment will destroy a towering structure of importance. The scoffer does not simply rebuff an admonition. This matter goes more deeply. The inclination to cynicism pushes away *all* admonition, *all* significance and *all* importance.

It would be instructive to study the response of Rashi to the instruction in *Parshas Zachor* (Deuteronomy 25:17-19): "Remember what Amalek did to you on the way, when you were leaving Egypt; he happened upon you [Hebrew: *korcha*], killed all your weaklings and attacked your rear guard when you were faint and exhausted. He did not fear G-d." The word *korcha* (from *kar* — cold) implies that Amalek not only attacked you, but also "cooled you off." The nations were afraid to battle against Israel. Then Amalek came and attacked. This situation can be compared to a pool filled with boiling water into which no person dared jump because they knew that they would be severely scalded. Suddenly a scoundrel appeared, and dared to jump into the pool. Although he was scalded, he succeeded in cooling off the pool sufficiently so that others were no longer afraid to jump in. In the same way, Amalek not only attacked Israel, its attack diminished the importance and stature of Israel in the eyes of the nations. Prior to Amalek's attack, the princes of Edom, the leaders of Moav and the residents of Canaan were deeply affected by *the admonition*, i.e. the fear of the G-d of Israel who had engineered the Exodus and split the Reed Sea. The water in the pool, so to speak, was boiling hot. With the emergence of the Nation of Israel, importance was born to the world, bathed in an aura of awe. But Amalek could not tolerate importance. Upon Amalek's attack, the nations of the world saw that Israel might indeed be vulnerable. Through this breach, Amalek hoped to destroy the entire structure of importance. This has been the ambition of cynics from the beginning. Their desire is to promote the power of skepticism that exists in the heart of mankind (and thereby undermine belief in G-d and in His dominion over man).

Rebuke will not change the character of Amalek. The actions of Amalek reflect the inability to accept admonition and authority. (But Jethro accepted admonition (i.e. understood the power and importance of G-d and Israel's mission to the world) when he witnessed the defeat of Amalek. It is for this reason that our Sages taught, "Strike the scoffer and the simpleton will grow wise."[9] They interpret "And Jethro heard"[10] as meaning that Jethro understood the lesson in Amalek's defeat.

The forefather of Amalek was Esau, the twin bother of Jacob. He did not simply sell his spiritual birthright to Jacob, "Esau disdained his birthright."[11] He *mocked* the importance of the birthright. To Esau, nothing spiritual is important. Going beyond the disdain of his ancestor Esau, the essence of Amalek is the drive to uproot spiritual importance from the human soul.

In the End of Days, all the nations will aspire to spiritual perfection, with the exception of Amalek. "In the end, Amalek will be destroyed." As the Torah makes clear, no matter how evil the nations may be, they are receptive to spiritual admonition. This opens the possibility of their eventual recognition of G-d's Kingship, and they can be salvaged. Not so Amalek, as its essence and nature lack receptivity to admonition.

Since Amalek was the first to oppose Israel and the Divine absolute, its rank is the "first of the nations." In the end, therefore, it will be the first to cease to exist. "In the end, it is slated for destruction." When history reaches its apex, everything will achieve spiritual completion; anything not complete will cease to exist. Since the very essence of Amalek is to uproot spiritual completion, Amalek perforce will cease to exist.

"Amalek arrived to battle against Israel in Refidim."[12] The Hebrew name *Refidim* may be broken down into *"rifyon yadayim,"* which means "weakness." Amalek's intention was to weaken Israel's resolve, to prevent Israel from receiving the Torah. It hoped to weaken Israel's determination, perseverance and tenacity. Ultimately, it was Israel's own weakening of resolve and diminished sense of the importance of Torah that brought about its punishment through Amalek's attack.

Whenever we describe the opposite of devotion to Torah study we use the phrase *"bittul Torah,"* the lack of appreciation of the importance of Torah. This expression implies and results in "the weakening of our hold on Torah."[13] When a person lessens his commitment to an enterprise and loses his understanding and appreciation of its significance, he weakens his grasp. In describing the battle with Amalek, where Amalek's goal was to cool Israel's commitment, "to lessen their grasp on the Torah," our Sages observed that ultimately the battle was the result of the fact that Israel had already weakened in its resolve.

Our task is to do the opposite, to constantly strengthen our grasp on Torah and to enhance its importance. We must not allow the cynical influence of Amalek to cool our ardor and enthusiasm. We must always strive to recognize the awesome importance of the majesty and honor of the Divine Torah.

Spiritual Repair and Completion in the End of Days
As taught by the Ramchal in Derech Hashem

When the Messiah arrives, the nations of the world will achieve a degree of elevated spiritual perfection. Their present deficiency, which involves a lack in their understanding of reality, will be repaired. Their present false beliefs as to what existence is about will be corrected. They will become different people and will automatically, instinctively, intellectually and spiritually react to this new reality. In the presence of the Messiah, also called the End of Days (Acharis Hayamim), all people will know that G-d is Creator and King of the universe, that He alone is the master creative force behind all of nature, history and reality.

As the light of Divinity grows stronger, people will instinctively begin to understand that which is expected of them; their values and conduct will change, they automatically will begin to observe Divine commandments because these will become a reflexive, spontaneous part of their new reality. Their new grasp of reality will define that which is important. The new reality will create universal behavioral conformity.

The importance and urgency of the Divine imperative as has been taught in Scripture and by our Sages will become an automatic response to a new perception of reality and importance. As the prophet Zechariah taught, "G-d will be King over all the earth: On that day, G-d will be One and His Name will be One."[14]

▸ An Additional Thought

Many individuals struggle to identify that which is truly important in their lives, while others merely profess true commitment. When we observe how they express their commitment, in their words and actions, it is apparent that they are beset by cynicism and the absence of true spirituality. Apply this analysis to what we value. How do we spend our time and our money, who are the people with whom we associate, in which frivolous pastimes do we engage, and what serious agendas, causes and people do we neglect? Many of us claim to be believers, yet our behavior reveals spiritual cynicism and indifference, an inability to recognize what is truly significant and consequential in meeting the expectations of Heaven.

---

1. *Numbers* 24:20.
2. *Rashi, Deuteronomy* 6:4.
3. *Exodus* 17:14.
4. *Exodus* 18:1.
5. *Sanhedrin* 63b.
6. *Sha'arei Teshuvah, Sha'ar* 3:148.
7. *Yevamos* 65:2.
8. *Proverbs* 9:8.
9. *Shemos Rabbah* 27:5.
10. *Exodus* 18:1.
11. *Genesis* 25:34.
12. *Exodus* 17:8.
13. *Mechilta Shemos* 17:8.
14. *Zechariah* 14:9.

THE SECOND RECEIVING OF THE TORAH ON PURIM

47

Based on *Pachad Yitzchok:* Purim 3

f someone were to ask you, "What is celebrated on the holiday of Shavuos?" the obvious answer would be, "The Giving of the Torah." Concerning the Torah we say, "*Torah ohr*, Torah creates light."[1] If you were then asked, "What is celebrated on Purim?" your reply would be, "*LaYehudim hayesah orah*, For the Jews there was light."[2] Concerning this light, we say, "Light is Torah."[3] In other words, the salient fact of Shavuos is Torah, whose definition is light. However, the salient event of Purim is light, whose definition is Torah.

What is the conceptual basis for this distinction? In the Bible we find that King David initiated a rule that has remained a Jewish law to this day.[4] At the conclusion of a victorious battle, the soldiers who engage in the battle and the soldiers who guard the armaments and supplies are to divide the spoils of war equally. King David enacted this policy during his war against Amalek. As we know, "Great things don't happen by chance."[5] To discover what provoked the enactment of this new rule, we must explore the unique character of the war against Amalek.

The redemption from Egypt is preparatory to the Covenant and the receiving of the Torah, i.e. the Covenantal process. This transition involved in receiving the Torah is the equivalent of a preparation for conversion to Judaism.

Indeed, all Jewish laws relating to conversion were derived by our Sages from the redemption from Egypt.[6] The process involved in receiving the Torah is the equivalent of conversion to Judaism.

In all redemptions subsequent to the Exodus, all enactments served to protect and preserve the Sinai Covenant. As G-d states in the Torah:

> *Even when they will be in their enemies' land, I*
> *will not grow so disgusted with them, nor so tired*
> *of them that I will destroy or abolish My Covenant*
> *with them. I will therefore remember the Covenant*
> *I made with their ancestors whom I liberated from*
> *Egypt, in the full view of the nations, through*
> *which I became their G-d.*[7]

Although the above passage indicates that the Covenant will ultimately stand forever, the Sages teach that the Covenant was threatened during the Persian Exile. It never actually collapsed thanks to Mordechai and his associates.[8]

"Kudsha Brich Hu, Yisrael v'Oraisa chad hu, G-d, Israel and the Torah constitute one singular unbreakable union."[9] From this passage we see that the life of the Torah parallels the life of the Jewish People. The above two kinds of redemption are reflected in Torah teachings. It is possible to grow in Torah by acquiring new concepts. It is also possible to grow in Torah by adding strength, depth and liveliness to Torah already studied. This corresponds to the relationship between the Jewish People and Torah during the above two redemptions. The redemption from Egypt caused Israel to enter into a Covenant with G-d, which called for their accepting the Torah, containing concepts and laws new to them. The Persian/Purim redemption brought about

the preservation of that Covenant, which had long existed. The Purim renewal of the Torah Covenant was an act of reaccepting the Torah, which injected a resurgence of strength into Torah knowledge that had already been learned.

The major "innovation" that marks the Jews' redemption from Haman's edict was that this was the first time in Jewish history that they experienced the fulfillment of the Divine promise that the existing Torah Covenant will be protected and preserved. The events of Purim caused another major innovation: the reaffirmation of the Covenant with G-d, and the mass reacceptance of the Torah. The Jewish victory over Haman uncovered a determination to bring renewed vibrancy into Torah already studied.

Israel's war against Amalek awakened Israel's soul to the realization that the reinforcement and strengthening of long-standing Torah knowledge was of equal and possibly greater importance than the aquisition of new Torah concepts.

We can now understand why King David enacted the new policy that the soldiers who fought the battle and those who guarded the supplies were to divide the spoils of the battle with Amalek equally. The brilliance of this law is that it reveals that there is equal value to the individual who increases his Torah knowledge and the individual who reinforces and strengthens learning already acquired. This concept was ingrained as a consequence of each effort to destroy Amalek. We can see how the reacceptance of the Torah in the time of Mordechai complements the Revelation of the Torah in the generation of Moses. Together they divide the spoils — he who goes to battle, and he who guards the armaments and supplies.

We return to our opening statements: On Shavuos we begin with Torah and conclude with light: *Torah creates light*. On Purim we begin with light and conclude with Torah: *Light creates Torah*. Now we understand what this means. The first acceptance of Torah (on Shavuos) gives rise to the light of Torah in our lives. *This* light generates a derivative, yet creative, new illumination that inspires our reacceptance of Torah (on Purim).

We can formulate this metaphysical process in this way: Shavuos equals the Covenant at Sinai and the acceptance of the Torah, which generates spiritual light — "Torah is light, *Torah ohr.*" That light, in turn, creates a self-regenerating energy that guarantees the protection of the Covenant when attacked.

Wars against Amalek, particularly that of Purim, represent such an attack on the bonds of the Covenant. On Purim, the "protective energy" not only protects the standing Covenant, it also generates fresh energies that catalyze the reacceptance of Torah.

Newly generated light invigorates Torah and the Torah Covenant — "*LaYehudim hayesah orah* [For the Jews there was light]. *Orah zu Torah*, light is Torah."

Indeed, the law remains in place to this day: Both those who engage in battle and those who protect the flank share the spoils equally. The Torah of Sinai and the Torah of Purim are equally relevant. How is this applicable to us? There is much light to be derived from Torah that we had not previously studied. Purim teaches that there is equal, and possibly even greater, light to be derived from reviewing and deepening our comprehension of Torah previously learned.

1. *Proverbs* 6:23.
2. *Esther* 8:16.
3. *Megillah* 16b.
4. *Samuel* 30:25.
5. *Maharal Tiferes Yisrael* 25 and *Gevuros Hashem* 19.
6. *Yevamos* 46b.
7. *Leviticus* 26:44.
8. *Megillah* 11a.
9. *Zohar, Vayikra* 73.

WHY IS THE MEGILLAH OF ESTHER FOREVER?

48 Based on *Pachad Yitzchok:* Purim 5

H ow are we to understand the following words of the Rambam? "All the books of the Prophets and Writings will be abolished when the Messiah comes, with the exception of the Book of Esther. The *Megillah* [of Esther] will survive, as will the Five Books of the Torah."[1]

To understand this, we must look back to our forefathers. When Jacob purchased the birthright from Esau, he said: "Sell your birthright to me as of this day."[2] Many commentators have tried to understand the meaning of the words "as of this day." They don't seem to have any connection with the beginning of the sentence. This phrase, however, does have a special meaning in the context of Purim.

When Jacob and Esau met after their separation of many years, Esau invited Jacob to accompany him to his home.

> *"My lord," replied Jacob, "you know that the children are weak, and I have responsibility for the*

nursing sheep and cattle. If they are driven hard for
even one day, all the sheep will die. Please go
ahead of me, my lord. I will lead my group slowly,
following the pace of the work that I have ahead of
me, and the pace of the children. I will eventually
come to [you], my lord, in Seir."³

These words of Jacob were never fulfilled, because Jacob never went to the residence of Esau in Seir. Our Sages teach that since it is not conceivable that something inaccurate would be said by Jacob, these words must have meaning in the context of the End of Days: *then* Jacob will go to Seir. The prophet Ovadiah (1:21) stated, "And saviors will go up — to judge the mountain of Esau." i.e., Seir.

There is no other way to understand this text. It was for this reason that Jacob placed special emphasis on the fact that he was buying the birthright "as of this day" from Esau. Without this emphasis, Esau could have made the following claim to Jacob: "I sold you the birthright; but just as you are making promises to me today that will be fulfilled far into the future, so too, the sale of the birthright will take place at the End of Days." Jacob therefore explicitly stated that the sale is taking place *today* and not at the End of Days. In view of the fact that Jacob is deeply rooted in spirituality and is continually aware of the End of Days, even Jacob's casual talk must be regarded as relating to the End of Days. This is in contrast to Esau, who is in possession of this material world only and who will disappear in the End of Days. Jacob's words, therefore, must be seen in the context of *today*, not in the context of tomorrow.

The Talmud says:

There are five verses in the Torah whose grammati-
cal structure cannot be clearly determined. Each
verse contains a phrase that can be linked to either
an earlier clause or a later clause. Among these
*clauses is "tomorrow."*⁴

When discussing Amalek's attack on Israel, Moses says, "Go, make war against Amalek, tomorrow, I will be stationed at the head of the mountain."[5] The word *tomorrow* can be understood in two different ways because it is unclear whether it is part of the previous clause or the next one. Moses may have meant that Joshua should do battle tomorrow, at which time Moses would stand on the top of the hill and pray. On the other hand, he may have meant, do battle today and tomorrow I will stand on top of the hill and pray; today you will not be in need of my prayers.[6]

The word tomorrow is also found in the Book of Esther (5:12): "Tomorrow, I am called to be with the king." Concerning this passage, the Maharal said that everything that relates to the defeat of Amalek belongs to tomorrow. As stated in Samuel I (30:17), "David defeated Amalek on the morrow." Why? Because "this day" belongs to Amalek. Amalek's defeat is something that can only take place tomorrow. It therefore turns out that the existence of Amalek in this world, today, beclouds the reality that will take place tomorrow. When Moses refers to Joshua's battle with Amalek, the use of the word *tomorrow* remains unclear.

You will note that this ambivalent emphasis also arises in the request of Esther for an additional day to battle Amalek in Shushan. The request was that "tomorrow we should be permitted to do that which we did today."[7] Why? Because within the boundaries of "today" it is not possible to achieve the total destruction of Amalek. The complete destruction of Amalek can only be accomplished "tomorrow."

We now return to the above quoted statement, that aside from the Five Books of the Torah, only the Book of Esther, *Megillas Esther*, will be relevant when the Messiah arrives. The other sacred writings are relevant today. These writings divide today from tomorrow. The entire *Megillah* of Esther, however, relates to "doing tomorrow that which we did today." For this reason it will not be put aside with the other sacred texts. It is a document that will be enforced fully in Messianic times, when Amalek will be destroyed forever.

---

1. *Mishnah Torah, Hilchos Megillah* 2:18.
2. *Genesis* 25:31.
3. *Genesis* 33:14.
4. *Yoma* 52b.
5. *Exodus* 17:9.
6. *Yoma* 52b.
7. *Esther* 9:13.

SEEKING SIMILARITIES IN ORDER TO ACCENTUATE DIFFERENCES

49 Based on *Pachad Yitzchok:* Purim 6

n the course of a Purim banquet one of the participants asked Rabbi Hutner the following: The poem *Shoshanas Yaakov* has been accepted throughout the world Jewish community as the theme song of the Purim celebration. We are also aware that deeply inscribed in the rejoicing of Purim is the mandate that we should become so inebriated that we will not be able to distinguish between 'cursed is Haman and blessed is Mordechai, *ad d'lo yoda.*'[1] In view of this, how is it possible that the poem, which so clearly spells out the difference between cursed is Haman and blessed is Mordechai, serves as the expression of the celebration of Purim?"

To answer this question we must understand and emphasize a basic principle: The reason we distinguish between two things that are externally similar is so that we will perforce recognize what distinguishes them inwardly. To the degree that we point out the similar externals, what distinguishes them inwardly becomes more blatant and significant. For this reason we go to special pains to recognize external similarities so that we will be able to understand the depth of the internal differences.

There are many examples of this in the Torah. One notable example is the casting of the lots on Yom Kippur to choose between two goats. One goat will be sacrificed to G-d and the other will be thrown off the cliff (Azazel).[2] The fate of each animal is so tremendously different that it is difficult to speak of both in one sentence. Here, where the inner differences are so very pronounced, pointing out the external similarities is crucial. Halachically, both goats must be precisely equal in height, in appearance and in value.[3] The individual who is given the responsibility for purchasing the animals takes special pains to see to it that their worth is equal. In its depth, the reality is so different. Taking pains to purchase animals that are externally alike makes possible our pursuit of the enormous difference that separates the fate and purpose of both animals.

The first hairy individual we meet in the history of our People (who sets the example and pattern for the hairy goats of the Yom Kippur ceremony) is none other than Jacob's twin, Esau, whom the Torah calls "the hairy man."[4]* In order to distinguish this individual from his brother, Jacob, we must dig to the deepest possible levels in order to understand that despite their external similarities, the true differences of personality, goals, values and the quality of their souls were so extremely different that there was no similarity at all. The prophet Malachi attests, "...certainly Esau is the brother of Jacob. I, [G-d] however, love Jacob and hate Esau."[5] We see here that the depth of the differences between them becomes clear only after we identify the fact that they are brothers.

---

* Jacob and Esau were twins, originating from the same biological roots. Esau was born first, with Jacob immediately after, holding onto his brother's heel. They appeared to be physically identical except for the fact that Jacob had smooth skin and Esau was hairy and ruddy. In G-d's plan, both brothers had the potential to equally inherit and effectuate the spiritual mission of their father, the patriarch Isaac. Both were destined to be numbered among the patriarchs. It was anticipated that the force for good in Esau would vanquish the force for evil. For a variety of reasons, this unfortunately did not happen. The descent of Esau into a primary force for evil is recounted in the Torah.

This is the awesome secret of the love of Isaac for Esau.[6] The differences between Isaac and Esau scream from the depths to the point where they must go through the most lofty and exalted comparison. The most sublime area in which Esau is similar to Jacob is the love Esau merited in the house of his father. Yet, their basic and deep distinction has its roots in the home of their father Isaac, particularly in the blessings each received from his father. In order for this distinction to operate in depth (that is so deep that it is inconceivable that there can be a greater depth), it was necessary that the enormous difference between the blessings that Isaac gave each of his sons be filtered through the similarity of his sublime love. Indeed, the progression of the blessings of Isaac to his sons begins with the love of Isaac for Esau. The differences are so much deeper because they originate in so sublime a love.

This prophecy of Malachi is fulfilled through us during Purim, during which we bring closer the obliteration of the seed of Esau and his evil descendant, Amalek.

Let us examine the Purim drinking celebration that is described as "*ad d'lo yoda*, until we are no longer able to distinguish." On this day, the day of the destruction of the progeny of Esau, a torch is kindled that is totally enlightening. This is the flame of the distinction that separates Jacob and Esau. This flame kindles our imagination to comprehend the depths of the distinction that separates these two, who are so very different despite their external similarities. We then drink to the point when we cannot distinguish between "cursed is Haman and blessed is Mordechai" — at that moment we are in the same position as that individual who has been assigned the task of finding two perfectly matching goats, one to be sacrificed to G-d, the other to be thrown off the cliff. At that very moment, this individual, too, is unable to distinguish which goat will be offered to G-d and which will be thrown down. This is the *ad d'lo yoda* of Yom Kippur, also known as Yom Ki'Purim (i.e. a day that is the mirror image of Purim). We uphold the purity of our father Isaac; that he was not deceived, that all along he understood how Jacob and Esau differed.

We become inebriated in an effort to discern the similarity between "he who is blessed and he who is cursed" so that later we will know how to send the cursed one to Azazel. We will then know precisely which goat is which.

In view of the great dangers involved in indulging in the delicate business of comparison, it is possible for us to deal with this matter only during the wine-drinking celebration of Purim, because it is at this feast "that the heart of the King is good because of wine."[7] While on the surface this quote refers to King Achashverosh, its inner meaning is that the heart of the King of the Universe was "good" in the "wine of distinction" through which He is constantly drawing the lines of distinction between Israel and the nations.

For this reason, *Shoshanas Yaakov* became the poem of Purim rejoicing. "Cursed is Haman, who attempted to destroy me: Blessed is Mordechai, the Jew." This is the lottery that determines which goat will go to Azazel and which is destined for holiness. It is not possible that this lottery take place other than in a situation where both contenders seem to be identical. It takes place through the Purim banquet while inebriated, not knowing the difference between the cursed and the blessed.

*Shoshanas Yaakov,*** the hymn of Purim, ultimately is a song celebrating the salvation and victory of the children of

---

**The *shoshanah,* often mistranslated rose, was the royal lily, an ancient symbol of sovereignty. (For this reason, Persia's capital was called *Shushan,* lily.) The lily can be found carved on ancient royal monuments and buildings throughout the ancient Near East. Therefore, the first two sentences of *Shoshanas Yaakov* may be freely translated as follows:

> *The royal sovereignty and dignity of Jacob was exalted, restored and jubilant when both Jew and Persian saw Mordechai resplendent in his royal purple robes. [He was viceroy of Persia in place of Haman.] You, G-d, are their salvation for eternity and their hope in every generation.*

The Jews of Persia had called out to G-d "from the depths." The restoration of Israel to royalty and the defeat of its primary enemy, Amalek, was a concealed Divine victory. The *Megillah* also conceals the Divine Hand, yet it foretells the End of Days, projecting the victory of Israel over Amalek.

Since *Shoshanas Yaakov* anticipates the victory of good over evil in the End of Days it is able to openly proclaim, "Cursed is Haman" and "Blessed is Mordechai." The concealment of *ad d'lo yoda,* of being "beyond knowing" will no longer be needed.

Jacob in the End of Days. Purim and *Megillas Esther* are a microcosm of the future Messianic victory. The song of Purim is a "New Song," telling of the victory of concealed and secret Divine forces.

---

1. *Megillah* 7b.
2. *Leviticus* 16:8.
3. *Yoma* 62a.
4. *Genesis* 27:11.
5. *Malachi* 1:2-3.
6. *Genesis* 25:28.
7. *Esther* 1:10.

PURIM AND YOM KIPPUR ARE ONE

Based on *Pachad Yitzchok:* Purim 8

ne of the most fascinating insights concerning Purim is that its "twin" is Yom Kippur. This concept is found in the *Sefer Likutei HaGra*, the assembled writings of the Vilna Gaon.[1]

The Gra bases his comment on the following Gemara: "The general structure of our festivals is that they follow a divided format: Half of the festival consists of obligations to G-d (i.e. prayer, special *mitzvos*) and the other half is for our enjoyment (i.e. festive meals, rest, friends, family, fine clothes, etc.)."[2]

The Gra writes:

> *Yom Kippur lacks this arrangement in that there is no half set aside for our personal enjoyment. On Yom Kippur we stand before G-d simulating angels, totally putting aside the fulfillment of our bodily pleasures. The activities of Purim are the*

*opposite: Most of the day is devoted in some fash-
ion to physical pleasure.*

Purim and Yom Kippur, therefore, are each mirror images of
the other. Each provides the missing half that the other lacks.
This is even indicated by their names: Yom Hakippurim is a Day
"*Ki-Purim*, similar to Purim." Together, they constitute one complete festival. This united festival consists of "a half that is for G-
d and a half that is for man."

Let us savor some of the sweetness of this spiritual honey. Our
Talmudic Sages debate the nature of G-d's ultimate reckoning
with the Patriarchs. G-d will say: "Your children have sinned
against Me." Isaac will answer: "Are they my children and not
Your children?" The Talmud then discusses the sins and merits of
the children, then "quotes" Isaac as saying: "If You [G-d] will bear
all of their sins, it will be good. If not, the responsibility for half
will be on me and half will be on You."[3]

Isaac's entreaty was interpreted by the great master of
Mussar [branch of Jewish thought] Rabbi Yitzchok Blazer
(Peterburger), who said that Isaac's response is explained in
the pronouncement of the Sages, "Master of the world, it is
revealed and known before You that our will is to perform Your
Will. Who prevents us from doing so? The yeast in the dough
[the evil inclination in our hearts] and our subjugation to foreign regimes [since these governments create obstacles to prevent our observing the positive commandments]."[4]

The above-mentioned obstacles are the basis for the division proposed by Isaac, "Half will be on me and half will be on
You." In fact, "the yeast in the dough, i.e. the force of the
inclination to evil is the opposing force which You, G-d, set
in motion."[5]

There were other men of renown who addressed a similar
complaint to Heaven. The prophet Elijah prayed as he confronted the worshippers of the Baal.[6] Elijah said to G-d; "Answer me
G-d, answer me: Let this people know that You are the L-rd G-d
and You will turn their hearts back in repentance." The commentator Radak, however, interprets Elijah's words to mean,
"You [G-d] are responsible for their backsliding and idol wor-

ship." How do we know that Radak's reading of Elijah's con-tention is accurate? We see elsewhere that G-d says, "…I caused them to sin [by creating the inclination for evil]."[7] Thus Isaac can rightly say, "half is Yours."

Why did Isaac also assume responsibility for half? Isaac said to G-d, "Indeed, it is I, Isaac, who created the second factor [of subjugation to foreign powers] which prevents Israel's full fealty to Your Will. I am responsible for the creation of Esau, who made possible Israel's subjugation to the gentile kingdoms. The exile and the subjugation of Israel to foreign governments is a direct result of the power of Esau. Therefore, I accept responsibility for Esau; 'half is my doing.'" (This concludes Rabbi Blazer's comments.)

The above conforms to the words of the Vilna Gaon. The two festivals, Yom Kippur and Purim, are "half for G-d and half for you." In effect, they are two halves of one whole. This whole, this unity, represents a deep cry, a scream that rises from the depths of the Jewish soul, "It is our desire to do Your Will [but we are prevented from doing so!]." Both reasons that prevent the Jewish People from serving G-d fully — the evil inclination and the enslavement of the Jews by other kingdoms — must be rectified. This is the point where Purim and Yom Kippur join. The combination of these two festivals brings about the elimi-nation of the two barriers.

Yom Kippur has the ability to remedy the first cause of sin: the power of evil. On Yom Kippur, we stand before G-d, shun-ning our physical needs. As a result of our emphasis on our spirituality over physicality, our impulse for evil loses its strength. Therefore, the angel who serves as "the prosecutor" in the Heavenly court on Yom Kippur has no opportunity, no "permission," to prosecute.[8] On Purim, the second force pre-venting us from serving G-d — that of the enslaving kingdoms descended from Esau — is eliminated. This happened in Persia at the time of the Purim miracle: "The fear of the Jews overtook the Persian population."[9] Between the two holidays, the obstacle to "Our desire is to do Your Will" is eliminated for all time.

Here we see the real meaning of the word *"Megillah"* in relation to *Megillas Esther. Megillah* has roots in two meanings: a scroll and "to reveal." In the scroll of Esther we see that the deeds of Esther and the salvation of Purim revealed the hidden potential desire of the Jews to do G-d's Will.

1. *Sefer Likutei HaGra,* Warsaw, 5549, page 308.
2. *Beitzah* 15b.
3. *Shabbos* 89b.
4. *Berachos* 17a.
5. *Berachos* 32b.
6. *I Kings* 18:37.
7. *Ibid.*
8. *Yoma* 20a.
9. *Esther* 8:17.

GIFTS TO THE ENEMY

51 Based on *Pachad Yitzchok:* Purim 12

The *mitzvah* of *mishloach manos*, sending gifts of food, is a unique aspect of the salvation brought about by Purim. Let us examine one of the emotions we feel concerning this special *mitzvah*.

In describing the four kings against whom Abraham went to war, the fourth king is called, "*Tydal, King of the Nations.*"[1] What is exceptional here is that when the Torah speaks of Tydal, he is not the king of a city or of a small nation. The Torah is clear that it speaks of him as a king over many nations. Our Sages have always seen the reference to Tydal as including a prophetic allusion to Edom and Rome, the Fourth Kingdom whose opposition to Israel is strikingly different from the opposition of the previous three kingdoms. The other three kingdoms were specific monarchies that ruled over a given territory at a given time, whereas "Rome" refers to the Jewish exile in the western world that includes many countries over a long period of time.

In post-Abrahamic days, the Fourth Kingdom is identified with Esau/Amalek, which became known as Edom/Rome. Rome is exceptional in that it spreads its anti-Jewish incitement to all nations. This aptly describes our present exile, the Exile of the Fourth Kingdom, which we refer to as the Exile of Rome. It is from Rome that Edom disseminates its poisonous anti-Semitic propaganda to all the nations of the world. It is in Rome that Edom makes his appearance as the king of many nations.

The saga of Purim is the first instance where we find Edom/Amalek/Rome allying itself with another nation in an effort to spread its hatred. Haman the Amalekite employs his poisonous incitement to activate his proxy, Achashverosh, King of Persia.

The *Medrash Rabbah*[2] informs us that when the Sages of Israel would travel to Rome in order to lobby for the needs of the Jewish community in the Land of Israel, they would carefully study the Torah portion of *Vayishlach*, which discusses the struggle between Jacob and Esau. It is this Torah portion which best demonstrates the Rabbinic teaching that "the experiences of the fathers are an indicator of what the children are destined to encounter in future generations." This particularly applies to Israel's relationship with Rome. And from the conflict of Jacob with Esau we learn of Jacob sending gifts to mollify Esau, which serves as a paradigm for paying bribes and tribute in later times.

There is no question that giving a gift to one's fellow is an expression of love and brotherhood. The Sages taught, "He who gives his fellow a gift must inform him in advance"[3] in order to intensify love. Picture, however, a person who is caught in the unfortunate situation where he feels compelled to constantly send gifts to his enemy in order to flatter him. The receiver knows the gifts are insincere gestures, so if ever the sender presents a gift in a gesture of true friendship he remains somewhat suspect: His reputation is that of one who sends insincere gifts. The above scenario describes the unfortunate situation of Jacob, who sent gifts to his murderous brother, Esau, in an attempt to mollify him.

And so it is that on Purim day, the day which celebrates the destruction of the power of Amalek/Edom/Rome, a day on which it is no longer necessary to travel to Rome to plead for relief, we finally experience a day on which we are not obligated to study the Torah portion of *Vayishlach* or feel the need to send deceptive, insincere gifts to mollify Esau. Today, on Purim, we are able to enjoy the purity of sending gifts to Jacob. In keeping with *halachah,* we first send gifts to Jews with whom we have had differences — precisely to emphasize brotherly love where it has not been apparent. In addition, we send *mishloach manos* to our closer friends, representing our friendship and love of every Jew.

1. *Genesis* 14:1.
2. *Genesis* 78:18, also 75:6.
3. *Shabbos* 10b.

MISHLOACH MANOS: SENDING GIFTS

52 Based on *Pachad Yitzchok:* Purim 21

We have previously mentioned the holy words of the Vilna Gaon, who expands on the teaching of our Sages that the "Day of Purim" and the "Day that is *Ki'Purim*," i.e. Yom Kippur, are similar. In effect they are halves of one whole. The Vilna Gaon bases his comments on the general halachic rule of festivals, that half of the day is given over to human pleasures and half to spiritual observances.[1] The exceptions are Purim and Yom Ha*Ki'purim*. Yom Kippur is "for G-d" — there is a total absence of bodily pleasures; while Purim is totally "for us" — the emphasis is on physical pleasure. The Gaon's insight is that these opposing qualities constitute a symbiosis between these two unique days. In effect, together they constitute one Yom Tov.[2]

What unique innovation do we find in this concept? What do these days have in common? On each, the Jewish People were rescued from an edict calling for their total destruction.

Following the sin of the Golden Calf, G-d instructed Moses, "Step away from Me and I will destroy them."[3] But G-d forgave them on Yom Kippur and rescinded His decision to destroy the nation. On Purim, Haman planned to "destroy, murder and obliterate all the Jews,"[4] until the tables were turned and the Jews were saved from annihilation.

Another comparison is in order. On Yom Kippur, both the edict and the salvation were known only in Heaven, in communications between G-d and Moses. No one on earth had any idea what was transpiring. On Purim, however, both the edict and the salvation took place here on earth, in the events described in the *Megillah*.

Both days reflect in their nature the character of the events with which they are associated. As the edict and salvation of Yom Kippur took place in the Heavens, the holy day is devoted to the spiritual. The events of Purim, however, took place here on earth, so that holy day is celebrated in an earthly fashion.

The uniqueness of each day is also reflected in the relationships it fosters between each person and his fellow. The Sages teach that repentance cannot be attained on Yom Kippur until strained relationships between "a person and his fellow are mended, until he mollifies his fellow."[5] The "mending" on Purim is accomplished through "sending gifts of edibles by each person to his fellow."[6]

The mending of relationships on Yom Kippur requires spiritual effort through introspection, words and apologies. On Purim, it is accomplished through gifts and guests at the festive meal, all of which apply to the physical. The result is that through the proper observance of the two related days — Yom Kippur and Purim — we have the opportunity to experience wholeness, respectively balancing each day's spiritual and physical components in ourselves and with our fellow man: Reconciliation on Yom Kippur, conciliation on Purim.

---

1. *Beitzah* 15b.
2. *Sefer Likutei HaGra,* Warsaw, page 308.
3. *Deuteronomy* 9:14, which recalls the incident described in *Exodus* 32:10.
4. *Esther* 3:13.
5. *Mishnah Yoma* 5.
6. *Esther* 6:22.

HALLEL ON PURIM

Based on *Pachad Yitzchok:* Purim 33

he Gemara asks, "Why don't we recite *Hallel* on Purim?"[1] It is somewhat of an anomaly that the commemoration of Israel's redemption from Haman's threat of total annihilation does not merit the saying of *Hallel.* The Talmud grapples with this problem and states that, "the reading of the *Megillah* is the *Hallel* of Purim." The famous commentator *Me'iri* states in his work *Beis Habechirah* that if a person is not able to read the *Megillah* for whatever reason, he is obligated to recite *Hallel.* It seems, however, that all the other Sages disagree with this position.

Why is there almost total unanimity among the Sages on this issue? Since the Gemara is insistent that one must fulfill the obligation to say *Hallel* on Purim by reading the *Megillah,* why would the actual recitation of *Hallel* be inappropriate?

We know that *Hallel* is recited only when the miracle it celebrates is a public event, when G-d's Hand in the miracle is obvious and known, such as on Passover, Shavuos and

Chanukah. *Hallel* is a public celebration that mirrors the nature of the miracle that took place. On Purim, however, the miracle took place in a secretive and hidden form. G-d's Name is not mentioned in the *Megillah*, and the Purim miracle took place in such a way that only a knowledgeable and perceptive person would have recognized that indeed a miracle had taken place. Therefore, the celebration of the miracle is concealed in the *Megillah* itself where it takes insight, hindsight and the talents of a detective to discern the miraculous nature of the events. A hidden miracle demands a "hidden form" of *Hallel* — the reading of the *Megillah*.

The Sages ask, what source is there in the Torah that informs us concerning Esther (i.e. where do we find an allusion to Queen Esther in the Torah)? They respond, the Torah says, "*Ve'anochi haster astir* — I will surely conceal."[2] (*Astir* is written with the same Hebrew letters as Esther.) Concealment is the nature of *Megillas Esther*. The *Megillah* does not replace *Hallel*. The *Megillah* *becomes* the unique form of the Purim *Hallel* in its own right.

▶ An Additional Thought

Even in our age, many individuals have merited experiencing G-d's open and obvious miracles. Even without such open miracles, every person experiences miracles that are often taken as commonplace — sunrise and sunset, birth and healing, wonderful fruits and delicacies — which are truly miraculous, viewed objectively. There are also hidden and private miracles that only a person who is spiritually sensitive can perceive and appreciate. In the presence of such miracles there is no explanation but the intervening Hand of G-d. Therefore, we daily thank G-d, "for Your miracles that we experience daily" in the *Shmoneh Esrei* prayer.

---

1. *Megillah* 14a.
2. *Deuteronomy* 31:18.

WHY IS PURIM THE ONLY FESTIVAL DESTINED TO LAST FOREVER?

Based on *Pachad Yitzchok:* Purim 34

Our Sages teach that when the Messiah arrives, the festivals will cease to be observed. There will be one exception — Purim. The *Midrash*[1] derives this unusual conclusion from a statement in *Megillas Esther* (9:28), "The memory of Purim will never cease from among their descendants." Why should a relatively "minor" festival be observed forever, while the basic and more significant festivals will no longer be needed? The following analogy will help explain this extraordinarily puzzling Rabbinic teaching.

Two individuals were given the following assignment: Identify your friends in the black of night. One individual was supplied with a flashlight. He identified his friends by shining a light in their faces. The second did not have a flashlight. He was compelled to identify his friends by listening to their voices and the sound of their steps. The first did a far superior job. Seeing people's faces is far more effective than listening to their distant conversation or to their footsteps. But the second person developed a unique talent. By training his ears to listen attentively, he developed a special sensitivity, much as a blind person develops a sensitivity that others lack.

When the sun rose in the morning, the first person turned off his flashlight. What value is there to a flashlight in the presence of sunlight? The second individual, however, had developed the talent of recognizing people in pitch darkness. He had acquired the ability to recognize people he couldn't see. This talent, which he developed and perfected during that long and dark night, remained with him during the next day, and the next.

To understand how this analogy explains the eternity of Purim, we must first understand certain principles. During a leap year, there are two months of Adar on the Jewish calendar, Adar I and Adar II. In almost all instances, the *halachah* insists that we observe a commandment at the earliest moment possible, but Purim is an exception. Here, the law mandates that we celebrate Purim and read *Megillas Esther* during the second month of Adar.[2] Why? Because there is an intimate relationship between the redemption of Purim and the redemption of Passover; between Purim and Passover that will take place thirty days later; between Adar II, which is the last month of the year, and Nissan, which is the first. *Purim must be linked to Passover because Purim describes the end of exile, the end of the long night of Jewish suffering, while Passover describes the beginning of salvation, the birth of redemption.* Just as the redemption from Egypt culminated in the word "*Anochi*, I" — "I am the L-rd your G-d who took you out of the Land of Egypt" — so too the redemption of Purim has a special *Anochi* of its own: "*Anochi haster astir*, I am the L-rd who will surely conceal."[3]

We learn this from a passage in the Talmud[4] that asks, "From where do we derive Esther in the Torah?" (What are the "roots" of Esther in the Torah, despite the fact that Esther lived many generations later?) The Talmud replies; "In the Torah it says '*Anochi haster astir.*'" ("*Astir*, I will hide," is written with the same Hebrew letters as Esther.)

What lesson do we derive from the two statements of *Anochi*? We learn that the Jewish People possesses two methods with which to connect with, identify and recognize G-d: The first is the public *Anochi* of the Exodus: "I am the Lord your G-d." [I performed public miracles when I brought you out of Egypt and gave you the Torah.] This *Anochi* can be compared to the person who identified his friends by shining a flashlight. There is a second way to recognize G-d: The ability of the Jewish People to recognize G-d's "*Anochi, I am*" when He is concealed in the darkness of exile. This is a uniquely Jewish talent — the ability to identify and understand the ongoing redemption of "*haster astir,* I will surely hide and conceal." Similar to the special talent of the person who trained his ears to recognize people at night by listening to their voices and the sound of their footsteps, the Jews recognize the presence of G-d's Hand in human events — even when it is not evident, but works through what the world calls "nature."

To what conclusion does this lead us? When the night of exile will be banished with the rising sun of the coming of the Messiah, when in the End of Days the Hand of G-d will be seen in all its strength and glory, G-d's presence will be so obvious that we will no longer require the "lights" provided by our holidays to perceive Him in historical events. At that time, the light of G-dliness will be thousands of times more powerful than the light of the sun. At that time, all of the holidays, which are rooted in the Exodus [*zecher l'yetzias Mitzrayim*], will pale in the blaze of the light of Divine Messianic Redemption.

There is, however, one exception. On Purim, during the long night of exile, the Jewish People developed the special ability to recognize G-d's Providence, even when concealed. This will remain our eternal possession even after the sun of the Redemption will rise. At that time all of the holidays will pale, except for Purim, "whose remembrance will never be forgotten by their descendants."

There are two types of light. The first is, "G-d is my light,"[5] and the second is, "Though I sit in darkness, G-d is my light."[6] The special quality of Purim is its ability to make us aware of the second form of light — the light that breaks through the cracks of darkness. That special light has a unique ability to guide man through darkness, even surpassing the normal light of the sun.

So too, the pearls of knowledge which shine through the darkness of the "beyond knowing," of the *ad d'lo yoda* of Purim, are especially precious because they are similar to the light that is capable of guiding man through darkness.[7]

▶ An Additional Thought

Passover is the holiday of spring, the first holiday of the new year. As vegetation breaks through the cold barren earth, as the rays of spring sunshine warm the ground and cast away the cold, the heart is stirred by feelings of redemption. When a year has two Adars, Purim takes place in the second, at the end of the year. Because Purim is the last holiday of the year, it must occur on the last month of the year. All attempts to destroy the Jewish People will end with the banishment of the darkness of exile and the breakthrough of the light of Redemption.

For this reason, the moment Purim departs we prepare for the new year by studying the laws of Passover. Our rabbis taught, "When Adar arrives, we begin to increase our joy." We rejoice in the knowledge that our enemies have been subdued, that the exile has ended. Passover is coming. It is a prelude to the great Redemption that will witness the rebirth and regeneration of the Jewish People as it rejoices in the arrival of the King Messiah. The study of the laws of Passover, which begin the day after Purim, bind Purim to Passover and lead us from darkness to light, from exile to the light of Redemption.

1. *Yalkut Shimoni Mishlei* 9.
2. *Megillah* 6b.
3. *Deuteronomy* 31:18.
4. *Chullin* 139b.
5. *Psalms* 27:1.
6. *Micah* 7:8.
7. *Megillah* 7b.

VIII PASSOVER AND LAG B'OMER

PASSOVER: BIRTH AND REBIRTH

55

Two unique moments of high emotional intensity punctuate the Jewish year: *Neilah*, the last prayer service of Yom Kippur, and *Kiddush* at the beginning of the Passover Seder. To the spiritually sensitive person, no other moments of the year compare to these special experiences in sheer depth and overwhelming emotion. Each of these moments arrives only after we have invested great emotional effort and significant preparation. *Neilah* is spiritual and personal. We achieve spiritual and emotional inspiration thanks to the cleansing effect of *Neilah*, the result of our long effort to achieve *teshuvah*, repentance.

The Seder, too, comes after much physical exertion — the intense weeks of pre-Passover cleaning, planning and preparation. Here too, we hope to have allowed the significance of the many enactments of Passover to sink in and to affect our thoughts, our psyche, our mood and our spiritual state. Passover is experienced through the Hagaddah, which dramatizes the birth of our Nation and its escape from the imprison-ing tomb of the Egyptian slave state. At the Seder we experi-ence this sense of exhilaration.

The intensity of *Neilah* is mostly personal in nature: I stood before G-d, I repented, I attempted to change my ways. Just days later, after Succos has passed, we confront the long, dark, cold winter which symbolizes alienation from G-d: failure, sin and exile. The winter months teach that the quest for human com-pleteness and happiness cannot be entrusted to the individual alone. When operating in isolation to overcome evil, alienation and exile, most individuals fail. The human being requires a sup-port system of family, friends, teachers, society and nation in order to direct, inspire and motivate his efforts. In recognition of the inability of the individual to banish loneliness and failure, G-d gave mankind the gift of a new mechanism, a new structure with which to fight the battle of life — the Torah. Family creativ-ity and national unity are at its foundation.

The first book of the Torah relates many incidents that describe how, despite initial successes, individuals working in isolation failed to change the course of history or transform humanity. These individuals, who lived prior to Abraham, proved incapable of bringing about the Messianic order. G-d, therefore, taught our ancestors how to create a new entity, to which he entrusted the responsibility for creating the new humanity — the Jewish Nation. The core and central structure of the Jewish Nation is the Jewish family.

▸ The Seder: A Family Experience

With the advent of spring, human hope is reborn. Nissan, the month of spring, is the first month of the Jewish Nation's year heralding the festival, Passover, the holiday of birth, freedom and renewal. Passover is the celebration of the birth of the Jewish Nation — a sacred collective of Jewish families. Therefore, in ancient times, the paschal sacrifice, the core of the Seder celebration, was a family event. Today, of course, we no longer have the Passover sacrifice, but the Seder remains intact as an annual family event.

The great preparatory efforts that culminate at the Seder *Kiddush* create within each of us a deep emotional awareness of transformation and birth. *Kiddush* is the very first act in the first dramatic moments of the Seder. The Seder marks our rededication to our responsibilities as free men and women. No longer are we slaves to Pharaoh: We are now free to serve G-d. "You are My servants, not slaves to slaves." The Seder recalls the first great act of Divine intervention in human history, the dramatic overthrow of the world's most powerful and advanced kingdom by force of the Divine Will — a singular, spectacular event which paved the way for the birth of G-d's own nation.

At Passover, we feel G-d's Hand operating in history. It is the first occasion when G-d revealed Himself before all of mankind as the controlling force of nature, as the master of history. Our rabbis teach that Passover contains within it the four hinge periods of life: the birth of the Jewish People as G-d's chosen nation; the conversion of each Jew to his new spiritual status as a member of *Am Yisrael*; the marriage of an eternal and indestructible nation to G-d and His agenda; and the creation of a unique spiritual society that would be dedicated to the worship and service of G-d. In the opening act of the Seder, G-d is revealed as the master of nature and history, the father of the Jewish Nation, the protector of the slave and the oppressed, the Creator of justice, human order and of a new spiritual society.

The father of each family stands at the head of the Seder table with the *Kiddush* cup in hand, in full realization that he is about to reenact and relive the historic moments of the Exodus. He looks at the gleaming Seder table and at the expectant faces of his wife, children and guests and senses that he is a witness to and a participant in the foundation of a new spiritual reality. He recalls that *Kiddush* means sanctity, reminding us that throughout hundreds of years of slavery, Jews maintained the integrity of the marital bond and resisted the contamination of Egypt's sexual depravity and licentiousness. Each of us feels, "I, too, was just freed from Egyptian bondage." This emotion brings with it a sense of the stocktaking of the family. Much as each individual is scrutinized on Yom Kippur, so too is the family scrutinized on Passover.

The fundamental concept of Passover is *areivus*, responsibility: the realization that salvation, *geulah*, cannot be realized through the individual alone but requires the collective efforts of the *am*, the nation. The Hebrew word *am* is a word that implies *with, together*, i.e. a collective. *Am* describes a unique concept, a sacred collective held together not by blood, language, culture, geography and dependence alone, but also by shared goals, ideals and teachings. The family is a mystical, spiritual entity. It exists in a covenantal relationship with G-d. Communal responsibility begins with the family and is founded on the familial bond. It is in the context of family that one learns that each individual is responsible for more than himself.

▶ Achieving a New Status

Why the intense preparations for Passover? Why are there so many laws and stringencies that strive for perfection and 100% removal of *chametz,* leavened products? This intensity, this striving for totality, is a reenactment of the Passover travail of the birth of a new revolutionary entity, *Am Yisrael.* This entity contains within itself the potential for human perfection and harmony. From the moment of the recital of the *Kiddush,* we put behind us the bleak, dark, cold night of winter. Suddenly warmth and sun break through, bringing life, hope and redemption. The Hebrew word *aviv,* spring, is rooted in *av,* meaning father. *Aim,* meaning mother, is similar to *am,* nation. From slavery, to family, to nation, we experience the presence of our new heightened status and spiritual reality.

Contrast the elevated Jewish family with the Egyptian failure to preserve family life. In the Torah, there are numerous references to the depravity and immorality of the ancient Egyptians.

The Seder is a celebration of children and family, of the sacred bond that unites father, mother, children, parents and grandparents. Our children make it possible to extend the past into the future. Our children are links in a golden chain that reaches back to the Patriarchs, to the Exodus, and stretches forward as it reaches the Messiah. The emphasis of the Seder is therefore on education, on children, on the children asking the Four Questions, on the search for the Afikomen, on the empowerment of our children, on the gradual transmission of the tasks, values, burdens, ideals and hopes set forth by our Torah to them. We are no longer slaves because a slave has no family.

By casting off the filth of Egyptian decadence, Israel was not only born, it also carried the seeds and the potential for eternal life. Our Sages teach that by the time they reached Mount Sinai, the Children of Israel overcame the depravity of Egypt and was restored to man's ideal status "prior to the sin of Adam." But this time, the New Mankind is born through the realization that perfection can only come about through *tikkun olam* — by reaching out to all of mankind in the creation of the Kingdom of G-d. Passover, therefore, marks the creation of that fruit-giving seed from which will grow human destiny, perfection and Redemption.

THE EXODUS: HISTORY'S TURNING POINT

56

O ne of the most significant points in world history is summarized in two crucial sentences in the Torah: "At the end of 430 years, all of G-d's forces left Egypt in broad daylight. This was a night of vigil for G-d *(Leyl Shimurim),* in anticipation of the Exodus from Egypt; this night remains for Israel a G-dly vigil for all generations."[1]

How does Rashi understand this term, *Leyl Shimurim*? It was a night of anticipation. For hundreds of years, the Creator anticipated this night. This was to be a night that would transform the world for all time, a night that would unleash universal forces that had been in readiness since the beginning of time. Until this moment, the religions of the nations were much the same; they all worshipped idols that represented forces of nature. Now there emerged a new nation — *Am Yisrael* — that recognized the true Master and Creator of history and nature. This new nation would comprehend the purpose of Creation and unleash spiritual forces that would bring Creation to fruition. Now, there was choice.

This was the night of promise designated from the time of Abraham as the night destined for redemption. Until this night, Israel was enslaved. Its potential to bring forth innovative forces was frozen. Now Israel would create new and vibrant realities, goals worth living and dying for.

"Hu halailah hazeh laShem, This was a night of vigil for G-d..."[2] Rashi explains: This is the night on which G-d said to Abraham, "On this night, I will liberate your children. On this night, the potential for which I, G-d, created this world will be released."

"Shimurim l'chol B'nei Yisrael l'dorosam, This night remains for Israel a G-dly vigil for all generations."[3] Rashi: The second time the word *shimurim* is used, it has an alternate meaning. It also means preservation. Israel is to be preserved and defended from those who would attack it. G-d said, "I will not permit the destroyer to succeed." The forces of redemption and creativity that give life value and purpose must be protected. Israel is the creative life-giving force of the universe. Through association with the newborn Nation of Israel, soon to receive G-d's Torah, a person is transformed into a dynamic and creative individual.

"L'dorosam, through all generations." In each generation, nations and civilizations will attempt to destroy this positive force. In each generation, we will have to fight for the ascendancy of Torah. The struggle against those who reject the Exodus, who reject the uniqueness of Israel's birth, who reject Israel's striving for truth, will continue until the end of time. In the End of Days, Israel will prevail and transform all of civilization. On that day, the L-rd will be King over all the earth.

This essay was inspired by Rabbi Mordechai Schechter.

---

1. *Exodus* 12:41-42.
2. *Exodus* 12:42.
3. *Ibid.*

THE
PASSOVER
PUZZLE

What follows is an inquiry into the Exodus, which is an effort to resolve the following questions:

Were our ancestors freed from slavery in Egypt due to necessity, due to their merit or because of the imperative to fulfill a Divine promise?

What were the cause, goal and purpose of 210 years of slavery?

Was this goal realized?

There are four basic approaches articulated by various sources as to why the Jews were freed.

1. Necessity: G-d snatched his People from the corrupting claws of Egyptian society because they had descended to the 49th level of immorality and spiritual impurity known as "*Mem*

tes Sha'arei Tumah, The 49 Gates [or Levels] of Defilement." Had they reached the 50th level, they would have become indistinguishable from their Egyptian taskmasters. Having lost their Abrahamic identity and character, there would have been no one left to redeem. Therefore, the Exodus was rushed. Israel left under pressure to leave before leaving would be impossible.

2. The Divine Promise: G-d promised Abraham in the "Covenant of the Pieces" that his descendants would be enslaved for 400 years and that at the conclusion of the enslavement they would be liberated and inherit the riches of the Egyptians.[1] Since they had now arrived at the conclusion of the 400 years, G-d kept His promise.

3. Merit: The Iron Furnace:[2] The purpose of the enslavement was to apply cultural shock treatment to the psyche of the Jewish People. By subjecting them to a debased, immoral and inhumane society ruled by a corrupt elite who lived a life of leisure and luxury on the backs of a degraded, suffering, enslaved population, the Jews would be purified and sensitized. The "purifying" experience of slavery, which we call "The Iron Furnace, *Kur Habarzel,*" would shock the Jews and cause them to emerge with a heightened sensitivity to the Divine challenge and to human needs, rights and values. After experiencing G-d's many miracles, they would be prepared to receive the Torah and live an uplifting life of spirituality by creating a Torah society that would transform mankind.

4. A Complex Perspective: We must keep in mind that the actual enslavement took place during a 210-year period. It is therefore impossible to generalize, since the descriptions and words of the Torah and of the Sages may apply to different periods of time and to different groups of Jews.

Originally, the Jews all lived in Goshen; later they dispersed throughout Egypt. At first, Pharaoh used gentle language and enticing methods to draw the Jews into what subsequently became enslavement. At times, the physical enslavement was backbreaking and inhuman. At one point, fearful that a Jew would become their liberator as was predicted by his advisors, Pharaoh ordered the drowning of all male children, thus threatening a holocaust which would have destroyed the Jewish People.

The Levites avoided the enslavement. Some Jews forgot their Abrahamic heritage, others held on to it. Some despaired of redemption while others believed G-d's promise and tenaciously looked forward to redemption.

In general, the Jews retained their Hebrew language, names and dress, and lived on a high level of family and personal morality. Rashi teaches that 80% of the Jews died during the plague of darkness: These were the Jews who were totally assimilated and were near spiritual extinction. Due to a lack of belief in G-d's power, many felt that liberation was beyond the possible (since no one had ever escaped from Egypt), and that the entire concept of a trek to the Land of Canaan through the desert was totally unrealistic. A marked change obviously took place when the enslavement ceased during the Ten Plagues prior to the Exodus. Each of the solutions must be viewed with the above in mind.

Our question remains: Had the Jews become more refined, which is reflected in the concept of the *Kur Habarzel*, the refining furnace, or had they reached the 49th level of defilement? We hope our analysis will provide a reasonable answer.

▸ How the Meshech Chochmah Views the Inquiry: The four expressions of Redemption and the four cups of wine evidence that the Jews lived exemplary lives

Various sources confirm that despite their long and cruel enslavement the Israelite slaves maintained their "Jewish" character. As taught in the *Mechilta D'Rabbi Yishmael, Masechta De Pischa* (and other sources):

Rabbi Eliezer Hakadar teaches, "In Egypt Israel surely possessed four commandments which made the continued existence of the universe possible.

1) They were not suspected of immoral sexual behavior;

2) As a rule, they did not practice slander;

3) They did not change their Hebrew names;

*4) They did not abandon their Hebrew language, culture
and national tradition."*

Using the above *Midrash* as his source, Rabbi Meir Simcha
HaKohen of Dvinsk, in his Torah commentary *Meshech
Chochmah*,[3] offers an astounding analysis. He largely bypasses
the concept of the "49 Gates of Defilement," and emphasizes the
high moral state of the Jews. He paints a picture of Israel prior to
their liberation in glowing and admiring terms.

In addition, he correlates "the four expressions of
Redemption" with the four cups of wine we drink at the Seder. On
Passover night we are obligated to drink four cups of wine. We
also know that the liberation from Egypt is celebrated through
the "four expressions of Redemption" enumerated by G-d in the
Torah: *v'hotzaysi* — "I will take you out;" *v'hitzalti* — "I will save
[your lives];" *v'ga'alti* — "I will redeem you [from slavery];"
v'lakachti —"I will take you [to Me as My nation]." The Meshech
Chochmah sees a direct correlation between the four expressions of liberation and the four cups of wine. Together, they offer
a surprising, masterful and uplifting insight into the meaning of
the Exodus.

Firstly, the four terms for liberation are not mere expressions,
but are descriptions of four types of liberation. The first is "*v'hotzaysi*, I shall take you [out of Egypt]." This is an allusion to the statement in Deuteronomy (4:34), "To remove a nation from the midst
of a nation just as you remove a baby from its mother's womb at
birth." The Jews were embedded in Egyptian culture. Many of
them were sinking into idol worship and had to be quickly extracted before they would totally sink into the decadence of Egypt. The
Jews had to be removed from Egyptian influence quickly, urgently.

The second expression is "*v'hitzalti*, I will save [your lives]."
The Egyptians were persecuting the Jews to a point where they
faced annihilation. There was a direct threat to their lives; particularly after Pharaoh's order to drown every newborn boy in

the Nile River. G-d's purpose was to save their lives from the hands of murderers.

The third expression is "*v'ga'alti*, I will redeem you." This expressed G-d's intention to redeem the Jews from the yoke of slavery, to liberate them from bondage.

The fourth expression is "*v'lakachti*, and I shall take you." "I shall take you to Me as My Nation. I will restore your spiritual and national identity and provide you with the Torah and a land, and I will be your King."

These four expressions refer to four benefits to the Children of Israel when G-d liberated them from Egypt.

1. G-d saved them from evil influences;
2. G-d snatched them from the threat to their lives;
3. G-d liberated them from slavery;
4. G-d restored their national and spiritual identity.

Now let us relate these concepts to the four cups of wine consumed at the Seder:

1. The first cup of wine at the Seder is *Kiddush*, the sanctification of the Passover holiday. *Kiddush* concludes with the words, "Blessed is G-d who sanctifies Israel and the festivals"("the set times"). Passover begins with the recognition that all people have the ability to sanctify time. The Talmud says, "Just as G-d sanctifies Israel, Israel sanctifies time and the festivals which are associated with time." As the Torah teaches, "This month (Nissan) will be for you the first of months." The month of Nissan is given over to you in the expectation that you will sanctify it. How can an individual sanctify something? Through holiness: If a person has the ability to sanctify, it implies that the person himself is filled with sanctity. When is a person holy? The Sages teach that sanctity derives from the ability of an individual to restrain him-or herself from illicit sexual activity.

Why is the Torah exhortation "*kedoshim tehiyu*, you shall be holy," found in the Torah next to the teaching forbidding illicit sexual involvement? Because wherever you find sexual discipline, you find holiness. A person who is circumspect as regards sexual morality is holy. Israel is able to sanctify the seasons because they are circumspect in matters of morality. From this we learn that when Israel was in Egypt, they lived exemplary moral lives. Had they intermarried or had they been promiscuous with their Egyptian neighbors, could G-d have extracted them from the Egyptians? The testimony to their holiness is a testimony to their ability to sanctify. *V'hotzaysi* does not only describe G-d's intervention to liberate them, it also describes a characteristic which Israel maintained during hundreds of difficult years.

2. The second expression (the third cup of wine) is *"V'hitzalti — and I will save you."* I will deliver you from those who scheme to kill you. The implication is that the Jews were endangered only by the Egyptians, but they lived in peace with each other. Once the Egyptian threat was removed, the nation was totally at peace.

From this we deduce that the Jews, with rare exceptions, avoided *lashon hara*. They did not speak ill of each other nor did they reveal secrets. They were not guilty of slander or tale bearing. They did not reveal confidences to their Egyptian taskmasters. They were not jealous of each other. How do we know that they were not jealous of each other? The source of tale bearing is jealousy, which is reflected in a lack of belief in G-d's goodness and providence. Jealousy arises when one does not believe sufficiently that G-d provides each person with his or her needs as He sees fit. Therefore, if the Jews did not gossip about each other, it indicates that jealousy was not common. The common Jew's faith was strong that everything G-d gives each of us is specifically appropriate.

This concept is found in the *Birkas Hamazon* where we say, "G-d sustains everyone in accordance with His Will." *Birkas Hamazon* begins with the words, "Blessed is G-d who sustains the world with goodness, grace, love and mercy. He gives bread to all, for His love is eternal. In His goodness, He has never denied us our needs." This prayer is an acknowledgement that no one receives more or less than what G-d wants him to receive. Applied to the Jews in Egypt, they understood that since G-d will take them out of a country that is harming them, the implication is that no one else wants to harm them. They lived in harmony with their fellow Jews. Each Jew recognized the supremacy of G-d and acknowledged G-d's Hand in everything. This understanding reflected a high quality of faith and contentment. In testimony to this quality, we drink the third cup of liberation at the conclusion of the *Birkas Hamazon*.

3. The third expression (and the second cup of wine) is "*V'ga'alti* — I will deliver you [from Egyptian slavery]." A slave is an individual who lacks the will to be independent, to be free, to accomplish, to possess his own family and possessions. Most slaves do not have the capacity to free themselves or the capacity for independence. They are secure in their slavery and are unable to cope with the responsibilities and challenges of freedom. They are satisfied to have their needs provided by their master and have lost the will to be free.

The Israelite slave was different. The fact that G-d said, "I am going to deliver you from slavery," indicates that the Jews remembered their origins as the descendants of Abraham, Isaac and Jacob. They never saw themselves as slaves.

Slaves lack identity. They feel alienated from their ancestors and are often denied rights to their spouse and children. They are regarded as property, not people. The Children of Israel, however, retained their Hebrew names. They named their children after their parents and grandparents. They remembered their origins and roots.

The trait of never accepting their slave status is the definition of *v'ga'alti*. Because they remembered their origins, we conclude the first section of *Hallel* with the second cup, celebrating the creation of the Jewish Nation.

4. The fourth expression (and final cup of wine) is "*v'lakachti eschem Li le'am,* I will take you to Me as My people." What accomplishment is celebrated here? The Jews never changed their language and culture. They constantly anticipated their liberation and future nationhood. They had aspirations and expectations of their establishment as a distinct and separate nation, as G-d had promised the Patriarchs.

The Hebrew word language, *lashon*, includes culture and nationhood. The Jews possessed traditions, observances and aspirations that were initiated by Abraham, as clearly indicated by the Covenants and promises recorded in the Torah. They recalled their past and never gave up on their future. They learned this from Joseph. Despite his prominence in Egyptian life, he said to his brothers, "It is my mouth that is speaking to you," i.e. I am speaking to you in Hebrew, the holy tongue.[4] It was Joseph who commanded that on the day of liberation his bones were to be carried back to the Land of Israel and buried in Shechem. To remind ourselves that we never abandoned our national aspirations in the face of the most abject conditions, we drink the fourth cup of wine at the conclusion of *Hallel*, which describes our future destiny and anticipated Redemption.

Why are the four types of redemption celebrated with wine? Why not four matzos? It is because the Jewish People is likened to the halachic regulations that govern wine. We observe the laws of wine in that we drink only wine that was handled by a Sabbath-observing Jew. Our insistence that wine be kosher is an allusion to the manner in which the Jew views himself vis-à-vis non-Jewish society. Were we not liberated because we maintained a wall of separation from the Egyptians?

Nothing points to the separateness of the Jew as much as wine. The rabbis established the laws of wine to prevent intermarriage. It was their conviction that because of the social effect of wine, as well as the ability of wine to dim the senses, the drinking of wine with non-Jews would blur the distinction between Jew and gentile and lead to intermarriage.

From the above, we see that despite the efforts of the Egyptians to enslave and obliterate the Jewish People, they retained their unique characteristics with stubbornness, idealism and self-sacrifice.

Not all the Jews were prepared to cast their lot with Moses. The Torah teaches that only one out of five Jews left, while the others died during the plague of darkness. The effects of Egyptian corruption and the fear of going into the unknown desert were felt by the majority. In the face of slavery and persecution, a minority refused to be subdued. They maintained their dignity, their family life, their faith and their hopes.

The Haggadah states that Israel excelled in Egypt: "This teaches that Israel was outstanding and excellent there." The

Meshech Chochmah acknowledges that despite this, the Jewish masses were corrupted by Egypt's idolatry and heathen ideologies. The picture that emerges is that while there were areas of moral excellence and a stubborn adherence to Hebrew language, culture, dress, names, the hope and anticipation of national redemption and an adherence to family and morality — they were still significantly affected in other ways by Egyptian idolatry.

The Meshech Chochmah's approach provides a key to the bondage of Israel and resolves the conflict between the various approaches:[5] The time had arrived for G-d's promise to Abraham to be fulfilled, but Israel did not yet possess active commandments that would enable them to be redeemed. Therefore, G-d commanded them to observe the *mitzvos* of the Passover Sacrifice, and of eating Matzah and Maror.*

▶ A Rebellious People: A Different View Based on Ezekiel 20 and the Ramban

The position of the Meshech Chochmah is forcefully contradicted by the words of the prophet Ezekiel:

> *Thus said the L-rd, Announce their ancestors'*
> *abominations to them! Say to them, "The L-rd G-d*
> *says: 'On the day I chose Israel, I took an oath to*
> *the seed of Jacob's house and revealed Myself to*
> *them in the land of Egypt. I swore to them, saying, I*
> *am G-d your L-rd. On that day, I swore to take them*
> *out of the land of Egypt to a land that I had*
> *searched out for them, a land flowing with milk*
> *and honey, the most beautiful of all lands. I said to*
> *them, 'Let each man throw away the detestable*

---

* It is difficult to designate the "author" of this sectioɪ.. it is based on a lengthy study of *Va'era* by the Meshech Chochmah. A new edition of his writings enjoys the lucid commentary of Rabbi Yehuda Cooperman. It was further expounded by the late Rabbi Isaac Bernstein of London. I have reformatted these sources in my own words.

things which you see. Don't defile yourselves with
the idols of Egypt. I am G-d, your L-rd.'

'(But) they rebelled against Me and did not want
to obey Me. None of them threw away the detestable
things they saw, nor did they abandon the idols of
Egypt. I decided to pour out My anger upon them and
pour My wrath against them in the land of Egypt.

'But I acted only for the sake of My Name, so it
would not be profaned in the sight of the nations
among whom they dwelled, for I had revealed
Myself to (the Israelites) in the nations' sight by
taking them out of the land of Egypt.' "[6]

Based on *Vayikra Rabbah,* Rashi points out that G-d's "hatred" of Israel's infidelity in Egypt was suppressed for over 900 years, until the time of Ezekiel, because of G-d's love for them. It was only because they were again so blatantly rebellious in his day that their transgressions in Egypt are recalled. G-d's message to Israel was delivered through Aaron who, according to the *Midrash,* exhorted the people to remain true to their holy destiny many years before Moses had the vision at the Burning Bush. Rashi points out that while some of the people always remained loyal to their heritage, huge segments succumbed to idol worship. These are the people who died during the plague of darkness.

Ezekiel is telling us that G-d did not destroy His People purely to avoid a desecration of His Name [i.e. so as not to destroy belief in Him on this earth]. This verse emphasizes that there were *no* positive reasons for Israel's redemption; that the merit of their forefathers and the Covenants that G-d had made with them no longer played a role in the Exodus. Israel fell so low in Egypt that the Rambam writes, "The plant which Abraham had planted was almost uprooted, and the family of Jacob went back to the mistakes and gropings of the rest of the world."[7]

Israel's redemption came as a result of their cries that stimulated G-d to "remember" [i.e. act upon] His Covenant with the Patriarchs: "G-d heard their cries and G-d remembered His Covenant with Abraham, Isaac and Jacob and G-d saw the Children of Israel and G-d took note."[8]

This contradiction is discussed by the Ramban, who tells us that the idea that Israel was permitted to survive in order to avoid the desecration of G-d's Name is an argument which is later offered by Moses and which caused G-d to forgive the people for the sin of the spies. The Ramban explains:

> It is not because G-d wishes to demonstrate His might to His enemies; G-d has no need to do this. But G-d created man to enable man to apprehend the Divine. G-d's purpose was thwarted by all the nations; they all became mired in sin and denied G-d. Only one nation, Israel, remained loyal to Him. Throughout Israel's history, G-d made known His omnipotence and thus became recognized by the nations of the world once again. If Israel were ever to totally rebel against G-d, G-d's link to mankind would be severed, and the purpose of Creation would come to naught. Therefore, that same Will of G-d with which He willed Creation, must guarantee the eternal existence of His People, for they are the closest to Him and know Him better than anyone else.[9]

G-d, therefore, withheld His anger from a morally bankrupt Israel. He preserved Israel's outer and empty shell in order to demonstrate His loyalty to Israel to the nations. It was also in recognition of the fact that G-d's design for the world and Israel's fate are so intimately intertwined that the Jewish People must increasingly and eternally be the bearers of the Divine glory on earth, come what may. There must always remain within Israel an indestructible core of holiness. This recognition opened the floodgates of G-d's love for His People. The Ramban continues: "This is the meaning of the verse 'For they are My Nation, sons who will never be unfaithful.' Therefore G-d is their savior. In all their sorrows, G-d suffers with them."[10]

According to Ramban, then, Ezekiel is teaching that there is an essential and eternal unity that binds G-d and Israel. Even though Israel had sinned previously, its unique core and character prevented its destruction. Israel must be eternal; it can never be destroyed, so that G-d's relationship with mankind can be maintained.

For this reason, G-d answered Israel's prayers in Egypt. It was at this point that the memory of their beloved fathers rose before G-d and triggered an unprecedented outpouring of love and mercy.

▶ Additional Insights and Solutions

1. The Torah states that the Jews left Egypt "*chamushim.*" This word can have two meanings: armed for battle; or the fraction 1/5. Rashi, quoting the *Midrash*, says that this means that four out of five Jews, those who had lost their faith, died during the Plague of Darkness. Thus, only 1/5 of the Jewish population left Egypt. We deduce that 4/5 of the Jews succumbed to Egyptian depravity, while those who were liberated had been loyal to the values of their ancestors.

2. Rabbi Yitzchok Hutner commented on a *Midrash* that says that immediately prior to the splitting of the Reed Sea, the ministering angels appealed to the L-rd not to free the Jews. The claim of the angels was that, "Both the Egyptians as well as the Jews are idol worshippers," therefore why liberate them? Rabbi Hutner stated that this claim is not to be taken literally, because the claim of these angels was not different from the claim the angels made when G-d declared His intention to create the first human being. Indeed, Adam and Eve could not have sinned at the time the angels raised their objection since they had not yet been created. The angels were concerned that a being possessing free will would not be capable of resisting temptation and of fulfilling the expectations of G-d, but would surely succumb to sin. In the same way, on the eve of the Exodus, which witnessed the "second Creation," of a new type of mankind — namely *Am Yisrael* — the angels expressed the very same fear.

3. The final cleansing and purification of the Jewish People would take place in the desert. With the giving of the Torah, the Jews would experience a spiritual, heightened existence and learn how to elevate and cleanse themselves from the filth of their Egyptian experience. The Torah repeatedly admonished the Israelites to

"Remember that you were slaves in the land of Egypt," meaning, "Do not repeat the depraved behavior that you witnessed in Egypt."

4. A fourth solution would combine the three solutions above: It is quite feasible that all the scenarios took place simultaneously. Egypt and the enslavement were degrading and dehumanizing. The Jews were deeply affected by Egyptian culture and paganism. Their personalities were seriously affected by the experience of slavery. Yet, they retained certain distinct Jewish qualities and drew strength from the tribe of Levi, which was not enslaved and had maintained the traditions of the Patriarchs. There was simultaneously a degree of degradation and a degree of stubborn retention of the qualities of their forefathers. While they had not yet received the Torah and were not yet righteous, they were many levels above their Egyptians neighbors.

5. We might also suggest that each of the above scenarios did not necessarily take place collectively, but individually. The experience of the Holocaust offers a poignant example. Some Holocaust survivors totally abandoned their faith and Jewish observance. Others were so motivated by the totality of their losses and their horrendous experiences that they were driven by a superhuman determination to rebuild and restore the Judaism of their parents. They married, created families, communities and yeshivos with unbelievable idealism, zeal and determination. Others lived in constant conflict. They were driven by both motives — not able to fully resolve the raging bitterness, conflict and hope in their hearts. The Jews in Egypt had lived through a protracted holocaust, witnessing the degradation and annihilation of their families through several generations. Their reactions to this experience could have gone to either extreme.

▶ The Word Exodus Implies Unloading Egyptian Degradation

n his *sefer Ohr Gedalyahu* on the Book of Exodus, Rabbi Gedaliah Schorr develops the view that the 49-day journey from the

Exodus to the Sinai Revelation constituted the process of refinement, which made possible Israel's transformation and preparation for the Revelation of the Torah and the Ten Commandments.

The purpose of the long trek in the desert that brought Israel to Sinai was to cut the bond between Israel and Egyptian society. This bond between Israel and the spiritual filth of Egypt was quite strong. Recall the following, "No slave was capable of breaking himself away from Egyptian degradation." Even slaves formed a strong bond with the degradation and moral turpitude that was so characteristic of Egyptian society. Israel's redemption from Egypt required much more than freeing their bodies. What was needed was the liberation of their souls from enslavement to Egyptian culture.

"Exodus" must be divided into two acts: freeing their bodies, and freeing their souls from Egyptian depravity, which involved unloading Egypt's spiritual and moral degradation. This process was the purpose of the 49-day trek to Mt. Sinai. They needed 49 days in order to enter the 49 Gates of Sanctity. As they departed Egypt, they entered holiness. As the refining process progressed, their attachment to Egyptian culture waned until they were able to totally divest themselves of their emotional and psychological ties to Egypt.

The *Zohar* interprets the term, *"Vachamushim alu,"* to mean that they exited all 50 gates of degradation. Every stage of divestiture from degradation is called *Yetzias Mitzrayim,* the Exodus from Egypt. The end of their journey was their arrival at Sinai. Each day's journey marked another stage, until they were prepared to accept the Torah. Upon their arrival at Sinai they had totally released themselves from their bond to Egyptian culture. As the Vilna Gaon teaches, "It was *at the moment* that they heard the Divine Voice, 'I am the L-rd, your G-d, Who took you out of the Land of Egypt,' that the process of divestiture from Egyptian degradation was completed." At that moment they were totally free.

The goal of the Exodus was receiving the Torah. At that point the refinement of their stature was completed. As G-d states in the Torah, "I will take you to be My nation, and I will be your G-d." And the *Mechilta* adds, "I am the G-d of all living beings; it is only upon you that I have placed My Name."

▸ A Kabbalistic Insight**

We must first abandon the myth that the Jews were thrust *in the early part of the exile* into physical poverty and misery. Experience teaches that the slide to corruption begins at great heights. As the holy *Zohar* teaches, the Jews in Egypt were, prior to the Exodus, steeped in evil and immorality. The security of wealth and the false tranquility of worldly success lured the Jews into a deceptive sense of belonging in Egyptian society. Their material success was the cause of their long descent to the forty-ninth level of defilement.

The *Midrash*[11] reveals the extent to which the Jews prospered in their foreign surroundings: "The Torah teaches, '*Vayagar Moav,* and Moav was sore afraid.' Another meaning of the expression *vayagar* bears the sense of being a stranger (*ger*). The Moabites felt themselves as strangers in the world. They thought: The Israelites went down to Egypt to sojourn there and took possession of it, renting houses to the Egyptians; as the Torah says, 'Every woman shall ask of her neighbor, and *migaras beisah,* of she who lives in her house, vessels of silver and gold.'"[12]

Another *Midrash*[13] indicates that it was universally acknowledged that the Jews in Egypt had achieved phenomenal success in their business endeavors, so much so that some Jews became landlords and the Egyptians were their tenants. This business success and all-consuming entrepreneurship later caused the Moabites to be apprehensive at the approach of the Israelite camp, fearing that the Israelites would clean them out of their possessions, as they had done to Egypt.

This *Midrash* further depicts the character and fate of the Jews who were drawn to the Egyptian lifestyle and copied their decadent ways: "Why did G-d, blessed is His Name, before Whom there is no respecting of persons, Who searches the heart and knows the secrets of men, bring darkness upon them? Because there were Jewish transgressors who had Egyptian patrons, who

---

** A totally new understanding of the Exodus is revealed by insights from the *Zohar* that I have excerpted from a book *Mateh Ha'Elokim* by Rabbi Eliezer Ben-David. It was was translated and adapted by Rabbi Yaakov Feitman in *Out of the Iron Furnace* (Shengold, *1975*).

lived in affluence and honor, who were unwilling to leave...
[These Jews were unworthy of redemption and died during the
Plague of Darkness.] For this reason, G-d brought darkness upon
the Egyptians for three days, so that the Israelites could bury
their dead without their enemies watching them."

The *Mechilta Shemos,* commenting on "*Vachamushim alu B'nei
Yisrael,* And the Children of Israel went up armed [out of the land
of Egypt],"[14] notes that the word *chamushim,* from the word
c*hamesh,* indicates the number five, teaching us that only one out
of every five Jews left Egypt. The *Mechilta* records various commentators on how many Jews were so enamored with the Egyptian
lifestyle that they did not merit to leave Egypt, and some of these
opinions are much higher than 4/5 of the Jewish population.

The overall picture seems to be that over the years, the wealth
initially acquired by the Jews in Egypt caused them to slide, sinking lower and lower into the corrupt Egyptian civilization. G-d
transformed their moral subjugation to Egyptian values into physical deprivation and slavery. Every hour brought the Jews closer
to the fatal fiftieth level of impurity. Eventually, the Jews were
trapped in moral bondage mirrored by their physical slavery.

In the beginning, even those who succumbed to the lure of
Egyptian culture thought they could also retain their Jewish identity. Seeking to live in both worlds, many fell by the wayside,
trapped by the powerful forces of Egyptian decadence. Until the
very end, however, many Jews retained some of their traditional
clothing, their Hebrew names and continued to speak Hebrew.
Our Sages tell us that because of this devotion to their Jewish
identity they merited to leave Egypt.

Egyptian bondage exemplified the archetypal *galus.* Entered
into willingly, it was only later that it developed into involuntary
servitude. *This exile, which was to be the template for all succeeding Jewish exiles, had to encompass every conceivable manner of
slavery: physical, cultural and moral.* The Torah makes clear as
early as G-d's Covenant of the Pieces with Abraham that the
Egyptians are to be blamed for only one aspect of Israel's slavery:

"Surely know that your seed will be a stranger in a land that is
not theirs and will be enslaved by them; and they shall afflict

them four hundred years; and also that nation whom they shall serve will I judge."[15]

▸ A Final Thought

What makes our inquiry so fascinating is that most Torah commentaries do not offer a comprehensive resolution to the various approaches above. The classical commentaries generally dwell on a particular solution, but rarely discuss all of the alternatives in an effort to present an all-inclusive picture. We have noted that the situation of Israel certainly changed during the 210 years of slavery from generation to generation, so that generalizations need to be placed in a specific context. This may be the key to explaining the nature of the Egyptian exile and of the Exodus. Unquestionably each of the approaches is true: Each reflects the situation at a different time, and from a different vantage point.

This chapter was inspired by Rabbi Moshe Eisemann's commentary on the Book of Ezekiel. (ArtScroll)

1. *Genesis* 15:13-14.
2. *Deuteronomy* 4:20.
3. On *Exodus* 6:6.
4. *Bereishis Rabbah* 93.
5. *Exodus* 3:16.
6. *Ezekiel* 20:5-10.
7. *Hilchos Avodah Zarah* 1:3.
8. *Exodus* 2:24-25.
9. *Ramban, Deuteronomy* 32:26.
10. *Isaiah* 63:8.
11. *Bamidbar Rabbah* 20:3.
12. *Exodus* 3:22.
13. *Shemos Rabbah* 14:3.
14. *Exodus* 13:18.
15. *Genesis* 15:13.

THE INNER
MEANING
58 # OF MATZAH

Why is matzah so basic to the celebration of Passover? Why is Passover called *Chag HaMatzos,* "the Holiday of Matzos" by the Torah? Why is this simple food a foundation of Jewish experience and ideology? Why has matzah come to symbolize human freedom?

Matzah has many aspects. It is the "bread of affliction," poor man's bread, eaten by slaves. It is also the bread of liberation and freedom. Let's attempt to plumb its many meanings.

Bread is the staff of life, but matzah is the most basic bread, the simplest food made by man. Matzah involves the amalgamation of the three basic elements that define civilized man: grain, water and fire. No external element beyond flour and water is permitted to define or influence its form. Matzah is made of flour and cold water — nothing more. If the mixture of flour and water was allowed to stand for more than eighteen minutes, the process of fermentation has already begun to take place. Yeast bacteria, found in the air, invade the dough, multiply by the millions and cause fermentation. The yeast microorganisms are an uninvited invading army, intruding on the flour and water mixture, helping themselves to a delicious meal of sugar molecules. As the yeast microorganisms multiply by the billions, they release the carbon dioxide gas that sours the dough, causing it to rise and become airy and light.

The intervention of this outside force is a symbolic expression of the intrusion of outside forces on man; forces that sway people from their chosen determined path and entice them to sin, compromising human independence, autonomy and choice. Yeast microorganisms begin their work independent of human will, independent of the person who combined the flour and water which constitutes the dough mix. Fermentation, i.e. *chametz,* represents these negative forces. It represents the inclination to evil, the urge to sin, the influence of alien ideas, pleasures and forces. It is the uninvited voice that sways us to ignore the presence and power of evil, until it is too late.

What is the difference between *chametz* (leaven) and matzah? Time. Nothing else. The ingredients are the same. By definition, dough made of flour and water that stands for more than eighteen minutes before it is fully baked becomes *chametz,* leaven. Because matzah is bread that is not leavened, it represents man in control of his passions — exercising his independent, disciplined will, uninfluenced by external forces. Matzah is the opposite of *chametz.*

To paraphrase Rabbi Chaim Friedlander, one of the giants of Jewish thought in our generation, fermentation demonstrates cause and effect in the world of nature. When we witness nature at work — apparently doing things by itself, without any outside intervention — we see how natural processes have the effect of concealing the Hand of G-d.

Matzos are baked quickly, in an effort to overcome the influences and limitations of time. We bake flat, crisp matzah in order to reenact the Exodus, when the Children of Israel fled Egypt in a hurry, as the Torah says: "You shall eat matzos during seven days…bread of suffering, for you departed Egypt in great haste."[1]

This *mitzvah* teaches that G-d's control of nature and history is above and beyond the constraints and limitations of time. G-d does not require cause and effect. He does not need time in order to accomplish His goals. On Passover, we too must emulate G-d and become creative spiritually by hurrying time, by acting with zeal and speed, by living life beyond time, in partnership with G-d who is above time and is timeless. We respond to G-d's Will by acting in defiance of nature, by breaking the limits imposed by time and nature.

The hasty departure of the Jews from Egypt was due to the Plague of the Deaths of Firstborn Egyptians, which convinced Pharaoh that if he did not respond to G-d's pressures without an additional moment's delay, all of Egypt faced immediate collapse and destruction. For Egypt to survive, Israel must leave immediately.

And for Israel to survive, Israel had to flee immediately. G-d forced Pharaoh's hand. He did this to teach Pharaoh and all of mankind that behind the normal course of events, which can be described as the workings of cause and effect, G-d's Hand compels the forces of history and nature to conform to *His* agenda. As the Maharal (Rabbi Yehuda Loewe ben Bezalel, a seminal figure in Jewish thought) explains, it was necessary that mankind become aware of the fact that the Exodus was the direct result of the Will and intervention of G-d.

What was the hurry? Why, after 210 years of slavery, did G-d finally decide to press the Egyptians to eject the Jews with speed and force? The Sages teach that the Jews had reached the 49th degree of decadence. As soon as they would enter the 50th degree, a development that was imminent, they would have reached the point of no return and would be beyond redemption. Once they would succumb to the infamous immorality, materialism, decadence and paganism of the Egyptians, their Abrahamic origins would become unrecognizable and they would sink into the morass of Egyptian society and disappear. (See Chapter 57 "The Passover Puzzle" for details.)

The Sages explain that each additional degree of decadence involved a geometric progression, something like the Richter scale where each number is ten times as great as the previous number. So long as Israel had not passed the 50th degree of impurity, their Abrahamic origins were still recognizable, though sullied. The Sages teach that during their 210 years of enslavement, the "Israelites, to their credit, had not changed their names, their culture, their language or their dress,"[2] clearly indicating that despite unremitting pressures and taunts they remained Jews in every way. The Hebrew names of the Jews as reported by the Bible demonstrate that they had continuously worshipped the true G-d of Israel and remained true to their heritage.

But after 210 years they were close to losing this heritage. They had to overcome the pressures of time by becoming a timeless, eternal people. This necessitated Divine intervention; G-d snatched His People from the jaws of history, by liberating them in such a way as to telescope time. Their miraculous liberation therefore defied the laws of nature, time and history.

The Maharal explains that it is for this reason that they were commanded to eat matzah when they observed the Passover of their liberation and for every subsequent Passover throughout all eternity. Matzah is the only food whose manufacture demands that it be created without time — beyond time as quickly as possible. The prohibition of leaven also teaches us that nature does not operate independently but is controlled by G-d. Nature is the Will of G-d concealed in the natural world.

Where applied to the human being himself, the Sages teach that the "puffed up" nature of *chametz* symbolizes the character trait of arrogance and conceit. The flat, unleavened matzah represents total humility. Humility is the beginning of liberation and the foundation of spiritual growth. Only a person who can acknowledge his shortcomings and submit to a higher wisdom can free himself from his own limitations. When we eat matzah, we internalize the quality of humility as the essence of faith. By not eating *chametz,* we rid ourselves of arrogance and self-centeredness.

In a symbolic sense, the Children of Israel had become "fermented" — to the point where they had almost become *chametz.*

G-d saved Israel from becoming *chametz*, which would have spelled Israel's destruction. It was the redeeming Hand of G-d which guaranteed that Israel would remain "matzah," the essence of humility, for all time to come.

For the above reasons, the words *mitzvah* and *matzah* are analogous. Our Sages teach, "*mitzvah she'haba'ah leyadcha al tachmitzena*, when a *mitzvah* comes your way, do not allow it to ferment"[3] i.e. when the opportunity to do a *mitzvah* arises, do it quickly. This teaching applies the urgency of baking Passover matzah with alacrity to all *mitzvos*. The Jew is expected to conquer time, to live beyond time, to associate his life with G-d, Who is timeless and eternal. The Jew never wastes time; the present is now — this is why it is so precious. The Jew employs time to bend this time-bound world to the goals of eternity. This is done by making time a precious commodity — by filling it with Torah, *mitzvos* and *chessed* (goodness).

1. *Deuteronomy* 16:3.
2. *Mechilta D'Pischa Shemos* 30:5.
3. *Makkos* 67.

THE THREE SONGS OF PASSOVER

59

O ne of the many ways in which Passover uniquely stands alone is that it is uplifted by the three great songs of our People which are recited in the course of the Passover holiday: *Hallel*, Psalms of Praise; *Shir Hashirim*, King Solomon's Song of Songs; and *Shiras Hayam*, the Song of the Sea, which Israel sang after they crossed the Reed Sea and witnessed enormous miracles there.

▶ *Hallel* — Songs of Praise

Hallel is comprised of King David's Psalms of Praise. It is recited on the two Seder nights, as well as on all eight days of Passover. However, there is a marked difference between the *Hallel* of the first two days (the "full *Hallel*") and the *Hallel* of the last six days, when we recite the abridged "half *Hallel*."

Hallel is a song of sanctity. It celebrates the victory of good over evil, but more so because the full *Hallel,* tied to the first two days of Passover, is an obligatory *Hallel.* It is linked to the observances of the Seder and to the *mitzvos* of the first two days of Passover. Eating matzah is obligatory on the first two days. While *chometz* is forbidden throughout Passover, matzah is optional on the last six days. From the above, one can see the first two days as the days of the engagement period of the Jewish People to G-d.

The Jews had departed through the great gates of Egypt; Pharaoh had acknowledged his defeat at the Hands of G-d, yet the Exodus was not yet complete. Suddenly Pharaoh changed his mind and decided to pursue the Jews. The Egyptians had not yet been defeated and the Jews would soon be confronted with the Reed Sea on one side of them and the Egyptians pursuing them on the other. The emphasis on the first two days is the transformation of Israel from a witness to G-d's miracles, into a People that plays an active role in its spiritual development. Through their sacrifice of the Passover lamb, one of the deities of Egypt, they demonstrated their spiritual release from Egyptian bondage. No longer were they slaves of Pharaoh; now they would serve G-d, the One and Only G-d of the universe.

▸ The Song of Songs

The second song is the famous Song of Solomon, the Song of Songs, which Rabbi Akiva called the Holy of Holies. This is the intimate inner sanctum of the love and marriage of the Jewish People with G-d. The Song of Songs, said Rabbi Yitzchok Hutner, "is the triumphant sound of the final great victory, when sanctity will define all of Creation, when even the optional part of life which we think of as being outside of the governance of the commandments will be transformed and be included in G-d's Kingdom, thus becoming sanctified by G-d's Will." The Jewish People was created to wage both battles: The battle against evil is waged with *mitzvos*, while the Song of Songs so powerfully expresses the battle for the free will of man, whose world will voluntarily become sanctified and become the force for the ultimate triumph of sanctity. This great Song celebrates the marriage of Israel and the Holy One Blessed be He.

▸ The Song of the Sea

The final victory of the saga of the Exodus does not reach its crescendo until the Reed Sea is split and the Egyptian forces are defeated in the most powerful manifestation of G-d's total control of nature and history. Now on the last day of Passover, the Jewish People sing the final Song of Passover — the song of the victory of G-d at the Sea and the defeat of the forces of Egypt. As Egypt lies in ruins, its will broken, the world witnesses the majestic triumph of G-d and His People. Evil is not only defeated; it lies totally decimated and destroyed.

▸ Who Were the Ancient Egyptians?

It is difficult for people living in civilized democracies to understand the mindset of the ancient pagans. Let us first visit the ancient Egyptian enemy that subjugated and nearly destroyed the Jewish People. It would appear to those of us who have read books about ancient Egypt, describing the riches and the glittering art discovered in the tombs of the Pharaohs, that ancient Egypt had reached the pinnacle of civilization, expressed in its art, architecture and technology. Yet we know from the Torah, as well as from hieroglyphic inscriptions and the historical record, that lying beneath a thin veneer of civilization lay naked cruelty and barbarism. With the exception of the aristocracy and the priests, the Egyptians were a nation of slaves.

Concepts such as the sanctity of human life, human dignity and human rights were ideals that would become known to the world only with the birth of Israel as a nation, which was just entering the stage of history.

▶ The Definition of *Mitzrayim*

The very word *Mitzrayim,* the ancient name of Egypt, derives from the related root words *tzar,* narrow and confined; *tza'ar,* pain; and *meitzar,* constriction of vision. For the Egptian elite, life was a combination of wanton pleasure, immorality, sexual caprice, magic and sorcery. The title of the ruler of Egypt, in Hebrew, *Paroh,* derives from the word *peh ra,* an evil, deceitful mouth, i.e. a person of dishonesty, deception and arrogance. It also implies *parua* — wild, uncontrolled, ruled by passion, wide open to evil forces and designs. Esau was called a *perah adam,* "a wild man." As the Torah says, "His hand was in everything evil, and everything evil was held against him." The word *perah* also is similar to *Paroh* — Pharaoh, a man out of control.

▶ The Message of the Song of the Sea

Having escaped this type of "civilization," the liberated Jews begin to chart their destiny with the singing of the Song of the Sea. What distinguishes the Song of the Sea is that in addition to being an ode of gratitude to G-d and a song of love for G-d, it immediately turns to the future responsibilities of the Children of Israel. This song is a formula for the future which was set forth at the very moment of Israel's creation. At the moment of the defeat of the Egyptian forces, Israel was finally truly free. So great was their exultation that the angels wished to join in singing the song of victory.

The majority of the Song of the Sea resonates with dreams of the future. It begins with "*Then* Israel will sing..." It concludes with "The chieftains of Edom *will be* confounded. ...Fear and terror *will* confound them. ...You *will* implant Israel on the mountain of Your heritage. ...The Temple *will be* established by Your Hands." Throughout the song, the future tense is heard.

The centerpiece of the song is a word with multiple meanings. "*Zeh Keili v'anveihu,* This is my G-d and I will glorify Him." The word *anveihu* has a number of meanings. The first is *naveh,* which means house, which leads commentator Onkelus to translate it as, "This is my G-d and I will — in the future — construct His Temple" in Jerusalem. The letters of *anveihu* also spell out *ani vehu* — I and He, suggesting, "I will do as G-d does; I will imitate G-d. Just as G-d is merciful, I too will be merciful," etc. *Anveihu* also means beautiful, which the Talmud[1] sees as a command — to beautify and exalt G-d through the observance of the commandments, with a beautiful *succah*, beautiful *tzitzis*, a beautiful *sefer Torah*, etc.

So powerful is this song and so deep are its messages, that the Sages said that "G-d Himself proclaimed: This is the song I longed to hear from the very day of Creation."

A few days after Israel sang the Song of the Sea, Amalek, the eternal enemy of Israel, the personification of evil throughout history, attacked Israel on its journey to Mt. Sinai. Amalek's goal was to prevent the Revelation of the Torah and the journey of the Children of Israel to the Land of Israel. While Israel was victorious in that battle, Amalek was not totally destroyed. After the battle, the Torah says, "...a hand is holding back the Throne of G-d."[2] The word throne, *kisei,* is written with the last letter *aleph* missing; the resulting word *kes* implies that the throne of G-d remains far from whole due to the continued existence of Amalek. In addition, the four-letter word for G-d in that sentence is spelled with only the first two of its four letters, *yud* and *heh,* implying that as long as Amalek survives, the very Name of G-d cannot be considered complete. The sentence concludes, "G-d will battle Amalek from each generation to the next."

Rashi says, "*The Hand of G-d is raised as He swears on His throne that the hatred and battle against Amalek will last forever. Why* kes *and not* kisei*? And why is G-d's name split in half? G-d has sworn that neither His name nor His throne will become whole until Amalek is totally obliterated — and when the name of Amalek will be obliterated, only then will G-d's Name and throne be whole again.*"[3]

Here we have a surprising insight. When Israel sang the Song of the Sea, is it possible that Israel anticipated Amalek's unprovoked attack? Is it reasonable to believe that Amalek, the personification of evil, is reflected in the text of the Song of the Sea? Could Moses have known in advance of the upcoming battle with Amalek, even as he celebrated the victory at the sea?

It would appear that there is an allusion to the battle with Amalek in the Song of the Sea. Though not explicit, it cannot be mistaken for anything else. This evidence is to be found in the sentence preceding, "This is my G-d and I will glorify Him." In this sentence[4] we find the same split Name of G-d, containing only the letters *yud* and *heh*. To demonstrate that this points to the upcoming war with Amalek, an examination of the full text of the Torah will confirm that the split Name of G-d, *yud, heh* appears in only two places in the Torah: here in the Song of the Sea, and later in association with the war with Amalek. We can assume that the mission of Israel immediately following the defeat of Egypt was to undertake responsibility for continuing the struggle of obliterating evil from the world until that task is completed. Having defeated the barbaric Egyptians, the Jews were soon attacked by the barbaric Amalek, who had no reason to attack them other than pure hatred of Israel and of G-d.

The sentence I am referring to is Exodus 15:2, "*Azi vezimras kah vayehi li l'yeshuah.*" "*Azi vezimra kah*" means "G-d is my strength and my praise." "*Vayehi* li *l'yeshuah*" — G-d will be "*li*" [to me] my future salvation. The word after the split name of G-d *yud, heh*, is "*vayehi,*" He will be, in the future. Amazingly, the word "*vayihi*" contains the missing two letters of the Name of G-d, *vav* and *heh* (the other two letters in "*vayehi*" are two *yud*s, which have also come to substitute for the four-letter Name of G-d in most texts). Here we find both an allusion to the future war against Amalek, as well as an allusion to the *final* war against Amalek, as a result of the four-letter complete Name of G-d mysteriously appearing in the text.

The above point is articulated by Isaiah, and by Rashi on Isaiah, in this manner: In Isaiah (12:12) the prophet says, *"Hineh Keil yeshuasi evtach ve'lo efchad…* Behold G-d who has delivered me! I am confident and unafraid! For my strength and song is *Kah"* (the abbreviated name of G-d, *yud hey*); *yud-hey-vav-hey* (the full four-letter Name of G-d) — *"vayehi,* (the word that completes the abbreviated name of G-d, *vav, yud, hey, yud*), G-d will be my salvation."

Here we again see the use of the split name of G-d, which is now followed by the full name of G-d, followed by *vayehi,* a word that contains the two letters that complete the Name of G-d. It also contains two *yud*s, which are an abbreviated form of the four-letter ineffable Name of G-d. Rashi says, "Up to this moment, G-d's Name was fractured; however, with the defeat of Amalek it will become whole again." As the Torah states, "A hand withholds the fractured throne of G-d, which will remain fractured until the day of G-d's final victory over Amalek."

The Netziv (Rabbi Naftali Zvi Yehuda Berlin, Rosh Yeshivah of the famous Volozhin Yeshivah in Russia), points out that the *siddur* calls the Song at the Sea a *"Shirah Chadashah,"* a "New Song." It is a renewing song — because in a deeper sense it will be completely fulfilled with the final Redemption.

What is the significance of the three Songs? Why do Israel's two major enemies appear in the Song of the Sea?

The Egyptian enslavement was the greatest challenge the Jewish People ever faced. This enslavement was to be the prototype of all of Israel's future punishments and exiles. Indeed it contained all of the elements and challenges of the "Four Exiles" the Jewish People would undergo through their long journey through history. Upon its escape from the Egyptians, Israel at its high point — at a moment of exalted joy — sings a song, a poem of triumph. This song contains three elements:

1) Victory: the defeat of Israel's enemy.

2) A vision of the future: the building of the Temple, the settling of the land, the receiving of the Torah, the creation of a society devoted to *mitzvos.*

3) A description of Israel's efforts to defeat G-d's leading enemies on earth, Egypt and Amalek.

G-d has prepared two sets of enemies for Israel, should it forget the lessons of the Egyptian enslavement. The people are enjoined to "remember you were slaves to Pharaoh. Don't behave like Egyptians; don't adopt their pagan, barbaric, inhuman, magic-filled way of life. If you do, you will encounter enemies placed there by G-d." These enemies remind us of our neglected duty and the special relationship we were meant to have with G-d. The Song of the Sea contains the two sets of Israel's enemies: *First* — the "Four Kingdoms/Exiles" — Babylonia, Persia, Greece and Rome. (Today we are still enslaved in the Exile of Rome.) *Second* — the "Seven Nations" — the Amalekites, Edomites, Moabites, Canaanites, etc., as enumerated in the Bible. Amalek/Rome is in both sets, incorporating elements of the Four Kingdoms and the Seven Nations. (Egypt is not counted among the Four Kingdoms because the Children of Israel were enslaved there prior to becoming a nation and receiving the Torah. Egypt does, however, combine all of the subsequent kingdoms and exiles.)

The message of the Song of the Sea to the Jewish People is eternal: If you obey G-d, you will live in your land, create an ideal society and elevate mankind. This process will lead to the arrival of the Messiah. If you betray G-d, your enemies will rise against you. Your enemies may have other names, but basically they are associated with the two sons of our forefathers who were separated from Israel and its Divine mission: Ishmael, the brother of Isaac; and Esau, the brother of Jacob. All of Israel's enemies belong to these two groups. We can defeat them only if we employ the weapons G-d has provided for us: loyalty to Him and to His Torah.

1. *Shabbos* 133b.
2. *Exodus* 17:16.
3. Rashi, *Exodus* 17:16.
4. *Exodus* 15:2.

THE MYSTERY OF LAG B'OMER

▸ **Many Puzzling Questions Surround the Little Understood Holiday of Lag B'Omer.**

hirty-three days following the first day of Passover, Jews celebrate a "minor" holiday called Lag B'Omer, the thirty-third day of the Omer. It is an oasis of joy in the midst of the sad *Sefirah* period that passes almost unnoticed by most contemporary Jews. Yet it contains historic lessons of such gravity that our generation must attempt to unravel its mystery. We may well discover that our own fate is wrapped in the crevices of its secrets.

The seven weeks between Passover and Shavuos are the days of the "Counting of the Omer," the harvest festivities which were observed in the Land of Israel when the Temple stood on Mount Moriah in Jerusalem. This fifty-day period should have been a time of joyful anticipation. After experiencing the Exodus from

Egypt on Pesach, Jews literally "counts the days" until they can relive *Mattan Torah* — the Revelation of Torah at Mount Sinai which took place on Shavuos, exactly fifty days after the Exodus. While the Exodus marks the physical birth of the Jewish Nation, the Giving of Torah completes the process through the spiritual birth of the Jewish Nation.

Each year, as we celebrate the Seder on Passover, we are commanded to see ourselves "as though each of us actually experienced the Exodus." It therefore follows that we should prepare ourselves during the *Sefirah* period (counting of the Omer) to once again accept the Torah on Shavuos — to make our freedom spiritually complete.

Clearly then, the *Sefirah* days should be days of joy, but instead, they are observed as a period of semi-mourning. Weddings, music and haircuts are not permitted; some men do not shave during this entire period. Yet on the thirty-third day of semi-mourning the holiday of Lag B'Omer occurs, the one day when our mourning is halted, when sadness is forbidden.

What is the reason for sadness during what should have been a period of joyful anticipation? The reason, the Babylonian Talmud tells us,[1] is that during this period, Rabbi Akiva's 24,000 students, who lived 1,850 years ago in the Roman dominated Land of Israel, died from a mysterious G-d-sent plague. Rabbi Akiva was the most revered Tanna of his day, whose insights and brilliant decisions fill the Mishnah and Gemara. Why did his students die? Because, the Talmud teaches, "they did not show proper respect to one another." However, Lag B'Omer (literally meaning the 33rd day of the counting of the Omer) is a day of celebration because on that day Rabbi Akiva's students ceased to die.[2]

▸ A Series of Unanswered Questions

This explanation leaves us with numerous unanswered questions. Why does this event, the death of Rabbi Akiva's students, tragic as it was, merit thirty-two days of mourning, when greater tragedies in Jewish history — such as the destruction of both Temples — are marked by a single day of mourning? In terms of numbers, the massacres of the Crusades, the Spanish Inquisition, the Chmelnitski pogroms and the Holocaust far overshadow the deaths of Rabbi Akiva's students. Why are the students given so much more weight?

Another question that arises stems from the fact that every event in the Jewish calendar was placed there by the Divine Hand because it conforms to a preset definition of the significance of the seasons and of history. Nature and history correspond and intermesh; certain days and periods are most suited to joy or to sadness. Why does the *Sefirah* mourning coincide with the joyous holidays of Passover and Shavuos, which in turn coincide with a time of harvest festivities? Even more importantly, how does the *Sefirah* mourning period, and its association with Rabbi Akiva, relate to the Giving of the Torah on Mount Sinai on Shavuos?

There also appear to be inconsistencies in the story itself. If Rabbi Akiva's students perished as a punishment for their sins, why should we mourn them? Didn't they deserve their punishment? In fact, why is Lag B'Omer a day of celebration? If what happened on Lag B'Omer was a cessation of the plague, wouldn't it be more fitting to set it aside as a single memorial day for the thousands of scholars who died, especially in view of the Talmudic statement that as a result of their deaths "the world became spiritually desolate"?[3]

We must also consider the connection between Lag B'Omer and the revolt against the Romans. Let us remember that the Temple was destroyed by the Romans during the Great Revolt in the year 70 of the Common Era. At that time, numerous factions fought each other bitterly, each vying for the loyalty of the Jewish People. Sixty-five years later, nearly all of the Jewish population was united behind the authority of the *Tana'im*, the great rabbi-teachers of the post-Temple era, of whom Rabbi Akiva was the most revered. One of Rabbi Akiva's most notable students was Rabbi Shimon Bar Yochai, who later authored the *Zohar*, containing the Torah's mystical teachings. What connection is there between Lag B'Omer and the revolt? And why do we sing of Rabbi Shimon Bar Yochai on this day?

And finally, why are all these questions not discussed openly in the Talmud or in the writings of our Sages?

The answers to these questions lie shrouded in the history of a turbulent age and in the mysteries of the Messianic era. First, we must understand that much of the material in the Talmud that deals with political matters was written with a keen sensitivity to the Roman censors. The Talmud could not speak openly concerning the political ramifications of certain events. In order to obtain a true picture of what happened, we must piece together the story from various historical sources and from Talmudic hints. Using this method, we can infer this scenario:

After the Second Temple was destroyed, Jerusalem and the surrounding countryside lay in ruins from border to border. Scores of thousands of Jews died in the fierce fighting and subsequently from persecution and starvation; thousands more were sold as slaves and forced into exile. Victorious General Titus erected a grand monument in Rome, the famous Arch of Titus, which stands to this day. Coins were minted bearing the inscription *Judea Capta* — "Judea is fallen." The Romans considered the Jewish Nation defeated and obliterated.

But even in defeat the spiritual leaders of the Jewish People struggled to rebuild Jewish life and recreate Jewish institutions. At this point, the Romans renewed their oppression of the Jews. In 135 CE, no longer able to tolerate Roman brutality, the Jews felt that the opportunity to restore their independence and rebuild the Temple was at hand.

A Jewish military leader named Bar Kosiba succeeded in organizing a fighting force to rid the Land of Israel of the hated Romans. Thousands rallied to his cause, including Rabbi Akiva. Some of Rabbi Akiva's contemporaries felt that a new revolt against the Romans was doomed to failure and urged the avoidance of bloodshed. But Bar Kosiba persisted and succeeded in organizing and training a superb military force of 400,000 men.[4] The Talmud relates that Bar Kosiba demanded that each recruit demonstrate his bravery by cutting off a finger. When the rabbis protested the self-mutilation, Bar Kosiba substituted a new test: Each recruit was required to uproot a young tree while riding a horse. Such was the level of their bravery and strength.

Many historians believe that the prospects for toppling Rome were very real. Various sources estimate that 10%–20% of the population of the Roman Empire at that time was Jewish. The pagan foundations of Rome were crumbling. Many Romans were in search of a religious alternative — which many of them subsequently found in Christianity in the following two centuries. Significant numbers converted to Judaism.[5] If the large numbers of Jews who lived throughout the Roman Empire could have been inspired and convinced to participate in anti-Roman revolts, and if they would have had the support of tens of thousands of sympathizers, there would have been a true possibility of success.

If the revolts succeeded and Jews from all over the world would unite to return to their homeland, Rabbi Akiva believed that the Messianic era — the great era of spirituality and universal peace foretold by Israel's Prophets — could begin. All Jews would return to the Land of Israel, the Jerusalem Temple would be rebuilt and Israel would lead the world into an era of justice, spiritual revival and fulfillment. Rabbi Akiva won over a majority of his rabbinic colleagues to his point of view.

Rabbi Akiva gave Bar Kosiba a new name: "Bar Kochba"— Son of the Star — in fulfillment of the prophecy, "A star will go forth from Jacob."[6] To Bar Kochba and his officers, all seemed to be in readiness. Rome was rotten and corrupt. Numerous captive nations strained at the yoke; rebellion was in the air. Bar Kochba trained an army capable of igniting the powder keg of rebellion and Rabbi Akiva lit it with one of the most dramatic proclamations in Jewish history — that Bar Kochba was the long awaited Messiah.

Discussing the Messianic era in his Laws of Kings (Chapter 11:3), Maimonides (known also as Rambam) says, "Do not think that the King Messiah must work miracles and signs, create new natural phenomena, restore the dead to life or perform similar miracles. This is not so. For Rabbi Akiva was the wisest of the scholars of the Mishnah and was the armor bearer of Bar Kosiba … . He said concerning Ben Kosiba that he is the King Messiah.

Both he and the sages of his generation believed that Bar Kosiba was the King Messiah, until [Bar Kosiba] was killed because of his sins. Once he was killed, it became evident to them that he was not the Messiah."

One of the greatest Torah teachers and leaders of all time, Rabbi Akiva could not have made this crucial and radical declaration, proclaiming a man to be the Messiah, unless he was certain. Rabbi Akiva added a new, spiritual dimension to the war of liberation. He attempted to merge the soldiers of the sword with his soldiers of the Book — his 24,000 students — each a great Torah scholar and leader. These outstanding scholars would become the real "army" of the Jewish People, a spiritual and moral force that would bring Torah to the entire world, overcoming anguish, suffering and the cruel boot of the corrupt Roman Empire. They would soon inaugurate a new era of peace, righteousness and justice, an era in which "the Knowledge of G-d would cover the earth as water covers the seas." The fact that the Jews were able to unite around a single leader separates this event from the great revolt of the previous century, when bitterly divided factions warred with each other inside the walls of Jerusalem even as the Roman army stormed the gates.

Bar Kochba's army achieved many initial victories and the rebellion raged for six years. Many non-Jews joined Bar Kochba's army as well. It is reported that it grew to 400,000 men — larger than the Roman Army. Bar Kochba was so successful that Hadrian called in all of his best troops from England and Gaul. Rome felt threatened as never before. On Lag B'Omer, it is believed by some, Bar Kochba's army reconquered Jerusalem, and we celebrate that great event today. Jewish independence was restored for four years. Many believe that Bar Kochba actually began to rebuild the *Beis Hamikdash*, the Temple. One writer believes that he completed the building of the Third Temple.[7]

There were two Roman legions in the country when the uprising began, one in Jerusalem and one near Megiddo. Both were decimated by Bar Kochba's men. Reinforcements were dispatched from what are today Jordan, Syria and Egypt but these, too, were mauled. Legion 22, sent from Egypt, disappeared from the listings of military units published in Rome. Scholars speculate that it was so badly beaten (most likely in the area of Lachish) that it ceased to exist as an organized force. The Jews apparently employed guerilla tactics, utilizing underground lairs, ambushing convoys and striking at night.

In desperation, Hadrian sent for his best commander, Julius Severus, who was then engaged in battle in far off Wales. Severus imported legions from Britain, Switzerland, Austria, Hungary and Bulgaria. The Romans were hurt so badly in the bruising campaign against the Jews, that upon returning to report to the Senate in Rome, Severus omitted the customary formula, "I and my army are well."

This was total war. In the middle of the effort to rebuild the *Beis Hamikdash*, the tide turned and Bar Kochba lost the support of Rabbi Akiva and the Sages who backed him. What had happened? Bar Kochba had accused his cousin, the distinguished *Tanna* Rabbi Elazar, of revealing the secret entrances of the fortress-city of Betar to the Romans and murdered him. (It is now believed that this betrayal was the work of Christians who wanted to undermine Bar Kochba, as they had their own beliefs in a messiah and did not want a second one.) Rabbi Akiva then realized that Bar Kochba no longer possessed the qualities that initially led him to believe that he was the Messiah.

▶ The Tragedy of Rabbi Akiva's Disciples

There was an additional spiritual dimension to the failure of Bar Kochba as well. Whether the spiritual failure of Rabbi Akiva's students was the only cause, or whether it was also the failure of Bar Kochba to rise to the spiritual heights expected of the Messiah is beyond our knowledge. For then — out of the blue — the horrendous plague *Askera* descended and struck Rabbi Akiva's students. The dream collapsed. For reasons that will probably forever remain obscure, the students of Rabbi Akiva were not considered by Heaven to have reached the supreme spiritual heights necessary to bring about the Messianic age.

Apparently, as great as they were, an important factor was missing. The Talmud tells us that, "Rabbi Akiva's students didn't show proper respect one for the other." Precisely what this phrase refers to we do not know. With greatness comes heightened responsibility, and with greatness comes a magnification of reward and punishment. Because of their failures and deficiencies — which would certainly be counted as minor in a generation such as ours, but which were crucial for great men on their high spiritual level — their mission, to bring the Messianic age and to fill the world with the teachings of Torah, was cancelled and they died a mysterious death.

With them died the Messianic hope of that era and for thousands of years to come. In the terrible war that followed, Bar Kochba and his army were destroyed in the great battles defending the fortress city of Betar. The war had been a catastrophe. Dio Cassius[8] reports the deaths of 580,000 Jews by Roman swords, in addition to those who died of hunger and disease. Some scholars think that the bulk of the Jewish population of Judea was destroyed in battle and in subsequent massacres. One historian believes that the Jews lost a third of their number in the war, perhaps more fatalities than in the Great Revolt of the year 70.

For the survivors, the failure of the Bar Kochba uprising marked the great divide between the hope for national independence and dispersal in the Diaspora. The trauma of the fall of Betar coming after the fall of Jerusalem effected deep changes in the Jewish people. The stiff-necked, stubborn, fanatically independent People that did not hesitate to make repeated suicidal lunges at the mightiest superpower of antiquity lost its warlike ambitions. The hope of the Jew for Redemption was to be delayed for at least 2,000 years.

It would be 2,000 years before there would be a Jewish fighting force. In the great and tragic defeat, not only were between 250,000-600,000 Jews killed, but the Romans were encouraged, once and for all, to uproot the Jewish religion and the Jewish People, to bring an end to their revolutionary hopes and their redemptive dreams.

It is for *this* reason that we mourn today. The mourning of *Sefirah* is not for the students alone, but for the failure of the

Jewish People to be worthy of the Messianic age, for the fall of the curtain on Jewish independence, Jewish hopes and Jewish Messianic ambitions. Every anti-Semitic outbreak which Jews suffered since that day, every pogrom, massacre and banishment that took the toll of so many millions during the 2,000-year bitter night of exile, must be traced directly to the failure of Bar Kochba — but ultimately, to the failure of the students of Rabbi Akiva. This was a tragedy of inestimable proportions to a war-ravaged world suffering under the bitter yoke of Rome as well as to the Jewish People. Rome did not fall at that time, but its fury led to the exile and dismemberment of the Jewish People.

Yet, on that very Lag B'Omer day 2,000 years ago, a new hidden light of hope emerged. In the midst of defeat, the *Tanna* Rabbi Shimon Bar Yochai emerged from his hiding place in a cave and revealed to a small number of students the secrets of the mystical *Zohar*. In the formulas, disciplines and spirituality of the *Zohar* lay the secrets that could bring about the coming of the Messiah. The *Zohar's* living tradition has kept that hope alive down to this very day. On Lag B'Omer the plague stopped, indicating that the Messianic dream was delayed, but it was not destroyed. It was to be nurtured throughout the generations and the stirrings of its realization enliven us today.

Because Lag B'Omer deals with the secrets of the future Messianic age, it is not discussed openly or understood as clearly as the Exodus or other events of the past. Whenever we stand between Passover and Shavuos — between our physical liberation from Egypt and our spiritual elevation at Sinai — we recall those chilling events of the Jewish rebellion against Rome.

▸ Lessons to Be Learned

Today we rejoice over the return of our people to *Eretz Yisrael* and to Jerusalem, the site of our destroyed Temple. History is bringing together so many crucial events: The history of our ancient past is once again coming alive in the land of our fathers. Clearly the days between Passover and Shavuos are filled with the potential and challenge of great spiritual growth. At the same time, these can also be days of spiritual failure, as the sin of the Golden Calf and the failure of Bar Kochba indicate.

There are significant parallels between our own age and that of Rabbi Akiva and Bar Kochba. Following a frightful Holocaust, which many believed would spell the end of the Jewish People, we experienced a restoration of Jewish independence — once more did a Jewish army score miraculous victories against overwhelming odds. Following the destruction of the great European centers of Torah scholarship, we witnessed the rebuilding of yeshivos in America and in Israel. We are experiencing an impressive revival of Torah study. The *teshuvah* movement has brought about a return to Torah for so many who had been alienated. Jerusalem and the Temple Mount are in our hands.

All around us, the world is in turmoil as violence, despair and corruption rage. Once again, the Jewish People have been entrusted with a great and frightful opportunity. Once again we have been given the potential to recreate a Jewish civilization of Torah greatness in our own land. Will we succeed or will our efforts be aborted because of our own failures, our own inability to respect the differences within the Torah community and unite the entire Jewish People to our cause?

The personality of Rabbi Akiva itself offers important lessons and opportunities. It was Rabbi Akiva who understood that "love your fellow as you love yourself" is the overriding principle which must be internalized by all Jews if our nation is to achieve its goals. Rabbi Akiva, too, is the quintessential *ba'al teshuvah:* At 40 years of age he was unable to distinguish between an *aleph* and a *beis*, yet he later rose to be Jewry's greatest Torah scholar.

Hundreds of thousands of Jews — Americans, Israelis and Russians — are today's potential Rabbi Akivas. The fate of Jewry and the achievement of Heaven's greatest goals are in the hands of this generation. Will we attempt to achieve them or will we withdraw into our own selfish cocoons by refusing to shoulder the historic responsibilities God has set before us?

It is not enough to wait for the Messiah's coming; we must toil to perfect our Torah lives and reach out to Jews everywhere, if we are to bring about his speedy arrival. Only if we learn from the lesson of Rabbi Akiva's students will we understand how very much the coming of the Messiah depends on us.

▶ Final Thoughts

We can now understand why it was Rabbi Akiva, of all the great rabbis and teachers, who said, "To love your fellow as you love yourself is a major principle in the Torah." The meaning of this Talmudic "innovation" and "insight" is puzzling. It is common knowledge that this statement is to be found *in* the Torah, in Leviticus 19:18, and that it is a major principle in defining the relationship that must prevail between one Jew and another. What is the new insight that Rabbi Akiva proposed in his statement?

The key to this problem is suggested by the great pre-modern sage, the Chasam Sofer (*Pituchei Chosam*), who proposes the following brilliant insight regarding the tragedy that befell Rabbi Akiva's 24,000 disciples: He says that there is a deeper meaning to Rabbi Akiva's phrase "*klal gadol ba'Torah* — a major principle in the Torah." A more profound interpretation is that this teaching is a major principle "concerning Torah" or "concerning the transmission of Torah."

"Love your neighbor as yourself" not only describes the ideal in human relationships. It must also govern an area where individual accomplishment often reigns supreme — in the intellectual area of the teaching, transmission and study of Torah.

The Torah was given at Sinai at a moment when there was total Jewish unity. The Torah states, "*va'yichan Yisrael neged hahar*," the Israelites encamped opposite Mount Sinai. *Va'yichan* is stated in the singular, which the commentator Rashi defines as meaning that Israel encamped opposite the mountain "as one man with one heart," i.e. in a state of total and perfect unity. From this, we derive the lesson that Torah can only prosper and accomplish its goals when the Jewish people are united. As this relates to Torah study, unity implies circumstances where individual intellectual creativity functions in an environment where love and caring override differences of analysis or opinion. This demands that in the community of scholars, there must exist a high regard for the views of fellow scholars. Each scholar is expected to promote his own scholarship while at the same time advancing and respecting the scholarship of others. Each scholar must make an effort to bring out the best in his colleagues, not to denigrate or downplay them.

The highest form of *love of fellow* must therefore be found among those who are engaged in the study and transmission of Torah. We are therefore obligated to love our fellow as ourselves in the process of transmitting, teaching and sharing our Torah with others. Who appreciated this insight more than Rabbi Akiva himself, whose 24,000 students died from the strange sickness which the Talmud calls *Askara,* because they "were not sufficiently respectful" of one another?

Let us remember that Rabbi Akiva had declared Bar Kochba the potential Messiah of Israel, that the world was a powder keg, that anti-Roman revolts were sprouting all over the Roman Empire, that the Jews believed that they had, with G-d on their side, the capacity to bring Rome down and create a world of justice, peace and respect for all human beings. They believed that these circumstances taken together would initiate the Messianic era.

We don't know the precise role played by Rabbi Akiva's students in the revolt against Rome. Were they scholars or scholar soldiers? Nor do we have proof that Rabbi Akiva taught this doctrine in the wake of the demise of the 24,000 students, but it appears to be obvious that this is the case. The fact remains that when the Sages recorded the ultimate reason for the failure of the great revolt, they did not point to the failings of Bar Kochba, his generals or his troops. They looked inward and realized that the failure was one of the spirit and of those who personified the spiritual life. The unity needed for victory was lacking. Perhaps the honor and respect Rabbi Akiva's students gave one another fell short of what Heaven expected of them.

Why is this Lag B'Omer legacy so important? The Jewish Nation is focused on history for one reason — to learn its lessons and act on them.

Note: *Medrash Koheles Rabbah* 11:10 confirms the above analysis, quoting the words of Rabbi Akiva who said, "'I had 12,000 disciples from Geves to Antiperes, all of whom died during my lifetime [between Pesach and Shavuos]. In the end, I had seven disciples, Rabbi Yehuda Bar Ilai, Rabbi Nechemiah, Rabbi Meir, Rabbi Yosi Ben Chalafta, Rabbi Shimon Bar Yochai, Rabbi Eliezer the son of Rabbi Yosi HaGalili and Rabbi Yochanan HaSandlar. The earlier [disciples] died because they envied the Torah accomplishments of their colleagues. You [the later disciples] must not repeat their error.' Immediately, they succeeded in filling all of *Eretz Yisrael* with Torah."

---

1. *Yevamos* 62b.
2. *Sefer Hamanhig 106, Beis Habechirah, Rabbi Menachem Hameiri* to *Yevamos* 62b.
3. *Yevamos* 62b.
4. *Talmud Yerushalmi Ta'anis* 4:5.
5. From *The History and Destiny of the Jews* by Josef Kastein, Garden City Publishing Co. Inc., Garden City, N.Y., 1936, pages 167-169:
In most parts of the world, the pagan, and more particularly the Greek population, was gradually inclining towards the fundamental beliefs and doctrines of Judaism as a result of coming into daily contact with it. This was the case in Rome, where Horace, Fuscus, Ovid, and Persius (members of the Senate) complained of the spread of Jewish ideas, and Seneca railed eloquently against the Jewish Sabbath day, because it was responsible for the waste of 1/7 of the working life of men. "The customs of this criminal nation are gaining ground so rapidly," he declared, "that they already have adherents in every country; and thus the conquered force their laws upon the conqueror." This was the case in Italy, Syria, Greece, and Asia Minor. Conversions to Judaism had become the order of the day.
6. *Bamidbar* 24:17. Rashi, Onkelus and Rambam state that this refers to the Messiah. See *Ta'anis* ibid.
7. Resnick, Leibel. *The Mystery of Bar Kokhba* (Jason Aronson, 1996) devotes three chapters to "The Bar Kokhba Temple," citing numerous sources.
8. Born only 30 years after the fall of Betar, Roman historian Dio Cassius recounts the story in his *History of Rome*.

IX SHAVUOS

WHY IS THERE AN OBLIGATION TO STUDY TORAH?

61

The trouble with most discussions concerning the human spirit and human potential is that very often you discover that you are talking to people who "live in the basement of a tall building." When you attempt to inform them that there is more to the building than the basement, that there are also upper floors that rise a hundred stories and more, that these floors are available to be lived in, that from the top floors the beauty, sweep and expanse of a great world can be seen — they will deny that the other floors exist. They will invariably invent all kinds of excuses for not seeking out the truth. "We've never been there; how can we be sure?" Then they will say, "We are afraid of heights; we're afraid to climb; it's dangerous; we may fall." Even when a few courageous individuals begin to talk about climbing to the upper floors, they are discouraged by their habit-frozen friends.

The inevitable result is that many of us remain in the basement of life, thinking that that's all there is to it. We continue to live on the lowest floor, unaware of the view and sunlight that exists on the top floors. Occasionally, we may catch a glimpse of a higher floor, we may see a picture of the life "up there," or hear a description of what it's like from someone who is filled with excitement about "the upper floors." But we can't bring ourselves to break old habits, to make a special effort, to find the courage to explore the upper floors.

The Torah was written for people who want to live life to its fullest on *all* floors of their potential, people who refuse to imprison themselves in the basement of life, people who have courage and the spirit of intellectual inquiry. Judaism is a movement for the development and discovery of human potential. It doesn't say, "Don't enjoy life." On the contrary, it says G-d placed so many pleasures and challenges on earth, He wants us to enjoy them by discovering how to use them to construct the "building" of our lives. In this tall building, we will live life to its fullest — on both the spiritual and physical levels. By developing all of our talents, by experiencing life as its Creator meant it to be experienced, we will succeed in climbing out of the basement and develop our full potential.

Judaism sees no contradiction between the physical and spiritual. It demands that the spiritual be the architect of the physical and that the physical serve the spiritual. Judaism mandates that the physical and the spiritual live in harmony, so that each human personality, each a "miniature world," can reach the heights, scale the great mountains and create a kingdom on earth in which G-d is King.

Another analogy: We often compare life to a flame. Nothing has greater potential than a flame, and nothing can be extinguished so readily — with the flick of a finger. In recent history we saw how "human beings" snuffed out the lives of millions of other human beings as nonchalantly as we might extinguish a match. Can we allow ourselves to live exclusively on the physical realm while the spiritual aspect of our personality is stifled or extinguished? We may lack sensitivity to music, beauty, nature or other people's feelings. We may even lack a sense of holiness or may not feel the presence of G-d in our lives. We may be all physical, all body, all instinct, with no spirit, conscience or soul. Like the flame, however, if we add fuel to our spiritual side, it will grow. If we deny it fuel, it will dim and soon become extinguished.

Mankind today puts its emphasis on the physical. Modern technology and the media have made it easy to be surrounded by the grossest sounds and sights — by music or TV that appeal exclusively to our basest instincts, but which ignore or debase our souls. If a bit of the spiritual still remains, it is easily subdued.

Recent surveys reveal that Americans watch an average of eight hours of television each day. If each week the advertisers and producers develop new ways to seduce and shock us with violence, pornography and stupidity so that we will continue to keep our eyes glued to the tube, how can we possibly find the time, the mind or the heart to explore the spiritual or the holy? How can we rise from the basement?

Nothing is as fragile as the spiritual. It must be cultivated, tended and cared for if it is to survive and grow. If not protected, it is easily shattered.

▸ The "Hobby" of the Torah Nation

The passion, quest and national "hobby" of the Jewish People is the study of Torah. We are described as the *Am HaTorah* — the Torah Nation. Prayer is man speaking to G-d; when we study Torah, G-d is speaking to us.

Torah contains truths about life and secrets of the purpose of the universe that are as deep as the sea. The spiritual Jew knows that the Torah is his or her key to spiritual growth. As such, it is the source of life in every respect. "It is a tree of life to those who grasp hold of it."[1] Virtually every kind of wisdom can be found in the Torah if one knows where to look. "Turn it over and over, for all is in it."[2]

How Did We Acquire the Torah?

A *Midrash* relates that before G-d gave the Torah to the Jews, He first offered it to each and every nation on earth. The Amelekites asked, "What does the Torah say?" G-d responded, "Thou shalt not murder." The Amalekites replied, "In that case, we cannot accept the Torah, because our society is built on continuous war and conquest. The very basis of our social structure involves teaching our youth the art of war and murder."

G-d offered the Torah to each nation in turn, and each nation rejected it in order to protect its "national interest" — until He finally offered it to the Jews. They did not ask, "What is in it?" Their immediate and unanimous response was *"Na'aseh v'nishma,"* i.e. "We will do as You command and then we will ask for explanations."

This *Midrash* does not describe a one-time event. Its intention is to describe the continuous confrontation between the Torah of the Jews and mankind's societies and nations. Even though mankind did not *accept* the Torah, they have managed to maintain an ongoing relationship with it through their association with the Jews and with the Jewish Bible. The nations of Western civilization have done this through Christianity, and Asia and Africa have done it through Islam. Each nation that values the Bible continues to have its own unique "relationship" with the Torah of the Jews. Much of Christianity and Islam consist of borrowings from the Torah.

Unfortunately, a good deal of the world's population, including most Jews who are not Orthodox, no longer accept the Torah as the word of G-d, as a set of commands to be obeyed, as a unique document which describes a historic dialogue between G-d and His beloved Chosen People.

A New Key to Torah Study

J ust imagine what would happen if belief in the authenticity of the Torah ceased to be a matter of religion or faith — something you have to *believe* in. What if facts began to emerge which proved the Torah's claims conclusively, scientifically and mathematically? What if these new facts were so compelling that sociologists, mathematicians, anthropologists, historians and professors of Bible would no longer be able to challenge them? What if the new facts had the power to convince us that the Torah is uniquely compelling, more compelling than this morning's latest scientific discovery? What if its claims could no longer be discarded by the cynical as "pious myth" or "blind faith"? What would people do if the Torah were scientifically proven to be exactly what it purports to be — the authentic, eternally relevant word of G-d?

As a matter of fact, a new scientific study of the Torah has emerged and has begun to influence thinking individuals. Even though the odds in favor of discovering hidden numerical structures in the Torah are mathematically remote and logically almost impossible, they are being found today. There are not one, but thousands of structural surprises in the Torah — all mathematically astounding! — that demonstrate its unity, uniqueness and Divine authorship. It is just these structures, patterns and codes which are the subject of ongoing research and investigation by teams of computer scientists and mathematicians who constantly discover additional structural revelations embedded in the structure of the Torah text.

I believe that in our lifetime, these Torah codes, discovered by authentic Torah scholars and statisticians, will create a new and compelling reality for thousands who will find that scientific and mathematical proofs are just the impetus they need to break old habits. They will discover that the Torah codes are just the beginning — that the Torah is filled with wonders and insights that have been defined and explained by our Sages for thousands of years.

They will discover why the Torah that was revealed to the Jewish People at Mount Sinai on Shavuos has been the intellectual and spiritual mainstay of millions of people over the millennia. Hopefully, they will join the Torah People as serious partners — and then they will understand that the Jew's obligation to study G-d's word is nothing less than a prescription for life itself.

---

1. *Proverbs* 3:18.
2. *Ethics of the Fathers* 5:26.

REVELATION: THE BASIS OF FAITH

62

▶ Does G-d Communicate with Man?

s it conceivable that G-d would place man on this earth without a roadmap? It is possible that G-d would leave man completely to his own devices, allowed to make his own decisions and set his own standards? Can *each* person decide right and wrong for himself, and for everyone else? Is mankind alone — or does G-d care enough so as to instruct us as to what He expects of us?

The most important idea in all of civilization is that G-d communicates with His creation. This is an idea that goes far beyond the belief that our world did not come about by accident, and that there exists a Creator who brought the world into being.

It is not enough to acknowledge that the Creator "exists." This Creator is also a loving and caring Father and King, a G-d Who relates, Who communicates, Who is intensely concerned with His creation. Basic to the Jew's belief is that G-d is a loving and caring Father. (Because we call G-d a "Father" and refer to Him as "He" does not imply that G-d is "male." Male and female apply only to animals and humans — G-d is neither. We use this language simply because we cannot meaningfully conceive of a deity entirely in the abstract.) As our "Father," He communicates His Will and His purpose to His children. If G-d never communicated with us, it would indicate that He has no message, sets no standards and doesn't care how we behave. It would indicate, too, that G-d is *less* than His creation — not infinitely more.

Man is a unique creation because he is the *only being* in the universe in whom G-d implanted "G-dly" qualities. What qualities make man G-dly and unique? Among these are the ability to speak, the ability to make free-will decisions, the ability to develop and refine the spiritual aspects of our personalities, the ability to reach beyond and above ourselves, the desire of the soul to reach higher — and the ability to communicate with the generations which came before us and with those which will follow us. It is these "G-d-like" qualities of speech and choice that make the certainty of communication with G-d so very essential.

The conviction that G-d communicated with our great-grandfathers, telling them in human language what He wants and expects of man for all time, is called Revelation.

▶ The Nature of "Revelation"

On Shavuos, we celebrate the giving of the Torah and affirm the historic Jewish belief that the "Ten Commandments" was spoken by G-d to, and heard publicly in the presence of our forefathers — close to three million people standing at the foot of Mount Sinai. On Shavuos we affirm that G-d is the author of the Torah that He revealed to the entire Jewish Nation, both through His public Revelation at Sinai, and in more detail through Moses our Teacher. The *Midrash* tells us that in addition to those physically present at Mt. Sinai, the soul of every Jew ever to be born was at the Revelation and accepted the Torah.

It is not difficult to understand why some people don't believe in Revelation — after all, we live in an age of skepticism and doubt, and few of us have been introduced to this idea as a serious possibility. Fewer still have spent the time required to study and investigate the events described in the Torah so as to come to a firm conclusion or understanding concerning Revelation.

It may be said that belief in "Revelation" is in some ways more important than the belief in G-d. If one believes that G-d exists, but does not concern Himself with the world, what difference does it make if He exists? If G-d created the universe, but is too busy "out there" in space to be concerned with man — if He has nothing to say, if He has no standards to set, no demands to make, then what function does G-d serve? If He is not interested in us, why should we be interested in Him?

▶ What Historic Evidence Is There for Revelation?

During the past four thousand years, the Jewish People survived the efforts of nearly every civilization to defeat and destroy it religiously, intellectually and physically, and has held to its claim that G-d spoke openly to the nation at Mount Sinai. How can the Jewish claim be so firm?

The Revelation of the Torah, and the many supernatural events which accompanied it, was a historic occurrence publicly witnessed by 600,000 male adult Jews. Counting their wives and children, approximately 3,000,000 people were present at Mount Sinai. Each father and his sons, each mother and her daughters participated in the Sinai Revelation: It was the major event in their lives. The spectacle itself was awesome; never before in human history had anyone seen and heard the voice of G-d. Naturally, the experience of this unique event was transmitted by word of mouth from parent to child and from them to succeeding generations. Every child knew the facts directly from his own parent. He did not need to be told by clergy to believe it.

Had the Revelation not occurred and had the Torah been written by a group of men who lived many generations after the Sinai event, as some people claim, the Jewish People would have rejected this preposterous claim being thrust upon them. Fortunately, an unbroken chain of thousands of years in the history of the Jewish People is based upon this historic experience and the certainty that all the events described in the Torah occurred. Through the ages, not one person denied that this truth was the major truth in their family tradition.

Today, in many families in which the certainty of this tradition has been lost, we still usually find that there is some form of Passover Seder. If asked where the family got the idea to participate in a Seder, most people will say that they do it because their parents did. Upon reflection, they will realize that their parents had a Seder because their grandparents did, who had one because their parents did — and so on, right back to the Exodus! As the Exodus predated the giving of the Torah by 50 days, they may be assured that if they have a tradition of a family Passover Seder, their great-grandparents were also present at Sinai.

Judaism is the only religion that dares to make the claim that G-d spoke directly to all of our Jewish ancestors. Other religions claim that G-d spoke to one designated "prophet," but never that an entire nation witnessed G-d's direct communication. Were they able to make such a claim, they would have done so. But it is impossible to make such a claim: It is impossible to get away with it if it is not true. The perpetrator would instantly be revealed to be a fake.

While some Jews may find the Torah difficult to live by, *no one* during our four thousand year history claimed that the Torah wasn't revealed to the Jewish People — not even the movements of opposition or rebellion against kings or rabbis, prophets or princes. Not one opposition group or party challenged the fact of Torah Revelation. The early generations lived close to the reality of the events. Acceptance was complete and unanimous. There were so many live witnesses to the many specific historic events in the Torah, and the Torah provides so many details, that it was impossible to suspect that an entire nation could be fooled.

Concerning the Revelation at Mt. Sinai, there was complete unanimity for thousands of years — until the emergence of the "Reform" movement in modern times.

The "pious hoax" they claim took place could never have been perpetrated on a nation so stubborn, rebellious, doubting and questioning as the Jews. Jews have always been this way, back to the time of Abraham and particularly during the generation of the Exodus. Furthermore, Moses, who was G-d's scribe in transmitting the Torah, was modest and truth loving. He resisted accepting the task G-d had given him, and finally accepted with great reluctance. The Torah points out that Moses was a poor speaker; a stutterer. If Moses had been like other kings and leaders, he would have portrayed himself as a god, as a perfect leader, as the originator of a great code of laws — not as a human being who sinned and was punished by G-d.

Nor could Moses have led the Jews to wander in the desert without a plan for feeding, clothing and housing them unless they had absolute faith that G-d would care for them. No people would have followed a leader into the desert without the confidence that this treacherous journey was G-d's Will and that G-d would look after them in that great barren space which lacked water and could not sustain life. The very fact that the 3,000,000 Children of Israel made it through the desert for forty years is in itself evidence of G-d's Hand in this impossible plan.

▶ How is Man Able to Discover Truth?

No other subjective source of knowledge and truth, such as sense perception (sight, sound, smell, taste), intuition, reason, insight or inspiration could be as reliable or as perfect as knowledge received through the direct communication of G-d. At Sinai, millions of people heard the same words at the very same time. Since man is subjective, since we all think differently and have differing opinions, likes and dislikes, we would all develop conflicting ideas of right and wrong and would never be able to agree on a universal standard which all of mankind must have if there is ever to be justice and peace on earth.

There has never been any record of a disagreement concerning the content of Revelation. Nowhere in the entire record of ancient writings, Jewish or non-Jewish, does anyone deny, question or doubt that the Revelation on Mt. Sinai took place. The first questioning of the origins of the Torah comes from non-Jewish sources and derives from the misunderstandings of translators which arose from the hundreds of inaccuracies in the translation of the Torah into foreign languages, as well as the lack of familiarity with the unwritten "Oral Law" (the Mishnah and Talmud), which is an integral part of the written Torah.

The Torah cannot be understood without knowledge of the Mishnah and Talmud. The Written and Unwritten Torahs are parts of one great body of truth and knowledge that can only be understood when studied side-by-side. For example, when speaking of the correct method for slaughtering animals for meat, the Torah says, "You shall slaughter as I have commanded you." Nowhere in the Torah are the details of this "command" provided. Where are the details found? In the Oral Torah. Another example is the exact structure, contents and process of creating *tefillin*. The commandment to wear *tefillin* is in the Written Torah, but the details are found only in the Oral Torah. There are many such examples.

▶ The Torah is Brutally Honest

Unlike all other ancient historical books and documents, the Torah never covers up or evades unpleasant truths. It is unashamedly truthful and tells things exactly as they are. Its teachings display the highest moral and ethical sensitivity — human failures or sins are constantly pointed out, even in our forefathers and other great moral heroes and role models. In the Torah, Moses himself is reproached for sinning and is punished by not being permitted to enter the Land of Israel. If Moses had written the Torah, as some claim, he would have eliminated those sections where G-d rebuked him for his reluctance to accept responsibility for his sins and impatience. Such an author would have told us fanciful and heroic stories of how he led the victorious Jews into the Land of Israel — *not* that he failed in his mission and was required to give over the leadership to Joshua. He would not have told the stories of how the people rebelled against his authority time and again.

Furthermore, the Torah contains numerous reminders that the People of Israel were at times disloyal, cowardly, ungrateful, stubborn and rebellious. Were the Torah not the revealed word of G-d, the Jewish People would never have accepted the many unflattering condemnations and criticisms it contains. People of ancient times (as well as now!) never wrote a document that so honestly chronicles its failings.

In fact, no People, other than one scrupulously committed to truth, would admit and even take pride in the fact that its origin was in slavery and idolatry. Each year, we repeat at the Passover Seder, "We were slaves to Pharaoh in Egypt" and "In the beginning, our fathers were idol worshipers." Ancient peoples, with the *one* exception of the Jews, consistently glorified their origins through myth and legend, always describing their descent from "kings and gods." They wrote only of their victories — never of their defeats. Only the Torah of the Jews is uniquely different and consistently honest. We may conclude that given all of these factors, the Jews — who presumably shared the same vanity as all ancient cultures — would not have authored the Torah. Only a Divine Being would give the world such a document and only from such a Divine Being would the Jews accept it as truth.

▸ Some Unique Aspects of the Torah

The Torah introduced hundreds of new laws and practices (the Tabernacle/Temple service, Sabbath, *Kashrus*, the laws of Sanctity, *tefillin*, *tzitzis*, etc.) and brought about a complete revolution in the life of each individual, each family and the entire nation. Some of these laws were given without an explanation. Many were difficult to adopt suddenly, particularly for a people long accustomed to living much differently. No one had even seen the objects described by the Torah, such as *tefillin* or a *mezuzah*. Yet, the entire nation completely revolutionized its way of life in each of many thousands of details. This could not have happened unless each Jew was deeply and unreservedly convinced that each of the 613 commandments represented G-d's law and G-d's Will, unless they were filled with love and awe of G-d and with the certainty that comes with experiencing revelation and prophecy.

The unique contents of the Torah are in themselves an indication of its G-dly origin. No human mind could have invented the elevated and sublime ideas, ideology, laws and systems of the Torah, certainly not in the cultural and religious environment that prevailed at that time. The thinking of every other "civilized" nation was diametrically opposed to the Torah in goal and practice. The peoples of the world and its great civilizations were steeped in war, idolatry, cruelty and inhumanity; their cultures and civilizations were based on values, standards and "morality" which ran opposite to all that the Torah teaches. The ancient world was an age of child sacrifices, of killing an entire family in compensation for a murder, of pagan magic and mutilation, of sexual aberrations, of prostitution as a form of worship, of cruel and inhuman slavery.

Suddenly, the Torah came on the scene and demanded a full day of rest for all, equality before the law, justice, morality, kindness and mercy. The Torah way of life, which was revealed in a vast, vacant desert to a People which had but recently been liberated from slavery, has preserved the Jewish People and has served as the supreme guide of life through nearly four thousand years of unbroken, dynamic, changing human history.

The Jew has lived in agricultural, urban, rural and industrial societies; the Jew has lived in the Land of Israel as well as in nearly every other country and society. Yet, the Jews have lived by the Torah and have been able to aspire to the perfect life through its laws despite the fact that it was given in the desert to a People who were slaves but 50 days before. In every time and every place, Torah laws are applicable and fulfilling. There is no man-made code of laws on earth so flexible, yet so unchanging and enduring. The Torah is a code that has survived for 4,000 years and continues to be mankind's most advanced legal system.

While archeology can never prove or disprove that G-d spoke to Abraham or Moses, archeologists have uncovered scores of the cities and towns mentioned in the Bible as well as the remains of buildings, documents, monuments, scrolls, records and tools. These discoveries substantiate in the minutest detail the descriptions of life and society given in the Torah. The Torah mentions hundreds of details of geography, chronology and genealogy; yet archaeology and its allied sciences have discovered nothing that contradicts the accuracy of the Torah. To the contrary, science is the Torah's staunchest ally.

▶ How Can the Same "Book" Speak to Both Young and Old?

Because it is of Divine origin, the Torah is able to appeal to people of every inclination, style and age. The mystic and the rationalist, the romantic and the intellectual, all discover that the Torah speaks directly to them. Through the Torah, child, adult and scholar "hear" the living Voice of G-d.

Our greatest minds have devoted their entire lives to the study of Torah and have found it to be inexhaustible. Unlike secular texts or books, you can never finish studying the Torah. No one has ever felt that he was able to fully master it or to outgrow it. The Torah is written in such a way that it "grows" as a person's mind develops and matures. Because the Torah is written simultaneously on many levels, it can be studied by a young child as well as a seasoned scholar; one can understand it superficially or plumb its esoteric depths. It remains an inexhaustible source of Divine wisdom and truth. No other "book" bears such unique characteristics.

Another important point to consider: Religions in the Western world, including the many branches and forms of Christianity,

Islam and Judaism, all consist of borrowings from the rich table of Orthodox Torah Judaism. In other words, the basic religious expression of all the many countries which practice *any form* of monotheism in North and South America, Europe, Australia and a large portion of Asia would not exist were it not for the ideas they borrowed from our Torah and their acknowledgement that the Torah is G-d's true word. The foundation and wellspring of all human monotheistic spiritual expression has its origins in the Torah. It is not logical for anyone to seriously consider any form of religious practice or belief without first carefully investigating and seriously considering the claims of Orthodox Judaism, since they are Torah-based and the foundation of all monotheistic religions.

▸ The Torah is Not a "Book"

We tend to think in scientific categories. Everything must fit into some neat group. There are countries, nations, religions, rocks, minerals and animals. This leads us to think that the Jews and the Torah must also fit into a category. And somehow, all things within that category tend to be regarded as equivalent. We tend to generalize, then, that the Jews must be a nation (or a religion) and that the Torah is a book. In actuality, however, these generalizations are inaccurate.

The most meaningful categories are those that are unique. Our universe is unique; man is unique; G-d is unique. So, too, His Torah, His People, His land, His language are all unique creations that fit into no other categories. They were created for the special purpose of bringing man closer to the goals and purposes for which he was created.

The unique Torah is G-d's greatest gift to mankind, the key to human happiness and fulfillment. Its secrets reveal a world of truth, grandeur, depth, challenge, meaning and achievement. It is a jewel that is yours to have if you possess the wisdom and maturity to make it your own.

THE INFLUENCE OF THE TORAH ON WORLD CIVILIZATION

63

T he influence of the Torah and its laws has been felt by civilization as a whole; so much so, that many of Western civilization's concepts of humanity, equality and justice are borrowed from the Torah. In fact, the social and religious ideas of most of the world's civilized people are rooted in it.

What are some of these principal values and ideals? Some of the ideas that have their roots in the Torah are the following:

- Equal justice before the law.
- Society can and will some day eliminate war.
- Man is essentially good and can aspire to greatness.
- Man is created in the image of G-d and has within him a G-dly soul. He is not merely an "intelligent animal."
- Fair labor laws.
- Universal compulsory education.

- Knowledge and education belong to every single individual, not only to the aristocratic elite who use their knowledge to control the ignorant.
- Sabbath, which demands that every human being, rich and poor, is entitled to a regular day of rest.
- Punishment must fit the crime.
- Government meat inspection.
- Humane slaughter of animals.
- Conservation.
- Ecological concerns.

Even more basic are the concepts that G-d is One; that He is unique, unseen, moral, ethical, loving, caring, kind, all-powerful and independent of magic and human control.

This list does not, of course, imply that the Torah and Western civilization live in agreement concerning life's values, but indicates that Western civilization has borrowed many concepts and ideas from the Torah and molded them to its own uses. Obviously, without *halachah* [Jewish law], many of the Torah's concepts remain ideas that are good in theory but are impossible to carry out. Yet the Torah remains the most relevant and influential document of human civilization. It continues to influence mankind and to motivate men and women to high spiritual goals.

Much more important than specific values or concepts is observance of the Torah itself. Despite centuries of "progress and development" by civilization — and the competition of other ideologies and philosophies over the ages — the most dynamic, committed and vibrant part of the Jewish People lives by the Torah and follows it in every detail.

▸ How Can We Decide Between Right and Wrong?

The Torah addresses itself to age-old questions which still challenge mankind. How are men to decide between right and wrong? How can we know the difference between good and evil? As we look around the world, we find many nations, peoples, groups, religions and philosophies with diametrically opposing views of what is "good and right." People disagree on the purpose and value of life. Some think it has no purpose — that mankind came about through a combination of accidents. Only the Torah provides a consistent, meaningful answer to these questions — together with a framework of laws and practices which make it possible for the system to work.

Tragically, today we see the results of the rejection of the Torah's universal messages to mankind. We are witnessing a rash of suicides among young people. Why live? Why respect society and its laws? Who are "they" to tell me what to do?

We have a generation of young people strung out on every drug you can name, destroying everything and everyone they touch, wrecking and destroying for the fun of it. They are attempting to escape from life and responsibility — seeking kicks — no matter who is hurt. If there is no G-d, or if He exists but doesn't care — why worry about the next person? Isn't it every man for himself?

For that matter, if life is an accident, if there is no G-d and no purpose, why worry about causes such as peace, civil rights or poverty? What difference does it make if the child next door is starving? Just turn up the television as loud as possible so you can't hear his cries.

If, however, we all have one "Father," if we are brothers and sisters, if we must care for each other because our Creator cares for us and if He wants us to love our neighbor because, like us, he is created in the image of G-d, then we *must* share with the poor, then we *must* care about the world.

How can we express that caring? Are there rules? Do I give my poor neighbor *all* the money in my pocket? What about me, and *my* needs? What about the next poor person who comes along? What about abortion, euthanasia, pornography, child labor, divorce, cheating on exams? Who is to determine right and wrong?

Who is to decide — the man who has a gang of hooligans to back up his ideas of justice? People who believe that the stars are G-d? People who believe that man is basically an animal? People who believe that economics is the most significant factor in history and morality?

Without Torah, without G-d speaking to man, without G-d giving man outlines, principles and rules, we would have no idea of what *good* is — and no idea of how to go about creating a good world. Many have revolted against evil, many have destroyed evil governments — but, without Torah, has anyone succeeded in creating an ideal society?

World Peace: A Jewish Invention

The idea that a peaceful world is desirable and possible has its origin in the Torah. The prophets of the Bible spoke of a day when mankind "shall beat their swords into plowshares and their spears into pruning hooks. Nation shall not lift up sword against nation, neither shall they learn war anymore" (Isaiah 2:4).

In the ancient world, war was seen as a permanent part of life, not an evil to be eliminated. Permanent peace as a national ideal is found only in the Torah. The Torah is the source of man's goodness, and only through the Torah can we remake the world.

The Torah's contribution to world society has only just begun. Eventually, its clear, universal messages will be understood by mankind: individuals and nations will learn that the One God above us is our supreme Master and that He wants us to live in harmony, with dignity and love for all.

HOW TO ACHIEVE ETERNAL LIFE

Based on *Pachad Yitzchok:* Shavuos 21:1

▶ Israel and the Torah are One

he Torah says that the letters of the Ten Commandments were inscribed on the Tablets. The Hebrew phrase describing the inscription is *charus al haluchos.* Our Sages teach: Do not pronounce the word as *charus* [meaning inscribed or chiseled]; instead, pronounce it *chayrus,* meaning freedom — i.e. freedom from the Angel of Death.

Note on Rabbi Hutner's interpretation: This quote from the Sages is actually an amalgam of several phrases. In Mishnah Avos[1] and Talmud Eruvin[2] we find the substitution of chayrus *for* charus. *In the former source, it indicates psychological freedom, in the latter source it is used in the context of national freedom. In Talmud Avodah Zarah[3], we note the opinion (citing a different verse) that were the Torah of Sinai never defiled, it would have exempted Jews from the attention of the Angel of Death. Rabbi Hutner takes the lib-*

erty of assuming that this latter view would in turn interpret the chayrus *reading as confirming freedom from death.*[4]

We may assume that there is a relationship between the concepts of freedom/immortality and the chiseling of stone if the Torah chooses to use words that imply both. The Talmud teaches that there is reason to think that if someone is present at the moment a person dies, he should conduct himself in the same fashion as he would were a *Sefer Torah* being consumed by fire. He would perform *kriah*, rending his garment in mourning, twice: once for the parchment and a second time for the writing on the parchment.

Thus, the departure of a soul is compared to the burning of a *Sefer Torah*. The soul is like the letters on the *Sefer Torah,* which are written on the parchment but disappear in the flames. Just as it is possible to separate the letters from the parchment, it is also possible to separate the soul from the body.

This separation of the text from the page, however, does not apply to the inscription chiseled on the Tablets that bore the Ten Commandments. These letters are *charus*; chiseled letters, not written letters. Chiseled letters are not like letters written with ink on top of parchment. They are chiseled into the stone and become an intrinsic part of the stone. They can neither be erased nor separated. The chiseled letters on the Tablets express and reflect the special relationship the Covenant created between G-d and the Jewish People at Sinai — a relationship as inseparable as letters chiseled into stone.

The Sages therefore taught that the chiseled inscription in the stone (*charus* = inscribed = *chayrus* = freedom) represents a unique, eternal relationship between the Jewish People and Torah. Rabbi Hutner infers further that this fusion of the Jewish Nation with Torah is so permanent that it overcomes the Angel of Death and grants the gift of eternal life. The Covenant achieved through the Tablets created an eternal bond between the Jewish People and G-d, not subject to Death.

The inner message of this teaching lies in the Sages' dictum that "Y*israel ve'oraisa chad hu* — the Nation of Israel and the Torah constitute a total and eternal unity." The body of Israel is rendered eternal by virtue of its soul, the Torah, being eternal. The two cannot be separated. We may, therefore, deduce that every individual who is attached to *Klal Yisrael*, the body of Israel, and who identifies with the Covenant of Torah, which was sealed with the Ten Commandments, achieves eternal life.

1. *Mishnah Avos* 6:3.
2. *Eruvin* 55a.
3. *Avodah Zarah* 5a.
4. *Shavuos* 21:12, also *Midrash Shemos Rabbah* 41:7.

X TISHAH B'AV

WHY DO WE
65 STILL MOURN?

A story is told that in the 1930s, the world-renowned *tzaddik*, the Chofetz Chaim, received a letter from a Jewish soldier who had been drafted into the Polish army. The soldier related that he was assigned to a remote base where there were no Jewish soldiers, no religious services, no kosher food and where it was impossible to keep Shabbos or any *mitzvah* at all. His question to the Chofetz Chaim: "How do I survive as an observant Jew in this forsaken place?"

The reply of the Chofetz Chaim is awesome: "If it is impossible for you to keep Shabbos, *kashrus*, or to *daven* or to keep *mitzvos*, don't be discouraged. There is one thing you can and must do. Whenever you have a free moment, speak to G-d, and whenever you speak to G-d, face east. Why face east? Because you will be directing your thoughts to Jerusalem. In so doing, you will reunite yourself with the Jewish People and with G-d. In fact, whenever a Jew faces Jerusalem in prayer — he or she is *in* Jerusalem." The Jew may not be in Jerusalem — but Jerusalem is always in him.

Most Jews in some way participate in a Passover Seder and observe Yom Kippur. The most dramatic moments of the Yom Kippur service occur just as the day is about to end. At the conclusion of this most sacred day, a long shofar blast is sounded, to which the congregation responds, "Next year in Jerusalem." The very same hope is expressed at the end of the Passover Seder. This is not a coincidence.

For many Jews, the wedding ceremony concludes with the singing of the phrase, "If I forget you, O Jerusalem, let my right hand forget how to function."[1] Then a glass is broken by the groom as a symbolic gesture of grief, so that even at their happiest moment, the newly married couple recalls the destruction of Jerusalem and the Holy Temple. This is in keeping with the next verse, "Let my tongue stick to my palate if I remember you not, if I set not Jerusalem above my greatest joy."[2] Synagogues around the world are built facing Jerusalem. Why is there so much emphasis on remembering Jerusalem in our lives?

To the world at large, the history of Jerusalem opens with its conquest by King David. For the Jew, Jerusalem is the place where man was created. Jerusalem is the city of King Malkizedek, the city in which Abraham, Isaac and Jacob worshipped, the city chosen by G-d to radiate direction and spiritually to all mankind. Jerusalem is the gateway through which all of mankind's prayers rise to Heaven. Jerusalem is the place where the *Shechinah,* the very presence of G-d, is felt more intensely than anywhere else on earth.

To the average Jew, numerous questions arise: What is the source of Jerusalem's uniqueness? Why is Jerusalem the only city mentioned in our prayers? What is the source of its holiness, the mystery of its origin? Why can G-d's Temple be located on this spot and nowhere else? Why is Jerusalem's status and destiny of such deep concern to scores of nations around the globe? Why is the Temple of such momentous importance? Why does a

Jew feel that a world without the Jerusalem Temple is a world alienated and desolate?

If you visit Jerusalem today, you will be moved by its beauty, its expanse, its bursting population, its thousands of Torah scholars and its scores of yeshivos. There is once again more *kedushah*, holiness, to be found in Jerusalem than in any other spot on earth. Jerusalem is teeming with Jewish life and with Torah. Why, then, do we still mourn its destruction?

The answer to these questions is to be found in our three daily prayers for Jerusalem. During the past 2,000 years, Jews have prayed, "Blessed are You, eternal G-d, Who *is building Jerusalem.*" This prayer, which is in the present sense, was recited through the past 2,000 years of exile, even as Jerusalem lay destroyed and desolate. Why? The Jerusalem Talmud makes an astounding statement: "The generation in which the *Beis Hamikdash* is not rebuilt is to be regarded as though the *Beis Hamikdash* was destroyed in that generation." The explanation is simple. When we mourn for the *Beis Hamikdash*, we are not mourning for a building that was destroyed 2,000 years ago. Our mourning must be directed to the realization that each generation is obligated to rebuild the *Beis Hamikdash* and that our failure to do so has little to do with politics, the debate over who has control over the Temple Mount, or the threat of the Arab nations to go to war if we disturb the mosques that sit atop the Temple Mount. The *Beis Hamikdash* will be rebuilt when a sufficient number of Jews make a commitment to change their lives. When will the Messiah come? As the Torah says, "Today, if you hearken to My voice."

Jerusalem is the beating heart of Jewish life. It is literally the eye of the universe; it is the one spot on earth where the presence of G-d is most evident and most concentrated. It is from Jerusalem that human fulfillment and the ultimate Redemption will flow. In Jerusalem, the Messiah will reign — and from there he will bring justice and love to a torn world.

Even though modern Jerusalem is a rebuilt and beautiful city, we still mourn because its heart and essence lies in ruins. When we speak of Jerusalem in our prayers, we are speaking of the

Temple and its service, of the intensity of G-d's presence in its Holy of Holies and of G-d's anticipated rule over Jerusalem — and over the entire world.

▶ Why Do We Need the *Beis Hamikdash*?

To what degree do today's Jews actually mourn for the destroyed Jerusalem Temple? Our lives are so rich, both physically and spiritually. We are so content with our families, our homes, our businesses, our pleasures and our prosperity as to make the destruction of the Holy Temple 2,000 years ago somewhat remote and of limited concern. Few people truly *mourn* for the Temple. Even fewer truly feel the absence of the *Shechinah*. For the rest of us, it is hard to imagine what would be added to the world were the Divine presence to be felt when the *Beis Hamikdash* is rebuilt on the Temple Mount in Jerusalem.

In one of the sad poems [*Kinos*] we recite on Tishah B'Av each year, the famous liturgical poet Rabbi Eliezer Kallir bemoans the absence of the Temple and the Divine presence. He then asks the following question, "What is left for us *here, here* in this world?" This *kinah* teaches us that both the Temple and the Torah rest on a principle to be found in this one word: here.

The Torah constantly reminds us, "The Torah is not in the heavens, but is very close to us, and its purposes can be accomplished *here* in this world." The message of Rabbi Eliezer Kallir is that it is not necessary to ascend to the heavens to find spirituality. Now that the Torah has been given, G-dliness and spirituality are to be found here on this earth and are accessible to all.

In his famous book, *The Kuzari*, Rabbi Yehudah Halevi is asked by the king, "Why is it that Christianity and Islam offer so many more promises and descriptions of Heaven and of the World to Come than are to be found in the Torah?" He replies that these religions have no alternative but to emphasize the world after death; in that way, no one can challenge anything they have to say. Also, there is so very little that they can offer in this world.

The Torah, however, has no need to delay its promises to the next world. Its emphasis is on this world because it has so much to offer in *this world*. It can, therefore, afford to speak little about the World to Come. The Torah challenges us to raise this world to perfection, to create the Kingdom of G-d *here*. It clearly emphasizes G-d's mandate: "I will be your G-d and you will be My people." Here, in this world.

There could be no greater challenge or promise. In many ways, the Holy Temple made this challenge so much easier to grasp and comprehend. In the Temple, it was clear to anyone who entered that the fulfillment of our spiritual yearnings is possible *here* in this world. In the Temple you could feel the presence of the *Shechinah*. As the Sages express it: "The Temple is testimony that the *Shechinah* rests among Israel." It is here that man's dreams, aspirations and hopes can be found and realized. It is here that a person who is troubled and vexed by failure and sin can be transformed. In the Jerusalem Temple, the awareness of G-d's presence was so intense and deep that no one could deny its power.

When the Temple was destroyed, the *Shechinah* was "like a bird wandering from roof to roof."[3] As a result, we were robbed of the one place on earth where G-d's presence and miracles were obvious and could be felt and seen readily by everyone. We were denied the awesome knowledge that "all of reality is here," because G-d's presence was so apparent to all who entered the Temple's gates.

As the exile progressed, we became increasingly alienated from this basic source of spirituality. The *Shechinah* seemed more and more remote. Today, many believe that to become intimate with G-d requires the intense study of mystical works such as the *Zohar, Kabbalah* and the writings of the *Arizal*. They believe that anyone incapable of mastering these deep studies should despair of achieving intimacy with G-d.

This is not the Jewish approach. To the contrary: A Jew who prepares a kosher meal; who is careful with the laws of *netilas yadayim* [hand-washing before the meal]; who recites each *berachah* carefully; who discusses words of Torah during the meal; and who recites the *Birkas Hamazon* [Grace After Meals] carefully, with intent — his table is referred to by the Mishnah as "*zeh ha'shulchan asher lifnei Hashem,* This is a table which is in the presence of G-d."

Even though the Mishnah employs this phrase, even though the Sages teach that every Jew's table can be thought of as an altar, the average person would still ask, "What does eating have to do with the G-d? Isn't He distant and removed from all things in this world?" The average Jew finds it difficult to believe that we can find the *Shechinah* here in our material world. This feeling of alienation and distance is the very definition of the *Churban*: This is the inner meaning of the destruction [*Churban*] of the Temple.

The *Sefer Hayashar* says that every person has "days of love and days of hate." When we have love, everything we do seems to happen without any effort at all. But when there is no love, everything is drudgery and seems so much more difficult to accomplish.

In our relationship with G-d, there are also days of love, days on which we are pleased with our lives and our accomplishments; days on which our Torah study and *mitzvah* observance are uplifting and inspiring. On those days, we are happy and pleased with our lives. However, when we feel alienated from G-d, when He seems remote, everything is difficult and nothing seems to succeed.

The essence of our lives should be an effort to live in the presence of G-d. Knowing that He is here with us, that He is present in our lives, is the true source of our joy and satisfaction. The moment we no longer feel G-d's presence, the moment we feel that He is displeased with us, everything turns black. We are experiencing the effects of the *Churban*. Contrary to popular thought, when we lament the *Churban*, we do not mourn the absence of an imposing building: *Churban* is the absence of G-d's presence.

The challenge to the Jew who lives in exile, in the absence of the *Beis Hamikdash,* is to create G-d's Temple within his own being. The purpose of the *Beis Hamikdash* was to inspire each individual to *become* a miniature *Beis Hamikdash*. We mourn for the *Beis Hamikdash* to acknowledge that we yearn for G-d's presence to return to our midst.

▶ Working Toward the Goal

A human being is made of body and spirit; each is dependent on the other. Our body's condition influences our thoughts. We feel instinctively that our bodies are capable of responding to spiritual thoughts, to spiritual motivations and aspirations. Our goal must be that our sensitivity to spiritual matters should become as keen as our response to physical pain and pleasure.

In the ideal person, body and soul, matter and spirit function in concert and harmony. In that person, body and soul are integrated and inseparable. In the ideal person, each is given the same attention and care. While few people achieve this, it is crucial that we recognize the goal.

How do we become a force for spirituality? We galvanize our own spiritual potential and affect others when we yearn for greater intimacy with G-d, when we place special emphasis on prayer, and on Torah study, *mitzvah* observance, ethical conduct, the proper upbringing of our children and the creation of an appropriate Torah environment in our homes. When we possess the vision to spend our time, our means and our creativity on uplifting the People of the Torah, it is then that we become a force for spirituality. As a result of these efforts, we can bring closer the day when the *Beis Hamikdash* will be restored.

When you sit on a low bench on Tishah B'Av and cry over the destruction of the Holy Temple, pay attention to the fact that the word "*eichah*" [how] with which the Book of Lamentations begins, can also be read as "*ayeka*" [Where are you?] through a small change of the vowels. When we mourn for the Temple, the question that is being asked of us is, "*Ayeka*, Where are *you*?" Where are you regarding spirituality and commitment? Why have you abandoned the Torah studies of your youth? Why have you become so deeply involved with your career and financial goals, at the expense of your spiritual growth? What have you done to develop your inner self?

This challenge becomes much more poignant for this generation, which has experienced the reconquest of Jerusalem, including the Temple Mount. It is as though G-d is saying to us: "You have come closer to accomplishing the ultimate goal than at any time during the past 2,000 years. Never before have I brought you so close to that place that has drawn the Jewish heart for centuries. Yet so many Jews are so distant from this holy place that they do not care if the Temple Mount finally belongs to them and they have no concept of the precious Jewish way of life the Torah holds for them. What are you doing to help them discover the wonderful, forgotten heritage that is rightfully theirs?"

We may not yet all live in Jerusalem, but Jerusalem lives in us. Our challenge is to expand the Jerusalem in us so that Jerusalem and its rebuilt Temple will become the spiritual center for all Jews and for all mankind.

Parts of this essay were inspired by Rabbi Shlomo Wolbe.

1. *Psalms* 37:5.
2. *Psalms* 37:6.
3. *Psalms* 102:8.

ISRAEL
THE FIERCE

66 Based on an unpublished lecture by
Rabbi Yitzchok Hutner

"Israel is the fiercest of the nations." This surprising statement was made by the Ramban.[1] Similar statements are found in the Talmud: "A *Braisa* was taught in the name of Rabbi Meir, 'Why was the Torah given to Israel? Because they are fierce, i.e. strong willed.'"[2] "This is what Rabbi Simeon Ben Lakish said, 'There are three who are strong who are distinguished with fierceness [i.e. strong, difficult to defeat]: Israel among the nations, the dog among the animals and the chicken among the fowl.'"[3]

In what possible way could Israel be considered fierce? Rabbi Yitzchok Hutner answers: What distinguishes the Nation of Israel as "fierce" is its capacity to suffer, to maintain its convictions and integrity in the face of adversity, pressure and persecution. This fierceness constitutes the foundation of the sanctity of Israel and forms the core of Israel's "chosenness." Since its birth during the Exodus from Egypt, Israel has been repeatedly persecuted, yet it has remained staunch, firm and loyal. Israel's loyalty in the face of persecution and oppression is founded on the deep mutual love between G-d and Israel.

What is the foundation of Israel's love for G-d? It flows from the knowledge that one's beloved will help him bear his burdens and suffering. Israel knows that G-d helps it bear oppression because of its willingness to suffer for His Torah. The ability to withstand suffering in the face of adversity is the rock bottom foundation of genuine love. Israel's love is demonstrated through its willingness to be the suffering servant of G-d, to work for Torah, to suffer for Torah, to uphold Torah in the face of pressure, oppression and persecution. Without deep commitment, love is an empty word. Without commitment, love becomes hollow, no more than the self-love and self-gratification so prevalent in contemporary Western societies.[4]

"Chosenness" and love go hand-in-hand. Every day prior to reciting *Sh'ma Yisrael* we say, "Blessed is G-d who chooses His People Israel with love." Israel is considered the Chosen People because of the unique bond of love and mutual commitment between it and G-d. This bond is so strong that the Sages describe it as "eternal and unbreakable": "The Holy One, Blessed be He, Israel and the Torah are one."[5] The love between G-d and Israel is therefore established on the willingness of Israel to bear the burden of suffering for Torah, for being a Jew, the burden of exile and persecution.

We now understand the meaning of the Ramban's unusual definition of Israel as fierce, a definition that explains how a nation that has always aspired to be as gentle as a lamb was cast in the role of a fierce lion.

"*Ki alecha haragnu kol hayom*, For Your sake we have been killed and have suffered through the long day of history."[6] This is our gift to our Beloved, this is the source of our greatness, the secret of our ultimate victory. To be the son of the king, or the wife of the king, implies a readiness to suffer for the king. And if your beloved is the King of Kings, ultimate victory will be the victory of victories, the victory of the gentle over the oppressor, the victory of the few over the many, the victory of the People of

Torah over all the oppressors, tyrants, bigots and idolaters of the world.

The leaders of our People always displayed this quality of fierceness. G-d challenges each Jew. Will we go the way of the majority who look for the easy way out, or will we display *azus* — fierceness, love, loyalty — the iron mettle of a people that recognizes the obstacles that have been placed in its way and is prepared to confront and challenge them?

The secret of our eternity is the ability to overcome, to persevere and not submit, to maintain our posture in the face of extreme pressures. And we do so knowing that a loving G-d and Father is at our side at all times.

1. *Ve'eschanan* 7:7.
2. *Beitzah* 25b.
3. Ibid.
4. See also *Nehemiah* 9:33.
5. *Zohar, Achrei Mos* 73.
6. *Psalms* 44:23.

XI YEARNING FOR REDEMPTION

YEARNING FOR REDEMPTION

A FEW INTRODUCTORY WORDS

67

The holidays teach us to sanctify time. Their agenda stretches from Creation all the way to Redemption. Creation, Revelation and Redemption are the recurring themes in each of the holidays, which together constitute the annual holiday cycle. These themes are also the theme of Shabbos.

In what other contexts do we encounter the effort to sanctify time? Where else do we inspire man to aspire to the Messianic Redemption? I see the above themes in two contexts aside from the festivals:

The first context is in the relationships between the central personalities of the Torah. The struggle for the refinement of mankind is most apparent in the struggles of eight sets of brothers. The conflict of brothers is a recurring theme in Scripture. If the holidays teach us to live above and beyond time, certainly the personalities who serve as our guides in history teach us how to sanctify and elevate civilization and humanity. This is the central theme of the first chapter in this section titled "Eight Biblical Brothers: *Fraternal Love and Redemption.*"

The second context is in the need to assure the unity of the Jewish Nation, especially as expressed during major transitional historic events. Probably the most outstanding and blatant manifestations of such unity first took place when G-d revealed Himself to Israel at Sinai, when the Torah was given. The second manifestation was on Purim, when the Jews reaccepted the Torah following the miraculous defeat of Haman. The second chapter in this section, "Israel's Unity as a Condition for G-d's Unity," reveals the first time Jewish unity played a central role in Jewish history, which resulted in the establishment of *Sh'ma Yisrael.* This chapter studies the saga of the reunification of Joseph with his brothers and his father, and the proclamation by his father, Jacob, of *Sh'ma Yisrael,* possibly for the first time in history, when he experienced the restored unity of his sons — an event that he had despaired of ever experiencing from the moment he learned that his son Joseph was allegedly devoured by a beast.

The national identity of the Jewish People is further explored in relation to the Land of Israel in the last chapter of this section, "Why Does the Jewish Religion Need a Country?" In it, the culmination of all historical processes are explained in the context of the final Redemption, for which we all yearn.

While not directly connected to the holidays, each of these chapters reveals concepts that are central to the festival's message.

EIGHT BIBLICAL BROTHERS: FRATERNAL LOVE AND REDEMPTION

68

t is accepted practice that Torah analysis, and especially the analysis of Torah events and personalities, is rooted in *Chazal,* the Sages of the Talmud and the *Rishonim.* This thesis, however, is my own. Yet when I mentioned my failure to find supporting evidence for my thesis in *Chazal* to a major Torah authority, his response was that "The theme does not require roots in the Sages because it is clearly and obviously rooted in *'p'shuto shel mikra,'* the obvious and apparent meaning of the Torah text."

There are, however, two additional concerns which need to be mentioned in advance:

In view of the fact that they were not blood brothers, to what extent do David and Jonathan legitimately belong among the brothers?

Can *Mashiach ben Joseph* (the Messiah, son of Joseph) and *Mashiach ben David* (Messiah, son of David), who have not yet entered the stage of history, be regarded as the eighth set in the progression of Biblical brothers?

I leave the above questions and their answers to the reader.

▶ Relationships in the Torah

While the Torah does not explicitly speak of the *Mashiach* [Messiah], it describes events, messages and the developing and maturing interpersonal incidents and relationships among brothers which are saturated with messianic significance.

Many think of the Torah primarily as a book of laws, but this is not so; above all, the Torah is a manual for the elevation and perfection of human society. This is why the first book of the Torah is almost totally devoted to the lives of our fathers, our mothers and their families and their dreams, challenges and struggles.

A major theme that runs through the Torah and the first books of the Prophets is the strained relationships between brothers. Indeed, mankind's first crime was the murder of the first human brother by his brother. It would seem obvious that a major goal of mankind must be to discover a formula by which brothers and sisters, even those who are G-d's chosen and most beloved, could live in harmony.

When the Torah is subjected to careful scrutiny, we observe that the quality of Biblical filial relationships is not at all static. There appears to be a dynamic, generational, Divinely guided progression. As we move from one Biblical set of brothers to the next, the quality of each relationship changes and progresses. Each set of brothers demonstrates an upward step in what appears to be a deliberate changing and evolving quality of relationships that progressively improves from one set of brothers to the next. We move from a brother who hates and murders until we reach a brother whose love demonstrates an unbelievable degree of self-negation in which his only motive is the promotion of the Will of G-d.

The Torah and our Sages describe these seven evolving and maturing filial relationships in great detail. Each of the seven sets of brothers represents a new major historic plateau. Each contains a lesson on how mankind is able to bring closer the era of the Messiah. Viewed historically, the saga of the seven sets of brothers appears to be the history of mankind.

The progress made by each of the seven sets is so striking that one might think that in tracing their story we might conjecture that we have been tracing the personality and spiritual development of a single individual who struggled, persevered and finally resolved his inner conflicts and totally refined his personality. Might it not be that our Creator has placed these biographies in His Book of Books to serve as living lessons to guide our lives?

The *Midrash Tanchuma*[1] reveals a frightening and alarming insight: *"Kol ha'achin son'in zeh es zeh,* All brotherly relationships contain elements of hatred of one brother for the other." Our rabbis are teaching that there often exists a tendency in precisely those people we expect to be dedicated to the other, to allow the fire of jealousy to create distances and rivalries that destroy their relationship. When Biblical brothers reach the point where they succeed in overcoming jealousy and hatred, the Biblical record we are about to examine indicates that they became prime instrumentalities in bringing Redemption closer. By uniting and resisting tale-bearing, jealousy and rivalry, brothers are capable of defeating those negative tendencies which tear them apart and instead bring about the ascendancy of forces of tolerance and empathy which promote both familial and national unity. Ultimately, we arrive at brothers who pave the way for the actualization of the Divine master plan for human self-realization and universal salvation.

Rabbi Yisrael Salanter taught, "The most difficult challenge confronting each human being is to break one negative personality trait." The impulse that motivates brothers to compete and hate is so deeply ingrained that when it *is* overcome, it plants the seeds for the promised Redemption.

According to the *Sefer Hashorashim,* the *Book of Word Origins* of the Radak, the word *ach,* brother, is at the root of *echad,* one. Forging ideal relationships between brothers is the basic ingredient for reaching the goal of the human enterprise in which the Jewish Nation serves as a light to the nations. Exemplary filial behavior motivates and activates all of human history. The goal of the Jew must be to bring civilization to a pinnacle of spiritual achievement, to the time proclaimed in *Sh'ma Yisrael;* as defined by Rashi, when *Hashem Elokeinu,* the Lord Who is *our* G-d, the G-d of the loyal segment of Jewry, will become *Hashem Echad,* the One G-d of all mankind, united as *achim,* brothers. The achievement of unity — progressing from brother *aleph* to brother *ches,* (the number eight in Jewish thought denotes meta-history and Redemption) — demands that Jews unite as *achim.*

We will now analyze the seven sets of Biblical brothers who dominate the Torah landscape. They provide us with a roadmap leading from the murder of Abel by his brother Cain, through the discord and hatred that characterized the relationship between Isaac and Ishmael, Jacob and Esau, and Joseph and his brothers.

The first break in brotherly hatred is the effort of Joseph to restore his relationship with his brothers and convince them that he bears no grudge over their former actions and accepts all the preceding events as the fulfillment of the Divine plan. This pattern is further broken when a radically new and refined relationship bursts forth, that of Ephraim and Menasheh, the sons of Joseph. The next step upward are Aaron and Moses, who subsequently develop an even more extraordinary kinship which sets the stage, generations later, for the highest and most exemplary "brotherly" relationship ever, that of David and Jonathan, who were not biological brothers, but brothers in a sublimely spiritual sense. They represent the ideal fraternal kinship, a relationship unprecedented and unduplicated in all of human history. Theirs is the road sign that points to the Messianic era.

▶ A Closer Look

Human history opens with a conflict of the first brothers, whose jealousy and hatred result in the murder of Abel by Cain. When Cain saw that his younger brother had earned G-d's favor, his strategy for regaining his temporal and spiritual kingly privileges, which are the birthright prerogative of the firstborn, was to murder his brother. The first crime committed by a human being was the murder of a brother by a brother. Resonating through history is Cain's ungodly rejoinder: "Am I my brother's keeper?"

The next two filial sets are Isaac and Ishmael, and Jacob and Esau. The issue we face here is identifying a genuine progression from the Isaac/Ishmael relationship to the next generation of brothers, Jacob and Esau.

While the Sages see Esau as the eternal competitor and antagonist of Jacob, this is not explicitly stated in the Torah text. To the contrary, Isaac never banished Esau; he loved him to the end and apparently became aware of his incorrigible negative traits only towards the end. The Torah never openly states that Esau shared the explicitly stated evil characteristics of Ishmael, of whom it says, "And he shall be a wild ass of a man: his hand against everyone and everyone's hand against him and over all his brothers shall he dwell."[2] The simple meaning of this verse, according to Rashi, is that Ishmael would "be an untamed brigand, a hated plunderer and warrior."

While Ishmael's banishment is described by the text in detail, in the case of Jacob and Esau, it was Jacob who fled his father's house while Esau remained at home. Looking at the *p'shat*, the plain meaning of the Torah, we might even believe that Esau was on a higher level than Ishmael, giving credence to their being a double link in the progression of the seven sets of brothers.

Ishmael was banished from Abraham's home because his corrupting influence could no longer be tolerated. In contradistinction, the Torah describes the seeming, yet temporary, reconciliation of Jacob and Esau: "And he (Jacob) passed in front of them and bowed to the ground seven times until he reached his brother (Esau). Then Esau ran to him, hugged him and fell on his neck and kissed him; then they both cried."[3] The Sages debate whether this was a full and sincere reconciliation. Even Rabbi Shimon Bar Yochai who taught that, "It is the accepted principle that Esau hates Jacob," says that, "Esau's compassion overwhelmed him at that moment and he kissed Jacob with his full heart."[4]

The Netziv in Ha'amek Davar says:

> *They both cried, to teach that at that moment Esau*
> *was overcome with love for Jacob, as was Jacob*

overcome with love for Esau. This also took place in later generations. When the children of Esau are filled with a pure spirit and recognize the exalted qualities of the children of Jacob, then the Jew is also aroused to recognize that Esau is indeed our brother, much as Rebbe (Rabbi Yehudah HaNasi) loved his Roman friend, Antoninus. There are other similar examples.

Nonetheless, this opinion does not reflect the consensus of *Chazal,* nor does it reflect the reality of subsequent history. Until recently, the Isaac/Ishmael rivalry receded, while the Esau/Jacob relationship as reflected in *Chazal's* description of the Esau/Israel rivalry came to the fore as the focus of Jewry's 2,000-year-old exile in which Esau/Edom/Rome are the evil antagonists.

Brotherly relationships take a dramatic and decisive about-face with Ephraim and Menasheh, the fifth set of brothers. The story of the unique blessing with which Jacob blessed his grandchildren Ephraim and Menasheh, the blessing with which Jewish fathers bless their children each Friday night, *"Yesimcha Elokim k'Ephraim ve'ch'Menasheh,* May G-d make you as Ephraim and Menasheh," is the key to that relationship. What is out of character and most intriguing about Jacob's blessing is that "Israel put forth his right hand and placed it on the head of Ephraim, who was the younger,"[5] thereby favoring the younger brother over the older. Following this crucial, shocking and truly provocative act, the Torah continues its narrative by telling us absolutely nothing more about it! The Torah's total and unexpected silence on this is almost shattering. With a dramatic and resonating silence, Menasheh accepted the fact that it was possible, for reasons of which he was certainly aware, that his younger brother had been chosen for the special role to which the older brother was normally entitled by reason of birthright. Most importantly, brotherly hatred ceased to be the dominant factor in brotherly relationships. With this act, a revolutionary new relationship emerged, opening the door to the possibility of Redemption, which in a more immediate sense led to the next step, the births of Aaron and Moses.

The unique relationship of Moses and Aaron demonstrates the key role fraternal relationships played in molding Jewish history. The Jewish Nation was created for the express purpose of transforming civilization. A key element of this improvement is bettering the manner in which people relate to each other.

The underlying factor that made possible the Exodus, the birth of Israel as a nation, and the Revelation at Sinai was the exemplary brotherly relationship of Moses and Aaron. It was radically unlike the negative relationships between Cain and Abel, Isaac and Ishmael, Jacob and Esau or Joseph and his brothers. Brotherly love created a unique partnership between two towering leaders that broke the logjam of 210 years of Jewish bondage and exile, and which facilitated the creation of two new crucial Jewish institutions: *Malchus*, kingship, awarded to Moses, and *Kehunah*, priesthood, awarded to Aaron. This new *ach* [brotherly] relationship made possible humanity's greatest moment, the Revelation at Sinai. When the Jewish People stood at the foot of Mt. Sinai they enjoyed total unity, as expressed by Rashi, *"K'ish echad b'lev echad,"* they stood united, "as one man, as though with one heart."

The unique relationship between Moses and Aaron is celebrated in Psalm 133, King David's ode to the Messianic age. *"Hineh mah tov u'mah na'im sheves achim gam yachad,* How good and how pleasant it is for brothers to dwell in harmony." This is how Rashi understands this Psalm:

> Only when Hashem, Himself, will sit in the Holy
> Temple together with the Jewish People who are
> called achim, *brothers, and* rayim, *friends — only
> then will G-d be* yachad, *will He and His People
> be united.*

How are Jews to achieve this ultimate "good and pleasant"? When we are reunited as one People in our own land, when we are again *achim*, united as brothers — only then will the Messiah come. The Radak comments:

> This refers to the Melech HaMashiach [the King
> Messiah] and the Kohen Gadol [the High Priest],
> who, in the Messianic Age, will be brothers in greatness without a shred of jealousy between them."

Psalm 133 continues, "Like the precious oil upon the head running down the beard, the beard of Aaron, running down the hem of his garments." This sentence demonstrates that Aaron, and not Moses, had the principal merit for bringing about the Exodus and the Revelation at Sinai. The Redemption from Egypt became possible due to two factors: first, Aaron's success in overcoming his jealousy of his brother, and second, Moses' refusal to accept the leadership of the Jewish People, and his insistence that Aaron's position as prophet and elder brother entitled him to Jewish leadership.

Rashi teaches that the Torah narrative describes seven days that Moses pleaded with G-d to appoint his brother Aaron the king and leader of the Children of Israel in his stead. Moses refused to accept the leadership of the Jewish People for one reason — to avoid usurping the prerogatives, prestige and honor of his older brother, Aaron. "I beg you, O L-rd," exclaimed Moses, "please send someone who is more appropriate" (i.e., Aaron, the one You are accustomed to send).[6] Moses finally relented when G-d said to him, "See, Aaron is setting out to greet you, and when he sees you, his heart will be glad."[7] Rashi adds, "It is not as you think, that he will resent you because you are ascending to greatness." The Talmud relates, "Said Rabbi Malachi, 'As Aaron's reward for, 'and when he sees you, his heart will be glad,' concerning the appointment of his brother, Aaron merited to wear the *Choshen Mishpat*, the breastplate of the High Priesthood, over his heart.' "[8]

Now we arrive at the high point. Contrast the murder of Abel by Cain with the fifteen chapters of I Samuel devoted to the description of the moving and dramatic saga of two men — each destined to be king of Israel — Jonathan, the son of King Saul, and David, the son of Jesse. Each should have hated the other; each had ample reason to murder the other. Jonathan rose above politics, pragmatism, family, succession and reality, aspirations that motivate all human beings. In a most dramatic and unexpected turn of events, Jonathan overcame self-interest, hatred, jealousy and ego. Jonathan sublimated his regal dreams and aspirations and those of his family to serve a higher purpose, the establishment of David's line of kingship, the *Malchus Beis David* from which *Mashiach* is destined to be born.

The selfless behavior of Jonathan is the greatest story ever told. This is the living gift and legacy of Jonathan, whose name means "G-d will give," and David, whose name means "beloved." As the prophet Samuel records, "The soul of Jonathan was bound up with the soul of David, and Jonathan loved David as he loved himself."[9] Then, "Jonathan removed his cloak and his tunic,"[10] symbols of royalty and kingship, and voluntarily presented them to David, acknowledging the providence and Will of G-d. Jonathan endangered and ultimately sacrificed his life so that his arch-competitor would survive the enmity of his father, Saul, and rule Israel in Saul's stead. This overwhelming act of brotherly love and self-effacement made possible the emergence of the House of David, the ultimate mechanism for human Redemption.

Note that Cain and Abel and David and Jonathan struggled over the same prize — who would wear the crown as G-d's representative on earth? While Cain tragically solved his challenge by murdering his brother, Jonathan resolved his by offering his own life, not only so David could live, but so that David would inherit Saul's crown. This total transformation, traditionally called a *tikkun*, a correction or rectification, completes the circle and serves as a paradigm for humanity.

David and Jonathan aspired to and reached the highest levels of human brotherhood. Are not all Jews — indeed, aren't all human beings — brothers? It was the sacrifice of Jonathan that established the Messianic line.

When David learned that Jonathan fell in battle, he spoke of him as his beloved brother; "I am stressed because of you, my brother Jonathan, you were very pleasant to me, your love for me was far more wonderful than the love of my wives."[11] Can anyone deny that David and Jonathan were "brothers" in a most sublime sense? The Book of Samuel clearly confirms that they were.

Examine each opposite end of our brotherly spectrum. Contrast the first set of brothers, Cain and Abel, and the seventh set of "brothers," David and Jonathan. Then contemplate the final, eighth set of "brothers" — *Mashiach ben Yosef* and *Mashiach ben David,* who are not yet on the scene. When they appear, however, as historic messianic personalities, they will bring the saga of the brothers to a close with the onset of the Messianic age.

In fact, it is the reconciliation of the two ultimate regal brothers in the guise of *Mashiach ben Yosef* and *Mashiach ben David,* who in the End of Days will bring the two competing tribes of Joseph and Judah into harmony, which will make possible the Messianic era of human spirituality, reconciliation, peace, justice and the rule of G-d over mankind.

Among the seven sets of brothers, two hold the key to the Messianic era: Joseph, who ruled over Egypt, and David, who ruled over Israel. Their descendants will be *Mashiach*: *Mashiach ben Yosef,* the son of Joseph, who will be followed by *Mashiach ben David,* the son of David, a descendant of Judah, who will restore Israel to its former glory. What distinguishes Joseph and David from the other five sets is that theirs was not a competitive relationship of enmity. On the contrary, theirs was a relationship of rejection and alienation from their brothers. At first, the brothers failed to accept and recognize the role that the G-d of history had assigned their brother, but later both Joseph and David achieved full reconciliation with their brothers. Both succeeded in restoring a relationship of harmony, trust and love. As David says in the Psalms, "for the sake of my brethren who are my comrades, I shall speak peace in your midst. For the sake of the House of Hashem, our G-d, I will request your good."[12] Brotherly relationships loom large because they constitute an essential foundation in the task of molding a unique people that bears the responsibility of bringing to fruition the Divine plan for human destiny.

The transformation in relationships between the seven sets of brothers from Cain and Abel until David and Jonathan sets a pattern. It calls upon Jews to internalize this new filial relationship to the point that we, too, become worthy to participate in the Messianic adventure. Only then can we succeed in transforming the Jewish community from one in which one segment distrusts and sometimes despises the other, into one in which each segment respects the other. The Torah did not envision a monolithic Jewish Nation, but one of many tribes. The grandeur of the Jewish national concept calls for each of the twelve "tribes" to march under its own banner, to demonstrate its unique style, and at the same time be capable of uniting under One King and One Torah.

Encouraging diversity within the Torah community is legitimate so long as each segment respects legitimate differences and lives in brotherhood and harmony. What makes this thesis so meaningful is that there are precisely eight sets of brothers, leading from Cain who murdered Abel; to Isaac who was alienated from Ishmael, causing eternal separation; to Jacob and Esau who, while they forever remain brothers, live in eternal competition and enmity until the End of Days when "Redeemers will arise on Mount Zion who will judge the Mountain of Esau;" to Joseph's brothers who were prepared to murder Joseph, but in the end achieved unity, reconciliation and repented their ways when they acknowledged that, "We are all brothers, the children of one father." Each of them represented facets of the same truth which must co-exist in peace.

Many centuries later, another attempt was made to bring about the Messianic Age. The relationship described in *"Hineh mah tov,"* the cooperation between two great leaders, nearly succeeded when Rabbi Akiva recognized Bar Kochba as the Messiah. Though they stood at the very precipice of a potentially great Messianic Age, their partnership failed. It is my contention that their failure was because the students of Rabbi Akiva were unable to attain heightened relationships, such as those attained by Ephraim and Menasheh, Moses and Aaron, David and Jonathan. The reason for the deaths of Rabbi Akiva's multitude of students is cited by the Talmud: *"She'lo nahagu kavod zeh bazeh,* They did not adequately honor each other." I believe that this failure to maintain absolute unity and respect for each other caused not only their own deaths but was the direct Heavenly cause of Bar Kochba's defeat, resulting in 2,000 years of Jewish exile and suffering, from which we are now hopefully emerging.

Much like Rabbi Akiva and his colleagues who rebuilt Jewish life following the devastating *Churban* [destruction of the Holy Temple and Jerusalem], our generation has experienced six great miracles: the miraculous rebuilding of Jewish life following a twentieth century *churban;* the reestablishment of Jewish sovereignty in the Land of Israel; the conquest of Jerusalem; the rebirth of the Torah world;

the *teshuvah* movement; and the liberation of Soviet Jewry. No rational person could have anticipated any of these events. Despite clear evidence of G-d's Hand, the overwhelming majority of Jews remain oblivious to the challenges and demands presented by these events. As a result, the Jewish world and the world at large face unimagined tests and dangers. Instead of marshalling our forces and intensifying our efforts to reach the non-observant, there exists much fragmentation and intolerance within the Torah world.

Our guiding light might well be Joseph, whom the Torah calls the *ba'al hachalomos,* literally the master of his dreams. It was he who reunited the twelve brothers to form one nation; it was he who restored peace to the House of Israel; it was he who demonstrated that it is possible to rise to extraordinary spiritual heights in a non-Jewish society, and yet raise children as loyal Torah Jews. It is Joseph alone among Biblical personages who is called by our Sages *hatzaddik* — the righteous.

Our seven Biblical brothers were among mankind's greatest personalities, men of unusual piety, principle, idealism and determination. Their lives represent the pattern on which we must design our own lives. They were real people who engaged in the ultimate struggle of life, the struggle to overcome the limitations of their humanity.

If their dreams and life's purpose are to be realized, these dreams must become our own dreams. We must learn not only from our ancestors' triumphs, but also from their failures and struggles, and reach the universal brotherhood they sought. While this may well seem an impossible challenge, is this not the challenge for which G-d has placed us on this earth?

1. *Exodus* 27.
2. *Genesis* 16:11.
3. *Genesis* 33:3-4.
4. Rashi quoting *Bereishis Rabbah.*
5. *Genesis* 48:14.
6. *Exodus* 4:13.
7. *Exodus* 4:14.
8. *Shabbos* 139a.
9. *I Samuel* 18:1.
10. *I Samuel,* 18:4.
11. *II Samuel,* 1:26.
12. *Psalm* 119:165.

ISRAEL'S UNITY AS A CONDITION FOR G-D'S UNITY

69

▸ The Trials of Joseph and the Origin of *Sh'ma Yisrael*

Does the Torah reveal the origin of *Sh'ma Yisrael*? Is it revealed anywhere with certainty? Let us search for clues in the words of our Sages. Logic would have it that *Sh'ma Yisrael* originated with our Patriarch Jacob, whose name was changed to *Yisrael*, Israel, after struggling with the Angel of Esau and prevailing.

When then did *Jacob* first utter *Sh'ma Yisrael*, the clarion call of *Am Yisrael*, the most succinct and powerful statement of our commitment and mission? I believe that the origin of *Sh'ma Yisrael* can be found in the saga of the rift between Joseph and his brothers, which concludes with their dramatic reunion and the subsequent reuniting of Jacob with his beloved son Joseph. In the process of unraveling the mystery of the rift and the reunion of the sons of Jacob and Joseph, we will uncover both the origin and the inner meaning of *Sh'ma Yisrael*.

From the very moment Jacob emerges victorious from his battle with the Angel of Esau until the end of the Book of Genesis, the word *panim*, face, is employed with unusual frequency. The face is a thematic thread that ties the text together and defines various seminal incidents.

Following his bout with Esau, Jacob exclaims, "I have seen G-d face to face." What is the significance of the emphasis on face in the Torah?

G-d is invisible, without body or physical form. If we wish to see G-d in the physical world, He can be "seen" by observing the human face. In what way is this true? Just as G-d is unique, so too each human face is unique. Since the time of Creation, billions of humans have walked the earth, yet each human face is different. No two faces are exactly alike. How many differently shaped ears, chins or noses are there? The phenomenon of the singularity of the human face exists despite the fact that each face is a composite of a finite number of variables. Magically, when finite variables are applied to the human face, in combination, limited elements produce unlimited results far beyond the mathematical potential of each individual element in combination.

The uniqueness of the human face is acknowledged by the Hebrew word for face — *panim* — which means "the inside," thus denoting the inner personality of each human being. In contrast, the English word "face" describes a secular value — the "outside" or external feature of a physical object. The word *panim* teaches that the human face reflects each person's unique soul and personality. As expressed by our rabbis, each person is an *olam katan,* a miniature universe. The face describes and portrays the soul, man's singular personality and the complicated world that exists on the inside of each person. The Torah describes how *Moshe Rabbeinu,* Moses, covered his face with a mask because its radiance was so dazzling that no person could gaze upon it.

A great Torah sage whose face radiates his righteousness and scholarship is often described as possessing a *hadras panim,* a spiritually radiant face that portrays his greatness. Indeed, some Torah sages were capable of looking at an individual's face and "reading" that person's personality and history. The face is far more than something we are born with. It is said that through his life's journey, each person creates his or her own face — a task that is completed at around age 50.

Joseph was the first individual to test the Torah system created by Abraham, Isaac and Jacob in the loneliness of exile. He accomplished this feat despite the fact that Egypt provided him with no Jewish home, no parents, no yeshivah, no teacher, no synagogue and no Torah support system. He was the epitome of the lonely man of faith. Each of our patriarchs was tested, but Joseph endured the greatest test of all. His was the test of rising to the pinnacle of human civilization, of empire, prestige, power and influence — yet remaining *Yosef Hatzaddik*, Joseph the Righteous.

Joseph proved that it is possible to function as the prime minister of the most sophisticated civilization while at the same time living the life of a Torah Jew. He succeeded in creating a sublime environment of *kedushah,* of holiness, in the isolation of his home and in the loneliness of his heart. He demonstrated that *kedushah* could emanate from within a human being outward. Joseph was in essence a recreation of our father Abraham. He accomplished his mission as the first exiled Jew who was successful in integrating the creativity of "modern" technology and worldliness with a supreme level of *kedushah* and *taharah*, elevated holiness and purity — all within the sordid depravity and licentiousness of ancient Egypt.

One of Joseph's greatest trials was resisting the effort of his master Potiphar's wife to seduce him.[1] Potiphar's wife was relentless in her pursuit of Joseph: She tried to entice him with words, by varying her seductive dress, by threats of imprisonment, humiliation and physical harm and by offering him huge sums of money.[2] According to one view in the Talmud, Joseph's resistance had nearly cracked and he was ready to yield to her demands.[3]

As Joseph is about to succumb to the woman's seductions, he suddenly recoils and flees. What prevented him from sinning? Rashi, the most respected Biblical commentator, quoting the Talmud states, "There passed before Joseph's mind's eye the picture of his father's face."[4] A sudden vision of his father's face in the window jarred Joseph's conscience and reminded him of who he is and of the unique stature of his father. Why did the vision of his father's face affect him so profoundly?

A clue to Joseph's relationship with his father Jacob can be found in the Torah's statement, "Israel (Jacob) loved Joseph more than he loved his other sons."[5] Rashi teaches that one of the reasons for Jacob's preference is that "the appearance of Joseph's face was the same as Jacob's." Is the fact that a son looks like his father sufficient reason for loving him more than his other children? This might sway the average person, but does it befit a person of Jacob's exalted spiritual and intellectual stature? Jacob — a most extraordinary human being — is regarded by our Sages as the greatest and most perfect of the forefathers. What is the true significance of Jacob's choice?

I believe that the key to this enigma can be found in the statement of the *Midrash Rabbah*, "Jacob's face was chiseled on the throne of G-d's glory." Our tradition teaches that G-d has neither a "throne" nor a "face" chiseled on this "throne"; the *Midrash* is therefore metaphorically teaching that in G-d's judgment, Jacob represented human perfection. Indeed, the Torah calls Jacob *"ish tam"* — the perfect man, the ideal human being. This is further substantiated by the statement of the Talmud, "The beauty of Jacob was similar to the beauty of Adam, the first human."[6] The father of all mankind is described by the Sages as the epitome of human perfection — and Jacob enjoyed a similar stature. The Sages further teach that "the face of Adam looked like the *Shechinah*" — it reflected the very presence of G-d.

Let us now assemble the above elements and attempt to arrive at a conclusion. When Joseph was about to succumb to the seductions of the wife of Potiphar, and the face of his father appeared to him, whose face did he see? He saw his father's face — none other than the "face" engraved on G-d's throne. He undoubtedly saw a second face as well: *his own face*, since Joseph's face and Jacob's face were the same. At his moment of confrontation with sin, Joseph was jolted into remembering who he was and what he represents. When he "saw" his father's face he remembered his unique mission and high station. He then understood that he could not possibly commit an immoral act.

We can now understand why Jacob loved Joseph more than his other sons. To Jacob, Joseph was the vital link in the chain that leads to human perfection, to the Messiah — to the fulfillment of life's goals — to the fulfillment of Jacob's purpose on earth.

We can now appreciate the deep significance of Jacob's dramatic words when, after 22 years of absence, he learned that his son Joseph was alive and well. Jacob exclaimed, "I must go to Egypt and see him before I die."[7] Jacob's emphasis on the need to see Joseph's face before he died underscores his desire to ascertain with his own eyes that despite the trials and experiences Joseph encountered during his long exile from his parents' G-d-fearing home, and the awesome transformations that certainly resulted from Joseph's high secular office in the palace of Pharaoh, his face had not changed. Jacob's dream was to see Joseph's face just once again, to be assured that it remained the same face that was emblazoned on G-d's throne.

For this reason, when Jacob is reunited with Joseph, Jacob exclaims, "I am now able to die, now that I have seen your face, now that I know that you still live,"[8] i.e., now that I know for certain that your face has not changed. Jacob knew that Joseph was alive prior to seeing his face, but he could only ascertain that the link in the chain of Jewish continuity and sanctity was alive and intact in his son by personally meeting him. Now he knew that the historic chain initiated by Abraham had not been broken.

These conclusions lead us to a surprising and revealing discovery as to when and how the key statement of Jewish commitment, the *Sh'ma Yisrael*, came into being. At the emotion-filled moment when Jacob and Joseph are reunited, the Torah relates, "Joseph fell on his father's neck and wept for joy." But what was Jacob doing at that historic moment? Rashi, quoting R. Yehuda'ai Gaon states, "Jacob did not fall on the neck of Joseph nor did he kiss him; our Rabbis are telling us that at that moment Jacob was reciting *Sh'ma Yisrael*." Was Jacob so pious that he was incapable of expressing personal joy? Why did Jacob find it necessary to recite *Sh'ma Yisrael* at that moment? Had he forgotten to recite *Sh'ma Yisrael* during his prayers that morning? If his purpose was to praise G-d for His kindness, why did Jacob not choose a more appropriate prayer such as, "Praise the L-rd for He is good, for His love and kindness endure forever?"

We are left with the inescapable conclusion that the sentence, *"Sh'ma Yisrael Hashem Elokeinu, Hashem Echad,"* did not exist and could not have existed prior to that seminal, crucial, historic moment, and that Jacob proclaimed it and coined it at that very moment. Prior to the encounter of Jacob and Joseph, the unity of the Twelve Tribes of Israel, the *B'nei Yisrael* — the sons of Israel — was shattered. During the 22 years of Joseph's absence, the *Shechinah*, the very presence of G-d that was ever-present in the homes of the Patriarchs, had departed from Jacob; his progeny was no longer whole, their unity was now dissolved. Joy had departed from Jacob's heart; his dreams for a united nation were shattered. The *B'nei Yisrael* — the twelve sons of Israel — no longer existed. But the moment Jacob was reunited with his son Joseph he could again be called Yisrael the victorious, not Jacob the downtrodden. Could Jacob have possibly exclaimed, "Hear, sons of Israel," prior to the reunion? So long as Jacob believed Joseph to be either dead or no longer the Joseph he once knew, the Sons of Yisrael no longer existed.

Picture the historic moment when Jacob saw Joseph's face. At that moment, the *B'nei Yisrael* were reunited and recreated. Jacob could now proclaim: *Sh'ma Yisrael*, Yisrael exists again; the force capable of bringing about the fulfillment of the Divine mission is again a reality. This mission was defined by Rashi, who says that the meaning of the words *"Hashem Elokeinu"* is that the L-rd Who is the G-d of those who obey Him, accept Him and proclaim Him King will become *"Hashem Echad*, G-d the One" and only One. When? When all mankind accepts Him as King. Thus will G-d become One and His Name One.

The reemergence of the face of Joseph and the reuniting of the sons of Jacob made possible the renewal of the mission of the Jewish People encapsulated in the timeless words of *Sh'ma Yisrael*. The rallying cry of the sons of Jacob was born at that historic moment.

When Jacob died with the words *Sh'ma Yisrael* on his lips, he died with the assurance that his life's mission was capable of fulfillment.

▶ According to the *Pri Tzaddik*

Rabbi Tzadok of Lublin, in his classic *Pri Tzaddik*, which is largely based on the *Zohar,* corroborates the above points. When Jacob presumed that Joseph was devoured by a wild beast, he feared that the Divine presence had departed from his own face. When he learned that Joseph was alive and that he was the ruler of Egypt, he feared the paganism and corruption of Egypt had negatively affected Joseph. For this reason, Jacob exclaimed, "I must go down to Egypt to see Joseph before I die," so as to determine that no change had taken place in the Divine presence on Joseph's face. Jacob knew that no one else but he had the ability to make this determination.

It was when Jacob saw Joseph that he was able to say: "*Sh'ma Yisrael,* Listen Children of Jacob," "*Hashem Elokeinu,* G-d who is our G-d," will become "*Hashem Echad,* the One and only G-d" and King of all mankind through our efforts.

Jacob was confident that that entity known as *B'nei Yisrael,* the united Children of Israel, was whole again. Now and only now was Jacob able to say these words, which resonate through the generations — *Sh'ma Yisrael.*

Jacob was then able to exclaim, "I can now die that I have seen Joseph's face." This was a positive confirmation that the Divine presence on both his own face and on Joseph's face had not departed and that the chain of tradition would continue intact.

1. *Genesis* 39:7-12.
2. *Yoma* 35b.
3. *Sotah* 36b.
4. *Sotah* 37b.
5. *Genesis* 37:3.
6. *Bava Metzia* 84a.
7. *Genesis* 45:28.
8. *Genesis* 46:30.

WHY DOES THE JEWISH RELIGION NEED A COUNTRY?

70

▶ The Uniqueness of Jewish Nationalism

❝**T**he Land of Israel without Torah is a body without a soul." The two, Torah and the Land, are in truth one, an entity that has the ability to make the Jew whole in body and in soul. As the Rambam says in his *Guide for the Perplexed*, "The chief aim of the life of the Patriarchs was to establish a nation that would know G-d and serve Him."[1]

First Abraham heard the Voice of G-d. He replied, "*Hineni* –– here I am, I am prepared to obey." Only then did G-d speak, "Go from your land, from your birthplace, from your father's house to the land I will show you." There, G-d promised to make him a great nation; and there He blessed him.

The Jewish Nation as a whole underwent the same process. First, following the Exodus, they became a People, free to choose. In the desert, they responded, "*Na'aseh v'nishma*, we will obey and we will listen." Only then did they receive the Torah, and only then was it possible to receive a land, the place in which to fulfill this commitment. It is there, in the Land of Israel, that the presence of G-d is felt by man. It is there that the Temple, the symbol of man's highest striving, once stood and will stand again.

Anyone who reads the Bible or prays from the *siddur* will be struck by an amazing revelation: The relationship of the Jewish People to its homeland is markedly different than the relationship of all other peoples to their homeland. Not only is it deeper and more intense — not only has it withstood the test of time — it is a loyalty and a yearning which is uniquely intellectual, emotional, religious, ideological, universal and messianic all at once. Abraham, our father, longed to establish a great human civilization that would "keep the way of the L-rd to do righteousness and justice." His descendants recognize that the land he was promised is the holy ground on which this is to take place.

How does the relationship of the Jewish People to the Land of Israel differ from the relationship of other nations to their homeland? What makes the Jewish relationship unique?

For most nations, nationalism was something that evolved, coalesced and emerged after groups of people lived together in a specific geographic area for centuries. National identity is often the end result of an unplanned sociological, economic and political development. A common language and a common historic bond gradually provided the cement for nationalist fervor. Often, it was the need to defend themselves against formidable outside enemies which forced them to unite.

The experience of the Jewish Nation in this respect is unique: As opposed to all other nations, the Jews are a "founded People." The creation of *Am Yisrael* was the product of an act of conscious will. It resulted from man's response to the command of G-d. What makes the Jewish People different is that it did not become established as a nation *as the result* of living in its homeland. Jewish history does not begin in the Land of Israel. On the contrary, it begins with a call to action, with the command of G-d calling to Abraham in Mesopotamia, telling him to leave his homeland and "go up to the land I will show you." The Jewish Nation didn't become a nation through natural accidents; it was "founded" by Abraham for a purpose. From the very beginning of Jewish history, the Jew had to "*go up*" to his land. The word *aliyah* implies being outside the land and going up. It describes a spiritual process as the basis for the physical process.

The Process of History

We can now understand why, to the Jew, the Land of Israel is more than a country: It is an integral part of a living historical process, a process which has been repeated several times throughout Jewish history. This process, which applies to the Jewish Nation as well as to the individual Jew, works this way: First, you must become a Jew. This means that first, you must drink from the living wells of the Torah and become a Torah Jew; only then can you come to the conviction that the Torah can be ultimately fulfilled *only* within the framework of an independent, self-contained society, free of outside influences, controls and impediments, subject to the rule of the Torah itself. Once you are filled with the desire to create a Torah society, once you come to the realization that the Torah dream can only be accomplished in the land promised by G-d to Abraham, Isaac and Jacob — only then are you ready to brave all odds and obstacles and "*go up*" to the Land of Israel to establish a Torah society. Our goal was and is to turn the Land of Canaan into *Eretz Yisrael*, the Land of Israel — the land "which the L-rd your G-d has His eyes on from the beginning of the year until the end." Let us see how this process took place in the life of the first Jew, Abraham.

Land of Promise

The history of the Jewish People begins with G-d's command to Abraham to abandon his birthplace and establish a new society in another land. The Torah does not open with a statement of theological principles or with the giving of the Torah on Mount Sinai. Before Abraham could hear G-d's Voice, he had to know G-d, believe in Him and recognize Him. Abraham, who rejected the idols of his father's house, had already become a man of faith in the true G-d: Only then could the Voice of G-d call to him.

> *And G-d said to Abram: Go forth out of your land,*
> *out of your birthplace and out of your father's*
> *house, to the land that I shall show you. And there,*
> *I shall make you a great nation...So Abram went,*
> *as the L-rd had spoken unto him..."*[2]

Jewish history is largely a history of the relationship of the Jewish People with the Land of Israel. The land and our right to possess it and live in it are a barometer of the quality of the relationship of the Jewish People with G-d. For this reason, the beginning of Jewish history can be traced to Abraham's journey to a land he had never seen, and from which his children's children were later to go into bondage in Egypt. Once freed from Egyptian bondage, the Jews went into the desert — an ownerless land — where the Torah was given on Mount Sinai. Only once the Jews received the Torah and became a Torah nation were they able to conquer the Land of Israel and ultimately build the Holy Temple in Jerusalem. But the Temple was not destined to last — their sins led to the destruction of the First Temple (586 BCE) and exile to Babylonia. Only after the people mended their ways, a remnant returned from the Babylonian Exile to the land. The land and the Temple were rebuilt again, but sins ultimately resulted in the destruction of the Second Temple (70 CE), the loss of Jewish independence and the crushing 2,000 year exile of persecution and wandering. The reestablishment of the Jewish homeland and of Jewish independence in our day was the *third time* the Jewish People returned to rebuild the Land of Israel.

The relationship of repeated exile and return is unique to the history of the Jewish People. No other nation in the world entirely left its homeland twice, yet returned centuries later to settle it anew.

▶ Why Do We Need a Land?

Why is it that only when Abraham discovered the one G-d, the Creator of heaven and earth, did the Almighty begin his relationship by demanding that Abraham leave his land and go to another? Why couldn't Abraham teach his neighbors about G-d and hope to change society in his homeland?

We see from subsequent events in the Bible that the Land of Israel, and Mount Zion in particular, was enriched with an extra measure of holiness from the time of Creation. The *Midrash* tells us that the first man was created from the soil of the Temple Mount;[3] the Binding of Isaac took place there; and Jacob's famous dream, which indicated to him that this spot was the "Gate of the Heavens," also happened on that spot. True to its spiritual richness, it was the location chosen by G-d for the building of the Holy Temple. From this concentration of holiness in Jerusalem, a special spiritual intensity radiates to the rest of the Land of Israel. It is for this reason that this territory is still known as the Holy Land. G-d did not want Abraham to simply leave his homeland, he wanted him to settle in *this land* specifically, because of its intrinsic ability to deepen the spirituality of its inhabitants.

Abraham was directed to go there for this reason, and because it was necessary for him to carve out a separate location for the building of a unique, G-d-fearing society. Apart from the powerful pagan society of Mesopotamia, in an area inhabited by weaker and diverse cultures, he would be able to stake out an area for a civilization built on Torah ideals.

▶ *Eretz Yisrael* — A Conditional Gift

When the people of Israel were forced into exile, only then did they realize how serious were the Torah's repeated promises that their sins would result in the destruction of their country. Only once they were in exile did they finally realize that the Land of Israel is a laboratory given by the L-rd to a People he had intended for this exclusive purpose: to use the land to carry out the *mitzvos*, to create a society that lived by the laws of G-d and to recognize Him as their true King. This society was to serve as a model to all of mankind, enabling mankind to overcome its flaws and heal. As articulated by the prophet Isaiah:

> *And many nations will go forth and say: Come let*
> *us go up to the mountain of the L-rd, to the House*
> *of the G-d of Jacob, and He will teach us of His*
> *ways, and we will walk in His paths. For Torah*
> *shall go forth from Zion, and the word of the L-rd*
> *from Jerusalem.*[4]

Throughout history, Jewish life in *Eretz Yisrael* was a *conditional gift*, bestowed for the purpose of service to the Creator and for the establishment of a righteous Torah society. The Jewish homeland is a Land of Promise: It is given to the Jewish People in return for their promise to do G-d's will by observing the Torah. G-d is patient. He never punishes immediately, but when He sees that His promises and the threats of His prophets are not taken seriously, He brings about destruction and exile. The Jew prays on every holiday, "Because of our sins, we were exiled from our land and removed from our soil, and we cannot go up (to Jerusalem) in order to appear and prostrate ourselves before You and perform our responsibilities, in Your Temple…"

As in the individual example set by our forefather Abraham, on a national level the Jews did not acquire the Land of Israel until they had reached the third phase of religious commitment: First they became a nation, then accepted the Torah and then acquired the land. Once driven from our land, we did not cease to be a nation, but we considered ourselves to be a nation in exile until we could return. Most nations ceased to exist, once their geographic homeland no longer held them together. Even if a sense of national pride remains with them, it usually does not last for more than a few generations. Because of the unique qualities of the Jewish Nation (containing, as it does, the elements that constitute an *am* — Torah, language, history, ancestry), it is the only nation that has gone into exile a number of times, each time returning to its land.

With its power to uplift every aspect of our lives, the Torah has traveled with us throughout the Diaspora. Judaism was and is practiced virtually everywhere in the world by G-d-fearing Jews committed to its *mitzvos*. Yet a complete Torah civilization — brought to fruition as G-d intended — must contain all the elements that make up every society: a land, government, army, judicial system and laws that pertain to agriculture, business and every other area of life. Only an independent people in control of its own destiny could properly observe the Torah's laws and create an ideal society. It is for this reason that the Jewish People was given a land and made an independent people, not so that we would become "a nation like all other nations."

Torah is meant to be lived in the Land of Israel, the place uniquely designated for its total fulfillment. The prophets continually warned of exile because the Jews were not carrying out their part of the agreement to mold the Land of Israel in the establishment of a righteous, moral and ethical society. The Torah requires the structure of a state so that it can influence every facet of human affairs — so that justice and morality would affect every aspect of human life. The Jews are not merely a religious body, they are meant to have an all-encompassing religious civilization.

▶ The Messianic Ideal

While many of the *mitzvos* of the Torah can be observed in any country, a significant number of commandments can only be observed in the Land of Israel. In fact, two thirds of the Talmud deals with laws that pertain to *Eretz Yisrael*. Total service to G-d requires a complete and total form of independent national life where all the *mitzvos* can be followed. When the other nations see the righteousness of Jewish national life; when they see how a sovereign Jewish society educates its youth, cares for its aged, fights its wars, protects its widows, celebrates its festivals, carries on its diplomacy and manages its economy, then, "all nations will know that the L-rd is G-d." In living by the light of the Torah, Israel will become a light to the world. The world would be elevated and redeemed, not through preaching, but through our living example.

The Messianic ideal calls for the People of G-d, living by the law of G-d, to live in the Holy Land of G-d — and to create there an elevated G-dly society. This Messianic ideal is the dream that sustained the Jewish People after the destructions of the First Temple and the Second Commonwealth. To return to Israel meant not only the end of exile and persecution, but also the resumption of full and genuine Jewish living. The Jew in exile vows, "If I forget you, O Jerusalem, let my right hand forget how to function."[5] The Jew dreams of Jerusalem and the rebuilding of the Temple because these are the methods whereby the *Shechinah* — the very presence of G-d — would return to earth in so concentrated a form that it would lead to the full Redemption of all mankind.

Each Passover resounds with the cry, "Next Year in Jerusalem." It was in Jerusalem that the freedom of the Exodus would be realized. Each time we pray, we face Jerusalem and the site of the destroyed Temple, without which no prayer for a better Jewish world, or any world, could be fully answered. To the Jew, the rule of G-d as King of all mankind becomes a possibility when G-d's People creates *a place* for G-d on earth from which His influence can be spread.

To the Jew, therefore, nationalism is the foundation of universalism. G-d can be King over all the earth only once the Jewish People accept Him — and from there, spread His holiness and message from the Holy City to the entire world. In other words — Torah teaching and Torah influence requires more than pious words; it requires an entire society — a nation — that lives a G-dly life in its country. This society has the power to transform mankind by showing that the G-dly life can inspire and transform all of human life, not an elite of priests or saints, but of each and every person.

For thousands of years, we Jews figuratively sat on our suitcases. When we pray for rain on Succos, we reflect on the hope that the Messiah might come any day and lead us to the Land of Israel. We study Torah laws relating to the Temple, government, agriculture and commerce with the same fervor we apply to the regulations of *kashrus* and family purity. We do not want to be unprepared for the return to Zion.

"The Land of Israel, without Torah, is like a body without a soul." The two, the Torah and the Land, are one. Together they have the ability to make the Jew whole again in body and in soul. Each needs the other for fulfillment; each is incomplete without the other. Together, they represent the goal of Jewish aspiration and hope.

Only when a person feels that he is not a complete Jew, or a complete person because he is deprived of the holiness of Zion and Jerusalem — when he realizes that the Torah life is fulfilled *only* when it is rooted in the land which G-d called holy, chosen, promised and beloved — is he fully able to experience the feeling of being in exile. He understands the full tragic impact of 2,000 years of Jewish homelessness and alienation.

No Jew can study the pages of the Torah, which speak of the yearning for *Eretz Yisrael,* and not feel this yearning. This yearning tells us that we are in *galus*, exile, both spiritual and physical. Not to *know* that you are in exile, not to feel and experience *galus*, not to feel a void in the personal and national sense, is not to be a Jew.

In this privileged generation, we see that G-d has once again entrusted us with the Land of Israel and with it, Jerusalem, the city associated with His most intense presence on earth. If the return to Israel in our own day is to have ultimate meaning, if it is to be lasting and permanent, the people who dwell there must show progress in building a model society ruled by the Torah's spirit and law. And no matter where we live, we must constantly be aware of our great responsibility to deserve this boundless treasure — Israel, the Land of Promise: our Jewish homeland.

Much of this material was previously published in the NCSY publication, Israel: Eretz Israel, Land of Promise, *edited by Dr. Michael Rosenak. Although this chapter has undergone many rewrites, some of the phrasing is his.*

---

1. *Guide for the Perplexed,* 111.51
2. *Genesis* 12:1, 2, 4.
3. *Bereshis Rabbah* 14:8, cited in Rashi, *Genesis* 2:7.
4. *Isaiah* 2:3.
5. *Psalms* 137:5.

XII CONCLUSION

THE MODERN REDISCOVERY OF G-D

71

n each and every age, Judaism has been challenged by the established dogmas of that particular era. Abraham, the founder of our worldview, is called by the Sages *ha'Ivri*, the Hebrew, the one who crossed to the other side. They explain the meaning of the term: "The entire world is arrayed on one side while Abraham stands alone on the opposite side." Like Abraham, Jews have grown accustomed to existential loneliness and isolation, to being challenged intellectually by the nearly unanimous views of thinking mankind that are contrary to the Torah's viewpoint. Other cultures are arrayed against our viewpoint; yet we march to a different tune and steadfastly stand our ground in the face of worldwide dissent.

At no time has this opposition been more intense and more devastating than in the modern age. With the rise of modern scientific method, Western man believed that he had acquired possession of the very keys to ultimate scientific truth and had unlocked the secrets of existence. For the first time in history, man was able to deceive himself into thinking that now, at long last, he was capable of bringing irrefutable proofs with which to demolish the mythologies and superstitions of the ancients, especially the Judaic claim to being the possessor of absolute revealed truth.

Battered by the frontal attack of the ideologies of modern man, Orthodox Judaism was largely eclipsed: it was abandoned for Communism, Socialism, secular Zionism and a host of other "isms." An Orthodox rabbi who had been a student at Harvard University 40 years ago stated that his fellow Jewish students "viewed 'Orthodoxy' as an obscure Jewish sect." When he took a course in philosophy, his Jewish professor asked him, "You seem to be an intelligent person: how can you be Orthodox?"

▶ The Crisis of Western Civilization

How very amazing it is to awaken each morning to discover in almost every daily newspaper how Western civilization's entire house of cards, its very intellectual edifice, is steadily crumbling and disintegrating brick by brick, assumption by assumption, dogma by dogma, discipline by discipline. In some sciences, such as astronomy and biology, we are first beginning to realize how relatively little we really know, despite the thrilling advances and discoveries of the past 400 years, concerning the mysteries of life. Each new discovery, each new voyage into space brings answers accompanied by even more advanced and difficult questions. As the mysteries unfold and reveal their truths, we are able to view reality with greater precision and inspect with greater exactness the intricacies of each structure and each system of reality. With each advance of technology — a new super computer, microscope or telescope — we realize how vast is the infinite universe, how many undiscovered new worlds exist that we did not suspect were present yesterday, how many new mysteries remain to be unraveled. To date, 50 billion galaxies have been discovered in this vast universe.

▶ The god that Failed

The above statements relate equally to our systems of government and economics, to the ideologies that determine our social and political system. Suddenly everything has become unhinged.

The great Soviet empire, which terrorized and threatened the world with its naked power, died in a whiff of smoke, without a shot fired. Shamefully exposed, it crumbled before our very eyes, its Iron Curtain torn asunder. This Red Empire was worshipped as a god, anticipated as a messiah; millions were martyred on the altar of its materialistic, atheistic dogmas. Masses rallied to its banner, abandoning home, parents and the traditions of generations. The Yevsektzia, the Jewish section of the Communist Party in Russia, was barbaric in its self-hating, anti-Semitic campaign to destroy Jewish life and its institutions. Synagogues were turned into barns; *mikva'os* were filled with dirt; rabbis were imprisoned, shot or exiled; Sabbath work was made compulsory; and the teaching of Torah became an illegal act. Then in a flash, before our very eyes, indeed miraculously, the Red illusion collapsed and disintegrated 50 years after it had begun, spurned and rejected by the masses and the nations it had subjugated. This great dogma, which had held the intellectuals and the universities in an iron vise and was the scourge of all civilizations, evaporated overnight as it was repudiated by its own advocates and its own professors of Marxist philosophy and Communist economics. Communism was revealed as an idol with clay feet, in the words of Arthur Koestler, "the god that failed."

Many factors — economic, spiritual, political and sociological — account for the fall of Communism. Its shockwaves have changed the world, with special impact on Israel and the Jewish People. We witnessed the historic liberation and exodus of Russia's Jews, the evaporation of the enmity of Eastern Europe to Israel, the impact of new realities on the PLO and Syria. Overall, the fall of Communism has heightened the confidence of mankind that it is possible, even when it hits rock bottom, to change course.

What toppled this cesspool of injustice, terror and oppression? There are the hundreds of stories of heroic "refuseniks" who revived Torah in the underground, but the one outstanding heroic event of spiritual bravery which we recall in the victorious battle against Communism is the poignant, dramatic, heroic moment when Natan Scharansky, about to be liberated, clutched his Book of Psalms — and like David poised with his slingshot against Goliath — took on the entire structure of communism when he refused to cross that bridge to freedom unless he was allowed to carry his Psalms with him. This symbolized his lonely, one-man spiritual battle of the will, in which the G-dly spirit of right and justice vanquished tyranny and inhumanity.

▶ The Collapse of Western Humanism

The sudden collapse of Communism both as an ideology and as a political system contains within it lessons which point to the fragile and tenuous existence of the West. In the midst of our victory celebration we must examine our own frailties and weaknesses if civilization is to avoid collapse in the long run.

In the post-Holocaust era we are witness to two parallel and contradictory events: the collapse of western humanism — the bankruptcy of western religion and morality (the utter silence of the "civilized" world during the Holocaust and the blindness of Europe to the realities of the Intifada in present-day Israel should suffice as examples), and at the very same time, the astonishing triumph of Western technology. This startling, fast paced technological revolution which demands freedom of thought, communication, knowledge, movement and a minimum of government involvement in human affairs was one of the major factors which caused mankind to turn its back on Communism and

Socialism. As a result, ideology has suddenly become irrelevant in the quest for the good life because secrecy, thought control, witch hunting and censorship destroy initiative and make technological progress impossible. Freedom, democracy and capitalism are victorious, not for philosophical or ideological reasons but for pragmatic reasons. They just work far better.

Having said this, and having saluted democracy and its basic freedoms, children of Abraham who are veterans of 4,000 years of human history know better than anyone else that without morality, discipline, goals and religious truths the "good life" becomes the "corrupt life" and is subject to eventual collapse. We know too, that the classical Jewish form of popular democracy, which creates Torah authority through broad consensus and which promotes the aristocracy of intellectual Torah scholars — open as it is to all economic and sociological classes — represents ultimate democracy, in its unique ability to promote excellence and creative leadership in an equilibrium between freedom and authority.

▸ The Fall of Rome

A good model which serves as an example of the vulnerability of a powerful, successful but corrupt civilization is the Roman Empire. Prior to its fall, it was at the apex of technological and economic mastery and achievement. It crumbled because its pagan underpinnings resulted in widespread human suffering, immorality, disillusion, demoralization and pessimism. This resulted in the collapse of the family, personal integrity and, in quick succession, the weakening of all of the institutions of religion, society and government. Ultimately, it resulted in the failure of the fabled Roman Legions to hold back Rome's enemies.

Our Western world must confront an identical challenge today. The very factors that undermined Rome threaten to undermine Western civilization. On one hand, the West continues its undreamed of accelerated progress in the areas of technology, information and science, while at the very same time it is descending to the depths of depravity. This is a result of the widespread proliferation of drugs, crime, violence, immorality, pornography, the acceptance of homosexuality and a general collapse of authority, values, family and institutions.

What must the role of Jewish civilization be in this environment? Are we a tiny minority religion, content to tend to our own internal agenda, or is the time coming to again become a factor in world history? Can we have an impact despite our insignificant numbers and the status of the Torah Jew as a minority, even among the Jewish People?

Many generations ago, when Judea and Rome clashed, when our Temple was destroyed and our national independence collapsed, Judaism contained within itself sufficient spiritual and intellectual force to transform the ancient world. Even as it lay prostrate in defeat, Judaism had a crucial impact and major effect on the Roman world. Even as the Romans erected their famous victory arch, the Arch of Titus to celebrate the fall of Jerusalem, thousands of Jewish slaves in Rome taught their masters the meaning of a life of discipline, principle, religious truth and grandeur through their obstinate adherence to the laws of Shabbos, *kashrus*, family purity and moral living. Eventually, a new religion, based originally on Jewish thinking, permanently superimposed a segment of Judaism's ideology on a bankrupt, pagan Roman world. It is believed by some historians that had Bar Kochba not failed — and had not Pauline Christianity offered the Romans an ersatz Judaism without the burden of *mitzvos* — the Western world might well have turned to Judaism.[1]

The question contemporary Jews must ask ourselves is, have we advanced sufficiently in the establishment of Torah institutions (from the ashes of the Holocaust) that we can create a force capable of influencing the thinking of others? In a world that is falling apart at its seams, a world in which old gods, ideologies and deceptions are daily crumbling under the weight of their irrelevance, does Judaism represent that viable alternative that is capable of electrifying, influencing and ultimately transforming today's world?

It is my conviction that the current spiritual and intellectual atmosphere is preparing the ground for such influences. A changing and rapidly moving scientific and intellectual environment is creating the fertile ground for Jewish ideology to again be in a position to effectively challenge the myths of Western civilization.

The ferment of ideas and the rapid progress of science and technology are gradually cleansing the poisoned atmosphere of the compulsion to deny G-d. This intellectual "need" has been the baggage of the human intellectual community since the beginning of the Enlightenment. Some of the changes come in a flash, while others evolve slowly. People are loath to surrender dogmas that have served them as crutches and which serve as the ideological rationalizations to uphold the corrupt habits and sloppy morality they have acquired. It is difficult for anyone to admit to a lifetime of error and even more difficult to actually change one's ways. But the fall of Communism and the lightning rapidity with which the universities of Eastern Europe instantly cleansed themselves of Marxist ideology and philosophy is evidence that people and societies are capable of change.

Ironically, the "Enlightenment" was one of the darkest eras in the history of the Jewish Diaspora. Its "light" can be compared to the "light" of Greece — which, from a Jewish point of view, darkened the face of the world for hundreds of years. The effect of this Enlightenment was to topple the walls of ghetto life and bring about a mass flight to Haskalah, reform, intermarriage, apostasy and general decay of Jewish life. The Enlightenment caused the greatest mass defection from Torah in Jewish history. It pushed Jewry to the edge of an abyss, to a mass betrayal of age-old traditions, that resulted in the weakening of loyalty to Torah and the undermining of the foundations of Jewish life. The Enlightenment was a repeat of the Chanukah story in modern dress. Toppled from its former glory, the loyal, observant Torah community was transformed into a weakened minority.

Torah Judaism is just now emerging from its long, dark night of decline. A major indicator of this radical revitalization is the near disappearance from the stage of history of nearly all the last generation's competing ideological and sociological trends in Jewish life. The emergence of the *Teshuvah* movement is a key factor in the revival of Orthodoxy. *Ba'alei teshuvah*, the newly Orthodox, make up 25% of the American Orthodox community outside of New York.

The *Teshuvah* movement is neither an accident nor an isolated phenomenon. It is the spearhead of a grand reversal of human history, a fundamental turnabout in the fortunes and outlook of the Jewish People. It represents a new and major factor within a rapidly evolving and changing intellectual and scientific world environment. Rabbi Aryeh Kaplan once said that the *Teshuvah* movement "is merely returning Jewry to its state of normalcy."

Just as the statues of Lenin and Stalin were toppled in city after city in Eastern Europe, the idols that once toppled Torah are themselves crumbling or crashing. The false ideologies and pseudo-sciences, the idolatries of Western man that claimed the loyalty of masses of Jews are gradually losing their glitter. The new environment is such that as modern exploration and science grows in sophistication it is rapidly becoming the ally of belief instead of its enemy.

▶ The Destruction of Faith

What are some of the major intellectual currents that destroyed the world of faith in general, and the Jewish world of faith specifically? And what are some of the profound changes that are taking place within their frameworks?

1) Socialism and Marxism: The false belief that man is an economic animal and that the problems of society and mankind would vanish if the means of production were taken from entrepreneurs and capitalists and forcibly given over to the workers. Everywhere, in Russia, in Eastern Europe and even in Israel's kibbutzim, this system has failed to produce the basics of human material needs. But most tragically, it has deceived, betrayed and enslaved masses of human beings who, suddenly awaking from their long nightmare, now realize that they were enslaved for no purpose.

2) Evolution: The idea of evolution was the keystone of the modern worldview. Darwin's theory and its derivatives, became the vehicles for the denial of G-d, of human uniqueness and human responsibility. The theory of evolution, elaborated into accepted "fact" by the scientific establishmenl, is coming under increasing fire. With the new sophistication of science and its instruments, the realization is dawning that no human scientific, technological or engineering achievement is remotely close to the intricate and majestic work of the Creator. The belief that anything constructive or important can come about through random chance was demolished. A new scientific concept called "Intelligent Design" is employing all the sophisticated tools of science and statistics to conclusively prove that our world is the product of intelligence and design.

The missing links, the bridge species, have not been found anywhere. Gradually, with the appearance of new instruments of research, new revelations and the publication of dozens of new books such as Dr. Michael Dentin's *Evolution, A Theory in Crisis,* science is becoming the handmaiden of those who believe in special Divine Creation, leaving the Darwinians behind as believers in dogmatic nonsense. A report in the *New York Times* on November 9, 1989, stated that the California State Board of Education will delete all reference to evolution as "scientific fact."

3) Biblical Criticism: The Reform and Conservative movements developed in the intellectual soil of the Wellhausian Doctrine of so-called Biblical (or Higher) Criticism. This doctrine denied the unity and Divinity of the Torah by employing literary criticism and pseudo-science to demolish the historic belief in Revelation that forms the foundation of Jewish civilization. Even today, these movements continue to dogmatically cling to these discredited, disproved theories which have been shattered by archaeology, by the new scientific study of the Torah, and by the works of Hoffman, Kassuto, Weissmandl, Witztum, Rips, Rosenberg, Yaniv and many others — all of which are gradually gaining in ascendancy.

4) Freudian Psychology: Freud defined the human being in animalistic, mechanistic terms, bereft of a Divine spark, of spiritual depth, and incapable of being motivated by ideals or spiritual goals. Freudian dogmatism attempted to banish right and wrong, good and evil, moral and immoral from the human psyche and vocabulary. Few, even in the world of modern psychology, any longer accept Freud's dogmas. In rejecting dogmatism in favor of pragmatic methods that work, psychology has lost its anti-G-d sting and need no longer be regarded as the enemy of faith.

5) Secular Zionism: While the modern return to Zion and Jerusalem is undoubtedly a miracle of historic significance, the notion that secular Zionism would solve "the Jewish problem" is no longer taken seriously, especially now that Israel has emerged as the central target for worldwide Jew hatred. Paradoxically, as other hatreds and rivalries decline, Jew-hatred increases in virulence and intensity, even in countries (such as Japan) which have few Jews. At one time, secular Jewish nationalism was seriously viewed by masses of Jews as a replacement for Judaism. In today's Israel, Torah and Judaism are thriving, while secular Zionism is a passé, discredited ideology. Israeli yeshivos of all kinds experience an 8% annual growth rate. The *teshuvah* phenomenon daily grows in intensity. Nowhere is the return to Judaism as strong as in the hearts of the grandchildren of those who once believed that secular Jewish nationalism was the panacea for Jewry's ills.

In fact, many Israeli Zionists have now become turncoats, as demonstrated by their determination to encourage the *aliyah* of masses of non-Jews. The anti-Torah movement of the extreme Israeli left is turning anti-Semitic due to their fear of the growing strength of the religious communities.

6) Hebrew: Even in an area as seemingly insignificant as the question of the origin of the Hebrew language, recent scientific language studies substantiate the ancient Biblical claim that Hebrew is the mother of all languages and not a late Semitic language which "evolved" from more primitive speech. This development is also destined to have a marked educational effect.

▶ The Challenge

t is no coincidence that the death of western ideology and the demise of Communism and the various forms of secular Judaism are taking place in tandem with the restoration of Jewish autonomy, the reconquest of Jerusalem and the Temple Mount, and the revitalization of Jewish observance and Torah study.

Yet old ideologies hang on, and the return to sanity is a process that requires time. But in today's world, in an era of rapid communication and human malcontent, we can anticipate that man's idols will crash and fall with accelerated rapidity. Our task is to replace false idols with the historic Torah faith for which mankind so desperately yearns. To succeed, we must display the same idealism, the same passion and the same devotion to Torah as our ancestors. We are here today as Jews because so many of them chose to brave all assaults on Judaism, even to the point of accepting death over apostasy. This is the challenge and the task of this generation.

While Torah Jewry remains a tiny minority within a tiny People, the lesson of our Torah is that spiritual forces have the power to vanquish armies, empires and ideologies that appear to be permanent and undefeatable. "*Yeshuas Hashem k'heref ayin*, The victory of our L-rd can appear in an instant."[2] We must remember also, "Blessing is not to be found in the obvious, but in factors which are hidden from view."[3] We know what these factors are: What is required is clear vision, effort and sacrifice. In a world distracted by technological toys and materialistic rationalization, is such a transformation possible? Our prophets have taught that it is. Our Torah teaches that the Messiah can come today: "*Hayom, im b'Koli tishma'u*, Today, [but only] *if* you will hearken to My Voice."[4]

---

1. Baron, Salo W., *The Social and Religious History of the Jews*, vol. 2.
2. *Minchah Le'Yehudah*, 27-28.
3. *Taanis* 8b.
4. *Psalms* 95:7.

REDISCOVERING OUR TRUE SELVES: THE CHALLENGE OF TODAY'S JEW

72

Think of a kite high in the sky. The string pulls with such force that it is almost impossible to hold on. The kite at the end of the string is long out of sight, but because we feel the kite's pull, we know that it is there.

One of the most amazing events in Jewish history took place when G-d took Abraham outside and said, "Gaze toward the heavens, and count the stars if you are able to." G-d concluded, "...So shall be your offspring."[1] It is obvious when we gaze at the heavens that the stars number in the billions and that it is impossible to count them.

What was the meaning of G-d's command to Abraham? It can hardly relate solely to the question of how numerous the Jewish People will become, because G-d's major concern is that the Jewish Nation be righteous, not numerous. The deeper message of Abraham's prophetic encounter is that in asking him to count the stars, G-d is demanding that he do the impossible. In effect,

He is telling Abraham that the mission He has set before him and his progeny is impossible! Despite that fact, G-d assured him that the promises He made to Abraham will be fulfilled.

The scene described above leads us to an obvious question. What is the purpose of a heaven filled with stars, if not to remind us that man, for whom the universe was created, is but a speck? Unfortunately, most of us live in cities where smog conceals the heavens. But if ever you are in a place where the stars can be seen in the millions, you realize that you are surrounded by a limitless universe. It is so overwhelming that its creation by an Infinite G-d is obvious. In attempting to "see" the universe, we realize that this is a task beyond our ability. This gives us pause: We comprehend that the G-d who created the universe directs us to "count the stars," so to speak, to understand that history and nature are beyond our comprehension. G-d and His world are impossible to see in their entirety. Our only window to G-d is through His creations and His deeds.

The essence of our being is that we possess an infinite soul. Many of us have stifled our attachment to our soul and we begin to realize that we are slipping. We have lost our grasp on reality. To quote Rabbi Jeremy Kagan, author of *The Jewish Self: Recovering Spirituality in the Modern World*:

> *By obscuring this essential connection, modern culture undermines the possibility of a genuinely grounded sense of self. This emptiness, this lack of being connected, shapes the world of modern man. The materialistic society, which surrounds us and consumes even the best of us, is a direct result of having lost our connection with true reality. We begin to feel that we are in essence functioning within a vacuum. We desperately search for something to fill the vacuum so that we can become whole again.*

We are constantly looking for fulfillment by filling our days and lives with things. We search for fulfillment through the things that are outside of ourselves. We live in the illusion that possessions, money and the pursuit of power and prestige can fulfill us.

We fail to realize that these things are mostly childish and fleeting, a grand illusion. The satisfaction attained through things quickly evaporates and leaves us even emptier than we were before. What we have done is to expand our vacuum, causing us to seek more things and still more things to fill our ever-widening emptiness. Some of us, when we grow up, realize that our true selves are within ourselves, that true fulfillment lies in the expansion of self, not in its contraction.

> *The loss of our connection with spirituality distresses us, still we have no idea as to where to turn to change our direction and to grow internally. The Torah, which views physical reality as an expression of a spiritual dimension, would seem to be a natural choice. But the same spiritual poverty that is at the heart of our problem also denies us access to the supreme tool. We cannot accept the Torah's legitimacy precisely because we have become so familiar with our restricted vision of reality. **

We know that we are not animals; that we possess the capacity to aspire to a world of spiritual growth and attainment beyond ourselves. The fact that we are endowed with the ability to speak, to transmit traditions from one generation to the next, to hope, to pray, to realize the existence of our true selves, to plumb our unique psychological, emotional and ideological selves, makes us aware of the fact that we have a soul. The fact that we are able to discern right from wrong, that we are endowed with a sense of shame, guilt, conscience and sin, as well as a sense of spiritual joy and elevation that provides us with genuine happiness that is far beyond the physical, makes us realize that we are much more than our physical and animal selves.

Sometimes spirituality comes to us through a profound closeness with another person — our spouse, a rabbi, a teacher, a scholar or a spiritual guide; sometimes through an event such as

---

*The passages of italicized quotes are from The Jewish Self: Recovering Spirituality in the Modern World *by Rabbi Jeremy Kagan.*

the death of a loved one, or the birth of a child or grandchild. Sometimes we are overawed by a natural scene, the beauty of a sunset, the power of a waterfall, a moment of quiet during a vacation or while standing on a boat looking at the infinite sea. There are so many uplifting, spiritual experiences in our lives *if* we would but allow ourselves to stop for a moment to experience and internalize them.

The Biblical Moses saw a bush on fire. When he saw that it was not burning down, he said, "I must change my course and investigate this amazing phenomenon. Why isn't the bush consumed?" Similarly, spiritual, emotional or intellectual experiences help us achieve, at least for a moment, a moment of realization: We understand with clarity that there is so much more to ourselves and our world than we allow ourselves to acknowledge. We begin to realize that both within our conscious selves as well as outside of us there exists a world of experiences, wonder, awareness and relationships to counterbalance the narrow vision that dominates our consciousness and the world around us.

These experiences force us to reevaluate the relevance of Torah in our lives. When we accept as final the very limited self-vision to which most of us have become accustomed, we squelch our deeper, inner self. Fortunately, we sometimes awaken to the fact that we have subdued any hope of achieving our true humanity. We realize that we have eliminated the possibility that we can fulfill our G-d-given potential, our talents, our abilities and the spiritual energies that exist within us. We realize that these things would make our lives rich, meaningful and fulfilling.

If we devoted serious time to studying one great Biblical personality such as Abraham, the founder of our People — who stood firm against the kingdoms and philosophers of his age — or Joseph, whose life challenges and experiences are so similar to ours, we would perceive that we are members of *a founded people* (a term coined by Eric Gutkind). This means that the Jewish People was founded by an individual who was driven by an ideal; a cause that he initiated in obedience to G-d's command.

Abraham founded a new nation because he discovered truth, not a safe haven, not a more fertile land, not the opportunity to plunder other nations or to achieve dominance or power. Instead, he created a society that would be guided by the one and only G-d. Instructed by G-d to leave his father's house, Abraham abandoned his source of power and influence to begin a new life, to establish a new and unique society of spiritual people who would be committed to a way of life that is intimately connected to the Source of life.

Our ability to connect ourselves with G-d's infinity, to reach beyond our individuality, is not something coincidental. It defines our humanity. Indeed, it is the only quality that distinguishes the human being from the remainder of Creation. Modern man views himself as a super intelligent animal or as the ultimate computer. But no animal will ever contemplate the Divine Will. No computer will every pray. Only man can consciously develop and integrate himself with Divinity. When we lose our ability to connect with G-d, when our prayer is rote, when our Torah study is superficial, when the celebration of our holidays does not deepen our connection to our history and roots, we forfeit our humanity.

The modern world, with all its technological grandeur, has so overwhelmed us that we forget those components that make us truly human. Today's Jew, to a very large extent, has lost his sense of the radical uniqueness of the Jewish People, of its history, its experiences and its Torah, because the rush of material life has blinded us to the many spiritual elements that define us. We have lost our ability to create and maintain our unique, spiritual selves and our connection with that eternal All-Powerful Being who created us and cries out to us to make our lives truly meaningful.

> If we find the Torah irrelevant when trying to determine our humanity and how to attain it, we must ask where the fault lies. Is it possible that this document, which has nurtured the soul of man throughout recorded time, has nothing of interest to say on a subject that so troubles our spirit? The Torah dom-

inated the lives of the most skeptical and scholarly people in history for thousands of years, and profoundly transformed and affected the worldview of every nation which came into contact with it.

It can't possibly escape us that almost all of current Western civilization was nurtured, influenced and revolutionized by the crumbs which fell from the majestic and regal table of the Torah People and its way of life. How can we explain the desire of nearly every major human civilization to rid itself of this source of human consciousness, conscience and purpose? How do we explain the fact that despite the attempt of every movement of modernity, Communism, Socialism, materialism and secularism, to assault our gates (and at times to almost succeed in demolishing us), we have survived and prevailed? Consider the fact that despite the wrenching and tumultuous rebellions and reformations which have been directed against classic Judaism during the past hundred years, the only powerful force, the only intellectual and spiritual movement which today engages the passion, devotion and loyalty of contemporary Jewish youth, is rooted almost exclusively to the powerful thirst of Jewish youth for Torah.

Yet, so many of us who already live within the house of Torah are not part of the burgeoning movement for Torah study or the movement to return our lost brethren to Torah. Interestingly, the Torah testifies about itself that it is not "an empty thing."[2] The Talmud expands this concept by adding the following words: "These words are not empty. If they appear empty, the emptiness is in you."[3]

We are left with the following question. If we "know" that the Torah is the rich source of a meaningful life, why are so many of us deaf to Torah's message? What is missing in our lives, in our education and in our awareness that leads us to live in a halfway house of Torah without allowing it full entrance into our minds and hearts? Why isn't it the major motivating force of our existence?

There has never been an observant community as wealthy, as influential or as powerful as ours. We are armed with all of the material, political, spiritual and intellectual blessings that should enable us to transform our own lives as well as the environment around us. The many crises which currently beset Jewry in every country of the world, particularly in our beloved *Eretz Yisrael,* are a Divine clarion call to set aside all else and do what our G-d demands. His demand is that we awaken, deepen our Torah roots, begin to devote a significant portion of our days to Torah study and play an active role in the many outreach endeavors to strengthen Torah here and in Israel. "*Ki heim chayenu, v'orech yameinu,* [The Torah] is our life, it is the length of our days."[4] The Torah is our essence. For our own sake, and for the sake of our children and communities, it must become the major focus of our lives.

1. *Genesis* 15:4.
2. *Deuteronomy* 32:47.
3. *Talmud Yerushalmi, Peah* 1:1
4. From *Ma'ariv* prayer.

INDEX

389, 392, 396, 406, 410-412

Shmoneh Esrei   51, 53, 54, 59, 76, 218, 298

Shofar 96, 112, 113, 117, 185, 224, 381

Shoshanas Yaakov   283, 286

Shulchan Aruch   193, 196

Sifri   262

Simchas Beis Hasho'evah,   see Water Libation Celebration

Sinai,   see Mount Sinai

Sirkis, Rabbi Yoel (Bach)   196

Slichos   78, 126, 131, 139

Socialism   425, 428, 431, 440

Socrates   202

Soloveitchik, Rabbi Joseph Ber   219

Song of Songs   163, 333-335

Song of the Sea   333, 335-340

Sophocles   202, 205

Soul   110, 112, 130, 132, 163, 189, 208, 240, 278, 284, 371, 376, 377, 421, 436, 437, 439

Spanish Inquisition   343

Spector, Rabbi Yitzchak Elchanan   240

Spirituality   40, 41, 43-45, 49, 99, 103, 110, 132, 138, 140, 196, 197, 209, 233, 253, 259, 281, 296, 306, 310, 358, 386, 406, 437

Spiritual light   95, 214, 279, 301

Succos   24, 32, 36, 87, 106, 107, 136-140, 142-144, 146, 148, 152, 155, 156, 158-160, 163, 165, 166, 168-172, 174-186, 267, 305, 420

Syria   346, 353, 427

Tabernacle   164, 238, 367

Tablets of the Covenant   23, 24, 59, 107, 122, 123, 131, 132, 145, 162-164, 183, 230, 231, 375, 376

Talmud   45, 82, 83, 93, 94, 106, 108, 130, 147, 150, 175, 179, 196, 198, 216, 227, 230, 235, 237, 239-242, 247, 250, 251, 253, 262, 268, 271, 281, 288, 289, 297, 300, 315, 337, 342, 344, 348, 366, 375, 376, 382, 388, 394, 404, 408, 419, 440

Targum Yonason   262

Tefillin   366, 367

Temple Mount   224, 350, 382, 383, 386, 417, 434

Temple,   see Holy Temple

Ten Commandments   41, 60, 61, 86, 88, 89, 107, 131, 133, 183, 259, 324, 362, 375-377

Ten Days of Repentance,   see Days of Awe

Tenth of Teves   237

Teshuvah Movement   192, 193, 350, 404, 431, 433, 440

Teshuvah,   see Repentance

Thirteen Attributes of Mercy   126, 127, 144, 145, 148, 149, 160-162

Tikkun olam   24, 31, 52, 308

Tishah B'Av   24, 237, 383, 386

Titus   344, 429

Torah, Receiving of   23, 32, 33, 51, 107, 113, 122, 123, 132, 134, 142, 162, 163, 242, 247, 264, 276, 277, 322, 324, 342, 343, 362, 363, 416

Torah study   26, 30, 54, 93, 99, 194, 201, 219, 229, 231, 232, 235, 236, 240, 241, 246, 250, 277, 279, 293, 350, 352, 356, 358, 359, 382, 385, 386, 427, 434, 439, 440, 441

Unwritten Torah,   see Oral Torah

Ushpizin   152, 156

Vilna Gaon   148, 163, 226, 243, 249, 288, 290, 295, 324

Water Libation Celebration   144, 165, 168-170, 172, 174, 175, 178, 179

Weismandl, Rabbi Dov Ber   149

Wolbe, Rabbi Shlomo   387

World to Come   31, 41, 43, 44, 139, 214, 384

Yetzias Mitzrayim,   see Exodus, the

Yizkor   87, 88, 89, 90

Yose ben Yochanan   229

Yose ben Yoezer   229

Yossi ben Yossi   79

Zechariah   42, 275

Zion   418, 421, 433

Zohar   41, 148, 150, 324, 325, 343, 349, 384